THE FAYUM LANDSCAPE

THE FAYUM LANDSCAPE

Ten Thousand Years of Archaeology, Texts, and Traditions in Egypt

CLAIRE J. MALLESON

The American University in Cairo Press
Cairo New York

First published in Egypt in 2019 by
The American University in Cairo Press
113 Sharia Kasr el Aini, Cairo, Egypt
200 Park Ave., Suite 1700, New York, NY 10166
www.aucpress.com

Dar el Kutub No. 26857/17
ISBN 978 977 416 883 3

Dar el Kutub Cataloging-in-Publication Data

Malleson, Clarie J.
The Fayum Landscape: Ten Thousand Years of Archaeology, Texts, and Traditions in Egypt / Claire J. Malleson.—Cairo: The American University in Cairo Press, 2019.
p. cm.
ISBN 978 977 416 883 3
1. Landscapes–Egypt
704.9436622

1 2 3 4 5 23 22 21 20 19

Designed by Adam el-Sehemy
Printed in the United States of America

For my parents

Contents

List of Illustrations

Black-and-White Figures

Color Plates

Between pages 130 and 131:

Acknowledgments

A great number of people supported me in this project, both during my PhD studies and while I was revising the text. I would particularly like to thank Nigel Fletcher-Jones and Neil Hewison from the American University in Cairo Press, who not only suggested they might like to publish my thesis but also provided invaluable advice, feedback, and encouragement. My PhD supervisors Steven Snape and Matthew Fitzjohn and my examiners Chris Eyre and Marco Zecchi offered many wise words and posed very helpful, difficult questions. Campbell Price, Cordula Werschkun, and Peter M. Robinson were endlessly supportive while I was preparing my PhD, as were my friends and colleagues in the School of Archaeology, Classics and Egyptology and the libraries at the University of Liverpool. My colleagues in the Department of History and Archaeology in the American University of Beirut have not only made me feel enormously welcome, but have also provided some crucial advice on parts of this book. Since 2007 I have worked with many archaeological missions in the United Kingdom and Egypt, and I owe a lot to the teams at Sedgeford Historical and Archaeological Research Project, Chester Amphitheatre, Giza (Ancient Egypt Research Associates), Tell al-Retaba, Elephantine (Deutsches Archäologisches Institut), Madinat al-Gurob, and Sais. My friends and family have known me at my best and my worst during this process, and I owe a great deal to Daniel Lawson, Pier Paolo Raffa, to my "five brothers and a million sisters" who keep me smiling, to my five "children" Rory, Benjamin, James, Amelia, and Robert, to my brother Tom, and to Emma and Niki. Many colleagues, friends, and family have read various drafts of this study as it progressed, and I am exceptionally grateful to everyone who offered their time and advice so generously, especially Ruth Binney and Marco Zecchi. Last, but certainly not least, I want to thank the people who first inspired me to 'do' Egyptology and Archaeology: Mark Lehner, José Pérez-Accino, Jan Picton, Mick Oakey, Keith Hazell, Naomi Payne, Neil Faulkner, and Patricia Graham.

Timeline

Chronology up to end of Roman Period based on Shaw (2000) unless noted otherwise (dates are approximate up to 664 BC).

Palaeolithic	700,000–7000 BP
Fayum Epipalaeolithic Cultural Phase (Qarunian)[1]	7530–6090 BC
Early Fayum Neolithic Cultural Phase (Fayumian)[2]	5480–4260
Late Fayum Neolithic Cultural Phase (Moerian)[3]	4620–3640
Lower Egyptian Neolithic and Egyptian Predynastic Period	5300–3000
Early Dynastic Period (First–Second Dynasty)	3000–2686
Old Kingdom (Third–Eighth Dynasty)	2686–2160
First Intermediate Period (Ninth–Tenth Dynasty)	2160–2055
Middle Kingdom (Eleventh–Thirteenth Dynasty)	2055–1650
Second Intermediate Period (Fourteenth–Seventeenth Dynasty)	1650–1550
New Kingdom (Eighteenth–Twentieth Dynasty)	1550–1069
Amarna Period	1352–1327
Ramesside Period	1295–1069
Third Intermediate Period (Twenty-first–Twenty-fifth Dynasty)	1069–664
Late Period (Twenty-sixth–Thirtieth Dynasty)	664–332
Ptolemaic Period	332–30
Macedonian Dynasty	332–310

Ptolemaic Dynasty	305–30
Roman Period	30 BC–AD 395
Late Antique/Byzantine/Coptic Period	AD 395–642
Ummayads	661–750
Abbasids	750–868
Tulunids	868–905
Ikhshidids	935–69
Fatimids	969–1171
Ayyubids	1169–1250
Mamluks	1250–1517
Ottomans	1517–1867
Muhammed Ali Pasha	1805–48
Khedival/Royal Egypt	1867–1953
Republic of Egypt	1953–Today

1

The Landscape: The Fayum

This province is the most remarkable and interesting of all the provinces of Egypt.[1]

—Major R.H. Brown (1892)

Other visitors . . . have also written in praise of the Fayoum, as "a true earthly paradise," "the garden of Egypt," "paradise of the desert." The stress has always been on the fertility and beauty of the land—by no means the only attraction of the Fayum to the modern visitor, but surely attraction enough, especially after the concrete desert of Cairo.[2]

—R.N. Hewison (2008)

For millennia the Fayum has been viewed as somehow different from the rest of Egypt. Not part of the Nile Valley but not remote enough to be considered one of the Western Desert oases, the Fayum has many unique aspects to it. The amazing qualities attributed to the region by Herodotus, the 'father of history,' in the fifth century BC were a source of fascination for later Classical scholars such as Pliny and Strabo, and attracted the first European pilgrims and explorers to the Fayum. The ideas they developed about the region, particularly those relating to Biblical events, became popular topics of debate in early Egyptology. The Fayum was the site of some of the earliest organized archaeological investigations in Egypt, by the British 'father of Egyptian archaeology,' Sir William Matthew Flinders Petrie, in the late nineteenth and early twentieth centuries. Amazingly rich discoveries of well-preserved Ptolemaic and Roman administrative and literary papyri, and life-like portraits found on Roman mummies in the region (known as the Fayum Portraits), meant that the Fayum became a major focus of attention for scholars studying those periods of Egyptian history. The Fayum is also home to some of the oldest archaeological remains discovered in Egypt. Around the shores of the lake, major Palaeolithic and Neolithic sites were noted during the early years of formal archaeology in Egypt, and have been under serious investigation since the mid-twentieth century.

The Fayum region is located to the southwest of Cairo and the Nile Delta apex, currently covering four thousand square kilometers. A lake, now known as Birkat Qarun, is situated in the northwest of the region and was historically fed by the Bahr Yusuf channel. The region is covered in 456 irrigation canals and drainage channels totalling 2,220 kilometers in length. In 2001 there was around 1,437 square kilometers of cultivatable land. These numbers are increasing every year. The region is separated from the Nile Valley by low-lying desert hills that are broken opposite Beni Suef where the Bahr Yusuf turns west to flow through a wide shallow valley toward the capital of the region, Madinat al-Fayum (ancient Shedet/Crocodilopolis/Arsinoë/Ptolemais Euergetes). The Fayum lands are essentially an inland delta, sloping gently down from the high point at the region's capital (c.23 meters above sea level), toward Birkat Qarun, which at the turn of the twenty-first century was 8 meters deep, with the surface at 45 meters below sea level[3] (see plates 1 and 2).

The geological history of the region has been much debated, and theories of how it was formed (created) have a colorful history. Following many decades of debate, geologists now generally agree that the Fayum depression—including the Qarun and Rayan basins—was formed by wind erosion over 1.8 million years ago in the early Pleistocene Period.[4] The Bahr Yusuf, which may well be a remnant channel of an older course of the Nile, is thought to have broken through the hills to the west of the Nile during the mid-Pleistocene (c.40,000 years ago).[5] The annual flooding of the Nile gradually carved many small rivers and channels into the basin, including two especially deep ravines now known as the al-Wadi and al-Bats drains, which, when viewed on a map, resemble two 'horns' or 'arms' emanating from the main river channel into the region (see plate 2). Over millennia, this flooding also deposited deep layers of fertile Nile silts into the region, spreading across the higher ground closer to the Nile Valley and down into the deepest part of the depression in the west. There was no escape for the flood waters, so a lake formed. The level of the waters of this lake varied each year through different seasons due to the annual Nile flood, and the average level has varied a great deal through history.

1. Google Earth image showing the Fayum in Egypt.

The major archaeological sites in the region are (see plate 3):

- Madinat al-Fayum (*šdt*/Crocodilopolis/Arsinoë/Ptolemais Euergetes): The capital of the region. Only a very few archaeological remains have ever been recorded, but there was probably a temple for Sobek here from at least the early Old Kingdom, and the city has been continuously occupied since then. The area where the majority of the archaeological remains have been found is known as Kiman Faris (Mounds of the Horseman).
- Kom W, Kom K: Two primary areas of prehistoric occupation remains on the north side of the lake.

- Widan al-Faras, Umm al-Sawan: Old Kingdom quarry sites.
- Qasr al-Sagha: Old Kingdom quarry town, Middle Kingdom temple and mining town.
- Seila: Old Kingdom pyramid, dated to reign of Sneferu.
- Abgig/Bebig: The site of the 'obelisk' of Senwosret I.
- Lahun/Kahun (*r-ḥnt*/Hetep-Senwosret/Sekhem-Senwosret/Ptolemais Hormou?): Pyramid of Senwosret II with associated cemeteries and town, which was reoccupied in the New Kingdom. The cemeteries were revived and expanded in the Ptolemaic/Roman Period.
- Biahmu/al-Sanam: Site of the ruins of two colossi of Amenemhat III.
- Kom Khelwa: Middle Kingdom elite tombs.
- Hawara: Pyramid of Amenemhat III, Ptolemaic and Roman cemeteries, and the 'Labyrinth'—so named by Herodotus, this monument gained legendary status. It is most likely that the 'Labyrinth' refers to the ruins of the mortuary temple of Amenemhat III.
- Madinat al-Gurob (*mr-wr*): Predynastic cemeteries, New Kingdom Palace town and cemeteries, Ptolemaic cemeteries.
- Madinat Madi (*ḏꜣ*/Narmouthis): Middle Kingdom temple of Renenutet and Sobek, Ptolemaic town and temple.
- Umm al-Burigat/Tebtunis (Tutun): Middle Kingdom cemeteries, Ptolemaic and Roman town and temples.
- Kom Aushim (Karanis): Ptolemaic and Roman town, temples, and cemeteries.
- Dimai (Soknopaios Nesos): Ptolemaic and Roman town and temples.
- Qasr Qarun (Dionysias): Ptolemaic town and temple, Roman fort.
- Kom Umm al-Atl (Bacchias): Ptolemaic and Roman town and temples.
- Kom/Kharabet Ihrit (Theadelphia): Ptolemaic and Roman town, and temples.
- Madinat Watfa (Philoteris): Ptolemaic and Roman town and temples.
- Kom al-Kharaba al-Kebir (Philadelphia): Ptolemaic and Roman town, temples, and cemeteries.
- Birkat Qarun (*?wꜣḏ-wr?*/Aqna/Tenhamet/Lake Moeris): The Fayum lake.
- Bahr Yusuf (*ḥnt?*/*ḥnt mr-wr*/Manhi canal): The primary watercourse into the region from the Nile.

Egyptological research about the Fayum has generally centered on either the issue of 'Lake Moeris' and the 'Labyrinth,' two highlights of the famous account of the Greek writer Herodotus,[6] or the aspects of Greek and Roman social and economic history revealed in the many rich archives of Ptolemaic and Roman papyri found in the region.[7] The impression given by the strong focus on the lake and the Labyrinth is that the lake was always seen to be the dominating feature of the Fayum landscape, and that the Labyrinth was thought to be the most significant monument in the archaeological landscape of the region. By looking at a wider range of sources, however, it is clear that perceptions of the Fayum landscape have not always been dominated by these features. The stimulus for much of the research in this book was my sense of discomfort with the lack of balance in past approaches to the Fayum landscape and the occasionally excessive amount of attention devoted to 'unwrapping' Herodotus's account of the Fayum.

This book is a history of ideas, a history of changing perceptions, and a history of the human–land relationship. It shows that when archaeology, texts, and oral traditions are brought together, those ideas, perceptions, and relationships are revealed to be both deeply imbued and manifested in the landscape, intertwined and overlapping into a rich palimpsest of historical nuances.

Ten Thousand Years of History

The archaeological materials, texts, and accounts included in this book cover a long span of history from 7500 BC to around AD 1900.[8] History is not a step-by-step linear sequence of events; changes in society, culture, or life can occur rapidly or slowly, they can 'regress' or become cyclical. People do not one day suddenly think, "Wow, I'm living in Ptolemaic Egypt, I should think this way, have these ideas and these perceptions today, instead of the ones I had last year when we were ruled by the Persians," but the inevitability of creating divisions, of breaking up that span of time into smaller chunks of time, is unavoidable when dealing with such a long history. The break-points in this book are based on the long-accepted divisions for the history of Egypt, which fall loosely in line with major changes in scripts and languages found in the texts examined here—from Egyptian hieroglyphs and Hieratic, to Demotic, Persian, Greek, Latin, Coptic, and Arabic, and finally European languages—although those divisions sometimes have very blurred lines. The continuation of ideas from one period into the next, and the fascination with far older beliefs that often resulted in ignorance of more recent ideas, has played a major role in shaping the ways people have engaged with and thought about the landscape of the Fayum.

The 'text-less' prehistorical periods (Epipalaeolithic, Neolithic, and Predynastic, c.7530–3000 BC) act as an introduction to the primary phase of traditional Egyptian history: the pharaonic period from the start of the Early Dynastic to the end of the Late Period (3000–332 BC). Both texts and archaeological remains are considered throughout the book. The archaeological remains provide tangible evidence of ways in which people physically interacted with the landscape. The locations of settlements, cemeteries (including pyramids), and temples provide some indications of what the landscape was actually like. In the case of the Fayum, the ever-changing level of the lake was the major factor governing people's choices, coupled with the natural resources of the region (stone for construction and the lake and land for procuring and producing food). The locations of, and spatial relationships between, architectural remains of houses, temples, cemeteries, and pyramids reveal a great deal about the ways in which the people of the region exploited and lived on the land, but it is the written record that illuminates the ways in which they thought about the landscape of the Fayum.

There is very little, if any, pharaonic material that can be considered to be 'geography' as we understand it today, and there are few written descriptions of landscapes. By studying the names given to the region, however, it is possible to gain insight into the contrasting ways the landscape of the Fayum was perceived. As outlined by Christopher Tilley, "place names are of such vital significance because they act so as to transform the sheerly physical and geographical into something that is historically and socially experienced. The bestowing of names creates shared existential space out of the blank environment."[9] Thus, by studying the names of the region, the perception of the Fayum landscape held by the ancient Egyptians is revealed. While there have been detailed studies of the religious geography (or sacred landscape) of the Fayum,[10] which firmly establish the primary role played by the crocodile god Sobek, there have been no studies of the way in which the names allocated to the Fayum, or different parts of the region, reflect ancient perceptions of the Fayum landscape. The textual material examined in Chapter Three derives from hieroglyphic inscriptions on private stelae and statues, as well as seal impressions and hieratic documents. This selection of sources includes examples of formulaic statements made to promote the image of the individual, as well as more private materials that reflect less structured ideas. Major groups of material presented include documents from Middle Kingdom Lahun, the New Kingdom Wilbour Papyrus, private statues and stelae from all periods, and the Greco-Roman Book of Fayum.

The most significant point arising from the pharaonic materials is that they make a clear distinction between the 'imagined' and the 'experienced' landscapes, the sacred landscape and the physical landscape in which people lived. Administrative texts and religious texts use different names.

The Names (3000–332 BC)

The place names used to describe the Fayum (the lexicography) yield information on how the region was perceived by the ancient Egyptians. Names of towns, cities, villages, and areas or locales can be hugely revealing about what people thought of a landscape. Often they are explicit descriptions of small locales, for example 'Lake Land,' 'Lake Opening,' and 'Great Green.'

Naming transforms what is a purely physical geographical landmass or area into something tangible, something with a boundary, something imbued with meaning. To quote Christopher Tilley: "The bestowing of names creates a shared existential space out of the blank environment."[11] By looking at textual and inscriptional evidence from Fayum monuments, and writings associated with individuals known to have lived in or had close ties to the Fayum, it is possible to gain insight into the institutions based in the region, as well as the activities that took place there. One thing that is important to bear in mind is that place names change a lot over time. There have been several previous studies about place names in the Fayum, usually relating to the issue of the name of Lake Moeris, but not many acknowledge that it is not appropriate to attempt to allocate a name to a place and assume that that place held that name, or the same meaning, throughout history. Pharaonic history in particular tends to be treated as one entity, often due to a lack of nuanced information, and people have tied themselves in strange knots attempting to figure out which name refers to which place, forgetting that even in a short space of time a place name can morph into something different simply due to small events, new stories, or shifting ideas.

Each of the various names given to the Fayum region during the pharaonic period, and to localities or specific places within it, provides significant information about the way the area was perceived.[12] Each of the various different names given to the Fayum was almost always restricted to specific contexts. In other words, different types of people used different names for places at different times. Texts that have a religious aspect (for example, texts from temples, priestly titles, and statue inscriptions dedicated to Fayum deities) use different versions of the name than texts that clearly relate to administrative activities, such as the titles of officials.

šdt (Shedet) was the name of the primary cult center for the crocodile god Sobek, and *tꜣ-š* (Lake Land) was the name used for the region in religious contexts, while *š-rsi* (Southern Lake) was the name given to the region in administrative texts. Some of the names for localities in the Fayum obviously carry meaning but appear to have been used only in restricted circumstances. For example, despite the fact that the name *š-sbk* (Lake of Sobek) is clearly linked to the primary deity, the crocodile god Sobek, it appears as a place name only during the Middle Kingdom and exclusively in administrative texts. The lake does not appear to have been specifically named. It was of course the only major inland lake in Egypt, so 'Lake' (*š*) was appropriate, but the idea that the lake was an embodiment of location in the realm of the gods may possibly be found in the name *wꜣḏ-wr* (Great Green).

tꜣ-š—Lake Land

This is the most prominent name for the Fayum, found almost exclusively in religious texts, priests' titles, and inscriptions dedicated to deities from the Middle Kingdom onward. This usage, in inscriptions, probably accounts for the fact that it is the best known name for the region. Other names occur on less permanent materials, such as papyrus. There are three primary variants of the 'spelling' of this name, each of which includes the lake hieroglyph (Gardiner sign N37) and either the land hieroglyph (N16) or the hills hieroglyph (N25). Visually, this group of signs clearly depicts a lake with land and hills—highly appropriate for the Fayum.

š-rsi—Southern Lake

The second commonly found name for the region appears in the Third Dynasty, but is generally found only in administrative contexts. *š-rsi*, 'Southern Lake,' is found with a variety of spellings, and the differences occur predominantly in hieratic spellings of the name. All the variants include the lake hieroglyph (N37) and the combination sign for 'south' (M24). Some hieratic examples indicate that the name may sometimes refer not to the region as a whole, but to a specific place, as the town sign (O49) is included.

š-sbk—Lake of Sobek (sometimes *š n sbk*)

It would be natural to assume that the names *š-sbk* and *š n sbk* referred to a lake connected to the crocodile cult within the Fayum region. While this may be possible, the name is found almost exclusively in hieratic administrative texts from Lahun, all dated to the Middle Kingdom, with just a few examples occurring later in the New Kingdom, all of them still clearly administrative. The hieroglyphs found in the name include the lake sign (N37), but also frequently the land hieroglyph (N23) as well as the crocodile hieroglyph to denote Sobek (I3 or I4).

wp-š—Lake Opening

One of the names that really plays on using hieroglyphs as visual images is *wp-š*. This name, 'Lake Opening,' is not only clearly describing a place within a landscape, but it also relies on the actual signs to convey a more complex pictorial visualization of this specific landscape. The name is only found in the New Kingdom Wilbour Papyrus and the Twenty-fifth Dynasty victory stela of Piy, but it is especially interesting for this study. 'Lake Opening' could mean one of two things. It could refer to a place where a lake opens out into several parts, divides perhaps or separates, or a place in which a lake splits up into rivers or canals. 'Lake Opening' could also refer to the beginning of a lake, the point of origin, or the rivers that run into the lake to create it. In the case of the Fayum lake, this could be the place in which the main tributary splits at the western end of the Gurob–Hawara corridor into the al-Wadi and al-Bats ravines. The writing of the name includes the bull horn hieroglyph (F13), which almost appears to be a visual onomatopoeia, with the bull horns resembling those two ravines running north and south from the end of the Bahr Yusuf (see plate 2). It could perhaps refer to the 'opening' of the region at the eastern end of that corridor, where the mountains of the Western Desert divide and the Bahr Yusuf turns west into the region. In most texts this area around Lahun does seem to be the area to which the name was attached. What is of even greater interest is the fact that the Arabic name for the lake, may be a corruption of Birkat al Qurun, 'Lake (of the) Horns,' suggesting that this image of the rivers dividing and resembling horns persisted throughout history. Based on the texts we can be certain that this name refers to a specific locality in the landscape around Lahun.

š—Lake

There are a few instances in which the name *š*, or 'Lake,' appears alone, with no additional descriptive words, and in the examples relating to the Fayum the name clearly refers to a lake in the region. Since this name was used in both religious and administrative contexts in the Middle and

New Kingdoms, the use of the name seems to have been somewhat flexible. Within the administrative examples there is a difference between very explicit references to a place or town (in the Wilbour Papyrus and Onomasticon of Amenemope) where a town sign is used, and more ambiguous examples on the statue of Sobekhotep (Berlin 11635),[13] where 'lake' might refer to either a place or a lake. In religious contexts 'lake' refers simply to a lake associated with a deity. The name is written simply, for example, Sobekhotep was *ḥ3ty-ʿ n š*, Mayor of (the) Lake. Here 'lake' is found written with the small tongue of land hieroglyph (N21). In other instances the hilly land hieroglyph (N25) is used. It is possible that in most instances this was simply an abbreviated form of *t3-š* given the religious context of most of the texts.

ḥnt—Henet

ḥnt is a somewhat ambiguous term, the translation of which is still not entirely clear, largely due to the fact that it is sometimes written using the 'lake' or 'pool' ideogram (N37) and sometimes with the 'canal' or 'channel' ideogram (N36). For a long time it was translated as 'swampy lake,'[14] meaning a generally watery landscape (but not a marsh). In more recent years this has been revised, and the term is now translated as 'waterway.'[15] The term appears fairly frequently in the Old Kingdom Pyramid Texts as an area or place within the landscape of the afterlife that has to be crossed, but it is clear from an examination of the Middle Kingdom Lahun papyri and the New Kingdom Wilbour Papyrus that there was a *ḥnt* that was a clearly defined type of body of water (within the Fayum). The Lahun papyri refer just to the *ḥnt*, but assuming that these documents were primarily internal correspondence then it is probably safe to suggest that anyone reading the letters would know which *ḥnt* was being referenced. The *ḥnt*s in the Wilbour Papyrus are all more clearly designated with a location, for example, the *ḥnt* east of Spermeru (a town south of the Fayum) and the *ḥnt* of *mr-wr*. This may seem like a tautology—'canal of the great canal'—but if *mr-wr* was the name of a town (see below), it is more acceptable.

The more descriptive name *r-ḥnt* (or *r-n-ḥnt*), 'Mouth of the Henet,' appears in funerary texts as a locality in the landscape of the afterlife, and in both religious and administrative documents as a place in the Fayum. The Twenty-fifth Dynasty Victory stela of Piy names *r-ḥnt* as the area of the Fayum in which *wp-š* is located:

 *pw ỉr.n ḥm.f r wp-š m r-ḥnt* (His Majesty went north to Wep-She in Ra-Henet)

It is instructive to note that in this instance the *ḥnt* in question was not described using a locality, it is not the henet of somewhere (as the *ḥnt* of *mr-wr* was, for example), but that the word *ḥnt* is a part of the place name itself. In the Book of Fayum it is apparent that this refers to the entrance area of the Fayum, near Lahun, and it is always assumed that the name Lahun is a modern form of the ancient name *r-ḥnt*.

 *mr-wr*—Mer-wer

It has long been accepted that the New Kingdom palace-town at modern Madinat al-Gurob was named *mr-wr*, 'Great Canal,' as this name appears soon after the founding of the town in the Eighteenth Dynasty. It is clear from Gurob papyri and the Wilbour Papyrus that *mr-wr* is a town. In all examples the town determinative hieroglyph is part of the name. The occurrences of the more specific *ḫnrt* or *pr-ḫnty* (usually translated as Harem) in *mr-wr* refer to an institution probably located in the Royal Palace at Gurob. This place name is so overtly descriptive of a local feature in the landscape that it is hard to imagine that the Mer-wer, 'Great Waterway,' is anything but the river course running from the Nile into the Fayum, known now as the Bahr Yusuf.

 *p3-ym*—Pa-yum

Perhaps the most fascinating name for the Fayum (or an area within the Fayum) is *p3-ym*, 'The Great Lake/Sea,' which incorporates a Semitic word for sea (*ym*). This name is phonetically almost identical to the Coptic root of the modern name Fayum. However, *p3-ym* occurs only very rarely prior to the Ptolemaic Period. In the Wilbour Papyrus, *p3-ym* (if indeed the name in that manuscript is *p3-ym*) does seem to refer to an area of the Fayum close to the entrance at the Nile–Fayum divide. In the Book of Fayum, *p3-ym* is a place within the sacred landscape, where Ra was thought to have been born.

 *w3ḏ-wr*—Wadj-wer (Great Green)

Whether or not this name applies to a location or place in the Fayum landscape is debatable.[16] A considerable amount of evidence suggests that 'Wadj-wer' was used to refer to the Mediterranean, but several Fayum texts, especially the Hymn to Sobek and the Book of Fayum, clearly designate it as being within the Fayum. It seems to refer more to a location in the landscape of the gods, the 'Great Green' (sea/lake) in which the gods dwell, and where Ra is born.

šdt—Shedet

It is usually stated that the 'capital' of the Fayum was known as Shedet (*šdt*), but every occurrence of this name is linked to the principal deity of the region, the crocodile god Sobek. The name never occurs independently in administrative texts. *šdt* was very specifically, and above all else, the dwelling place of Sobek, and the name first appears at the beginning of the First Dynasty. The root of this name could lie in several words, each of which provides insight into how this location or place was perceived by the ancient Egyptians. *šd* (Artificial Lake), *šdyt* (Pool/Well), and *šdy* (Ditch) all seem potential candidates, and each suggests a very different type of landscape feature. It is entirely possible that the use of the root *šd* reflects a general notion of a body of water within the landscape, fitting in perfectly with all the names given to the region. The root of this name, *šd*, which implies something that is not natural, may well be at the root of the myth that appears in the account of Herodotus and the Book of Fayum, drawn from the creation mythology first found in the Hymn to Sobek, in which the idea that the lake was dug by men or gods is an important theme.

That the main variants of the writing of this name depend on which deity is being referred to becomes apparent when its use is analyzed. With just one exception, if the deity is Sobek as a form of Horus then the Shedet 'determinative'—a 'booth' with the bucranion emblem (a bull's head) on it—is used. An example can be found on a fragment in the Petrie Museum, from Hawara (UC14794, see plate 4). The inscription reads *ḥr ḥry-ib šdt*, or 'Horus dwelling in Shedet.'

If only Sobek as a sole deity is referred to, then that determinative is not used, as can be found in the false door of Ka-nefer, an Old Kingdom priest of Sobek of Shedet (BM1324):

ḥm nṯr sbk šdt (Priest of Sobek of Shedet)

Part of the inscription on the lap of the Middle Kingdom statue of Ren-seneb demonstrates this most clearly,[17] as here both Sobek and Horus are referred to individually, and Shedet is spelled differently for the two gods:

ḥtp di nsw sbk nb iwnw sbk šdt ḥr ḥry-ib šdt (An offering which the King gives to Sobek Lord of Innu, Sobek of Shedet, and Horus who dwells in Shedet).

In the Middle Kingdom Hymn to Sobek, the earliest occurrence of the specific Fayum form of Sobek, Sobek-Shedty, appears. As this writing is not restricted to either hieratic or hieroglyphs, the spelling cannot be said to be a result of different scripts. Early occurrences of *šdt* in the Pyramid Texts are some of the only examples in which the town-sign determinative was used, suggesting that the location was indeed not only a location in the sacred landscape but also a town. The designation of 'capital' for Shedet is questionable given the total lack of any individuals with administrative roles linked to the town, other than priestly roles.

Based on the early occurrence of the name, this town (or cult center) was clearly founded by at least the Fifth Dynasty, and the name reflects one aspect of ancient perceptions of the landscape. The possible roots of the word—ditch, artificial lake, or well-like-pool—all carry the notion that the body of water in question is not necessarily natural. The location of *šdt*, at the end of the Bahr Yusuf where the river divides into numerous smaller channels running toward the Fayum lake, on the highest and probably driest area in the region, is a natural and obvious location for a major town. It would have been an ideal location from which to monitor goods traveling from anywhere in the region toward the Nile, and vice versa. For this reason, the lack of people with administrative titles associated with the town is especially perplexing. In fact, it strongly suggests that the region was administered from outside.

The name of the Fayum lake has changed over time. As is shown above, the ancient name is not really understood, if it indeed even had a name other than 'Southern Lake.' The earliest occurrence of what is perhaps the most 'famous' name for the lake seems to be in Herodotus's *Histories*, where he appears to name it Lake Moeris or Lake of Moeris. Later, what may be a name for the lake (although this, too, is unclear) appears on medieval Islamic maps, where the names Aqna and Tenhamet appear as 'labels' for the Fayum lake. The name Birkat Qarun does not seem to have been recorded before the eighteenth century.

The Bahr Yusuf was perhaps originally named *mr-wr*, as explained above, but in most medieval Islamic texts it is named al-Menha canal or the Manhi canal. The name Bahr Yusuf appears in the thirteenth century, and almost certainly derives from local legends that attribute the creation of the channel to the prophet Joseph.

There is just one ancient dedicated 'map' depiction of the Fayum region: The Book of Fayum, which is one of the most spectacular papyri to have been found in Egypt. Its contents have roots in far more ancient traditions, but the preserved copies of the papyrus date to the Roman Period. The document is a visualization of the religious landscape of the Fayum, and takes the form of a pseudo-map of the region with every sacred aspect included: the lake, the land, shrines, and temples. The text is heavily laden with religious meaning and is almost incomprehensible, in part because it is almost certainly a Roman version of far older writings and the scribes may well not have understood much of what they were transcribing. This text, discussed in Chapter Three, conveys deep-rooted beliefs about the sacred landscape of the Fayum, which may, in its entirety, have been thought of as a 'temple' of Sobek. The river was believed to be the embodiment of the mother goddess (the Celestial Cow), from whom the sun god Ra was born into the lake, in order to allow him to rejuvenate each night as he passed through its waters, and to sustain the gods each day with offerings as he passed across the sky. Osiris, the embodiment of the fertility of the land, was protected from the malevolence of the god Seth, the embodiment of the desert, by Horus in his crocodile Sobek form along the banks of this river, known as the Henet.

Changing Landscape

The most influential piece of writing on the Fayum ever produced, the Greek account of Herodotus, was written in about 445 BC during the Late Period, when Egypt was under Persian rule. From the moment it was first disseminated, this account deeply affected the way people viewed the Fayum. At the very least, it shaped how the Fayum was written about. The actual influence on the people living in the Fayum is impossible to gauge. It is difficult to write about the Fayum without mentioning Herodotus, and indeed most written accounts of the Fayum begin and end with considerations of his account and the remains of the sites and monuments he described. In Chapter Four, the account is placed in its historical and cultural context.

Following what is traditionally seen as the end of the classical Egyptian pharaonic period were the Ptolemaic and Roman periods (332 BC to the fourth century AD). Because the Fayum was undoubtedly a place of interest for the rulers of the time, this period is especially significant in the history of the Fayum, not least because the landscape was dramatically transformed by major interventions into the hydrology of the region. There are many standing remains of temples and towns from the period. Astounding quantities of papyri have been found in the region that provide extraordinarily rich and detailed accounts of life in the Fayum during this period. The textual and archaeological records extend as late as the early Byzantine Period in the fifth to the sixth centuries AD. As a result, the Ptolemaic and Roman Fayum has been studied extensively. Due to the abundance of material, texts from the Fayum have been used to study the Ptolemaic and Roman history of Egypt as a whole. While there are well-preserved remains of temples (now heavily restored), several of the settlements and cemeteries have sadly been lost, not only due to the passage of time and major changes in land use, but also as a result of the activities of individuals in search of caches of papyri and other saleable artifacts.

One positive result of the 'recovery' of such vast quantities of papyri is that a great deal is known about the administration of the towns and temples of the region in this period, and several detailed studies of the settlement systems and landscape of the Fayum have been completed.[18] The scholarly work on the huge corpus of texts from this period is outlined in Chapter Four, alongside descriptions of the relevant archaeological remains in the region. As with the textual evidence from the Ptolemaic and Roman Fayum, the amount of archaeological exploration that has taken place on sites dating to this period is extraordinary; the results are summarized here. Outside the study of administrative materials in their own right, much of the focus of the work on the Fayum texts has been on understanding the names used for the Fayum and its villages/towns, and on locating those places, particularly the hundreds of known villages, as well as Lake Moeris and the Henet of Moeris.[19]

Alongside the study of the 'internal' records from the Fayum in Chapter Four is an examination of the contemporary writings of so-called 'classical scholars'—the geographical and historical works of Strabo, Diodorus Siculus, Pomponius Mela, Pliny, and Claudius Ptolemy—as well as a small selection of letters that record the activities of visitors to the Fayum during the first and second centuries AD. During the Ptolemaic and Roman periods, the Fayum was a prime tourist attraction. Drawn by the descriptions in the account of Herodotus, many visitors went to the region to see the crocodiles, the lake, and the Labyrinth. Their accounts and letters attest to the enduring perception of the Fayum as being embodied by these three aspects. It is these works that had such a great effect later on European writers, primarily due to the status of Greek and

Latin writings in the early European education system. The views held by Greco-Roman visitors seem utterly disconnected from what is known about the reality of urban and rural life in the Fayum at this time, and they seem to overlook totally the many contemporary 'wonders' of the region. The Ptolemaic and Roman temples must have been truly wonderful then, and the towns would have been bustling hubs of society, but the motivation behind the accounts was historical, and as a result we have no accounts describing perceptions of the Fayum landscape as it was at that time. Instead, the visitors' accounts are of a temporalized imagined ancient (sacred) landscape.

Legendary Landscape

Writings that have rarely been included in accounts of Egypt (although they are attracting increasing attention) are the works of medieval Islamic scholars, which are presented in Chapter Five. This material dates from the eighth century to the mid-fifteenth century AD, spanning a gap often left blank in histories of Egyptology. Following the Islamic conquest of Egypt in AD 642, the earliest medieval account of the history of Egypt (dating to c. AD 790) was written by Ibn 'Abd al-Hakam. During this time, the science of geography was rapidly advancing and many renowned Islamic scholars contributed a great deal to the understanding of the nature of the earth and its dimensions. It is the contributions of the 'historical' geographers (more anthropological works) that are of greatest interest. These individuals produced works that are easily classifiable as human geography in today's terms. They studied the routes from one province of the Islamic empire to another, recorded borders, and took copious notes from merchants and travelers regarding the locations of towns, their produce, and their taxation systems. They recorded tales about 'marvels' of different nations (monuments, natural wonders), noted the most significant ancient monuments and stories about them (for example, the pyramids), and generally commented on the nature of different regions of the countries. These authors provide insight into the perceptions of Egypt held by visitors from elsewhere in the Islamic world. Only a very few of these scholars were native Egyptian Arabs, and if they were, it is likely that their Muslim Arab identity was stronger than their Egyptian identity. The Fayum region during this period was, like many parts of Egypt, still predominantly occupied by Coptic Egyptians. The Muslim Arab ruling elite remained confined to Cairo and the north, and their perceptions of the Fayum region were colored by several factors, notably the shared beliefs found in the Bible and the Qur'an, their nationality, their location in Egypt, and their reason for being in Egypt.

The religious ties between Islam and Christianity are vividly represented in medieval Islamic accounts of the Fayum, and indeed these accounts are the only records of what are certain to be Coptic Christian traditions about the Fayum landscape. The most significant aspect of the Fayum in the eyes of medieval Islamic scholars was that it was created by the prophet Joseph—an important figure in both the Bible and the Qur'an. It is likely that Coptic tradition linked Joseph to the creation of the region. This story, when told to Muslim visitors, was easily accepted because it involved a familiar figure. The medieval Islamic scholars, like all travelers, often compared the landscape of the region they were visiting with that of their home nation. More than one scholar noted that the river of Fayum was more remarkable than the Euphrates or Tigris, even though the reality may well have not been so idyllic.

One of the most significant elements of their ideas about the landscape of the Fayum is their perception of its location. Cairo (Fustat) was one of the most important cultural centers of the Islamic world, and most scholars probably did not venture beyond its outskirts, collecting their information about Egypt from merchants who traveled throughout the country. Thus the medieval Islamic perception of the Fayum was based on the experiences of people who traveled to the region from Cairo, resulting in a strong directional perspective. Their perception of the region was shaped by the route taken by the merchants to the region from Cairo, across the desert. This journey from Cairo to the Fayum, crossing the desert, led to a perception that the Fayum landscape lay outside the landscape of Egypt both physically and psychologically. It was distant and hard to reach, and not really integrated into Egypt.

The medieval Islamic perception of the region developed over time, with writers borrowing ad hoc from each other, often repeating the accounts of earlier scholars without question. The end result was that the Fayum landscape was perceived to be divine, having been created by Joseph with inspiration from God. It was also distant from 'their' Egypt (Cairo) and reachable only after undertaking a dangerous journey. The perception that the region was divine and linked to Joseph was also held by some of the later European scholars, somewhat ironically based primarily on different sources.

Explored Landscape

The final group of materials to be considered (presented in Chapter Six) comprises works of 'modern' European writers, generally in the form of travel accounts. From the sixteenth century, European travelers started to visit Egypt in increasingly large numbers. Their perception of the landscape was shaped by what they had read in the classical accounts of Herodotus, Pliny, and Strabo, and to a large extent they divorced the modern Egypt of the Mamluks from the ancient Egypt of the pharaohs. Modern Egypt was a place that, in their eyes, needed transforming, while ancient Egypt needed studying. Their perception of the Fayum was frequently shaped by their 'knowledge' of the Labyrinth and Lake Moeris of Herodotus. The travelers who were in Egypt to experience its modern, exotic, 'oriental' culture, not its ancient culture, visited the Fayum for its rich game hunting. Their perception was naturally shaped by the rich resources the region provided for these activities.

These writings are typical early orientalist works, and are studied in an appropriate context. Works such as those by Edward Said (1978), Donald Reid (2002), and Elliot Colla (2008), have influenced the way these accounts are treated here. To a large extent their perceptions of Egypt shaped the approach taken by early Egyptologists, and many of these perceptions are still apparent today. In Chapter Six the accounts are placed firmly in their cultural and historical context. They are not taken at face value—the 'views' of the landscape they portray do not always reflect reality. Rather, they reveal perceptions of the Fayum landscape shaped by the writers' cultural sphere, nationality, social status, personal studies, and 'place' in Egypt.

The Transmission of Texts

One of the key factors affecting the history of the study of the Fayum is the unavoidably monumental effect the 'Classical' Greek and Latin accounts had on early Egyptology. This makes it is appropriate here to outline how the Classical texts were transmitted and received, in order to fully appreciate how and why they played such a huge role in shaping perceptions of ancient Egypt, especially the Fayum.

The beginnings of Classical scholarship lie in the early records of what had previously only been orally transmitted (Greek) poetry in the seventh century BC, resulting in small-scale circulation of written works. By the fifth century BC a book trade existed in Athens, and small private collections were forming. In the fourth century BC the first academic institutions with libraries were founded, with the Mouseion and its library in Alexandria established in 280 BC by Ptolemy Philadelphus. By the end of the second century BC the great age of Greek Classical scholarship in Alexandria had come to an end, but people continued to study the older works. The partial destruction of the library in Alexandria in the first century BC did not prevent it from being used. Strabo, for example, was able to study in Alexandria.[20] Inspired by the Greek scholars, Latin literature had started to appear in the third century BC. Education consisted primarily of the study and interpretation of Greek poetry. In addition, an interest in history began to develop. Under Augustus the book trade flourished and the appearance of the codex and use of parchment provided easier production and greater durability of texts. As a result, many works were copied, ensuring better preservation of the texts. The rise of Christianity but lack of suitable Christian texts led to the use of Greek Classical works in religious education.[21]

Between the fourth and seventh centuries AD Greek texts were translated into Syriac in the East, and Greek and Latin books were preserved in monasteries in the West. During the eighth century a revival of learning and education occurred in Europe, schools were attached to cathedrals and monasteries, and copies of Classical Latin texts started to be reproduced again.[22] Perhaps ironically, given the value that had been placed on Greek works during the Roman Period, Latin—rather than Greek—began to be viewed as the language of education and religion, and knowledge of Latin became a marker of cultural status.[23]

The fact that scientific and philosophical works were highly valued by Islamic scholars meant that the Classical age of Islamic scholarship included many studies of Greek works, and during the ninth century AD many Greek Classical texts were translated into Arabic and Persian. The focus on astronomical, mathematical, and geographical texts, however, meant that the more literary works (for example, Herodotus's *Histories*) were overlooked. Contemporaneous with this Islamic translation movement in the East, there was a revival of learning in the Byzantine West during the mid-ninth century. By the mid-eighth century, paper making, learned from the Chinese by the Arabs, had passed across into Western Europe, facilitating greater ease of reproduction. During the ninth to twelfth centuries the Classical Latin texts were copied and studied. Many Greek Classical texts found their way to Italy, sparking a brief interest in them in the ninth century. By the twelfth century, education had shifted from the monasteries into cathedral schools, Greek texts found their way into the curriculum via Latin translations (often based on Arabic translations), and Islamic learning was filtering into Europe via Spain. It should be borne in mind that education was essentially aimed at the instruction of the clerical classes, namely men destined for service in the church who needed to be versed in Latin in order to preach the Bible.[24]

By the thirteenth century the first universities had been established, and they, too, focused on the education of men destined for the Church. During the Renaissance, Classical texts were translated into several contemporary European languages, making them far more accessible. Alongside this advance, the educated classes increasingly valued knowledge of Latin as a means of impressing social peers. The early fifteenth century saw the earliest European collecting expeditions to the East in search of new manuscripts for the study of Greek and Latin Classical and Biblical texts, and some of the first court patronage of book collections and libraries.[25] The first Greek grammar was produced by the English Franciscan friar Roger Bacon in the thirteenth century, but it was not until the fifteenth century that scholars really showed any great interest in the Greek works, when the desire to read the authors referred to in the Latin works led to the employment of many Greeks as translators and teachers. Several Greek works were translated into Latin in Italy during the early years of the Renaissance, and in 1457 Pope Nicholas V (who established the collection of manuscripts in the Vatican library) ordered translations of Herodotus, Strabo, and Ptolemy.[26]

The invention of the printing press in the late fifteenth century led to a huge increase in the availability of Latin texts. The press at the Sorbonne in Paris produced large numbers of Latin texts and the Aldine press in Venice was dedicated to the production of Greek works. The increasingly tight Church control over the Bible led to a decline in its use as a Classical text—no longer could scholars debate the meaning and translations of the work. In 1590 Pope Sixtus V oversaw the production of the Latin Vulgate Bible, which, after a few changes by his successor Clement VIII, became the standard (unchangeable) text for the Catholic Church until 1926. During the fifteenth and sixteenth centuries both Greek and Latin studies flourished in France, Budé producing Latin translations of Greek works, and both Latin and Greek texts were translated into French.[27] The first partial translation of Herodotus's *Histories* into Latin was by the Italian scholar Battista Guarino in the early fifteenth century, and by 1452 a full translation had been completed by Lorenzo Valla.[28]

Following the Renaissance rediscovery of the many Egyptian obelisks in Rome, during the sixteenth century European scholars and pilgrims started to make trips to Egypt. Interest in travel to Egypt for exploration and to see the ancient monuments described in Classical works started to grow, and visitors started collecting antiquities for their patrons. By the mid-seventeenth century many of these travelers were publishing accounts of their exploits, which led to increased interest in travel, exploration, and collecting in Egypt. Work by Jesuit scholar Athanasius Kircher triggered a surge of interest in the translation of hieroglyphs, which previously had been shrouded in mystery;[29] Kircher unfortunately made no real advances. This increasing fashion for travel to collect antiquities and manuscripts increased the desire to gain access to more of the Classical geographical works and to acquire information on the countries to which the collectors were traveling. While traveling, scholars encountered local (oral) folklore, which during the Middle Ages was accorded similar importance to the Classical texts.[30] There can be no real doubt that early Renaissance travelers to Egypt held this view, and the stories included in many early European accounts display a blend of Classical and oral traditions. Due to the epic nature of the events and heroic deeds of the characters, folklore often captured the imaginations of travelers and their readers more readily.

The first ever *Description de l'Égypte* was written by the French diplomat and historian Benôit de Maillet in the late seventeenth century,[31] although this title is now synonymous with the far grander and more ambitious monument of a 'book' produced by the much later Napoleonic expedition in the early nineteenth century. The eighteenth century can easily be viewed as the birthplace of Egyptology as it is understood today. The works of travelers/explorers such as Englishman Richard Pococke and Danish naval officer Frederick Norden became guides for future travelers and included highly detailed accounts of the sites and monuments they encountered in Egypt. Naturally, they wanted to discover new sites and 'wonders,' but they also all sought to discover the 'famous' sites known from the Bible and the Classical Greek and Latin histories of Egypt. The Labyrinth and Lake Moeris of Herodotus were high on that list. This led many travelers and scholars to the Fayum, and eventually resulted in exploration of the region as a whole and the discovery of the numerous other (more tangible) Ptolemaic and Roman remains it contained.

The earliest 'Western' studies of medieval Islamic historical and geographical works were undertaken by (principally French) orientalists and philologists in the nineteenth century. They looked primarily at the language itself—medieval Persian or Arabic. The works were also valued for the insights they provided into the early Islamic state, medieval Islamic history, and medieval science, and for their contribution to Western understandings of the early Islamic faith. Certain genres became the focus of interest for specific groups of scholars, that is, mathematics, astrology, astronomy, geography, cartography, or history. Simultaneously, during the early to mid-nineteenth century Egyptology as we understand it today was becoming established. Egypt became more easily accessible to Europeans after the invasion of Napoleon in 1798. During the late nineteenth century the Service des Antiquités was founded. There was initially interest in the value that some of the Arabic and Persian material held for Egyptologists. Gaston Maspero, the second head of the Antiquities Service, studied the French translation of the anonymous *Akhbar al-zaman (l'Abrégé des merveilles)*,[32] acknowledging the value of the work. His wider knowledge of Islamic works is apparent in the fact that he noted that many passages were borrowed or copied from al-Mas'udi, Maqrizi, and Murtada. This interest was only briefly held in Egyptology, however, and only rarely since Maspero have Egyptologists considered these texts. A summary of the few works that have considered medieval sources is presented by Okasha El Daly (2005). It includes Penny Wilson and David Jeffreys, but the list is not long.[33]

The quest to 'find' the wonders described by Classical scholars is not really over: relatively recent publications show that Lake Moeris and the Labyrinth are still topics of debate.[34] Advances in Egyptology mean that far more attention is now paid to broader questions relating to the history of occupation in the region and the use of the Fayum landscape. One serious barrier to producing long histories of the Fayum (or indeed any area of Egypt) is the almost complete fragmentation of the study of the history of Egypt into many distinct subjects: Egyptology (the history, language, and art of ancient Egypt), Egyptian archaeology (more scientific studies of material culture, ancient technology, settlements, and activities of daily life), Classical history/archaeology (Ptolemaic and Roman periods), Classical studies (the traditional Classical Greek and Latin texts), Coptic studies (Coptic as a language and Christianity in Egypt), and Medieval studies (texts and archaeology of Arab–Islamic Egypt).

The Landscape: The Fayum

The natural form of the Fayum region—an inland delta contained within the boundary of desert hills—not only makes it an ideal case study for a long history of the relationship between people and the clearly bounded land they inhabit and experience, but also is responsible for major developments in the ways in which humans interact with their environment. From the earliest exploitation of natural resources in Egypt with the beginnings of agriculture in the Palaeolithic/Neolithic, to the first land-altering interventions into the hydrology of Egypt in the Ptolemaic Period, and some of the earliest excavations in Egypt during the nineteenth century AD, the Fayum landscape has always invited people to take advantage of it and to speculate on how it came into being. The ways people have lived in, altered, and studied the land of the Fayum region have shaped and been shaped by their perceptions of the landscape. It is that relationship which forms the focus of this book.

2

Academic Landscape: Theory in Archaeology and Geography

> Landscape has to be contextualised. The way in which people—anywhere, everywhere—understand and engage with their worlds will depend upon the specific time and place and historical conditions. It will depend on their gender, age, class, caste, and on their social and economic situation. . . . They will operate on very different temporal scales, engaging with the past and with the future in many different ways. [1]
>
> —Barbara Bender (1995)

It is generally accepted that the term 'landscape' originated in sixteenth-century Germanic and Romance languages as a word to describe paintings of natural scenery—*landskip*. The painters of romanticized landscapes of the Renaissance Period were inspired by the pastoral genre of the Classical poets, including Homer, Virgil, and Ovid, and influenced by the increasing availability of the printed Bible and exposure to the strange and foreign landscapes described in it.[2] The notion of the wild, untamed, and beautiful landscape became a key theme of the Romantic poets of the nineteenth century, with William Wordsworth being the most influential proponent. This was in part a reaction to the rapid industrialization of Britain, and also stimulated by a growing interest in Classical authors. In England it coincided with the wars with France, the decline of the Ottoman Empire, the beginning of the industrial revolution, and the rise of the British Empire. All these factors contributed to advances in science and travel. As a result of discomfort with the perceived destruction of their ideal landscapes, the Romantic poets looked backward in time and 'temporalized' the landscape. They romanticized the antiquity of the land and any monuments within it, as if they wanted to freeze the landscape in a past time.[3]

In the mid-twentieth century a series of publications discussing the English landscape and the relationships between humans and land had a great influence on geographers, historians, and archaeologists. Renowned British archaeologists such as Sir Cyril Fox (author of *Personality of Britain* (1932)), Jacquetta Hawkes (author of *A Land* (1951)), and English landscape historian William George Hoskins (author of *The Making of the English Landscape* (1955)), became fascinated with the ways in which different landscapes had been created by people and how those landscapes themselves affected the lives of the people living in them. Hoskins was a major advocate of having an active engagement with the landscape in order to fully appreciate the fact that landscape was a palimpsest of history shaped by mankind (terminology he borrowed from Ordnance Survey archaeologist and early exponent of the use of aerial photography in archaeology O.G.S. Crawford). Hoskins is (wrongly or rightly) seen to be the 'father' of landscape history, and the popularity of his television series (*Horizon: The Making of the English Landscape* (1972) and *Landscapes of England: An Exploration* (1978)) and accompanying books (*English Landscapes* (1973) and *One Man's England* (1978)) had a major impact on how geographers, historians, and archaeologists thought about the landscape. Hoskins undoubtedly romanticized the landscape. He was deeply disturbed by the wave of post-war industrialization and had a great love of the Romantic poets, particularly Wordsworth. As a result he looked into the landscape seeking a time in which his notion of the ideal English landscape existed—populated by the humble rural working-class, devoid of urban and industrial expansions.[4]

In the United States, influential geographer Carl Ortwin Sauer (professor of geography at the University of California, 1923–57) also turned to the past to find what he perceived to be the purity of the wilderness. He had been deeply affected by the industrialization of his 'home' landscape (in California) and, like Hoskins, believed that the landscape was the result of the interventions of men. For him landforms were both the object of cultural expression and the medium through which culture was expressed. Sauer's students at the Berkeley School of Cultural Geography had a major influence on thinking about landscapes for most of the second half of the twentieth century. For both Sauer and Hoskins the landscape was objective, external, and material. It could be seen and assessed. They advocated the idea that observations of landscapes, and representations of them in maps and photographs, were the (only) empirical facts that were required in order to understand the history of the human–landscape relationship.[5]

From the 1960s onward, stimulated by the many new exciting computing technologies becoming available, there was a growing focus on scientific methodologies in geography and archaeology. Classification, quantification, and mathematical spatial analyses became increasingly popular. This highly abstracted way of thinking did not last long, however, and during the 1980s archaeological scholars began to focus on self-reflection, placing emphasis on elucidating the influences responsible for shaping the way we think. They now posed questions such as: What has affected our perception? How is our perception formed? This school of thought was led by British archaeologist Ian Hodder[6] (former professor of archaeology at Cambridge University, currently professor of anthropology at Stanford University, California) and was termed 'post-processual.' Several of Hodder's students at Cambridge University (1977–99) were equally influential and contributed a great deal to debates on method and theory in archaeology. Examples include Canadian archaeologist–anthropologist Bruce Trigger,[7] who examines how contemporary society and politics affect archaeological interpretations, and British classical archaeologist Michael Shanks, co-author of several key archaeological theory works with another of Hodder's students, Christopher Tilley.[8] Tilley was a major advocate of phenomenology in archaeological interpretation of landscapes, focusing on intuitive thinking rather than reliance on scientific 'people-less' interpretations.

This trend in archaeological thinking draws heavily on theories and approaches borrowed from geography, most particularly the newly emerging field of cultural geography. The development of cultural geography was driven by Barbara Bender (professor emeritus of heritage anthropology at University College London),[9] Denis Cosgrove (professor of geography at University of California Los Angeles), and Stephen Daniels (professor emeritus of cultural geography, University of Nottingham).[10] They advocate the idea that landscape is a way of seeing, a Western and elite construction deriving from Renaissance ideas, and that the word 'landscape' represents a way of thinking and, as such, is an expression of cultural, political, and economic power.[11] Cosgrove was interested not only in examining the material remains in order to gain an understanding of how humans shaped the landscape, but also in investigating how that landscape shaped the people who lived in it, and then how they reacted to it. He seeks to move away from conclusions based on merely viewing the landscape, and toward conclusions based on living within it—how it affected people, not what they saw.[12]

One of the few examples of an overtly theoretical approach to landscape in Egyptology is the work of leading British Egyptologist/archaeologist David Jeffreys (director of the Memphis Survey Project and until recently based at the Institute of Archaeology at University College London), who looks at the cognitive aspects of the geographical relationships between two major cult sites—Memphis and Heliopolis.[13] Janet Richards (director of excavations in Old Kingdom cemeteries at Abydos and curator of Egyptian collections in the Kelsey Museum of Archaeology, University of Michigan Ann Arbor) approaches the study of Egyptian temples as manifestations of sacred landscapes with a very explicitly theoretical approach.[14] Jeffreys and Richards look at the ways in which monuments can be seen to reflect ancient Egyptian ideas about sacred landscapes. Richards shows that the temples are essentially 'models' of the sacred aspects of the Egyptian landscape, with various elements of the temple representing different parts of the landscape, for example the floodplain or the desert. Jeffreys takes a broader perspective, looking at the placement of monuments in the landscape and the importance of views across landscapes between major sacred sites.

The research that gave rise to this book was not conducted in chronological order, in fact almost the exact reverse, and that approach undoubtedly shaped my way of thinking about the Fayum landscape. The first set of materials I examined was European travel writing and early Egyptological works, in the hope that they would yield snippets of information about fragments of monuments found by those travelers in the Fayum, which had subsequently been forgotten. I was hoping to make new 'discoveries.' Reading these materials revealed that Classical Greek and Latin historical and geographical writing played a dominant role in the formation of European ideas about the Fayum, especially Herodotus. People were almost obsessed with Herodotus and his description of the Fayum. Those Classical works essentially shaped early, idealized images of landscape, and so, in order to understand the roots of the sixteenth- to twenty-first-century ideas, Herodotus's *Histories* and later works by authors such as Pliny and Strabo needed to be examined.

In an attempt to balance a Eurocentric approach and the potential for revealing 'other' (non-European) notions of landscape, as well as investigating some of the influences on early orientalist Egyptological scholars such as Edward William Lane, I studied medieval Islamic geographical and historical works. My awareness of the value of medieval Islamic writing to the study of the history of Egyptology was without doubt a result of classes I attended with Okasha El Daly at University College London while he was in the middle of research for *The Missing Millennium: Ancient Egypt in Medieval Arabic Writings* (2005). These sources have long been overlooked as sources of information in Egyptology. They did not play a role in early Egyptology for the simple fact that they were relatively inaccessible and only became widely available and published in European languages (usually French) in the mid- to late nineteenth century—after Egyptology became established. To be blunt, the fact that archaeology as a discipline was founded at a time when non-Western scholarship was deemed to have little or no value also played a major role in Egyptologists' ignorance of Arab and Persian scholars. I am not suggesting that the material is valid as a tool for understanding ancient Egypt (for that topic see El Daly (2005)), but rather aim to highlight the fact that those works are just as valuable to the history of Egyptology as the regularly studied and quoted works of Classical scholars such as Herodotus. Islamic historical and geographical works provide a valuable non-Western source for perception of the landscape, and reveal a very different image of the Fayum.

Finally, based on the overwhelming preponderance of nostalgic, temporalized, imagined perceptions of the ancient Fayum landscape, it was obvious that ancient Egyptian archaeology and textual material had to be included in my study. This opened up the possibility to examine ways in which ancient Egyptians perceived their landscape, and this revealed the origins of later perceptions. The 'Chinese whisper' effect became apparent. It was only by studying the biographies of the later European writers and the sociocultural environment in which they worked that influences on how older ideas about the landscape were transmitted could be unraveled. As a result, it is now possible to show that the ancient perceptions of the landscape have in many ways actually persisted to this day.

How Is Our Perception of Landscape Formed?

The ideas about landscape held by Hoskins typify European, and most especially English, reactions to natural landforms. The notion that the land(scape) embodies beauty and fertility is apparent in some of the earliest Western written accounts of landscapes of Egypt. Classical poets idealized nature, fertile landscapes, and a pastoral way of life, while Romantic poets extolled the beauties of the unadulterated, unmodernized, feminine landscape and the vestiges of antiquity held within it. Orientalists introduced notions of the beauty of the wild, untamed, masculine desert and mountain landscapes. The intellectualizing of the landscape undertaken by cultural geographers and landscape archaeologists of the late twentieth century—the belief that the landscape is an expression of cultural values, a view or perspective that can be held only by educated scholars—cannot alter history. It cannot be denied that the way in which historians and archaeologists think about certain areas of land or certain regions of the earth has been shaped, or at least heavily influenced, by the ideas of our predecessors. If we are to be fully self-reflective, the influence of the intellectual heritage of thinking about landscape must be acknowledged in our own thinking about past landscapes. As archaeologists, our approach to investigations is unavoidably bound up in our notions of what ancient people might have perceived—notions that are formed by contemporary theoretical approaches. Unless we are fully aware of the influences on our own perceptions, we cannot begin to challenge our preconceptions.

One major issue in landscape archaeology has been the problem of implanting modern conceptions of value and meaning into interpretations of ancient landscapes based on archaeological research alone. By examining written evidence of perceptions of the landscape from different points in history, it is possible to illustrate the very different and simultaneously very similar ways in which different groups of people perceive the same landscape. The sets of materials examined in this book derive from different contexts. The pharaonic material illustrates the perception of people who inhabited their own landscape, and their interaction with that landscape. The Greco–Roman and Islamic materials illustrate the perceptions of people for whom this landscape was alien and unfamiliar, even though they 'owned' it and utterly transformed it—the Greeks much more so than the Arab–Islamic inhabitants, as the Fayum was a major center of Greek occupation. The European writers approached the landscape with well-formed perceptions prior to arriving there. Their writing illustrates the contrast between premodern and modern conceptions of landscapes. Unlike any earlier writers, they knew about ancient Egypt; Egyptology was an emerging discipline in its own right, their perception was shaped by an increasing understanding of ancient Egypt, and thus, inevitably, their perceptions shaped those of modern Egyptologists.

How we can approach an understanding of the heritage behind perceptions of a landscape was outlined in Bender's introduction to *Landscape: Politics and Perspectives*, as quoted at the head of this chapter.

The idea that social and cultural status as well as the specific time and place of engagement with a landscape have an effect on a person's perception of that landscape is fundamental to this book. For that reason, each source is placed into historical and sociocultural context and the contemporary landscape of the Fayum (irrigation, temples, settlements) is presented. By examining (where possible) the authors' biographies, it is possible to gain a better insight into their accounts, and a better understanding of how their perception of the landscape was constructed, what affected it, and how those influences are reflected in their accounts—thus also revealing what affected later accounts and perceptions. For example, how does a person's background, nationality, or place in history affect their perception of a landscape? What effect do their religious beliefs, their social status, or their own reading and research have? In what way has the general perception of the landscape over time affected the way in which archaeologists approach the landscape and the interpretation of the ancient landscape?

Physical Landscape and Perceived Landscape

One theme that became apparent as I reviewed the material was a clear division between two aspects of the landscape: the 'real' and the 'imagined.' This, to some extent, could be seen to mirror the two sides of the landscape debate—landscape as a physical object shaped by people, and landscape as a subjective notion or idea. Bender summarizes a concept that is applicable to many landscapes: "Landscapes are both spatial and temporal, . . . they serve as palimpsests of past activity, . . . are half imagined or something held in memory."[15] There are two concepts to explain subjectively held ideas of landscape: that landscapes can be temporal, and that they can be imagined. The ideas about how imagined temporalized landscapes are formed derive, in the main, from Said's *Orientalism* (2003[1978]).[16] The notion that imaginative geography and history help people intensify their sense of identity by heightening the differences between 'there' and 'here' and between 'then' and 'now' (and ultimately, for Said, between 'them' and 'us') is most overtly apparent in the genre of materials utilized by Said: Western travel accounts of Egypt. However, it can be traced to the earliest sources consulted here. The pharaonic concepts of there/here and then/now are demonstrated via religious beliefs, with deities and the afterlife being them, there, and then, while daily life is us, here, and now. The knowledge held of the geographical reality of the 'here and now' does not necessarily affect the historical/geographical ideas of the 'there and then.'

In this book, these ideas are translated into the concept of the imagined landscape and the experienced landscape. The imagined landscape is a construction based on a subjective notion of the landscape derived from external influences, including what a person has read in earlier travel accounts and literature, what the person has been told, and long-standing well-established, communally-held religious ideas. It could be called the 'sacred landscape,' although that term is more often used to refer to physical manifestations of religious ideas in the form of temples. The imagined landscape is imbued with meaning; the landscape itself and the sensations and emotions it evokes are the subject of interest, and take many forms. The experienced landscape (contra Cosgrove's use of the term 'experienced') is the perception derived from an objective interaction with the landscape. This perception of the landscape is based on the here and now, generally unaffected by any preconceived ideas about the meaning of the landscape but rather formed based on a direct interaction with the land. As Julian Thomas notes in *Landscape: Politics and Perspectives*, "an objective and distance perspective view on landscape has much in common with strategies of monitoring and surveillance."[17] In some instances the perception of the experienced landscape is actually a direct reaction to the perception of the imagined landscape: the landscape is not what it was expected to be, and thus is reevaluated on the basis of 'real' experience.

The experienced landscape is the objectified, 'viewed' landscape, the perception of the physical nature of the landscape. The imagined landscape is the subjectified, idealized, temporalized landscape, usually an idea of an ancient 'pure' version of the landscape.

Whose Landscape Is Being Perceived by Whom? The Role of Folklore and Tradition

In the late 1990s there was a general movement in many branches of academia and popular culture that reflected a growing sense of discomfort with the history of western attitudes toward Asia and Africa—so-called 'colonial guilt.' Landscape historians, anthropologists, and geographers started to employ more ethnographic methods and investigate indigenous notions of landscape. The idea that landscape is a Western construction was seen to be reflected in the large-scale mapping programs undertaken by European powers in their Eastern empires, for example by Britain in India or Australia. 'Accurate' and scientific mapping and the recording of physical landscapes came to be seen as symbols of power, often imposed on indigenous populations. The cognitive maps created in some cultures came to be seen as unscientific but nonetheless highly valuable reflections of a deep and more meaningful engagement with the landscape. In many instances this was tied up with contemporary reclamation of land by native populations.[18]

One source of indigenous perceptions of landscape is myths and legends—traditions not regularly recorded in written form by those inhabitants. These traditions are, however, often recorded by travelers. Folklore could be seen as one of the primary ways in which we can understand the perceptions of landscapes held by people removed physically, culturally, or temporally from ourselves. This is expressed best by Tilley:

> To understand a landscape truly it must be felt, but to convey some of this feeling to others it has to be talked about, recounted, written or depicted. . . . If stories are linked with regularly repeated spatial practices they become mutually supportive, and when a story becomes sedimented into the landscape, the story and the places dialectically help to construct and reproduce each other. . . . Narrative is a means of understanding and describing the world in relation to agency. It is a means of linking locales, landscapes, actions, events and experiences together. . . . In its simplest form it involves a story and a story-teller. . . . A narrative must of necessity always be written from a certain point of view. In relation to the past and written from the standpoint of the present, narrative structures play a similar role to metaphor—they describe the world in fresh ways, bringing new meanings and new senses. . . . Every story involves a temporal movement in addition to the spatial one—they describe the world in fresh ways, bringing new meanings and new senses.[19]

In essence, stories help create landscapes. They help secure the significance of, and the meanings held by, a place in a landscape—to anyone who hears the story. The transmission of the story perpetuates the perception of the landscape held by a specific person or group of people, and can shape the perceptions of anyone who hears or reads the story.

What I aim to do in this book is to unravel the palimpsest of perceptions of a region. While I am not in any way attempting to propose a new approach to landscape, I illustrate that it is only possible to have an appreciation of changing perceptions of a landscape by incorporating material from a very wide date range (here, almost ten millennia, from c.7500 BC to AD 1900) and embracing methods developed in a number of different disciplines. Landscape studies appear in many different subject areas, and I have borrowed ideas from geography, cartography, Classical studies, archaeology, art history, literary studies, philosophy, ethnography, and anthropology.

In this book the focus is on the way people perceive the landscape of the Fayum. Rather than adopting the ideas posed by Bender, Cosgrove, and Daniels that the concept of landscape implies a way of seeing,[20] I adopt the more traditional approach of taking landscape to mean the physical environment and the ways people have interacted with it and thought about it, and why. I combine approaches advocated by Hoskins and Hodder. The chapters in this book evaluate the ways in which people viewed a particular area of land that, in their minds, was a clearly defined and unique landscape. It is not simply their perception of the region, but also more specifically their perception of the physical landscape forming the region that is of interest here. What qualities did they perceive the land to be imbued with? The key distinction is between the 'experienced' and the 'imagined.' The perceptions of each writer were based on their experience of the landscape either directly or through having read about it, and often took the format of a descriptive account of the physical form of the landscape, the crops, towns, and monuments. But in many instances this description is not as straightforward as it might appear. The influences on the writer, both physical and psychological, have to be considered. What expectations did they have before they arrived in the landscape, and what were those expectations based on? In what circumstances were they experiencing the landscape: as a merchant, a tourist, an antiquities dealer? Where were they from? What were they comparing this landscape to? All these factors have a significant impact on the perceptions of the writers and their accounts.

The imagined landscape is a landscape that has not been physically experienced, not visited. The writer is imagining what the landscape is (or was) like at a certain point in time, based on what they had read or heard. Importantly this term also applies to the landscape that cannot be experienced because it is mythological, the landscape as it appears in creation legends and in stories about past times. The imaginary landscape is frequently the landscape imbued with the most meaning. It is often the description of the creation of the landscape—an event that is clearly not possible to experience but that results in a perception of the landscape that is heavy with religious meaning and often temporalized and idealized. Perceptions of this landscape are, naturally, significantly affected by the writer's beliefs.

The experienced landscape is the landscape of 'reality.' It is the physical form of the landscape, and perceptions of that landscape which are based on more purely rational thinking. This landscape can be (and usually was) measured, recorded, mapped, and managed. This is the landscape that appears in administrative documents. It is the landscape exploited by humans for the resources, and in most cases that exploitation was 'state'-run and thus had a great deal of bureaucracy associated with it. This landscape is devoid of any meaning; people had no real emotional attachment to this landscape.

How are these two different ways of perceiving the landscape related? Is it possible for the writer to describe both their perception of their experience of the landscape and their perception of the imagined landscape? In many instances the writers do incorporate the imagined landscape into the real/experienced landscape. Particularly for the earlier writers, this is not a problem at all—the two perceptions coexist. The landscape becomes a palimpsest of intertwined ideas, beliefs, traditions, and remains of human interventions and interactions.

3

Landscape of the Lake: The Ancient Egyptian Fayum (7500–332 BC)

> It is a remarkable fact that despite the vast numbers of finely sculptured records to be found on the monuments erected by the Ancient Egyptians, there is nothing of the nature of a map, nor any inscription that is capable of providing us with a clear notion of the geographical and cosmological views held by them.[1]
>
> —John Ball (1942)

Despite an apparent lack of explicit descriptions in geographic texts, it is in fact possible to gain insight into ancient Egyptians' ideas of their geographical surroundings—their landscape. The locations of the remains of towns and temples provide information on the nature of the land (for example, its habitability or suitability for cultivation) and help us understand what shaped people's experience of the landscape, answering questions such as: Which landscape features did they live near? What could they see? Which environmental factors may have affected their daily lives? The ability to 'people' the landscape is perhaps unique to the study of ancient Egypt; it is not often in archaeology that we are able to put names to individuals living in the past as easily as we can for the elite in Egypt.

One of the most strikingly apparent phenomena when looking at all the combined evidence of Pharaonic activities in the Fayum is that the activities appear to have been restricted to a very small portion of the region. It seems highly likely that only a relatively restricted area of the Fayum was actually habitable. The dominant feature of the ancient Egyptians' landscape in the Fayum was the lake, but not as it is known today. The lake of the fourth to the second millennia BC was a considerably larger expanse of water, filling at least seventy-five percent of the region. The sacred landscape of *tȝ-š* was intimately linked with the fact that the expansive marshy lands were an ideal habitat for crocodiles and thus the worship of the crocodile god Sobek/Sobek Shedty. The Fayum also had a unique place in the bureaucracy of Egypt, clearly defined as an administrative zone named *š-rsi*. Interestingly, it was never defined as a nome within the standard ancient Egyptian system of regional divisions.

The Fayum: Pharaonic History

As is the case throughout Egypt, the preservation of archaeological remains in the Fayum is highly variable. This is a result of the traditional archaeological focus on the more 'obvious' remains of temples and tombs, the inevitable loss of ancient settlements as towns grow and expand over time, and the effects of the constantly changing watercourses, with millennia of flood silt deposits obscuring and obliterating archaeological remains. Further factors affecting what we know of the history of the Fayum are the almost fanatical zeal with which people sought to locate the sites mentioned in Classical texts, and the fact that Flinders Petrie led most of the early excavations of Fayum sites (1888–1920). These factors had both positive and negative outcomes. It is hard to truly ascertain if the distribution of archaeological evidence in the Fayum reflects ancient settlement patterns and land use or is a result of choices made by archaeologists. Generally speaking, the early surveys of the region (see Chapter Six) defined the sites that have been explored. Sites with highly visible remains are naturally far more likely to attract attention, and it is only in recent years, since the 1990s, that survey methods enabling archaeologists to detect 'invisible' remains have become more readily available in Egypt, meaning that a large proportion of remains has already been lost to cultivation and expanding towns (as is the case globally). It is important to look not only at the remains found in the region but also at the history of the excavations in order to understand why some sites have yielded 'better' results and more information than others, and to be aware of how that inevitably affects our potential to understand ancient activities in the Fayum and ancient perceptions of the region.

Prehistoric and Predynastic Periods (500,000 BP–3000 BC)

Stone tools dated to the Lower Palaeolithic (500,000–250,000 BP) provide the earliest evidence of human activities in Egypt. During the Middle Palaeolithic (250,000–70,000 BP), periods of heavy rainfall across North Africa supported both seasonal and permanent lakes in the Western Desert, and there is evidence of exploitation of natural resources (mining) along the Nile

Valley at that time. Gradual climate change during the Upper Palaeolithic (c.70,000–24,000 BP) led to a shift toward far more arid conditions, which appears to have drawn people out of the desert toward the Nile, where resources (especially food) were now more easily available. Archaeological evidence from Late Palaeolithic sites (24,000–10,000 BP) suggests that people occupied desert campsites seasonally, exploiting various types of food resources (fishing, hunting, and gathering wild grasses and tubers). The Western Desert gradually became uninhabitable due to increasing aridity, until the Neolithic early Holocene wet phase (8,800–7,000 BP) when average rainfall across North Africa increased. Exceptionally high Nile levels and unpredictable floods meant that the valley became uninhabitable, but increased water availability in the desert regions made the Western Desert once again suitable for people to occupy, and Neolithic sites provide evidence for groups of people living in semi-permanent camps, herding cattle and hunting, collecting and processing wild grains.[2]

The picture is far from simple, however, and it has to be borne in mind, especially for the Fayum, that localized regional changes may well fall outside the general pattern of overall climate change. Most scholars have equated (noncatastrophic) higher floods with better agricultural opportunities in Egypt, due to a larger expanse of silt deposits being available after the waters recede. In the Fayum more water means a higher overall water level as water cannot escape the basin, and therefore in fact less land available for use. The Fayum basin becomes more attractive for agriculture when the waters are lower; hence the irrigation projects that sought to drain the region via canals. However, the annual cycle of the inundation means that there is usually some land available in areas affected by flooding after the waters recede, revealing fresh deposits of fertile silts.

The earliest evidence for human activity in the Fayum dates to the Nile Epipalaeolithic, roughly contemporary with the Saharan Early Neolithic (c.7000 BC), found along the northern shores of the lake. For decades, long before scientific archaeological investigations began, the area was renowned for being rich ground for collecting ancient flint implements.[3] The work of many scholars, including British geologist Hugh Beadnell,[4] pioneering archaeologists Gertrude Caton Thompson and Elinor Gardner[5] for the British School of Archaeology in Egypt (1924–28), and K.S. Sandford and Anthony Arkell[6] of the University of Chicago, laid solid foundations in the first half of the twentieth century. These have been built on more recently by Fred Wendorf and Romuald Schild,[7] Bolesław Ginter and Janusz Kozlowski

(Krakow),[8] and a team from the University of Michigan led by Robert Wenke.[9] The current combined Dutch–American surveys led by Simon Holdaway and Willeke Wendrich have allowed for far more nuanced conclusions, unraveling the complex chronology of occupation around basins along the north lakeshore during prehistory in the Fayum (see plate 5).[10]

Around the northern perimeter of the lake are dense concentrations of remains, primarily lithics, burned plant materials (charcoal), ceramics, and animal bones. Caton Thompson and Gardner argued that the distribution of the sites possibly related to the changing ancient shoreline of the lake, and most subsequent studies have had the same hypothesis, using radiocarbon dates from habitation remains (for example, charcoal from hearths) to provide a chronology of the variations in the ancient lake level. They make the assumption that people have always chosen to live along the lakeshore. This, however, may well not be the case.[11] Recent work in the northern Fayum has shown that a number of smaller basins were probably more influential in determining changing locations of human activity than the primary lake was, and that most 'sites' show short-term, repeated use depending on which resources were available.[12]

The sites date from around 7500 to 3300 BC. They contain the earliest evidence of cultivation of domesticated cereal crops in Egypt, dated c.4700 BC.[13] One of the biggest problems facing archaeologists attempting to reconstruct the early history of the Fayum is the fact that many of the earliest survey missions in the region (except those of Caton Thompson and Gardner) simply collected the lithics they found littering the desert surface, making it very hard to determine the true extent of ancient activities. Additionally, the nature of the archaeological remains means that it is almost impossible to determine how long the 'sites' (areas of scattered pits and hearths) were in use, or how frequently they were reused/revisited.[14]

Holdaway and Wendrich demonstrate that we should not see this time period as a simple forward-moving 'evolution' of cultures, but more as a gradual intermingling of ideas and adaptations to local and regional environmental fluctuations.[15] But the generally accepted chronology based on recent radiocarbon dating is that the Fayum Epipalaeolithic (Qarunian) lasted about fifteen hundred years from circa 7530 to 6090 BC, the early Fayum Neolithic (Fayumian) lasted about twelve hundred years from circa 5480 to 4260 BC, the late Fayum Neolithic (Moerian) lasted around a thousand years from circa 4620 to 3640 BC, and the Fayum Predynastic dates cover circa 4170 to 3360 BC.[16]

Qarunian (Epipalaeolithic) sites have been found on the northern shores of the lake and in the southern regions of the Fayum. These consist of scatters of artifacts and fish/bones with minimal evidence of the exploitation of wild plants, which is interpreted as showing that the sites were in use by transitory groups of hunter–fishers. Fayumian (early Neolithic) remains are also found on the north shore as well as in the southwest regions of the Fayum.[17] The most significant Fayumian sites are Kom W and Kom K in the north, identified by Caton Thompson and Gardner and extensively studied by Holdaway and Wendrich. At both sites many firepits were uncovered, and at Kom K the remains of basket-lined storage pits containing the preserved remains of domestic cereals were found, providing firm evidence of the development of agriculture in Egypt. Other features of the Fayumian culture include handmade ceramics, lithics (sickles), grinding stones/grinders, and objects made from non-local resources. These artifacts indicate that these people traveled away from their camps to procure specific items,[18] and are suggestive of a more complex economic system.

Only a small number of sites in the Fayum can be considered Moerian (late Neolithic, 4620–3640 BC), and it has been suggested that this indicates an 'abandonment' of the region.[19] They show no signs of habitation, and the people staying there seem to have relied on seasonal fishing for subsistence. Aspects of the Moerian lithic assemblages mirror those found in Buto-Maadi culture sites along the northern Nile and into the Delta (c.4000–3400 BC), and it has been suggested that the Buto-Maadi traditions grew out of the Fayum late Neolithic culture.[20] Although there are sites in both the northern and southern regions of the Fayum dated to the Predynastic, there is still some debate surrounding their association with the main Nile Predynastic phases (Buto-Maadi or Naqada cultures, 5300–3000 BC). To complicate matters, radiocarbon dating suggests that the Moerian and Fayum Predynastic may in fact represent different aspects of one contemporaneous culture.[21] One theory is that the Moerian is in fact different in material culture but contemporary in date with the Fayumian. That difference is a result of the fact that these were people who lived in closer proximity to the lake and thus naturally relied on different subsistence methods, namely, more fishing.[22] Since the Fayum is essentially on the border between the Western Desert and the Nile Valley, it seems likely that the people in the area were affected by both of those distinct cultures, while retaining their own cultural identity.

These earliest inhabitants of the Fayum lived in an environment that would be barely recognizable to us today. The lake covered the majority of the region, rising to as high as 20 meters above sea level, making everything but the desert edges of the Fayum uninhabitable. However, this lake-based environment provided the means for subsistence. People could rely on seasonal fishing and hunting, combined with farming and herding, in both instances 'tied' to some extent to the lakeshores. Crocodiles and hippopotami were certainly present and would have been a threat to these people, but they were also a resource. The earliest Fayum dwellers were naturally opportunistic, and it is highly possible that the area represented a chance to settle and engage in more sedentary and reliable farming, in a move away from their earlier nomadic and transitory life. Beside the lake, they would have been able to exploit the rich natural resources of fish and edible wild plants, as well as good land for cultivation of domesticated crops and raising herds of sheep and goats. The Fayum was both physically and temporally a transition point for the development of settled culture and agricultural activities in Egypt.

Early Dynastic Period and Old Kingdom (3000–2160 BC)

The earliest signs of urbanism in Egypt (mud-brick architecture, nucleated settlements, official buildings) appear during the Buto-Maadi cultural phase, in the Naqada II Period (3500–3200 BC). Hierakonpolis in Middle Egypt is the 'type-site' for the emergence of settled life along the Nile Valley, primarily a result of the extensive and highly focused research that has been conducted there. Here, and at various other sites in Egypt, there is strong evidence that people started to come together and settle permanently in increasingly dense villages.[23]

During the final phase of the Predynastic Period (Naqada III, 3200–3000 BC), a unified 'state' emerged in Egypt. Evidence from cemeteries points toward increasingly stratified communities, with elite members able to equip their graves richly with objects made of gold and semiprecious materials. Hierakonpolis and Abydos became major centers, as attested by both settlement remains and increasingly elaborate burials. Tomb U-j at Abydos covers 66.4 square meters and contained large quantities of Egyptian and Palestinian ceramics—evidence of well-established trade routes. The beginning of the pharaonic, or Dynastic, period is marked by the presence of the name of just one king in textual evidence (pot-marks, jar labels, seal impressions) across Egypt, identifying that ruler as the sole ruler of the country.[24]

The Old Kingdom (2686–2125 BC) is perhaps best known as the age of the great pyramids. Archaeological remains of massive funerary complexes clustered in the north between Giza and the Fayum are the most obvious landmarks of increasing economic success, which followed the development of complex organizational structures for overseeing large-scale construction projects that involved huge teams of laborers and skilled craftsmen. Access to and control of natural resources became important, and much of the Old Kingdom evidence in the Fayum is indeed associated in some way with exploitation and management of resources.

Not a great deal is known about activities in the Fayum during the Old Kingdom. In this period the lake level was at around 15 meters above sea level, give or take 5 meters,[25] which left just a small area of unflooded dry land surrounding the area of modern Madinat al-Fayum. Based on a sealing of Narmer found at Tarkhan (Petrie Museum UC59522), it is clear that Shedet (*šdt*) as a cult center for the crocodile god Sobek was founded at least as early as the First Dynasty. In addition, evidence from the Fifth–Sixth Dynasty pyramids texts of Unas, Pepi I, and Pepi II shows that a cult of Sobek in *šdt* was well established by the middle of the Old Kingdom. There is archaeological evidence for Old Kingdom activities in the Fayum at Lahun and Seila and in the far north at the quarries of Umm al-Sawan and Widan al-Faras. Close to the better-known Twelfth Dynasty remains at Lahun there is a small early-Dynastic cemetery dating to around the Second Dynasty, excavated by Petrie at the beginning of the twentieth century. He uncovered 104 graves, some of which contained very fine quality objects. Nearby Kom al-Iswid and Dimiqshin also yielded a small number of later Old Kingdom cemetery remains.[26]

The existence of ancient quarries in the deserts to the north of the Fayum was noted in 1905, and the area was first explored by Caton Thompson and Gardner in the 1920s. It is important to consider whether the northern quarry zone along the Gebel Qatrani was thought of as part of the Fayum. Basalt quarries and associated camp/settlement areas at Widan al-Faras and gypsum quarries at Umm al-Sawan have been dated to the Old Kingdom, with reuse in the late Roman Period,[27] but the fact that the basalt was used in royal funerary complexes at Giza and Saqqara could suggest that the quarries were thought of as being a part of the Western Desert. However, the existence of a road running south from the Widan al-Faras quarries to Qasr al-Sagha appears to link the sites to the Fayum.[28] The lake in the Old Kingdom was at least 15 meters above sea level, meaning that Qasr al-Sagha would have been close to edge of the lake—very much within the Fayum region. The presence of a quay at that site does strongly suggest that this was the case.

The lack of any reasonable evidence to date this quarry road is problematic. The lack of any signs of use/wear on the paving slabs makes it hard to visualize how large numbers of blocks could have been transported from the quarries to the lake, but the suggestion that the paving acted as a foundation for wooden 'runner' planks is plausible.[29] A large number of circular depressions and Fifth to Sixth Dynasty ceramics were found at both the basalt quarries in the Gebel Qatrani escarpment at Widan al-Faras and at Qasr al-Sagha. These closely resemble features interpreted as temporary hut foundations found at the Old Kingdom quarries of Umm al-Sawan (to the north of Widan al-Faras) and Hatnub (close to Amarna),[30] providing a clear link between Widan al-Faras and Qasr al-Sagha and suggesting that this road was indeed used during the Old Kingdom. The physical and temporal links to the northern quarries certainly show that they were perceived to be part of the landscape of the Fayum during the Old Kingdom. In all likelihood the blocks were transferred to boats at Qasr al-Sagha and transported south through the deeper channels in the flooded lands of the Fayum to the main river channel of what is now known as the Bahr Yusuf. From there they could go north through Nile channels (the Bahr Libeni, which runs north toward Memphis, may be a remnant of older major river channels) to the royal funerary complexes at Saqqara and Giza.

A small step pyramid at Seila in the eastern Fayum was discovered in 1899.[31] Exploration and excavation works took place in the 1930s, 1960s, and 1980s, and the monument has been dated to the reign of Sneferu by the remains of a statue and two stelae found during excavations in 1986–87.[32] It is thought to be one of seven similar pyramids built along the Nile Valley that acted as both symbols of royal power and administration and local centers of worship for the royal cult.[33] The presence of this small monument here is evidence that the region was included in the countrywide administrative network of resource management.

Evidence for Old Kingdom activities in the Fayum is not restricted to the archaeology of the region itself. Inscriptions in private tombs belonging to officials who clearly had links to establishments in the Fayum have been found in Giza, Saqqara, Abusir, Deshasha, and Tihna al-Gebel. The earliest textual evidence for Fayum activities attests not only that the cult center at Shedet was established as early as the reign of Narmer in the First Dynasty, but also that the very specific hieroglyph used to designate this cult of Sobek was already in use at that time. A seal impression found by Petrie at Tarkhan (UC59522) bears images of several crocodiles,[34] one of which is depicted on a standard, and also has the distinctive booth sign surmounted by a bucranion (bull head). The sign is well known as the 'determinative' for the cult of Sobek in Shedet from later inscriptions, usually transliterated just as *šdt*.

The earliest occurrence of a name for the whole region appears early in the Old Kingdom in the Third Dynasty tomb of Meten (*mtn*). This tomb, found close to the pyramids at Abusir, was first recorded by Richard Lepsius,[35] and can now be found reconstructed in the Berlin Neues Museum (Berlin 1105 (tomb) and Berlin 1106 (statue)). Meten held many administrative titles during the reign of Sneferu, one of which was 'Chief of the towns of the Great Estate of (the) Southern Lake (*š-rsi*).'[36] A fragment of an inscription naming an 'Overseer of all acacia trees of (the) Southern Lake (*š-rsi*)' was discovered at Lisht and may well also belong to Meten. The titles found in the block from Lisht are rare, and the closest parallels all date to the Third Dynasty, and most particularly to the tomb of Meten, leading to the hypothesis that the Lisht block came from his tomb.[37]

A false door from Dahshur currently in the British Museum (BM1324) belonged to one of the sons of the pharaoh Sneferu, Ka-nefer (a common name in the Old Kingdom). His massive mudbrick mastaba (number 28, to the southeast of the much later pyramid of Amenemhat II) was excavated in the late nineteenth century by Jacques de Morgan.[38] Ka-nefer was overseer of the pyramid of Sneferu (at Dahshur). He was also a priest of Sobek of Shedet.[39] Mastaba G2150 in the western cemetery on the Giza plateau is among a group of large stone mastabas probably laid out during the reign of Khufu. G2150 also belonged to an individual named Ka-nefer (*k3-nfr*). This mastaba does not name him as son of Sneferu, and the dating of this tomb suggests that the Giza and Dahshur Ka-nefers were two different individuals who by coincidence both acted as priests of the same cult. This tomb was first explored by Lepsius in 1842 and fully excavated by George Reisner in 1906/1911–13. The inscriptions are now held in the Boston Museum of Fine Arts (34.58, see plate 6). The mastaba contained nine burial shafts and was in use from the end of the fourth into the early fifth Dynasty.[40] Ka-nefer had various titles, including priest of Shedet.

Shedu (*šdw*), whose tomb was found at Deshasha (south of the Fayum in the Nile Valley), held several titles, including 'Overseer of the Fields,' during the Sixth Dynasty, probably under the reign of Teti.[41] The tomb contains a series of typical Old Kingdom 'daily life' and craft scenes, including one showing woodworking with the description, "Strengthening the staff (of office) of (the) Southern Lake (*š-rsi*)."[42] A group of Old Kingdom rock-cut tombs at Tihna al-Gebel (just north of Minya) was first discovered by Petrie in 1887 and later explored by George Fraser in 1890.[43] Tomb 14 appears to belong to an individual named Khenwka, and in the inscriptions is a nome list that appears to include *š-rsi*.[44] The tomb was in poor condition, but at least one title was discernible: 'Chief of the Gangs of the South.' This is the only occasion when *š-rsi*, the Fayum, appears in a nome list of the pharaonic period. Adding to the evidence of the two known priests of Sobek of Shedet, there is also good evidence for the existence of a cult center in Shedet in the Old Kingdom in the Pyramid Texts. The pyramid of Unas has one spell (275) that includes the line, "Unas becomes the Great One in Shedet." In the pyramids of Pepi I and Pepi II, spell 582 states, "I govern as Sobek who is in Shedet (*sbk imy šdt*)."[45]

The Old Kingdom evidence shows that the cult of Sobek in *šdt* was well established, and that *š-rsi* was defined as an administrative area/estate early in Egyptian history. It is impossible to know if the occurrences of 'Southern Lake' in the tombs of Meten and Shedu are evidence of *š-rsi* as an established place name or descriptions of a place. Is it 'the' southern lake or 'Southern Lake'? It seems highly likely that *š-rsi* began as a description of the area and then became established as the name for the region. This reveals two interesting points. First, the fact that 'Lake' was chosen clearly shows that it was a highly significant feature in the landscape. Second, the fact that this is the *southern* lake reveals that the naming took place north of the Fayum. Even if 'north' and 'south' are modern conceptions based on knowledge that the earth is a globe with two poles, the word *rsi* clearly designates a location upstream, which in Egypt is 'south.' The titles are clearly administrative titles, and therefore the need to allocate a description/name to the area almost certainly came from the fact that the resources of the Fayum were being exploited and that there were officials allocated to manage those resources.

The issue of the central 'control' town for Egypt, and indeed the issue of centralized organization, is under debate, but most of the evidence points to the fact that the majority of Egypt's officials and organization were housed in the north at Memphis (modern Mit Rahina, ancient *mn-nfr*) or perhaps at the town close to the pyramids at Giza (modern Heit al-Ghurab). Both sites are north of the Fayum. All the evidence for this administration comes from outside the Fayum, and while this may be due simply to a lack of evidence as a result of loss of archaeological remains, it does indicate that the region was administered externally. The very descriptive title held by Meten—Chief of the towns of the Great Estate of (the) Southern Lake (*š-rsi͗*)—is perhaps the most revealing piece of evidence for the status of the Fayum as an estate, probably belonging to the pharaoh with several towns. Sadly the locations of these towns are lost.

There is no evidence to suggest that the name 'Lake Land' (*tꜣ-š*) was in use at this time. The evidence suggests that this second name for the region came into use during the Middle Kingdom and the growth of the cult of Sobek.

First Intermediate Period (2160–2055 BC)

Following the reign of Pepi II (2278–2184 BC), the rule of Egypt was no longer in the hands of one pharaoh. The Seventh and Eighth Dynasties consisted of numerous rulers, none of whom was in power for very long, and little is known about them. The First Intermediate Period is usually defined as a time of instability and civil conflict, based on the lack of a sole ruler, and texts describing a state of chaos in towns and villages. Around 2125 BC a line of southern rulers appeared, about whom a great deal more is known, and it was they who finally succeeded in unifying Egypt once again under the rule of one pharaoh in 2055 BC.[46]

There is very little evidence of activities in the Fayum during this period of change in Egypt. However, directly to the east of the southern part of the Fayum, the town of *nn-nsw* (modern Ihnasya al-Madina, Greek Herakleopolis Magna) became the ruling base of the northern pharaohs in around 2160 BC. No contemporary settlement remains have been detected to date, but the large associated cemeteries to the west of the town at Sedment in the narrow strip of desert between the Nile Valley and the Fayum region attest to major First Intermediate Period occupation in the area. It is almost certainly significant that the name of the chief deity of *nn-nsw*—Herishef—means 'The one who is upon his Lake' (*ḥri͗-š-f*).

The earliest evidence for the name of the locality *r-ḥnt* (possibly the root of Lahun) appears in the biographical inscription of the tomb of the nomarch Ity-Ibi at Asyut.[47] Several important tombs were first documented in 1799 at Asyut by the Napoleonic expedition, the publication of which is still invaluable, as the tombs have suffered considerable damage since then. The tombs were studied and recorded by numerous scholars during the nineteenth century, and the key publication of the inscriptions was made by Francis Llewellyn Griffith (1889). The tombs became the subject of a recent reevaluation and have been carefully documented by a German–Egyptian mission, which began work in 2003.[48] The inscription in tomb III, belonging to the treasurer Ity-Ibi, is heavily damaged, but what fragments remain do give a hint at Ity-Ibi's view of some events during the First Intermediate Period. The context in which *r-ḥnt* occurs is in a section describing a journey north after fighting (with southern leaders) has finished. What this inscription does provide is the earliest evidence for *r-ḥnt* as a Fayum location.

Middle Kingdom (2055–1650 BC)

The southern rulers who gained control over all of Egypt came from Thebes, and it is now recognized that the Middle Kingdom began with this reunification during the Eleventh Dynasty circa 2055 BC. The first king of the Twelfth Dynasty (Amenemhat I, 1985–56 BC) relocated the principal royal residence to the north, to a new town called *iṯ-t3wy*—Itj-tawy (probably Lisht) just north of the Fayum.[49] The Twelfth Dynasty is sometimes seen as an Egyptian Renaissance,[50] with a flourish of temple building, remarkable and exquisitely crafted funerary and religious art, the development of new and complex styles in literature and poetry, and the construction of many highly structured, obviously planned settlements associated with state-run projects (for example, quarries and pyramids).

The Middle Kingdom is by far the best-represented period of pharaonic history in the Fayum. Temples were constructed at Shedet (Madinat al-Fayum), Qasr al-Sagha, Madinat Madi, Biahmu, and possibly at Abgig. There are private 'nobles' tombs at Kom Khelwa, and two major royal funerary complexes are located in the Nile–Fayum corridor at Lahun and Hawara.

This period is considered to be the Golden Age of the Fayum, during which major hydrological works took place, many monuments were erected, and the region became both highly significant and prosperous. There is one frequently repeated assumption about the Fayum during the Middle Kingdom: that Amenemhat I engaged in major irrigation works in the region (although sometimes this work is credited to Senwosret II).[51] There is evidence for Middle Kingdom interventions into the hydrology of the region at the Gadallah dam, but the remains cannot be dated to a specific reign.[52] This notion—that the pharaohs intervened into the hydrology of the region in a significant way—is perhaps born more out of legend than fact. While the evidence certainly does point toward some control over the water entering the region between Madinat el-Gurob and Lahun in the Middle Kingdom,[53] there is very little real evidence to suggest that human interventions had any major effect on the Fayum landscape prior to the Ptolemaic period. Indeed, the other dams in the region (Shedmu, Dimikshin, and Bahlawan) have been dated to the Ptolemaic and Roman periods.[54] Despite the proliferation of repeated assertions that there were major developments in Fayum agriculture during the early Middle Kingdom, at present there is in fact a real lack of evidence to support those statements.[55]

Nonetheless, the region did become more important during the Middle Kingdom, and perhaps the key sign of this is that both Senwosret II and Amenemhat III erected their pyramids on the boundary of the region at the Nile–Fayum divide, at Lahun and Hawara, respectively, and that the cult of Sobek grew almost immeasurably. Additionally, after his death up until the Roman period, Amenemhat III was worshipped as a deity. It is hard to find ways to understand the trigger for the apparent surge of interest in the Fayum region during this period. The establishment of a new royal residence and administrative center at Itj-tawy—the new 'capital' of Egypt of the Twelfth Dynasty—certainly would have drawn people south from the older centers at Memphis and Heit al-Ghurab. It is possible that a desire to perhaps retain some kind of links with the First Intermediate Period center at *nn-nsw* (Ihnasya) may also have been behind the increased interest in the Fayum. Without new evidence, we can probably never fully understand this phenomenon.

The earliest Middle Kingdom archaeological evidence in the region dates to the reign of Amenemhat I (1985–56 BC). While the lack of evidence makes it impossible to know if he constructed a new temple at Shedet, there is one statue attributed to him that is thought to have originally come from the site. This was seen by Lepsius, George Schweinfurth, and Petrie, close to the Ptolemaic Sobek temple at Kiman Faris.[56] The statue was 'rediscovered' in the 1990s and described as the lower part of a pair statue of Amenemhat I with Bastet seated on a throne.[57] The difficulty with this is that it may not have originally been situated there, as the removal and transport of statues between different temples in Egypt was common.

Better evidence of interaction with the sacred landscape of the Fayum comes from the reign of his successor, Senwosret I (1956–11 BC). The so-called 'obelisk' of Abgig now stands in a roundabout in central Madinat al-Fayum. The earliest report of this monument dates to the mid-seventeenth century, when Father Johann Michael Vansleb visited the region and stopped at the village to see the 'needle' standing in the middle of a field (see Chapter Six for details of his exploration of the Fayum).[58] This monument, often called an obelisk, is 12.9 meters tall, made from red granite, and has inscriptions on four sides and a rounded stela-like top (instead of a pyramidion pointed top). It stood on a 3.6-meter square limestone base. By the time the inscriptions were recorded accurately by the Prussian expeditions led by Lepsius (1842–46), the monument had fallen and only three sides were visible. Even then, they were heavily damaged and very little was legible.[59]

There has never been any archaeological evidence to suggest that there was a larger enclosure or temple at the location. The 'obelisk' seems more likely to have been a part of an open-court shrine of some kind, possibly linked to solar worship. Several deities are represented on the monument in the scenes of offerings (Montu, Ptah, Atum, Amun, Re-Horakhty, Isis, Nephthys, Thoth, Min, Horus of Letopolis, Sheshat, and Sobek), but Marco Zecchi notes that the 'obelisk' should not be seen as evidence of any specific worship of their cults in the Fayum, as it is not a symbol showing local beliefs.[60] The presence of these deities on the monument was more a way for Senwosret I to establish his presence in the region.[61] The text of the inscriptions fits within a genre known as *königsnovelle*, which is found on other monuments from the reign of Senwosret I. The king is described engaged in various activities, such as temple construction, restoration, or endowment, making it similar in some respects to autobiographical texts.[62] Just why this monument was erected in this location is really tricky to determine, and it is not impossible that it was moved from another location at a much later date. However, the fact that the village in which it was found lies at the 'head' of the al-Wadi drain, one of the major natural ravines in the region, may be significant.

Outside the Fayum, Senwosret I commemorated the region on his 'White Chapel' at Karnak. On the western façade, at the base of two columns, offering bearers personifying various different regions in Egypt are found, as well as topographic features. The Fayum does not occur in the main list of nomes, but *š-rsi* does appear in one scene.[63]

While there are no archaeological remains clearly dating to the reign of Amenemhat II in the region, there is one very important monument dating to the reign of his successor Senwosret II: the pyramid at Lahun. The site is perhaps better known for the remains of the town to the east next to the valley temple (see plate 7). Petrie discovered the town site (which he named Kahun) near the Lahun pyramid during explorations in 1888–89, undertaken with the explicit aim of preventing an "inexperienced German team" from working at the site.[64] Petrie spent several seasons focused on work in this area, not only at Lahun/Kahun but also at Hawara and Madinat al-Gurob. Why Senwosret II chose to locate his pyramid so much farther south than any of his ancestors is hard to assess, but the possibility that this decision reflects the increasing importance of the Fayum region during the Twelfth Dynasty cannot be ruled out.

The name Lahun or al-Lahun is believed to derive from the name *r-ḥnt* (mouth of the waterway), which seems to have been used to denote the region at the entrance to the Fayum, around modern Lahun.[65] This place name occurs only rarely, and never in documents from Lahun itself. The name *r-ḥnt* in this area of the Fayum primarily occurs in later texts: the New Kingdom Wilbour Papyrus and the so-called 'Victory Stela' of Piy from the Twenty-fifth Dynasty. It seems plausible that if this area was known as the 'mouth' of the Henet, Senwosret II may not only have been trying connect with the newly emerging importance of the region but also have chosen the spot specifically to locate his funerary cult with a symbolically highly significant place name.

Archaeological remains from within Kahun point to the fact that it did not simply function as a workers' town for the pyramid builders and

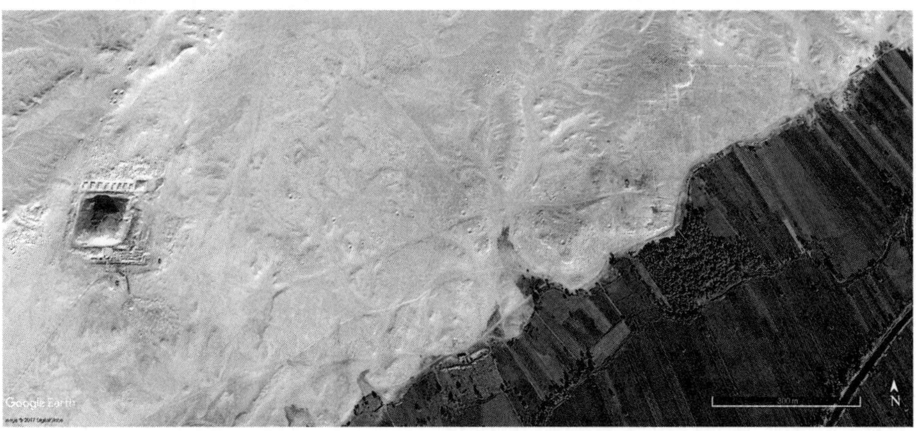

2. Google Earth image of Lahun area.

3. Google Earth image of Kahun town.

home for the priests and officials of the pyramid cult. Like many other so-called workers' towns or pyramid towns, it functioned as a base for regional administration. Petrie's extraordinary work in this site unarguably ensured the preservation of the remains, and the artifacts from the site can be found in several collections across Britain, primarily in the Petrie Museum in London and the Manchester Museum. Two separate groups of papyrus documents were discovered at the site that relate to activities within the temple complex and the town during the reigns of Senwosret III and Amenemhat III. The papyri from the temple archive can clearly be shown to derive from one unified collection of documents belonging to one scribe, Horemsaf,[66] and show that the funerary cult of Senwosret II was being maintained for up to four generations following his death. The papyri from the town are less of a 'collection' but are certainly contemporary, showing that the town was probably still active in the later Twelfth Dynasty into the reign of Amenemhat IV.

Within the two collections it is apparent that there were two different 'places' at the site: Hetep-Senwosret, which according to most scholars was the name for the town site, and 'Sekhem-Senwosret,' which was the name given to an area designated for the temple administration.[67] The two collections of papyri are held in two different museum collections, the Petrie Museum in London and the State Museum in Berlin. The London archive is now fully published (see Collier and Quirke 2002, 2004, 2006), while the publication of the Berlin archive (primarily from the temple complex) is ongoing by Ulrich Luft. The exact nature and locations of the two different 'places' named in the archives has much been debated,[68] and it is unclear if there was more than one town at the site or if the two 'places' refer to two different institutions in one location. In a detailed reevaluation of all the documents, Zoltán Horváth (2009) proposes that the upper, western part of the town was Sekhem-Senwosret and the lower part with the large mansion-like dwellings was Hetep-Senwosret.[69] What is clearer, however, is that there were several temples there: the funerary temple and valley temple of Senwosret II, as well as temples/shrines (or, at the very least, cult areas in the primary temples) for Sobek, Hathor, and Anubis.[70]

The documents in both archives are all administrative, and additional evidence for administrative activities is provided by the remains of seal impressions found in heaps in several places in the town. Texts from the town papyri name a nearby location 'Lake of Sobek' (*š sbk* / *š n sbk*), or 'Northern Lake of Sobek' (*š sbk mḥty*), and occasionally just 'Lake' (*š*). They also refer to *ḥnt* as a place within the region. Within the corpus of letters found in the town, many open with a standard formulaic greeting that praises *sbk šdty ḥr ḥry-ib šdt*: "All the concerns of the Lord LPH are secure and flourishing in all their places through the favour of Sobek Shedty Horus residing in Shedet" (UC32210 lot VIII.1).[71] The fact that the names 'Lake Land' *tꜣ-š* and 'Southern Lake' *š-rsi* do not appear in these texts is noteworthy, but may be due to the fact that this is principally an administrative archive relating to activities within one town area. It is possible that these documents in fact do not refer at all to the Fayum as a region, but instead relate to the estate of the mortuary complex of Senwosret II. The complete lack of reference to *š-rsi* as a region does suggest that the perspective of the officials based in Kahun did not extend beyond their own estate, and upholds the theory that *š-rsi* was the name given to the region by the external administration. The texts place the vizier, the most important official below the pharaoh, in the town, as well as treasurers of various offices, high-ranking overseers of several institutions, high stewards, secretaries, accountants, and many different officials, including those in charge of stores.[72]

An offering table fragment found by Petrie at the site does belong to a mayor of *š-rsi* (and *wꜣḏ-wr*, 'Great Green'),[73] but this is likely to come from the local cemeteries, and it is perhaps unsurprising that an official for the broader region chose to be buried or was granted a burial close to the pharaoh. This is one of the only occurrences of the name *š-rsi* on an object found within the region, and it may be possible that this official, although buried at Lahun, was actually based elsewhere. The occurrence of *w3ḏ-wr* in this context is of interest as this place seems to be (based on later evidence) more connected with the sacred aspect of the landscape, the waters of the realm of the gods.

At some point during the mid-Twelfth Dynasty the northern quarry sites may have been revived. While there are no Middle Kingdom archaeological remains in the quarries themselves, a settlement was established and a small temple was built at Qasr al-Sagha, north of the lake. Excavations in the town over several seasons by a joint German–Polish mission led by Joachim Śliwa have revealed a typical Middle Kingdom 'planned' town:[74] orthogonal, laid out to one unified plan, and walled. The site has been dated to the late Middle Kingdom / Second Intermediate Period, and lies on what would have been the northern edge of the lake during the Middle Kingdom, about 15 meters above sea level. It is estimated that it could have been occupied by up to twelve hundred people living in thirty distinct 'house' units. To the west of the town is a large contemporary cemetery. The material culture is typical of this type of settlement, and combined with the architectural evidence it indicates that the town was built to house the officials and administrators, craftsmen, and overseers possibly associated with the basalt quarries at Widan al-Faras. The dating of this settlement and the renewed exploitation of the quarries ties in well with the major temple-building program initiated by Amenemhat III.

A survey along the southern edge of the region in 1966 by Dieter Arnold showed that at Kom Khelwa/Ruqayya the remains of a substantial Middle Kingdom tomb complex were preserved.[75] In the 1980s the tomb was investigated fully by a mission based at Madinat Madi (University of Pisa), led by Edda Bresciani, as part of a regional survey of this southern edge of the cultivated area. The tombs at Kom Khelwa are rock-cut into a low outcrop of limestone, the roofs of which collapsed long ago. The lower portions of the inscribed pillars were sufficiently well preserved to provide some information on the tomb owner. His name and primary titles are also known from a statue found in 1981.[76] The tomb belonged to Wadj—*ˁḥm* priest, Chief Lector, Treasurer/sealer of Lower Egypt, Sole Companion, One who sees the beauty of the King in holy places, Overseer of the priests of Sobek, Sole one of Horus of Shedet, Governor of the sanctuary of the south and the sanctuary of the north, Governor of Nekheb, One who enters into the most holy parts of the temple, Pure of fingers, Stolist of Horus Shedty, and Overseer of the fields.' Clearly, Wadj was an important official.

The fact that Wadj chose to locate his tomb on this southern edge of the region is interesting because there are no known major temple or settlement remains any closer than Madinat Madi and the site is some way away from the center and main Sobek temple at Shedet. The fact that this tomb is not at Hawara or Lahun, close to royal funerary complexes, may indicate that the tomb dates to the earlier part of the Middle Kingdom, prior to the foundation of the pyramids at Lahun and Hawara. The presence of this tomb on the southernmost tip of the Fayum is a good indication that there must have been a major settlement somewhere nearby. Activities along the southern edge of the Fayum may have been an extension of those along the western Nile Valley at Herakleopolis (*nn-nsw*) and the desert cemetery at Sedment. It is not uncommon at all in Egypt for settlement remains to be 'missing' from the landscape. In many locations along the Nile there are extensive cemeteries with no apparent evidence of the towns where the buried individuals must have lived. Invariably this is due either to the fact that the ancient town remains have been destroyed by the inevitable development of the town over time or the obliteration of remains by the constant fluctuations in the course of the Nile and smaller river courses. The fluctuating water levels and changing shape of the landscape of the Fayum would have had similar effects.

The southern site of Tebtunis/Umm al-Burigat (to the east of Kom Khelwa) was first investigated properly by Bernard Grenfell and Arthur Hunt in 1899–1905, and is best known for extensive Ptolemaic, Roman, and Coptic remains. The site has been occupied continuously since at least the Middle Kingdom.[77] Grenfell and Hunt opened hundreds of tombs and excavated houses within the Roman quarters, where they found the large quantities of papyri that made the site so famous. Sadly the site was heavily and systematically looted for years, with a brief pause while it was investigated in the 1930s by an Italian team. The site once again fell prey to the *sebbakhin* (the people who quarry sites for mudbricks to use as fertilizer) and dealers until the late 1980s, when work was resumed by a combined French–Italian mission.[78] The history of looting at the site resulted in hundreds of papyri appearing on the antiquities market. Sadly their true provenance is lost along with the information that this kind of detail can reveal if proper excavations are conducted.[79] The presence of a Middle cemetery Kingdom here, and hints at the presence of a temple in texts show that this area was certainly occupied at this time.

4. Google Earth image of Biahmu.

With the reign of Senwosret II's successor Amenemhat III came the elevation of the Fayum to an even more significant status. Given the lack of sufficient evidence, the question of whether or not Amenemhat III (1831–1786 BC) made any major interventions in the hydrology of the region and/or expanded agricultural activities in the Fayum is essentially still impossible to answer with any certainty. He undeniably paid a great deal more attention to the region than any of his predecessors had done and initiated a major temple-building program in the Fayum during his reign.

The so-called 'pedestals' at Biahmu are arguably among the most enigmatic monuments in Egypt (see plate 8). The earliest descriptions were made by the Greek traveler–scholars Herodotus, Pliny, and Strabo. Herodotus described them as pyramids, with statues of the pharaoh on thrones seated on top. Similar descriptions were offered in most accounts until the medieval Islamic governor of the Fayum compiled a more accurate report based on having actually visited the site, describing two "idols" of stone, "built in the natural soil," with ancient writings on them, similar to the pyramids and temples.[80] Until about the sixteenth century AD, two seated colossi were probably still present on thrones, but from at least 1737 all that remained were the base pedestals of the statues.[81] During his season in the Fayum in the late nineteenth century, Petrie conducted excavations at the site over six days. His record and theoretical restoration of the monument are still considered reliable. Based on the dimensions of the preserved pedestals and the few fragments of the statues (a nose and clothing pieces, plus nome figures from the throne bases), he estimated that the original colossi would have been around eighteen meters tall, making them the same height as the Colossi of Memnon in Luxor. The two statues had a walled courtyard in front of them measuring around 24 by 29 meters. Petrie noted that the courts were almost certainly paved since he detected a 'uniform spread' of limestone chippings, and there were 'stairs' leading down from the statue bases to the courtyard paving level.[82]

No other remains have ever been found in the area around these pedestals (possibly because no archaeological work has taken place there since Petrie's time), bringing into question their function and purpose. Since at least 1737 there has been a road running between the statues from Madinat al-Fayum toward the lake (it now runs into the village of Biahmu), which Petrie believed to be evidence of the purpose of the colossi: as a monumental 'entrance' to the Fayum. Until the construction of the Aswan High Dam in the 1960s, the area around the pedestals flooded during the inundation. Indeed, it was probably the fact that Herodotus saw them from a distance surrounded by water that led him to believe they were far larger monuments within the lake itself. The level of the lake during the Middle Kingdom was around 15 meters above sea level and the Biahmu monuments sit just above this level, meaning that they did actually sit on the 'edge' of the region close to the lake. This makes Petrie's hypothesis that these colossi acted as a monumental 'gateway' to the Fayum leading to Shedet plausible. The apparent lack of evidence of a temple attached to these colossi is perplexing, and any analysis of this monument has to be undertaken with extreme caution until more information is available. The Colossi of Memnon appeared to be isolated monuments in the floodplain for many decades, but recent work has brought to light clear evidence that they were just one part of a major temple.

From later religious texts we know that the region itself was perceived to be the embodiment of a temple of Sobek, and these monuments may actually have marked the entrance to that 'imagined' temple, just as colossi flank the entrances to many later temples. Fragments of inscriptions found at the site date the monument to the reign of Amenemhat III, although it is impossible to know at what point in his reign they were constructed. The colossi are clear evidence of how significant the region was to this pharaoh, and when combined with the hydrological data they provide a clue about just what the landscape may have looked like. Only a small area of the Fayum region was habitable, but it was a considerably larger area than was accessible during the Old Kingdom. Perhaps part of the reason for the increase in royal interest in the region was the fact that there was more land naturally available for exploitation.

One other point worth noting in regard to the colossi is that they seem to act as an entrance to the inhabited areas of the region from the north. The name of the region (*š-rsi*) already hints that it was 'viewed' from the north, but this monumental 'gateway' (or temple) suggests that unlike today—when we look at a map and can see that the 'entrance' to the region through the Nile–Fayum channel is from the east—the region was 'engaged with' from the north. This phenomenon of an 'upside-down' perception of the region is made very explicit in the Book of Fayum. The way we 'see' the region today is shaped by Cartesian geography—the mapping of the globe and an appreciation of what is north and south. Without this knowledge visions of landscapes are not seen from a bird's-eye perspective; they are created based on experience at ground level, which is always relative to where you place yourself.

Very little remains of the ruins of Middle Kingdom Shedet, but columns dating to the reign of Amenemhat III found by Labib Habachi (1937) near the ruins of the Ptolemaic temple do provide some particularly interesting evidence of the Sobek temple in Shedet constructed by that pharaoh.[83] Habachi found fourteen red granite papyriform column fragments that he believed were deliberately broken up for reuse in the construction of the Ptolemaic temple. The columns clearly all belonged together, and nine had fragments of inscriptions preserved that can be pieced together to show that the inscription was a dedication text to the pharaoh (the living Horus), who constructed a monument for 'his father' Sobek of Shedet, with a columned hall, which had granite floors and doors of electrum.[84] Excavations in the area where the columns were found showed no other evidence of a temple at that location, and some scholars have argued that the fragments probably came from Hawara, due to the fact that throughout Egyptian history it was not uncommon for temples to be dismantled for the stones to be reused elsewhere.[85] The fact that Petrie excavated other inscribed granite blocks from within the ruins of the Ptolemaic temple pylon[86] does back up a theory that the blocks found by Habachi were probably also remains of Ptolemaic reuse of earlier materials, although it is ultimately probably impossible to know from where the blocks came.

5. Seated statue of Rameses II at Kiman Faris (Crocodilopolis), 1980. *Photograph by R. Neil Hewison.*

The description of the temple in these inscriptions clearly suggests a major cult-temple dedicated to Sobek of Shedet / Sobek Shedty, constructed by Amenemhat III. Prior to the New Kingdom there is very little evidence of major stone-built cult temples for gods, so if these fragments were from a Sobek cult temple at Shedet they would indicate the exceptional nature of Amenemhat III's dedication to the Sobek cult in Shedet. As Zecchi points out in his study of the cult of Sobek in the Fayum, given the fact that this pharaoh did indeed dedicate temples to Sobek elsewhere in the Fayum (for example, at Hawara), it would seem strange for him to have ignored the primary cult center for the crocodile god.[87]

There are numerous other inscribed fragments in museum collections around the world that probably come from Madinat al-Fayum. Petrie noted when he was working at the site that the area was being cultivated and that many blocks were being lifted and removed, so it is probably safe to assume that many were sold. There are many blocks in collections with a provenance of 'the Fayum' naming Sobek of Shedet or Sobek Shedty.[88] Some of these blocks could come from Hawara rather than the Sobek temple at Shedet, but they all attest to the incredible proliferation of temple construction activities in the Fayum undertaken by Middle Kingdom pharaohs. The connection between Sobek and Horus was emphasized, and

6. Remains of the temple of Sobek at Kiman Faris (Crocodilopolis), 1980.
Photograph by R. Neil Hewison.

the very specific form of Sobek—Sobek Shedty—first appeared during the reign of Amenemhat III, along with *tꜣ-š*, the 'new' name for the sacred landscape of the Fayum.

The only preserved cult temple in the Fayum is officially dedicated to 'Renenutet, the living one of Dja'—Madinat Madi. The temple dates to the end of the reign of Amenemhat III and the earliest years of Amenemhat IV, and was expanded considerably during the Ptolemaic period. Until the 1930s, Egyptologists thought this site to date exclusively to the Ptolemaic and Roman periods, but excavations by Italian missions in the later temples uncovered this important Middle Kingdom temple. Despite the fact that it is dedicated to the cobra goddess of the harvest, Sobek–Horus of Shedet plays a key role in the temple and appears in many inscriptions.

The temple of the Twelfth Dynasty is relatively small (10.5 by 9.7 meters), with a columned portico in the front and a transverse hall with three recessed niches at the rear. In the niches are depictions of rituals being performed by Amenemhat III for either Renenutet or Sobek.[89] Within the temple Renenutet appears in the role of attendant of the two deities (Sobek–Horus and the pharaoh), and the legitimacy of royal power is expressed through the father–son relationship of Sobek and Amenemhat

III. In return for the offerings being made by the king (in the scenes), Renenutet provides him with protection, while Sobek very specifically provides 'good products of the Lake Land' (*t3-š*), which symbolically ties the notion of legitimate royal power to the Fayum in this instance.[90] Marco Zecchi sees this temple as an expression of the "perfect parallel between the economic and agricultural exploitation of the region by the ruling dynasty and the legitimization of the royal power."[91] By choosing to dedicate a temple to Renenutet—protective goddess of the harvest—Amenemhat III was making it clear that agriculture was a key element in the relationship between the pharaoh/royal power and the Fayum.

The location of this temple is especially interesting because it appears to be extraordinarily remote. Just as the tomb of Wadj at Kom Khelwa attests to what must have been important areas of occupation along the southern tip of the Fayum, this major temple on the southwestern edge of the region surely has to be read as evidence of the existence of a major town nearby, possibly lying hidden under the Greco-Roman town next to the temple. The fact that the temple was built in the desert might be an indication that it was not plausible to construct a major temple within the fertile area of the Fayum due to year-round high water levels. It is of course possible that there were other temples in the fertile area of the Fayum and that these remains have simply not been preserved, but it is hard to

7. Google Earth image of Madinat Madi.

8. Google Earth image of Hawara.

envisage a situation in which a temple of such importance, built in stone—a rare occurrence for the Middle Kingdom and testimony to the significance of this temple—would be constructed in an out-of-the-way location. For a temple to be built anywhere there has to have been a strong motive behind the choice of location. As discussed above, the location of the Biahmu pedestals on the edge of the flooded zone appears to have been perceived as the 'entrance' to the occupied area/Shedet. Quite what the motive was behind this choice of location for a temple is impossible to determine at present, but it is important to remain aware that this location clearly held some significance in the sacred landscape of the Fayum. During the later Roman occupation of the area, it acted as an outpost for the routes to the western desert oases, and the presence of the Twelfth Dynasty temple might indicate that this location played a similar role during the Middle Kingdom.

The Fayum owes much of its fame to Herodotus, but Hawara—location of the mudbrick pyramid of Amenemhat III—is an exceptional case. The description of the Fayum by Herodotus is dominated by the fantastic nature of the enormous lake and the overwhelming size and complexity of the Labyrinth. Herodotus's account is discussed at length later in the book (Chapter Four), but it is important to note here that his description of the Labyrinth has undoubtedly shaped the way in which scholars think about the site of Hawara—and the Fayum as a whole. It probably affected the way in which the Ptolemaic and Roman inhabitants of the region perceived the region, the site of Hawara, and the religious geography of the Fayum. As is discussed in the chapter on early travelers, the first European explorers in the Fayum all went with the explicit desire to find the fabulous Labyrinth. Initially it was believed that the temple at Qasr Qarun was the Labyrinth (at that time they did not realize that Qasr Qarun was not even built when Herodotus visited the region), but by 1819 when Giovanni Belzoni visited the Fayum he was certain this was not the case (see plate 9).[92] By 1827, when Edward William Lane wrote his account, "some modern travelers" agreed that Hawara was the location of the Labyrinth,[93] and Petrie pronounced in 1912 that he had identified the site of the Labyrinth temple at Hawara in 1888.[94] Since then, this theory has been accepted almost without question and a huge amount of energy has been put into determining the form of the Labyrinth at the site.

The issue of the form of the Labyrinth at Hawara has caused scholars many problems. Reconciling the scant and inconclusive archaeological evidence from the few excavations at the site with the elaborate descriptions of an enormous and complex temple has been virtually impossible. Since the first suggestion that Hawara was the site of this famous monument, people have created reconstructions of what the temple might have looked like, paying varying amounts of attention to the physical remains found in the ruin field south of the pyramid. Several detailed studies have been dedicated to this project, such as *Pharaoh's Gateway to Eternity* (Uphill 2000). It is probably fair to state that if this site was *not* considered to be the home of such a famous monument, the ruins would be simply seen as the remains of the mortuary temple of Amenemhat III. There is so little evidence at the site of anything more than a standard funerary temple that it is hard to build an argument that it bore more importance for the ancient Egyptians of the Twelfth Dynasty than any other royal mortuary complex. Even Petrie admits that "from such scanty remains it is hard to settle anything"[95] and notes in his journal that "the plan of it is hopelessly gone."[96] The most extensive study of the exploration and archaeology of Hawara is the monumental work by Inge Uytterhoeven.[97]

There is, however, ample evidence to suggest that Sobek played an unusually important role in this temple complex, as many fragments of individual and group statues of the crocodile god have been found at the site, which can be dated to the Middle Kingdom.[98] Elsewhere in Egypt there is further evidence of this temple. A quarry inscription in Wadi Hammamat from an expedition led by Senwosret, overseer of stone-cutters, provides what could be read as evidence of a Sobek temple at Hawara. The inscription shows that the mission of the expedition was to obtain stone for 'ten statues of five cubits seated upon a throne,' and to deliver them to Ankh-Amenemhat living forever and ever in the 'House of Sobek of Shedet.'[99]

There is a great deal of evidence of activities in the Fayum in textual sources found outside the region, and it is these sources that provide a lot of examples of the new name for the sacred landscape of the Fayum—*tꜣ-š*—and Sobek Shedty. The huge numbers of private stelae and statues dedicated at the important pilgrimage site of Abydos means that there is a large quantity of inscribed material from this period available for study. Many of these stelae contain autobiographical information about the owners, providing us with an invaluable source of information on not only different roles played by people in ancient Egyptian administration but also the more personal activities of individuals and the locations in which they lived and worked. In addition to this, the development of literary works during the Middle Kingdom that were valued enough to be copied repeatedly—often to the point of canonization—and have been preserved in much later papyri can provide much more nuanced insight into the way society, humankind, and the known world were perceived by ancient Egyptians of the time.

Sobek and Sobek Shedty in Shedet

The prominence of the cult of Sobek of Shedet during the Middle Kingdom means that there is ample evidence of individuals being connected to the Fayum via their role in temple activities at this time. Zecchi provides the most comprehensive overview of the role of Sobek in the Fayum (for all periods), listing all the relevant objects and inscriptions.[100] Many demonstrate that the Fayum was a hub of religious activities during the Middle Kingdom, and Zecchi convincingly argues that links to the Fayum via Sobek were used as tools of legitimacy by several pharaohs, proving the importance of the region to the royal court and the pharaohs.

Among the numerous stelae set up in individual shrines at Abydos during the Middle Kingdom, there are, as perhaps could be expected, several that belong to individuals with links to the Fayum, now held in the Cairo Museum (CG and JE numbers refer to the stelae registration numbers). The list includes a wab priest, *wꜣb ꜥꜣ n sbk šdty* (CG20616),[101] and an overseer of the priests of his cult, *ỉmy-r ḥm nṯr n sbk šdty* (CG20562),[102] an overseer of the Southern Lake of Sobek, *ỉmy-r pr š-rsỉ sbk* (CG20070),[103] and a 'chief' of Sobek Shedty, *ḥry-tp n sbk šdty* (CG20075).[104] Although such a conclusion is essentially impossible to prove, it is tempting to assume that these individuals were all based at the temple of Sobek in Shedet.

A group of funerary statuettes in a private collection (Favre) in Switzerland could potentially also come from Abydos, but they more likely come from cemeteries in or around the Fayum. A statuette of Sobekhotep (an overseer) has been dated to the reign of Amenemhat III and includes formulae for offerings to both Sobek Shedty Lord of the Lake Land (*sbk šdty nb tꜣ-š*) and to Ptah Sokar.[105] The offering formula on a small (damaged) basalt standing statuette of a deputy of Atfih (east of the Nile opposite Meidum) names Sobek Shedty, and a seated statuette of Ren-seneb, a district official of sentries, bears an offering formula dedicated to Sobek Shedty and Horus who is in Shedet (*sbk šdty ḥr ḥry-ib šdt*).[106] The fourth statuette in this group names a deity about whom little is really known: Osiris Ity, one who is in the Lake Land (*ꜣsir ity ḥry-ib tꜣ-š*).[107] Wild notes several other statues that name this deity, namely five Middle Kingdom and nine Late Period ones. This list was expanded by Zecchi, who notes that this deity appears in the late Twelfth Dynasty.[108] In addition to the statuette published by Wild, *ꜣsir ity ḥry-ib tꜣ-š* appears on a statue in the Metropolitan Museum collection (66.99.6) (which also has offerings dedicated to *sbk šdty nb tꜣ-š*) and on two statuettes in Cairo (JE 43095 and JE 43093). *ꜣsir ity ḥry-ib tꜣ-š* also appears on a coffin (unknown provenance) that was usurped during the Third Intermediate period by Takelot II.[109] Zecchi lists three further unprovenanced Middle Kingdom statues bearing offerings to Osiris (Ity) who is in the Lake Land and to Sobek Shedty: in Berlin (10/66 and ÄM31210), in Strasbourg (1382), and in Copenhagen (AIEM 88).[110]

The Louvre in Paris holds at least three Middle Kingdom statues with inscriptions that place the owners in or near the Fayum. Again their provenance is unknown, although the catalog suggests the Fayum as its origin based on the inscriptions mentioning Sobek Shedty and the 'Lake Land.' Louvre E10985 is a basalt cube statue of Ta dated to the Thirteenth Dynasty that bears an offering to Sobek Shedty and 'Osiris who is in the Lake Land' (*sbk šdty ꜣsir ḥry-ib tꜣ-š*).[111] Louvre E11196 is a composite statue of Wadjiwer with offerings to Sobek Shedty Horus who is in Shedet. Interestingly, his father was named Nefershedty, spelled using the specific Shedty hieroglyph, which suggests that this family was closely linked to the Fayum.[112] This appears to be the only occurrence of Shedty in a personal name. Louvre

E11053 is dated to the reign of Amenemhat III and belonged to Amenemhat-ankh (Ameny-ip), who was the chief of priests and *ḥry šstꜣ n st wrt m ꜥḥ-wr m šdt m tꜣ-š*, 'Chief of secrets of the great place in the great palace in Shedet in the Lake Land.'[113] This inscription is one of the very few that provides information on a non-temple establishment in Shedet. Based on this inscription it is possible to state that there must have been a palatial building or compound for the pharaoh in Shedet during the Middle Kingdom.

To summarize, this group of inscriptions contains a variety of different titles and dedications relating to Sobek, Shedet, and the Fayum:

- *sbk šdty*, Sobek Shedty: Occurs frequently, with the name always written using the specific Shedty hieroglyph.
- Sobek Shedty as *nb tꜣ-š*, Lord of the Lake Land: Occurs on the statue of Sobekhotep (Favre collection)[114] and Metropolitan Museum statue 66.99.6.
- Sobek Shedty as *ḥr ḥry-ib šdt*, Horus in Shedet: Occurs on the statue of Renseneb (Favre collection)[115] and Wadjiwer (Louvre E11196).[116]
- Sobek Shedty who is *ꜣsir ḥry-ib tꜣ-š*, Osiris dwelling in the Lake Land: This is attested on the Louvre statuette of Ta (E10985).[117]
- *ꜣsir ity ḥry-ib tꜣ-š*, Osiris Ity who dwells in the Lake Land: This is attested in at least six inscriptions.
- The Palace in Shedet, *ꜥḥ-wr m šdt m tꜣ-š*: This is attested on the statue of Amenemhat-ankh (Ameny-ip) (Louvre E11053).[118]

Based on this large group of statues and stelae it is apparent that *tꜣ-š* is the 'home' of the Fayum deities: Sobek Shedty, the specific Fayum Sobek crocodile God; Osiris in the Lake Land; and Osiris Ity in the Lake Land. While it is impossible for this list to be exhaustive, the absence of any other name for the region in these inscriptions and the fact that *tꜣ-š* only ever occurs in relationship to the Fayum deities strongly suggests that *tꜣ-š* was the name given to the sacred landscape of the Fayum—the landscape in which the gods dwelled.

Literary Texts

The Middle Kingdom is often considered to have been the Golden Age of ancient Egyptian literature, and dozens of compositions were used as 'school' texts and copied for hundreds of years, probably by hundreds of trainee scribes. Many of these texts are only preserved on papyri dating from the New Kingdom, and in many cases they are incomplete and therefore hard to translate, leaving many questions about their underlying meaning. Many of the texts have the appearance of simple tales of activities involving private individuals or the royal court, but all have a much deeper meaning and were frequently intended to be 'teachings,' much like Biblical parables. Some were a means of expressing religious beliefs, but all reveal a great deal about how at least a small part of ancient Egyptian society perceived certain aspects of the world around it.

What is best described as a 'hymn' in praise of the king is preserved on one Eighteenth Dynasty papyrus held in the Pushkin Museum in Moscow. The first translation of the text appeared in 1956, and the composition was divided into two parts.[119] Since then, further studies have shown that these two parts almost certainly belong together and are often also linked to a major annals inscription dating to the reign of Amenemhat II discovered in the Ptah temple at Mit Rahina (Memphis).[120] These three texts are best studied as one group.

The Memphis annals inscription is preserved on two main blocks that were reused in the construction of the New Kingdom Ptah temple. The first (smaller) fragment was discovered by Petrie in 1908 in front of the west pylon,[121] while the larger fragment that was beneath a Ramesside statue base was noted in 1974 and recognized as part of the same inscription.[122]

The inscription records the income and expenditure of a temple during the reign of Amenemhat II and may well not actually be from a temple at Mit Rahina. It is only possible to guess at its original location.[123] The activities recorded include expeditions to obtain raw materials for making statues, temples constructed, and arrivals of notable visitors. In this list of activities, Amenemhat II is said to have spent some time in a palace in the Fayum, specifically the 'Palace in the Southern Lake Land in the island of Senwosret I,' *ḥtp nsw m ꜥḥ n tꜣ š-rsi iw n nswt bity ḫpr-kꜣ-rꜥ*. While there, he took part in fishing and fowling, activities often deemed to be highly symbolic, linked with fertility and humankind's mastery of the chaos of nature. This is followed by a record of deliveries to the temple of 1,350 fowl and 459 fish, presumably the catch from the hunting expedition.[124] This inscription is of particular interest because it is the only occurrence of this extended name for the region—*tꜣ š-rsi*, the Southern Lake Land. It is possible that the name reflects the fact that this is an official royal inscription, but it could be an attempt to unite the two aspects of the Fayum landscape, sacred and administrative (imagined and experienced).

The section of this inscription relating to the Fayum activities stands out as being somewhat different in character to the rest of the text, less formal and more narrative.[125] John Baines actually compares this to the Old Kingdom tomb of Meten. It is tempting to consider the fact that there is some kind of connection between the activities (hunting, fishing, and fowling) and the Fayum landscape that caused this alteration in style, perhaps subtly reflecting ancient Egyptians' attitude toward and perception of the Fayum as an 'unworldly' landscape that held more sacred meaning.

Steven Quirke considered the event recorded in the Memphis annals to have been the inspiration behind the more literary texts in the stories 'The Sporting King' and 'Fishing and Fowling' in the Moscow papyri.[126] The parallels are indeed remarkable. The papyri are sadly fragmentary, which makes translation and interpretation difficult. Much like other Middle Kingdom 'stories' (for example, the tale of Khufu in the Westcar Papyrus), the papyri depict the royal court at leisure, and therefore the text reveals aspects of ancient Egyptian ideals. In these texts the landscape is very much the background for the activities: the activities take place because of the landscape.[127] The landscape seems to exist for the pleasure of the elite. It is an alternative world, described in idealized terms, much as it is in European nineteenth-century poetry.

The 'Sporting King' and 'Fishing and Fowling' texts traditionally were engaged with as two separate compositions, but they are increasingly recognized as most probably having been written on one papyrus, if not actually also being one tale with two parts, one royal and one nonroyal.[128] The story in the 'Sporting King' is introduced as being a speech given to the king by Sehetibreankh, describing the activities of the king, 'He of the Two Ladies, Hunter,' in the Fayum. Despite the severe damage to the manuscript, it is possible to discern that the hunting party arrives in the 'Palace of the Fayum' (*ʿḥ tꜣ-š*) and that the activities that follow take place in the area.

> He of the Two Ladies, Hunter, foremost . . . to the Red Crown as noble of the crew . . . ? Life! Prosperity! Health!, our lord, your setting is in the cool field . . . united with eternity . . . in supplies. . . . Women the children of the king shouting delight, receiving . . . proceeding in peace . . . in a ferry for crossing (?) shore . . . land, in the palace of the Land of the Lake (*tꜣ-š*).[129]

Later in the text the palace is mentioned again, and the Fayum (*tꜣ-š*) is mentioned at least twice more. The landscape described in the poem is lush, rich with marshes, birds, trees, canals, pools, and fish. The mention of what may be an abbreviated form of the name of the Middle Kingdom residence at Itj-tawy—*iṯw* (the full form is *iṯ-tꜣwy*)—combined with the setting of the tale in the Fayum really does point to the conclusion that the poem was composed by a scribe in the court of the Twelfth Dynasty pharaohs in Itj-tawy. It is tempting to consider that it was written in 'praise' of the Fayum landscape.

The non-royal 'Fishing and Fowling' poem is far better preserved and therefore much easier to translate and study. It is not so obvious that the activities take place in the Fayum, but the landscape is described using almost identical terms to those in the 'Sporting King.' The marshes are rich with birds, fish, and trees:

> The fish are pierced on the spear, I kill at each chance. There is no stopping my harpoon, I make bundles of white bulti-fish.[130]

> Spend time . . . in the midst of the water over the mouth . . . with the shrubs in two lines, reeds at my back for matting beneath me, the cover . . . birds roaming with no end to their passing.[131]

In a rather fragmentary part of the manuscript (section C),[132] the statement 'Let me teach you of the Lake of Sobek the western land' (*sbꜣ.i tw š n sbk tꜣ imnty*) occurs at the beginning of a list of places in the Fayum and the Delta. It is in section A (which Quirke places at the end of the text) that the Fayum plays a more obvious role.[133] This part is a joyous celebration of fishing and fowling in the marshes. One line reads: 'Happy day when we arrive going down to the field!' Another reads, 'Happy day for Sobek Lord of the Lake Land' (*hrw nfr sbk nb tꜣ-š*).[134] Burnt offerings (fish, birds, geese) are made to Sobek (Lord of the Lake Land) several times in the poem. The location in which the activities of Section B[135] take place is less obvious. The landscape is clearly marshland, but there is one small clue that this may also be set in the Fayum near the end in the lines: 'I might go down to the rivers on the month and fifteen-day festivals and go down to the Lake.'[136] While this could be any lake, the references to Sobek of the Fayum in the other sections strongly suggest that the 'Lake' is the Fayum lake.

'Fishing and Fowling' and the 'Sporting King' name the region as *tꜣ-š*, and refer to *š n sbk.* The landscape of the Fayum is described in terms that make it the ultimate fertile, rich, and pleasurable landscape. It is an idyllic landscape in which to pass leisure time, for royalty and nonroyalty alike. The poems are of course idealized images, and if they were indeed composed by scribes in the Fayum or Itj-tawy it is unsurprising perhaps that they chose to use their 'own' landscape as the setting for the activities. The Fayum would certainly have been a marsh-like landscape rich in wildlife, and most likely was ideal hunting grounds for fish and birds. The fact that the region is named *tꜣ-š* as opposed to *š-rsỉ* shows that the poems refer to the sacred landscape of the Fayum, the landscape of the gods, and therefore it is perhaps unsurprising that the landscape is described in such idealized terms.

Hymns

During excavations at the Ramesseum in 1895–96, Flinders Petrie and James Quibell discovered a Thirteenth Dynasty tomb shaft containing a box of papyri. Now known as the Ramesseum Papyri, the collection is held in the British Museum in London and the Ägyptishes Museum in Berlin. The papyri were in poor condition as the tomb had certainly been affected by inundation waters, and the mounting process in the early twentieth century unfortunately did further damage to the manuscripts. The documents represent a collection of some of the most important ancient Egyptian literary and religious works, including the 'Tale of Sinuhe' and the 'Eloquent Peasant,' as well as medico-magical texts and spells.[137] Among them are two hymns dedicated to Sobek of Shedet / Sobek Shedty (P.Ramesseum 6; BM EA10759).

The first hymn opens with a statement that Sobek arose from the primeval waters / the flood and is lord of low-lying lands and desert edges, of land where fishing and fowling takes place, and ruler of river-streams. The hymn extols the virtues and character of Sobek, who is *nb tꜣ-š*, who 'cleaves a way through' *r-ḥnt*, and is 'great of might' in *nn-nsw* (Herakleopolis / modern Ihnasya al-Medina, 'capital' of the Herakleopolitan Dynasty during the First Intermediate Period), among other epithets. Sobek Shedty, Horus dwelling in Shedet—*sbk šdty ḥr hry-ỉb šdt*—is described as both fearsome and loving, and the son of the goddess Neith.[138] The second poem is longer, but once again is dedicated to Sobek Shedty, Horus dwelling in Shedet. He is said to travel the Lake Land (*tꜣ-š*), cross the Great Green (*wꜣḏ-wr*), and be 'rescued' in the great Henet (*ḫnt-wr*) by Nun. He is the son of Osiris (naturally, being Horus he would be the son of Osiris) and of Neith. In this poem Sobek is described as being more powerful than all other gods, adored by all.[139] His first epithets place him in a cult-place at Lahun (*r-sḫwy*) in the Lake (*š*), which he entered via *r-ḫnt*.[140] He is adored/pacified by 'those who are in the flood'; he opened the lakes and is ruler of river-streams.[141] There are few direct references to the Fayum in the hymn, but Sobek is clearly placed in the region within the hymn via the Fayum-specific spelling of 'Lake.'

This hymn, while explicitly written in praise of Sobek, is a description of the sacred landscape of the Fayum and, importantly, is the earliest record of the Fayum creation theology. The overtly religious nature of the text means that the boundary between the landscape experienced by people and the landscape of the gods (found in the afterlife) is somewhat blurred. The fact that Sobek is said to 'cleave' a way through *r-ḫnt* strongly suggests that this locality was perceived to be a passage into the region. The occurrence of *w3ḏ-wr* in this text indicates that the 'Great Green' was a part of the Fayum sacred landscape. The 'great Henet' is not a location found in any other Fayum text, but a *ḫnt* is a type of waterway and the 'great' *ḫnt* in this text may well be symbolically placing Sobek in every *ḫnt* of the Fayum simultaneously. The core elements of Fayum mythology are that Sobek enters the Fayum via the *ḫnt*, is the son of Neith, enters the Lake (*w3ḏ-wr*), and then crosses the *t3-š*. His 'rescue' by Nun in the great Henet may refer to his birth. It is this framework on which the later Book of Fayum was probably constructed.

The Fayum certainly gained a new identity during the Middle Kingdom. The development of the Fayum creation story in the cult of Sobek, made explicit in the Hymn to Sobek, was almost certainly connected with major new religious institutions appearing in the region during this period. There must have been an influx of royal court officials, administrators, scribes, and skilled craftsmen associated with the construction projects around the region, and without doubt the Fayum became a hub of activities. The two aspects of the landscape—the imagined sacred landscape in which Sobek, or Sobek Shedty, ruled and the experienced landscape, the locations in which administrative activities took place—existed side by side, and the management of the sacred landscape was probably a major part of the daily life of many priests.

The landscape they experienced was the stimulus for the imagined sacred landscape. It was lush and green, rich in fish, good for hunting larger dangerous animals (crocodiles and possibly hippopotami), and probably fertile and good for agriculture even if there was not a great deal of land that remained above water long enough for significant areas to be used for crop cultivation. Regardless of the lack of firm evidence of any major interventions in the hydrology and irrigation of the region during this period, there is no doubt that the tradition that maintains that Amenemhat III was responsible for 'creating' the region, for managing the landscape, is justified. The significance he placed on the Fayum landscape cannot be denied. What can perhaps never be known is just why he chose to do this, but just as the 'Amarna revolution' was not an overnight change in the religious system of Egypt, this interest and investment in the Fayum landscape was not a sudden event.

The New Kingdom (1550–1069 BC)

Most sources suggest that there was an increasing lack of central rule during the Thirteenth Dynasty in Egypt (1773–c.1650 BC). It was, once again, a period in which many pharaohs followed in quick succession, possibly still all based in Itj-tawy. Egypt lost the control it had gained over Nubia during the reign of Sobekhotep IV,[142] and the country fragmented, with Asiatic rulers—the Hyksos—controlling the north from Avaris (modern Tell al-Daba). Simultaneously, powerful local leaders emerged in the south and a line of rulers emerged in Thebes. Evidence of the precise nature of the end of Hyksos rule and the reunification of Egypt under Theban king Ahmose (1550–25 BC) is confused, but it is clear that Ahmose led a specific campaign against the Hyksos, resulting in the founding of the Eighteenth Dynasty.[143] The New Kingdom (1550–1069 BC), although seen as one cultural phase, divides into two periods: pre- and post-Amarna. The dramatic events of the Amarna period, instigated by Akhenaten (Amenhotep IV, 1352–36 BC), probably barely had any effect on the lives of most ancient Egyptians, but culturally the Ramesside period (Nineteenth to Twentieth Dynasties) was markedly different to the earlier Eighteenth Dynasty.

There is no archaeological evidence for a building program in the Fayum during the New Kingdom to match that of the Middle Kingdom, but the establishment of a new palace foundation opposite Lahun at Madinat al-Gurob shows that the region continued to play a significant role in the pharaonic royal court during the Eighteenth Dynasty. Other information about the region during the New Kingdom can be gleaned from inscriptions belonging to Eighteenth Dynasty mayors of the Fayum, and the detailed registers found in the Wilbour Papyrus, and New Kingdom Onomastica reveal a great deal about the administration of the Fayum landscape during the Ramesside period. What is most notable about the landscape of the Fayum during the New Kingdom is the apparent lack of interventions by Rameses II. Although his name occurs in Fayum texts, there is no evidence of any major temple building program here during his reign. Given the scale of his building program at many sites across Egypt, his 'absence' from the Fayum is intriguing. It suggests that he did not consider the region important and felt no need to mark his presence on the sacred landscape or pay homage to the local deity in the way he did at so many cult temples in Egypt.

Excavations at Madinat al-Gurob have rather a troubled history. During his 1888–90 seasons in the Fayum, Petrie worked at Lahun, Hawara, and Gurob. Needless to say his attention was spread rather thin, and his assistant Walter Hughes-Hughes, who led the work at Madinat al-Gurob, kept notably poor records of his excavations. The final publication by Petrie contained some basic plans, but a great deal of information was lost and the site continued to be heavily plundered.[144] Objects that clearly came from Gurob continued to appear in the Fayum, and in 1903 Petrie sent Charles Currelly and Leonard Loat to the site while he worked at Ihnasya (*nn-nsw*, Herakleopolis) to the south. The pair concentrated primarily on the cemeteries, and Loat noted the discovery of a small village close to the site. The reports are minimal, however,[145] and it has not been possible to relocate the village. In 1901 local farmers began 'exploring' the site, and following their discovery of the now-famous head of Queen Tiye, in 1905 Ludwig Borchardt visited the site for one day and compiled more detailed plans of what little he could see, recognizing that it was the remains of a palace, rather than a temple. In 1920, Guy Brunton and Reginald Engelbach attempted further excavations at the site but were hampered by a lack of adequate maps and plans and the extensive destruction of the site due to looting.[146] Until the early 1980s the site was occupied by the Egyptian military, and today part of the archaeological area of the palace and cemeteries is still military land.

Survey and some small excavation work conducted by the University of Liverpool led by Ian Shaw took place between 2005 and 2012.[147] Following the 2011 Revolution in Egypt, the Liverpool team became aware of previously undocumented elite cemeteries to the southwest of the palace area, which had recently been looted. Work to study the materials discarded around the burials is ongoing. The agricultural land to the east of the main site is currently being investigated for evidence of the harbors noted in several texts. The mission is now led by Marine Yoyotte from the IFAO.[148]

The foundation of the palace has been dated to the reign of Thutmose III, a conclusion based on the discovery of stamped mudbricks in the enclosure wall and on evidence in the Wilbour Papyrus (discussed later), which indicates that it was still occupied during the reign of Rameses V. The reports from early excavations are somewhat sketchy, and various attempts have been made to reconstruct the site based on the scanty remains.[149] What is evident is that a large walled enclosure containing two large buildings formed the core of the site, with a spread of settlement and industrial buildings outside that enclosure, running along a high ridge immediately to the west of the floodplain. There is evidence of a columned building within the enclosure, and the early work indicated the presence of a temple to the west of the enclosure.[150] No ancient remains other than ceramics and a scattered spread of small faience fragments are visible on the surface today, although the layout of the site and the enclosure walls is apparent in aerial photographs. The question of the identity of the walled building, and by inference its purpose, has always been based on the occurrence of the names and titles of several scribes, overseers, and servants of a 'harem' (*ḫnrt* or *pr-ḫnty*) of *mr-wr* (or *š*) in papyri and inscribed on objects and stelae found at both Gurob and Kahun.[151]

Archaeological and textual remains attest to the presence of royal women at the site, and it is known that the palace was home to ancient Egyptian royal women and children. Some of the evidence (foreign ceramics, and the occurrence of foreign names in texts) suggests that foreign women in diplomatic marriages with Egyptian kings were also resident here. Evidence shows that the palace was a center of local administration, and as it was a land-holding institution this is perhaps to be expected. There is a great deal of material, both archaeological and textual, which suggests that the town was a center of textile production. It is clear that there was also an industrial area producing items of faience, copper, bronze, and possibly also glass objects, and there is ample evidence for the administration of and daily activities relating to agriculture.[152] That the Fayum was 'home' to royal women is one of the longest-held traditions in the region that still endures today, preserved in Islamic histories, but surprisingly not present in Greek texts.

The papyri from Gurob have never been fully published, or indeed ever comprehensively studied as a group, but a summary by Fredrik Hagen provides a valuable overview of this collection, which is currently held in the Petrie Museum.[153] Some items included in an earlier publication of Gurob papyri actually come from Kahun. They were grouped with Gurob material because they were New Kingdom in date.[154] The bulk of the actual Gurob archive dates to the Ramesside period—the reigns of Seti II, Rameses II, and Merenptah. Hagen notes that the papyri consist principally of temple archive documents, primarily the 'journal,' which includes records of deliveries of fish, oil, bread, and beer, temple income in the form of tax-grain, receipt of textiles, arrival and departure of officials, and lists of workers arriving and being sent elsewhere.[155]

There is a great deal of evidence of individuals associated with the 'harem'—*pr-ẖnty* or *ipt-nswt*—in *mr-wr*, primarily in papyri, meaning that there can be no doubt of the identity of Gurob as a royal women's palace.[156] For example, Seti was 'Royal scribe and Overseer of the Royal 'beauties' of the harem in Mer-wer' (*ỉmy-rꜣ nfrw(t) n pr ẖnty m mr-wr*); Nakht was 'Overseer of the Harem in Mer-wer' (*ỉmy-r jpt nsw (n) [m]r-wr*); Hori was 'Overseer of Mer-wer' (*ḥꜣty-ꜥ n mr-wr*); and Su-ner was 'Scribe of the Harem' (*sš ỉpt nsw*), to name just a few.[157]

9. Google Earth image of Madinat al-Gurob.

New Kingdom Mayors of the Fayum: The Sobekhotep Family

There is an important group of statues and a tomb belonging to an influential family of royal treasurers and mayors of the Fayum that dates to the reigns of Thutmose III, Amenhotep II, Tuthmosis IV, and Amenhotep III (c.1479–1352 BC). Key to understanding the genealogy are two individuals named Sobekhotep, who held mayoral titles in the Fayum during the New Kingdom under the reigns of Amenhotep II and Tuthmosis IV. Sobekhotep I has two statues (Berlin 11635 and Marseille 208).[158] He was the son of Kapu, a mayor of the Fayum, and inherited the title from his father under the reign of Amenhotep II. Sobekhotep I was also 'Overseer of the bird-pools of entertainment,' 'Overseer of cattle,' 'Overseer of the double granaries,' and 'Overseer of works,' as well as governor of the 'Northern Lake' and the 'Southern Lake.' He was father-in-law to the other Sobekhotep (II), to whom he passed the Fayum titles.

Sobekhotep II had a tomb on the west bank in Thebes (TT63)[159] and was mayor of the Fayum and treasurer during the reign of Tuthmosis IV. He was the son of Min (treasurer under Thutmose III) and father of Paser (mayor of the Fayum under Amenhotep III).[160] Betsy Bryan suggests that scenes in the large and exceptionally well decorated (now mainly destroyed) tomb of Sobekhotep II (TT63) act as a 'Fayum memorial' commemorating the strong ties to the region held by Sobekhotep II and his wife Meryt (nurse to the daughter of Tuthmosis IV, Tiaa, she also had connections to the Fayum). In the tomb Sobekhotep II is named as 'Overseer of the priests of Sobek of Shedet, greatest of entertainers of Sobek of Shedet and Mayor of the Fayum.'

The third known mayor of the Fayum during the Eighteenth Dynasty is Itunema, father of Amenemhat and owner of a large stela dedicated to Herishef, excavated at Sedment by Petrie.[161] Bryan dates the stela to late in the reign of Amenhotep III.[162] This family remained close to the region, Sedment being the necropolis of *nn-nsw*/Herakleopolis.

Overview of the family and their titles:

Kapu
Reign of Amenhotep II
Title: Mayor of *š* (title identified on Berlin 11635)

Sobekhotep I
(son of Kapu and Meryt I, who are named on Berlin 11635 and Marseille 208)
Reign of Amenhotep II

Statue Berlin 11635, dedicated to Amun-Ra and Sobek Shedty, Horus in Shedet.

Titles: Mayor of *š*
Companion of the Lord of the Two Lands in the islands dwelling in *tꜣ-š*
Overseer of the bird-pools of entertainment
Overseer of cattle
Overseer of the double granaries
Overseer of works
Overseer of the Priests of Sobek Shedty

Statue Marseille 208, dedicated to Sobek-Shedty, Horus in Shedet and Sobek-Shedty, Osiris dwelling in *tꜣ-š*. Contains biographical text describing a trip to *tꜣ-š*.

Titles: Companion of the Lord of the Two Lands in the islands dwelling in *tꜣ-š*
Overseer of bird-pools
Overseer of the priests of Sobek-Shedty
Mayor of *tꜣ-š*
Mayor of *š-rsi mḥty*

Sobekhotep II

(son of Min; married Meryt II, daughter of Sobekhotep I; son Paser; identified in TT63)
Reign of Tuthmosis IV
Tomb TT63
Titles: Mayor of *š-rsi*
Mayor of *š-sbk*

Paser

(identifed in tomb of his father Sobekhotep II, TT63)
Reign of Tuthmosis IV years 20–30, Amenhotep III
Titles: Priest of Sobek-Shedty
Mayor of *š-sbk*
Overseer of the Treasury

Itunema

(father of Amenemhat, identified on stela of Amenemhat from Sedment)
Late reign of Amenhotep III
Title: Mayor of *š-rsi*

There is a further royal connection to the Fayum during the Eighteenth Dynasty via monuments of Queen Tiaa, wife of Amenhotep II. Betsy Bryan discusses a statue fragment belonging to her that came from ruins in Madinat al-Fayum (CG 1167) and includes the inscription, 'Great Royal Wife, beloved of him, beloved of Sobek Shedty [of Shedet].'[163] Tiaa's granddaughter, also named Tiaa, was cared for by Meryt, wife of Sobekhotep II.[164]

This group of officials and their wives clearly had exceptionally strong ties to the Fayum during a period in which the region held specific significance for the pharaoh. The biographical text on the left side of Marseille 208 (Sobekhotep I) is easily comparable to the earlier Middle Kingdom literary texts regarding activities in the Fayum:

> An offering which the King gives for the Ka of the Governor Sobekhotep. He says, "I accompanied his majesty, I was the sole companion of the lord of the two lands (?), When his majesty spent a moment in enjoying himself and entertaining himself in his tarrying time, in traversing the bird-pools of the Lake Land."[165]

It is perhaps possible to detect a gradual line of promotion from one generation to the next in this family. Kapu and Sobekhotep I were both mayor of *š*, which was probably a town in the region at this time (see section below on Wilbour Papyrus). Sobekhotep I was also named as mayor of *tꜣ-š* and *š-rsi mḥty*. In this context it seems likely that *š-rsi mḥty* refers to the northern part of *š-rsi*—the managed measured landscape—and the role of mayor of *tꜣ-š* might imply that he was in charge of 'managing' the sacred landscape. His successor was mayor of both *š-sbk* and *š-rsi*, the entire managed landscape of the Fayum, while his son Paser is named as mayor of *š-sbk*, which might indicate that Sobekhotep II was promoted from mayor of *š-sbk* to mayor of *š-rsi* and that he handed the title of mayor of *š-sbk* to his son. Itunema may or may not have been related to this family but, based on the dating of his stela, he was probably the successor to Sobekhotep II as mayor of *š-rsi*.

This group of material beautifully illustrates the intertwining of the sacred 'imagined' landscape of the Fayum and the experienced 'real' landscape. These men were overseers of priests of Sobek of Shedet / Sobek Shedty, as well as mayors of either *š*, *š-rsi*, *š-sbk*, *š-rsi mḥty*, or, very unusually, *tꜣ-š*. What is especially interesting about the story of the king visiting the bird-pools of *tꜣ-š* is that this is likely to be an account of an actual event, and in this instance the name for the sacred landscape is used (*tꜣ-š*), not that for the 'real' landscape (*š-rsi*). This actually helps us understand the name *š-rsi* as referring specifically and only to the administered aspect of the Fayum landscape. *š-rsi* may perhaps mean the measured lands?

The Wilbour Papyrus and Onomastica

The ten-meter-long Wilbour Papyrus is considered the most important non-religious pharaonic papyrus ever discovered, consisting of twenty-five 'pages' on two sides written in 102 columns.[166] The document records estate landholdings of 2,800 plots of land between Minya and Madinat al-Fayum, which were all measured during year 4, in the second month of inundation, days 15 to 29, and on the first day of the third month of inundation, during the reign of Rameses V (c.1142–50 BC).[167] Alan Gardiner considered the contents to be much like the famous English Domesday Book. The papyrus was acquired by the Cairo Museum in 1928–29 from a dealer in Luxor, which means that the original archaeological context of the manuscript is unknown. The papyrus was eventually bought by the Brooklyn Museum in New York, with funds donated by the Wilbour family—hence the name.[168] It has been published in full only once, by Gardiner in 1941–48. Subsequent studies include those by Menu (1970) and Katary (1989). The document comprises two texts. Text A is on the recto, covering lands from Madinat al-Fayum to Minya. Text B on the verso covers only *khato*-lands of the pharaoh.[169] Text A is broken up into four distinct sections, each covering a different geographic area. These were recorded on different (consecutive) dates (in the second month of inundation). The plots of land were each measured and recorded under headings that detail who owned which piece of land. In some cases the recipient of the revenue was also recorded. A great deal of the land in the region was owned by Theban mortuary estates of the temples of Tuthmosis II, Amenhotep II, Horemheb, Rameses II, Rameses III, Rameses IV, and Rameses V.[170]

The document reveals a great deal about the management of Fayum lands, including the locations of estate fields, the estates owning land, and individuals involved in the management and cultivation of fields:

- The mayor of *š-rsi* had authority over lands (§43, §46),[171] and in one line is named as Ipuy (B§13).
- The mayor of *mr-wr* had authority over lands (§2x5–15, §42, §45) and in one line is named as Seti (B§12).

- District scribe Pentwere administered the lands under the authority of the mayor of *mr-wr* Seti (B§12).
- A deputy named Meryre was involved in apportioning the harvest tax from land cultivated for the *ḫnrt* (harem) in *mr-wr*, under the authority of an individual named Penhasi (§27).
- 'Controller' Penhasi (probably the same as the Penhasi from §27) administered land belonging to the *ḫnrt* in *mr-wr*. Some of the fields were located in new land east of *š* (§39).
- A priest named Hori had authority over the apportionment of taxes from land, including the harvest from fields measured to the west of *wp-š* (§17).
- A priest named Sunero had authority over land belonging to a temple, fields measured around *mr-wr* (§14). He administered land belonging to the pharaoh—under the authority of a priest named Amenemuia—the fields of the temple of Sobek located in the region of the pond of the *ḥnt* of *mr-wr*.
- A priest named Amenkhai had authority over land of the 'sunshade which is in *š*' (§26).
- A priest of the temple of Sobek Shedty named Ramessuiskhapesh had authority over land belonging to the pharaoh. Some of the fields were in the region of the pond south of the *ḥnt* (B§25).
- A priest of the 'sunshade which is in *š*' named Henufe had authority over land belonging to the pharaoh (B§35).
- An unnamed overseer of the king's apartments of the *ḫnrt* in *mr-wr* had authority of lands belonging to the pharaoh (B§21).
- An overseer of cattle named 'Ankhu had authority over land belonging to a temple, fields located to the southwest of *mr-wr* (§18).
- The cultivator Hori worked in the region (§2x–15) on land under the authority of the mayor of *mr-wr* (§46, §45). This may be the same Hori who raised cattle and managed land for the *ḫnrt* of *mr-wr* (§111, see also §135).
- A cultivator named Sobeknakht worked on land around the temple of Sobek and around *mr-wr* (§15).
- A cultivator named Amenha worked for Penhasi on fields belonging to the *ḫnrt* in *mr-wr* (§39).

- Fayum institutions that owned land or received taxes:
  - Temple of Sobek Shedty (§12) (? *ḥr ḥry ib tꜣ-š*)
  - Temple of Sobek Lord of Shedet, which is in *r-n-ḥnt* (§20)

  - Temple of Amun Lord of the thrones of the two lands in the midst of *š* (§24)
  - The *ḫnrt* (harem) in *mr-wr* (§27, §39, §111, §278, B§21)
  - The landing place of the pharaoh in *mr-wr* (§37, B§12)
  - The sunshade which is in *š* (§39, §41, B§35)
  - The temple of Sobek (B§26)
- Areas of land measured in the Fayum:
  - Land around the temple of Sobek (§13, §15, §19, B§12)
  - Land around the temple of Sobek Lord of Shedet (§20, §24)
  - Land around *mr-wr* (§13, §14, §15, §16, §18, §45, B§12, B§13)
  - Land around *š* (§13, §16, §39, B§26)
  - Land around *wp-š* (§13, §16, §17)
  - Land in the region of *wp-š* (B§12)
  - Land in the region of *p3-ym* (§13, §16, B§13)
  - Land around the *ḥnt* (§32, B§25)
  - Land around the *ḥnt* of *mr-wr* (B§26)

There are obvious differences between the named institutions and the areas of measured land. The temple of Sobek, the temple of Sobek Shedty, and the temple of Sobek of Shedet could all be one and the same temple or part of the same complex, but the fact that the latter is stipulated to be in *r-n-ḥnt* suggests perhaps that at least two different temples are being referenced. Several lakes are referred to in the text, but all are attached to an estate. *š* on its own is written with the town determinative in §39, B§26, thus it can be safely assumed that *š* was a town in the Fayum in these two instances. In sections §13 and §16, land is measured around *š*, but the town determinative is missing. Elsewhere, in sections §24, §26, §39, and §41, a chapel named 'Sunshade which is in Lake' or 'Sunshade of Re-Horakhti in Lake' and the 'Temple of Amun in Lake' are referred to, and in these instances the spelling also omits the town determinative. The fact that several temple-like institutions are placed in *š*, and that land can be measured around it, clearly suggests that *š* was a specific place, and more than likely was a town. It seems plausible that what was primarily a temple complex during the Middle Kingdom grew into a large town during the New Kingdom, and has since expanded to become the city of Madinat al-Fayum.

š-rsi had a mayor, but it owned no lands and no fields are measured around it, suggesting that this name does indeed refer to the whole region. While it cannot be doubted that *š-rsi* refers to the Fayum, there are questions surrounding *p3-ym*. This is the earliest known occurrence of this name. Gardiner argues that the spellings of the area named *p3-y(wm)* or *p3-m(ʿ)y* were corrupted spellings of a name *p3-ym*—the ancient derivative of the Coptic Pa-yum (literally, 'the lake'), which is thought to be the prototype of the Arabic name Fayum.[172] Three places are located in *p3-ym* (*p3-ywm* / *p3-mʿy*): Tent-poid, Pen-ne, and Ta-ʿabay. Thus it is highly likely that this name refers not to a specific place but to a region or area.

The name *mr-wr* clearly refers to a physical place around which fields are measured, with a mayor, but it was the institutions of the *ẖnrt* in *mr-wr* and the landing place of pharaoh in *mr-wr* that owned land. The *ḥnt* of *mr-wr* was an area around which fields were located, but it is impossible to know if the *ḥnt* referred to in sections §32 and B§25 is also the *ḥnt* of *mr-wr* or a different *ḥnt* in the area. The name *wp-š* refers to a place around which land was located (§13, §16, §17), and from this context it appears to be a specific place, or town. But in section B§12 *wp-š* is referred to as a region, perhaps suggesting that like *p3-ym* it was an area, not a town. The name *r-ḥnt* appears only once, as part of the epithet of Sobek Lord of Shedet as the location of a temple. *š-sbk* is referred to as the location of the king's apartments, but 'Shesobek' could in fact be a personal name in this instance (Text A§32).

The context of this document makes it clear that all these references are to places and institutions in the Fayum. This is a highly objective record of the landscape, hence the lack of references to *t3-š* (which only occurs once in an epithet of Sobek). All the locations mentioned—*š*, *š-rsi*, *mr-wr*, *ẖnrt mr-wr*, *ḥnt mr-wr*, *r-ḥnt*, *ḥnt*, *wp-š*, *š-sbk*—are locations of land or locations of land-owning institutions or individuals who manage land. It is clear that each designation is a different place. For instance at *mr-wr* there is a Henet, a harem, and a landing place of pharaoh. While this document does not provide any insight into the perception of the imagined landscape, it does contain a significant amount of information regarding the management of the sacred landscape of the Fayum at that time—the temples, chapels, and important establishments in the region. The region is *š-rsi*, 'Southern Lake.' The locations are: 'Lake,' *š* (town); 'Mouth of the Henet,' *r-n-ḥnt* (area); Mer-wer, *mr-wr* (town); Shedet, *šdt* (town); and Wep-she, *wp-š* (area). The temples and chapels are: 'Sunshade in Lake' (chapel), a temple of Sobek of Shedet in 'Mouth of the Henet,' and a temple of Amun in 'Lake.' In Mer-wer there is a Henet nearby, a harem within the town, and a landing place.

What this document reveals is that from the point of view of the Egyptian state, the significant places in the Fayum all lay in the east, close to the Nile, along the Nile–Fayum channel. The inner parts of the Fayum do not appear at all, and by simply looking at the number of times *mr-wr* appears in the document it is apparent that this town was the most significant (administrative) center for the period in the region.

Closely related to this record of landholdings are the Onomastica, which were essentially lists of places and things compiled in an attempt to classify and order the world. The Onomasticon of Amenemope is perhaps the most important in this group. This text was drafted at the end of the Twentieth Dynasty, and there are nine copies of the document in varying states of preservation. The author, Amenemope, was attempting to draw up a catalog of the universe, on earth, in water, and in the world of the Gods, classified hierarchically.[173] Lines 313–419 list the towns of Egypt, but the author faced some difficulty when ordering the towns of the Fayum due to the fact that for the region it was not possible (as it was for the Nile Valley) to simply list the towns from south to north. The tradition of lists of towns and estates can be traced back to the Old Kingdom 'processions' of estates presenting offerings in tombs. Both *š* (written without the town sign) and *mr-wr* appear in the Onomasticon of Amenemope, but *r-ḥnt* and *šdt* are missing.

There is considerably less evidence for interventions in the sacred landscape of the Fayum during the New Kingdom. By comparison with the Middle Kingdom, no major new temples were constructed and there is no evidence of any New Kingdom alteration to the Middle Kingdom temples. However, there can be no doubt that the region was still considered of major importance, especially as a royal center. The location of the royal 'harem' at *mr-wr* (Madinat al-Gurob) has to be significant. What was it about this part of the region that attracted the pharaoh to install a palace here? The fact that the extant copies of the Middle Kingdom texts 'Fishing and Fowling' and 'Sporting King' are dated to the New Kingdom may be a clue. The tradition that the region was rich and fertile, good for fishing and hunting, and that a connection to the Fayum in some way legitimized the rule of the pharaoh may have been factors. The fact that the most 'recent' pharaohs of the Middle Kingdom had been buried in the Fayum in the Lahun–Hawara area at the entrance to the region may also have drawn the king to this part of the Fayum. What might also be worth considering is that by locating *mr-wr* close to the main river, the site was more (easily) accessible from the south, which was the location of the 'capital' of Egypt during the New Kingdom (Thebes).

The Third Intermediate Period (1069–664 BC)

There is a general dearth of archaeological evidence dated securely to the Third Intermediate Period or the Late Period in Egypt, so the lack of tangible evidence for activities in the Fayum for these periods is unsurprising. The Twenty-first Dynasty is notable for the fact that every king, with the exception of the first ruler, was called Rameses. Following the death of Rameses XI (1099–69 BC), which marks the end of the New Kingdom, Egypt was still nominally united under the rule of one pharaoh, but a powerful line of priests and commanders were essentially controlling the south of Egypt. In the north, the rulers moved to a new central residence at Tanis. The remains of major temple complexes as well as royal tombs prove Tanis's importance, but no contemporary settlement remains have ever been found there, and the continuing role of Memphis as a nominal 'capital' is really known only from textual evidence. Settlement remains have only been found at a few Delta sites, Tell al-Daba and Sa al-Hagar (Sais), for example, as well as Tell al-Retaba in the Wadi Tumilat, although the lack of evidence may be more a circumstance of the traditional focus of interest on the earlier pharaonic periods. What is known about Egypt between 1069 and 332 BC derives primarily from funerary and temple sources, such as inscriptions on statues and sarcophagi. Our knowledge is therefore weighted heavily toward religion, and political information gleaned from private statue inscriptions. The Third Intermediate Period (1069–664 BC) was generally a period of political fragmentation, localized pockets of civil unrest, and increased diversity in the population due to an influx of people from Nubia and Libya.[174]

The chronology of rulers for the period is as confused as the other intermediate periods. The pharaohs of the Twenty-third Dynasty were contemporary with rulers of the Twenty-second, Twenty-fourth, and Twenty-fifth Dynasties. The rule of Egypt shifted between different powers, and for part of the time there were at least two rulers, one for the south and one for the north, with a recognized boundary at al-Hiba, just south of the Fayum. The presence of Libyans in high positions in Egypt is apparent from the early Twenty-first Dynasty, and by the Twenty-second Dynasty this included the role of pharaoh. The throne of Tanis passed to the chief of the Libyan Meshwesh tribe, Sheshonq I, in 945 BC.[175] The influence of Nubia becomes more apparent later in the Third Intermediate Period. Agreements were reached between Nubian rulers and Egypt, and they were officially recognized as pharaohs, at least in southern Egypt. Piy (also known as Pi('ankhy) or Piankhy) advanced north into Egypt in around 730 BC in an attempt to curtail the territorial expansion of a northern prince, Tefnakht.[176] This campaign was recorded by Piy on a monumental stela that was found in 1862 at the Amun temple in Napata at Jebel Barkal in Sudan by Said Pacha (Cairo Museum JE48862, 47086–47089).[177]

The Victory Stela of Piy

The Victory Stela of Piy is a detailed historical record of the campaign, listing the places the troops passed through and the temples at which they made tribute, and is therefore an invaluable source of evidence for the names and approximate locations of towns in Egypt for this period, as well as the names of the local leaders.

Having captured Herakleopolis (*nn-nsw*, modern Ihnasya), they sailed north:

 *pw ir.n ḥm.f r wp-š r m r-ḥnt*—His majesty went north to *wp-š* (Wep-She) in *r-ḥnt* (Ra-henet).

Here they found the entrance to the town of Per-Sekhemkheperre barred and heavily protected. The town soon capitulated, and they continued north to Mer-Atum, and then on to Itj-tawy (Lisht). While this one mention of *wp-š* and *r-ḥnt* does not really provide any information on any aspect of the Fayum, it shows that these names continued to be used for this part of the region or these places for a considerable length of time.

The Fayum Papyrus

One of the most important sources for any study of the Fayum is the so-called Book of Fayum, preserved in several of copies and referred to as an ancient 'bestseller.'[178] Although this document dates to the Roman Period and was clearly composed in the Ptolemaic Period, the contents are obviously based on the far older pharaonic Fayum creation myths and local Sobek cult, and so it is included in this chapter.

Two principal papyrus documents form the basis for most studies. It is actually not known with certainty if these papyri were found in the Fayum, but that is the usual assumption based on the content of the text. The two principal papyri were 'discovered' in 1859. They were probably found together, but were broken up into several large fragments (a common practice employed at the time to increase the income of the person selling the material) and sold to various collectors in Luxor and Naqada, where the markets for antiquities were far more lucrative than the Fayum. Two large pieces from one roll were taken to Cairo, where they were deposited in the Egyptian Museum. The fragments of the second roll were bought by Lord Amherst (now in the Pierpont Morgan Library collection in New York; see plate 11) and Reverend Hood (now in the Walters Art Museum in Baltimore; see plate 10). Since this first 'discovery' many other fragments have come to light, and sections of the text have been identified in temple inscriptions and on coffins.[179]

The primary fragments of the papyrus, known as Boulaq I & II (in Cairo), Amherst and Hood (named after the men who bought them), derive from two large papyrus rolls that were clearly composed by two different scribes. They form two halves of one 'book.' Because there are many other fragments of various sections of this book, written at different times, it is possible to determine that the text and layout of the first of the primary rolls (Boulaq I & II) contain numerous scribal errors.[180] Nonetheless, this papyrus should be considered one of the masterpieces of ancient Egyptian sacred art.

The book takes the form of a highly religious pseudo-map of the Fayum, "a treatise on the sacred landscape of the Fayum."[181] The composition date remains something of a mystery, but it was clearly based on a local Greco–Roman interpretation of the Fayum creation theology. Throughout history various versions of the core Egyptian creation myth were manipulated in order to elevate different deities to the principal roles. Usually a local deity was assimilated with Horus or Osiris, or a local feature of the landscape became the location for the emergence of the gods from the primeval waters on the sacred mound, the battle between Horus and Seth, or the location of a piece of the dismembered body of Osiris. In the Book of Fayum the lake was the location for the creation events and the waters in which the sun god Ra was rejuvenated each night. The desert surroundings were seen as a manifestation of Seth threatening the fertile lands that were protected by Horus (Sobek of Shedet).[182]

All the preserved versions of the text date to the Roman Period, but the foremost scholar on this subject, Horst Beinlich, considers the work to have been compiled during the Ptolemaic Period as an attempt by Fayum-based priests to describe the sacred landscape of the region after the dramatic transformation caused by early Ptolemaic irrigation works (see Chapter

Four).[183] There had been a huge revival of the scribal traditions in Egypt during the early Roman Period, and religious texts were written and copied in hieroglyphs (usually reserved for inscriptions), hieratic, and demotic (previously only used for recording everyday secular transactions).[184] As a result, there are copies of the Book of Fayum in all three scripts; many of the larger examples written in hieratic have notations in demotic. This thriving scholarly environment, in which highly educated and skilled elite scribes were writing and copying key texts for theological specialists in the scriptoria ('Houses of Life'), acted to preserve the cultural memory of Egypt.[184] The Greco–Egyptian priests and scribes in the 'House of Life' in Shedet (which features prominently in the Book of Fayum) were educated in long-held Egyptian beliefs about creation, local theology relating to Sobek and Sobek Shedty, religious language, various different Egyptian scripts, and the sacred landscape of the Fayum. They had the imagination and skills not only to compile what they knew about the Fayum creation myth but also to develop a highly innovative way of illustrating these ideas.

The Fayum scribes clearly selected elements to include in the Book of Fayum from the vast array of ancient Egyptian religious 'books,' found most often in funerary contexts, illustrated on coffins or papyri and on the walls of royal tombs. The Book of the Celestial Cow and the Book of Thoth are both reflected in sections of the Book of Fayum,[186] although it is highly possible that all these elements already existed in oral tradition of the Fayum creation theology. The 'encyclopedic' nature of the text also resembles the earlier Onomastica, in this instance listing the religious institutions in one area and providing a description of the landscape.[187] In this genre of writing the ancient Egyptian scribes/priests were attempting to order their known universe by listing and describing places and things.

The document as a whole was clearly intended to have some of the qualities of what we now understand to be a map. Other map-like images exist from earlier in Egyptian history, on Middle Kingdom coffins where the afterlife is sometimes set out in a geographical form resembling a map. There is one other example of a map from ancient Egypt that, unlike the Fayum Papyrus, is clearly an administrative document: the Turin mining map, which dates to the Nineteenth Dynasty (c.1150 BC) and is a relatively accurate map of the locations of gold mines in the Wadi Hamammat.[188]

The principal documents are P. Boulaq I, bought by Luigi Vassalli at Deir al-Medina c. 1859 (JE 95571/CG 58040), and P. Boulaq II, bought by Auguste Mariette in Luxor c. 1859 (JE 95662). This version is exquisitely rendered in a fine script. Hood was purchased in Luxor by Reverend Hood c. 1859 and later purchased by the Walters Art Museum (Walters Art Gallery no. 10.738 and 10.803). Amherst was purchased by Lord Amherst in Luxor or Naqada c. 1859 and later bought by the Pierpont Morgan Library (Amherst Egyptian Papyrus 8.1–8.5). An unillustrated version is preserved, again as two parts, on the walls of the temple of Kom Ombo, a major cult center for the crocodile god Sobek. The inscription is in a corridor dated to the reign of Tiberius (AD 13–47).[189] The coffin of Ankhrui from Hawara has three illustrations resembling those in the papyrus version of the text.[190] Several very fragmentary papyri bearing hieratic transcriptions of the text are held in Vienna and Paris (Louvre).[191] These sections are thought to derive from the same original document. Further small fragments are held in Denmark, and a fragment was discovered in Tebtunis.[192]

The book can be divided into eight sections and was designed to be read from left to right. This is highly significant. The Fayum landscape in this papyrus is 'viewed' from the north: the west is on the right and the east on the left, with north as the lower edge and south as the top. Thus, reading from left to right, the 'journey' begins in the east, moving along the channel to the lake in the west, where the sun god 'dies.' The section depicting the night-passage (rejuvenation) of the sun god through the lake had to be read right to left (west to east), showing the rebirth in the east in the morning. This 'view' of the Fayum from the north, looking toward the region from the main administrative centers, is found in earlier materials, and in all medieval accounts the 'entrance' to the region is seen as being in the north, not via the Bahr Yusuf. Later European travelers almost always made their trip to the Fayum from Cairo, across the desert. The image of the world we are so familiar with, with 'north' at the 'top' is really a very recent phenomenon, only possible since Cartesian geography ascertained that the earth is a globe revolving on an axis. To understand the map properly you have to visualize it as 'upside-down' to a modern mind.

The first part of the document depicts the river/canal—the *ḥnt* (Henet)—(filled with fish and birds), the opening of which is flanked by two hills, with various deities represented on either side, their cult places named. Next is the personification of the wet-lands (the *ḥnt*), the goddess Meret-weret, with her arms raised and two more rivers/canals shown (probably the two ancient ravines now known as al-Wadi and al-Bats drains). A version of the Book of the Celestial Cow is written above and below her body, followed by the lake containing the god Ra (in the water), possibly depicted being symbolically born of the goddess, and two divine barques (boats) carrying Sobek. The third section also represents the lake, depicted as a long oval surrounded by named deities. Within the lake are images of key gods, including the celestial cow Ihet, a large Sobek crocodile, and Neith the mother of Sobek represented as a hippopotamus carrying a crocodile. This section represents the stages of the transition of the sun god through the night. A complicating factor here is that because the journey has to be from west to east this section had to be read from right to left.

The second roll of papyrus begins with the fourth section of the book, but because this is less well preserved some of the reconstruction has proven trickier for specialists. The beginning of the fourth section is dedicated to temples in Shedet, followed by the journey of the sun across the sky (east to west), with images of all the gods in a crocodile form receiving sustenance (offerings) from the sun god. The fifth section concerns the 'House of Life of Ra-sehet,' with a depiction that can be loosely interpreted as a ground plan of the building. The sixth section is dedicated to a place named 'Acacia of Neith.' The seventh section describes the founding of the temple of Shedet, which equates with the creation of the lake. The text states that the lake was dug by the gods 'with their own hands,' which is highly likely to be the root of the story told by Herodotus that the lake was 'man'-made or artificial. This in turn probably grew out of the name itself: the root of the name Shedet—*šd*—can be translated as 'to dig.' The final section is a symbolic and conceptual 'summary' of the idea that the lake is a temple of Sobek, rounded off with a note from the scribe that this was the end of the text.[193]

Landscape of the Book of Fayum

t3-š—the Lake Land

This is the name given to the region, which is a temple of Sobek of Shedet and Horus dwelling in Shedet.

ḥnt—the Henet

The Henet is the embodiment of the mother of Ra, the celestial cow Ihet, and the embodiment of the waters/cow goddess named Mehet-weret. Thus, it is the *ḥnt* that brings life to the region by giving birth to Ra (he is 'born' in the lake). The *ḥnt* is depicted as both a channel of water, with fish in it and fertile banks on either side, flanked by the desert, and as the goddess Mehet-weret, with two other channels of water emitting from her elbows (the two 'horns'/ ravines of al-Wadi and al-Bats).

š—the lake

The lake is depicted twice. First it appears as the birthplace of Ra, with divine barques to transport the sun god, accompanied by Sobek. In the second scene it is a long oval and forms a passage for the sun god through the night. This lake is also a temple of Sobek. The lake measures 100,529 and 92,000 (cubits?).[194] It is made explicitly clear that this lake in the Fayum was 'dug' by the hands of the gods.

w3ḏ-wr—the Great Green

It is difficult to really understand what is meant by *w3ḏ-wr* in this text, but the contexts in which it is referred to imply that this is a mythical place of the gods, and that the lake of the Fayum is seen as an embodiment of that lake in which the sun god and Sobek (as Ra) were born. The word *w3ḏ-wr* has been interpreted to mean the Fayum by some scholars, but other occurrences have led to people interpreting this term to mean the Mediterranean Sea. There is no doubt that it refers to a large body of water, so perhaps in the context of the Fayum Papyrus, if the lake of Fayum had always just been referred to as 'the Lake' (*š*), by naming it *w3ḏ-wr* it was imbued with greater meaning and importance.

Land of the Lake

The translation of this text is especially difficult, as it is filled with obscure statements as well as being fragmentary in places. It may also have become corrupted via repeated copying.[195] Additionally, because the text is laden with arcane symbolic meaning (as might be expected from such a religious document) and is an amalgam and adaptation of various different myths, it is incredibly difficult to interpret some sections. This is the only known ancient Egyptian 'map' of a real landscape (that is, not a map of the land of the afterlife) that is purely religious in context. While it clearly aims to document the physical characteristics of the landscape, they are immortalized and placed in the realm of the gods. Thus they are also temporalized—placed in an ancient time before man was created. This is the most explicit unification of the experienced and imagined landscape. The temples and shrines of the region are not simply placed 'upon' this landscape, they are the landscape. The entire region is perceived to be sacred, the entire region is a temple of Sobek, and the religious institutions are just the outward expression of this phenomenon. The Fayum is perceived as the place in which creation took place, which is able to sustain all the gods of Egypt with its abundant fertility, with the waters of the lake and the Henet being crucial elements of this fertility and abundance.

The mythology conveyed in the document recalls the Hymn to Sobek of the Middle Kingdom, and should be considered a late record of that creation theology. The account of Herodotus seems also to contain some elements of these traditions, and, as will be outlined in Chapter Five, it seems highly likely that the later traditions found in medieval Islamic records probably record a Coptic version of the same story, but altered to fit with Christian doctrine, removing the 'pagan' deities and placing the prophet Joseph and God at the center of this creation.

4

Changing Landscape: Herodotus and the Greco-Roman / Late Antique Fayum (450 BC–AD 642)

> Marvellous as the Labyrinth is, the so-called Lake of Moeris beside which it stands is perhaps even more astonishing.[1]
>
> —Herodotus (450 BC)

> This Nome is the most noteworthy of all in respect to its appearance, its fertility, and its material development. It also contains the wonderful Lake of Moeris, which is an open sea in size and like a sea in colour; and its shores, also, resemble those of a sea.[2]
>
> —Strabo (first century BC)

Having experienced many years of foreign rule and dynamically changing cultural influences, by the fifth century BC Egypt was ruled by a Persian dynasty. Following the end of the Twentieth Dynasty, traditionally seen as the end of the New Kingdom (1069 BC), the Egyptian state underwent nearly four hundred years of upheaval, now known as the Third Intermediate Period: Twenty-first through Twenty-fifth Dynasties (1069–664 BC). In the mid-eighth century BC, Piy, a Kushite prince, extended his influence north across all of Egypt, as documented in the Stela of Piy (see Chapter Three). This new dynasty of southern rulers did not succeed in fully centralizing government in Egypt. The north was nominally controlled by Assyria, and it was the Assyrian vassal ruler Psamtek, based in Sais (modern Sa al-Hagar), who eventually managed to centralize government and reunify Egypt into a single stronger state in 664 BC: the Twenty-sixth Dynasty 'Saite' Period.[3]

Greek documents attest to a growing relationship between Greek states and Egypt during this period. By the mid-seventh century BC the appearance of trade centers in Egypt named after Greek islands suggests that there was an active Aegean population within Egypt, and the city of

Naucratis (in the Delta) was founded by Milesians. The period of Saite stability was broken in 525 BC with the Persian invasion led by Cambyses.[4] The first line of Persian rulers (the Twenty-seventh Dynasty) generally went to great lengths to establish themselves as fully Egyptianized pharaohs, respecting Egyptian religion and carrying out repairs to temples, as well as maintaining the established Egyptian bureaucratic systems.[5] This Persian rule lasted until 404 BC, thus it was Persian Egypt that Herodotus experienced.

The most influential center of learning at this time was Ionia, led by the city-state of Miletus, and it was here that Anaximander and Hecataeus, two of the most important and earliest geographers, started working in the sixth century BC. Anaximander is credited with being the first scholar to create a map of the known world, although it is unclear whether he believed the earth to be a sphere or a cylinder, as there is no surviving commentary that might have accompanied the map. Hecataeus is credited with having created the first written account of the known world. Ionia is considered to have experienced its own Enlightenment during the sixth century BC and, according to Herodotus, it was the place in which the most informative maps were made. These scholars, to some extent, rejected the fanciful tales of Homer. They sought to explain natural phenomena via rational and scientific thinking.[6]

During the fifth century BC, scholarly activities began to move in new directions. An interest in ancestry developed, and with it, the desire to trace genealogical links to deities. At that time these studies had to be based almost entirely on oral sources and traditions, and they are now seen as forerunners of history as a discipline. Generations were a method of dating events and providing a chronological context for events.[7] It was in this world of transition that Herodotus traveled to Persian Egypt, with the aim of gathering 'historical' information and examining the spectacular natural and man-made phenomena he encountered.

Herodotus imbued the Fayum landscape with ancient meaning, but the ways in which his account has been received, translated, interpreted, and studied have added more layers of meaning to that landscape as people sought the Fayum of Herodotus. His account really was the first to begin intertwining ancient beliefs with his perceptions, which were shaped by his own life and experiences, his engagement with the Fayum landscape, the people he met, and the traditions he encountered.

Herodotus (484–c.430 BC)

Other than the fact that Herodotus was born at Halicarnassus in Turkey circa 484 BC to a noted Greek family, little is known of his life. He traveled extensively as a young man, possibly visiting Egypt as well as Greek lands, and then settled in Italy.[8] At the beginning of his one preserved written work, he outlined his aims and objectives: to preserve the memory of the past by recording the great and marvelous achievements of Greek and Asiatic peoples, and to show how they came into conflict.[9] This was his only work, and the title eventually given to the work, *Histories* (meaning researches), and the fact that he was the first scholar to present an account of times before his own, led to him to become known as 'the father of history.' The account was known in Athens prior to its publication in any form, which took place during the early years of the Peloponnesian war (late fifth century BC).[10]

The perceived value of Herodotus's *Histories* as a reliable historical work has wavered a great deal through time. The other 'father of history'—Thucydides—who was almost a contemporary of Herodotus (he lived c.460–400 BC) introduced the idea that 'history' had to be a truthful account of facts. For almost two thousand years, until 1566, when French printer and classical scholar Henri Estienne published his work *Defence of Herodotus*, Herodotus's *Histories* received little attention or respect in scholarly circles, and he was even named 'father of lies' by some Classicists. The principal underlying difference between the ways in which these two historians dealt with their sources is that Herodotus reported all he heard, making it clear that he did not believe everything, while Thucydides collated several reports of events, chose which he thought was most plausible, and then recorded only that version, aiming to be more rational, applying Ionian thinking.[11] Herodotus and Thucydides were traditionally compared to and judged against each other, but they are now each valued equally as very different writers with different motives and styles, each giving a different perspective on history within a classical Greek framework.

There can be little doubt that Herodotus's style was influenced by epic/Homeric poetry as well as the more contemporary concerns with genealogy. Since the eighth century BC the dominant genre in Greek writing had been epic, or Homeric, poetry. This poetry was founded on elements of historical reality,[12] but as with all good legends, the facts were increasingly distorted and exaggerated over time. The purpose of epic poetry was to both educate and entertain the reader or listener. In general, until the fifth century BC, nothing was recorded in writing. Rather, dissemination relied on oral transmission. A key feature of Homer's work is the fact that he regularly idealized nature.[13] His landscapes consist of a central city surrounded by pleasant countryside inhabited by farmers. He organized the landscape into three aspects, based on the level of human intervention it had undergone: city, fields, and pasture lands. This is illustrated most vividly with a description of a 'map' inscribed onto the shield of Achilles in the *Odyssey.* The Egyptian landscape is described by Homer as being "rich countryside" with a "smoothly flowing river" (Book 14, ll. 257–84), and he conveys an explicit sense of wilderness in some passages.[14]

The new style of historical writing Herodotus developed ran along a line between the more Ionian or 'scientific' style of reporting and the traditional literary and poetic 'historical' tales. History as a discipline or literary genre did not exist as such. Herodotus was presenting the results of his inquiries into how and why things had come to be the way they were and attempting to answer such questions as: Who built the monuments and for what reasons?[15] To some extent, Herodotus aimed to 'iron out the kinks' in Homer's works, in much the same way that 'pro-Herodotus' scholars do for *Histories* today.[16] While, unlike many Ionian scholars, Herodotus did not attack Homer as being fanciful (he in fact accepted his work and modeled his own upon it), he also followed the Ionian spirit of science, treading the ground between the two. He believed firmly in the idea that if a tradition exists in two countries, it is from the older of the two civilisations that the tradition derived.[17]

Herodotus's sources and methods are issues of great debate. Some scholars suggest that the seeming lack of 'truth' in his accounts is a result of the unreliability of his sources. They argue that as he was questioning subordinate priests and ill-informed guides who frequently did not know the answers to his questions, their responses were to a greater or lesser extent somewhat imaginative.[18] These scholars essentially validate Herodotus and lay the blame for the lack of 'accuracy' in his account firmly on his sources. The great temporal distance between his period and the ancient events and characters who built the fantastic monuments has to be considered. At the time Herodotus was writing his account—the Late Period in Egypt—the construction of the pyramids was as far removed in time as we are now from Herodotus, so the priests and 'guides' he questioned could hardly have been expected to 'know' much about that history.

He spent a great deal of time with Greek people in Egypt, especially priests, who were probably very settled by then. Greeks had been living in Egypt for between two hundred and three hundred years at that point, and were probably very much Egyptianized. However, Egypt's ancient history can have been nothing other than mysterious to them, based on snippets of information gleaned from oral accounts of pharaohs and from temple records. Even those who could read Egyptian would have struggled to understand inscriptions, just as anyone but a specialist today might struggle to read medieval English, French, or German, or even Latin. Additionally, oral sources are naturally biased by the influences of the individual and corrupted by the repeated passing of information from one person to the next, as well as intentionally altered to suit a specific purpose or intention. The information would have been affected by the temporal distance from the events, and by the individuals' personal engagement with or experience of the events. The local Egyptian population may have been striving to emphasize the greatness of their civilization to Greek visitors by stressing the significant age of their traditions.[19] It is also possible that Herodotus wrote as if he were a dragoman: in order to engage his audiences he livened up his accounts of events, adding drama.[20] It could even be considered that the Greek occupants of Egypt may have been 'more Egyptian than the Egyptians'—proud of their new home nation and keen to extol its virtues, just as many expats/migrants are in an adopted country. Herodotus's account of Egyptian history is notoriously one of the most 'unreliable' sections of his work.

On the other hand, the 'anti-Herodotus' scholars contend that Herodotus's account is almost entirely fabricated. The suggestion is that his apparent acknowledgment of sources—"the priests say," "the Egyptians say"—was a means of validating his record. They feel that it was his way of giving credibility to stories he perhaps created himself, and that his references to different 'types' of sources is methodical and formulaic, governed by a set of rules. The seeming agreement between sources is another mechanism of validation. This view contends that no statements can be taken as evidence of Herodotus actually visiting any of the places he discusses, and, indeed, many of the scholars who argue against any reliance on Herodotus believe he did not set foot in many, if any, of the places in Egypt he claims to have visited.[21]

In many respects, Herodotus's account of Egypt is dominated by his descriptions of wonders, simply because Egypt had far more wonders than any other nation. Of particular fascination was the spectacular size of things, notably the pyramids and the Labyrinth, as well as 'epic' characters such as Moeris, Rameses, and Sesostris, with whom the monuments were associated, and their exploits. Additionally, natural features and creatures, such as the Nile, the flood, crocodiles, and hippopotami, were included in his account as 'wonders.' The curiosity that led him to inquire about how Egypt's monuments were constructed, and his dissemination of the details of these enquiries, can be considered a reflection of a particularly Greek way of thinking.[22] Herodotus seems to have made a particular point of finding ways to emphasize the differences between Egypt and the 'known world' via symmetries. He saw everything in Egypt to be the opposite of everything in Greece, or the opposite of something on the opposite side of the known world. The Nile in Egypt is the opposite of the Danube; the Scythian (northern European) rivers are natural, while the Egyptian canals are man-made; the Scythian people inhabit their landscape, while the Egyptians create theirs. This fondness for symmetry, or equally opposing aspects of life, was essentially a Hellenistic way of thinking.[23]

Herodotus gathered the material for this account while traveling (assuming he did indeed travel), and his sources were varied, including extant written accounts and local oral sources. In Egypt (which was Persian at that time), his sources included priests and indigenous Egyptians, whom he appears to have questioned at length. His sources can be divided into four categories: evidence of physical remains, such as inscriptions and monuments; knowledge, or orally gathered information and 'facts'; 'folk' tales and traditions, namely communally shared stories; and his own logical reasoning about events. His method of inquiry was to ask why things were the way they were, and here the question of comprehension should also be considered. Were Herodotus's questions fully understood, and did he fully understand the answers, given the likelihood that very few Egyptians would have understood Greek at that time? Additionally, it is important to remember that he had no way of understanding any of the inscriptions he may have found. Another factor to consider is that naturally, as with any tourism in any era, guides will always provide an answer to any question asked of them, even if they do not actually know the correct answer. Any potentially boring answers will always be enlivened, as storytelling plays a major role in any tour guide's repertoire. Thus, Herodotus's many questions may not have always been answered entirely factually.[24]

Herodotus is sometimes considered to have been a better geographer than he was a historian.[25] His account is filled with geographical information. He regularly recorded distances between places and the dimensions of lakes, rivers, and other natural formations (although these distances are one of the factors used in the arguments against his credibility). Herodotus's method was to compare the distance he was presenting to known aspects of the Greek world. He described the borders of the country and all the major physical attributes and rivers, as well as attempting to explain the 'cause' of them. He gave names of towns and cities and the different regions of the country, although the majority of these were situated in the Delta. He considered natural and man-made phenomena to be of equal interest and value.[26]

The account was written principally for recitation, not private reading, and thus is poetic in nature. Several authors suggest that there is some evidence that Herodotus himself read sections of his account to audiences. His audience was undoubtedly Greek and his book was written for Greeks, and was essentially about the Greeks or, more precisely, how the Greeks compare to other nationalities.[27] There are a number of papyrus fragments of copies of the *Histories* primarily from Oxyrhynchus, all dating to about six hundred years after the initial composition of the account.[28] The oldest preserved manuscript copy of the entire work is Codex Laurentianus 70.3, which dates to the tenth century AD. The work was translated into Latin in the 1450s by Loreno Valla, making it far more accessible. The earliest printed (Greek) edition of the *Histories* was compiled by Aldus Manutius and printed by Aldine Press in 1502–04. An edition translated into French by Pierre Saliat appeared in 1555–56.[29]

Histories

Herodotus's *Histories* covers Greco–Persian relations. In tracing the histories of Persia and Greece, he essentially wrote a history of the world known to him. Each country is described, including the plants and animals, the people, and the 'wonders.' Egypt's place in the *Histories* is attributed to its importance to the Greek world at that time and the popular interest it held in fifth-century Greece. It was also a way of introducing the background to the invasion of Egypt a hundred years previously by the Persian leader Cambyses. In 525 BC Egypt fell under Persian rule and became attractive to the Greek world. It was an agriculturally rich and desirable nation, but it was perceived to be in a state of decline due to invasions by 'less sophisticated' rulers (Assyrians, Nubians, Persians).[30] If Herodotus did travel to Egypt, he went there in around 445 BC. He described the country as far south as the first cataract, and although there has been some doubt that he traveled any farther south than Memphis and the Fayum, it is generally believed now that he did visit Thebes.[31] While Herodotus's account of Egyptian history is exceptionally confused—the author of a major study of Herodotus goes as far as to say it is "partial, chronologically preposterous and of little value,"[32] his descriptions of monuments and anthropological observations of social custom, domestic habits, and religion are generally valued as useful. His presentation of Egypt is particularly positive, because it had a notably larger number of 'marvels' that required description and explanation than any of the other nations. Herodotus had a favorable attitude toward Egyptian culture, believing many aspects of it to be superior to other countries.[33]

The Fayum and Lake Moeris are mentioned in several places in his description of Egypt. He states that he "had from the priests another striking piece of evidence about the country: namely that in the reign of Moeris the whole area above Memphis used to be flooded when the river rose only 12 feet."[34] In his account of the sacred animals in Egypt he mentions that:

> the strongest belief in their [crocodiles'] sanctity is to be found in Thebes and round about Lake Moeris; in these places they keep one particular crocodile, which they tame, putting rings made of glass or gold into its ears and bracelets round its front feet, and giving it special food and ceremonial offerings.[35]

Later in the account he relates that the activities of Moeris were among the most famed activities of the pharaohs: "Moeris, who is remembered by the northern gateway he built for the temple of Hephaestus and the lake with pyramids in it, which were constructed by his orders. The extent of the lake and the size of the pyramids I will mention later on."[36]

In the section dedicated to discussion of the gods and kings of Egypt, Herodotus describes how, after the reign of Sethos (a priest of Hephaestus), there was a period in which there was no sole ruler of the country. Egypt was divided into twelve regions, and:

> to strengthen the bond between them, they decided to leave a common memorial of their reigns, and for this purpose constructed a Labyrinth

a little above Lake Moeris, near the place called the City of Crocodiles. I have seen this building, and it is beyond my power to describe; it must have cost more in labour and money than all the walls and public works of the Greeks put together. . . . The pyramids, too, are astonishing structures, each one of them equal to many of the most ambitious works of Greece; but the Labyrinth surpasses them. . . . Inside the building is of two storeys and contains three thousand rooms. . . . The upper rooms . . . I did see and it is hard to believe that they are the work of men; the baffling and intricate passages from room to room and from court to court were an endless wonder to me.[37]

Of the lake he had more to say:

Marvellous as the Labyrinth is, the so-called Lake of Moeris beside which it stands is perhaps even more astonishing; the circumference of it is 3600 stades, or 60 schoeni; . . . in shape it is elongated, running north and south, and its greatest depth is fifty fathoms. Now this immense basin is obviously artificial, for nearly in the middle of it are two pyramids, standing three hundred feet out of the water (with their bases an equal depth below water), and each surmounted by the stone image of a man sitting on a throne. The water in the lake is not supplied by natural springs (the country hereabouts being excessively dry),[38] but has been brought from the Nile through an artificial duct, and flows in during six months of the year, and out again into the river during the other six.[39]

The people who live here told me that there is a subterranean passage, running westward into the interior of the hills above Memphis, by which the water of the lake reaches the Libyan Syrtis. I was anxious to know what had been done with the soil which had been removed when the lake was excavated, and when I asked the people who live near the lake to enlighten me about this, I had no difficulty in believing their answer—for I remembered the story of a similar thing that happened at Nineveh. . . . They tunnelled a passage . . . and every night they dumped the soil they took out into the Tigris. . . . Just the same method, I was told, was adopted in the excavation of the Lake . . . : they dug it out, and flung it into the Nile, and knew well enough that the Nile would carry it away and get rid of it.[40]

Herodotus cannot in his wildest conceptions have imagined the attention these passages would attract from so many scholars for so many millennia. Whether he visited the Fayum or not, the impression given is that the Labyrinth was a highly significant monument, and that the lake was a monumental aspect of the landscape—its most dominant feature. In general, Herodotus's focus was on the most notable achievements of the ancient rulers and the epic deeds of heroic characters, so that where those achievements involved interventions in the landscape, a perception of that landscape is presented to the reader.

The problems encountered when approaching Herodotus's record of the Fayum begin with the question of whether or not it is an eyewitness account. The school of thought that accepts *Histories* as an eyewitness account also accepts that Herodotus's sources on Egypt were unreliable: he was dependant on sources whose knowledge was based on local traditions and tales that were long-held and entrenched, but which had morphed considerably over the hundreds of years since ancient traditional pharaonic Egyptian culture had faded. According to Alan Lloyd (1975) and Chris Eyre (1991), these exaggerated stories are imagined, but not in a deliberate attempt to mislead readers. They argue that Herodotus went to the Fayum, asked about the monuments he saw, and was given answers. He may well not have fully understood the answers. The answers were based on local oral traditions and folklore, and he, wanting to entertain his audiences, gave the stories an extra gloss.[41] Describing the temple as a labyrinth was providing the Greek audience with a point of reference they could understand. Equally, describing the lake as having a circumference the size of the coast of Egypt was emphasizing the size of this wonder. There can be no doubt that what he learned about the Fayum landscape—a man-made landscape of the monumental remains of the works of great pharaohs—inspired him and provided him with the material to create an especially entertaining image of the Fayum for his audience.

In 1985, O. Kimball Armayor presented a highly critical view of Herodotus's description of Lake Moeris and the Labyrinth.[42] His initial frustration is with the way "all modern treatments of the Labyrinth un-critically assume the autopsy of Herodotus and Strabo at the outset."[43] Armayor dismisses the possibility of any such 'great lake' existing in the Fayum at all, based on the (incorrect) 'fact' that "geology and archaeology alike have shown that no such enormous lake is likely to have stood in the Middle Kingdom or even the Old Kingdom Fayum, much less that of the fifth century BC".[44] Based on his methodology, Armayor assumes that everything Herodotus describes in the Fayum is imagined and derived from Ionian legends and story-telling traditions. He is quick to criticize Egyptologists for constructing their archaeologies around Herodotus's descriptions of the Fayum, carefully finding ways to rectify the account with the evidence.[45] In actual fact, as shown in Chapter Three, it is highly likely that the region was indeed dominated by a lake until the dramatic hydrological interventions of the Ptolemies about two hundred years after Herodotus was in Egypt. The entire region below the naturally elevated central region at the 'end' of the Bahr Yusuf (just west of Madinat al-Fayum) was flooded probably to about fifteen to twenty meters above sea level. The Biahmu pedestals stand about fifteen meters above sea level. The region was known as the 'Lake Land' far back in history, because it was that—the land of the lake. Herodotus certainly would have encountered this vast flooded area.

The details Herodotus provides regarding calculations of sizes or distances of the lake were either estimated or provided to give an impression of enormity, not the lake's actual size (Waters gives other examples of Herodotus's manipulation of numbers).[46] Herodotus made estimates at geological time: the Delta was formed in ten to twenty thousand years but Lake Moeris was only nine hundred years old, emphasizing the relative youth of Lake Moeris and greater likelihood that it was not a natural feature.

Herodotus's belief that the Fayum was man-made might be explained if the later Book of Fayum—the record of the Fayum creation theology—is taken into account. In that text, which contains a more detailed and certainly more elaborate version of the beliefs about the Fayum landscape that are found in the New Kingdom copies of the Middle Kingdom hymns to Sobek (see Chapter Three), it is stated that the Fayum was cut by the hands of the gods. It is possible to then appreciate Herodotus's tale of the Fayum having been made by men—his belief that it was not natural—as a 'twist' on that part of the Fayum theology, or perhaps a misunderstanding by either Herodotus or indeed by the Fayum priests themselves. It may also relate to the symmetry he was constructing: rivers and lakes in Egypt are man-made, in contrast to the natural rivers of Scythia. It is also not impossible to see his description of the spectacular Labyrinth temple as somehow being a reflection of the ancient belief that the entire Fayum was itself a temple—the embodiment of a temple of Sobek—although that requires an enormous leap of imagination. Herodotus's statement that the waters flowed into the region for six months and out for six months might possibly relate to the aspect of the Fayum theology in which the god was described traveling across the land toward the lake in the day and back through the lake during the night. The notion that something was moving toward the lake then away from the lake may have been misconstrued as meaning the waters themselves.

The Lake Moeris 'Problem'

Because Herodotus is at the heart of the debate, it is appropriate to address the issue of the name Moeris and its transmission from pharaonic Egypt to modern times. The tangled issue of the identity of Lake Moeris (or Lake of Moeris), presented by Herodotus as a great wonder, has been addressed by several scholars and proven to be highly contentious. The earliest European scholars traveling in Egypt during the sixteenth and seventeenth centuries assumed that the Fayum lake (Birkat Qarun) was Herodotus's Lake Moeris,[47] and indeed many traveled to the Fayum explicitly to see this 'wonder,' or the Labyrinth (see Chapter Six). While a few people questioned the notion that Moeris was the ancient king responsible for creating the Fayum canal/river and the lake, and many discussed the plausibility of the measurements Herodotus provided for the size of the lake, there was no real debate about the origin of the name. The first major study of the issue of Lake Moeris was by French scholar Edme Jomard (1812), in which he discusses the lake of Moeris of Herodotus, Strabo, Pliny, and Ptolemy in comparison with Birkat Qarun. At this date the chronology of Egyptian history was unknown, and he could not have been aware that the lake described by Herodotus was not the same as the lake described by the later writers. The Ptolemaic transformation of the landscape that totally changed the lake took place after Herodotus wrote about the Fayum.

During the late nineteenth century, efforts to manage the irrigation of Egypt, which concluded with the construction of the first Aswan dam in the early twentieth century, led engineers to consider the hydrology of the Fayum lake. Between 1881 and 1894 an American lawyer-turned-engineer and Egyptologist Frederick Cope Whitehouse wrote over twenty papers on the matter of Lake Moeris, Wadi al-Rayan, and Fayum irrigation (see Chapter Six). In a large report compiled by Major R.H. Brown for the British Army, which was clearly intended to be a highly detailed account of the physical geography and hydrology of the Fayum from an engineering perspective, the author could not escape "the speculator's will-o'-the-wisp of Lake Moeris."[48] Brown's account indeed ended up being titled *The Fayum and Lake Moeris*. In all these cases the authors were interested solely, and almost to the point of obsession, with 'finding' Lake Moeris, comparing the Fayum lake/Birkat Qarun to Herodotus's description and seeking ways to explain the discrepancies.

The matter of the ancient name of the lake was first addressed by prominent German Egyptologist Karl Heinrich Brugsch in two articles (1892, 1893).[49] Brugsch (1872) had already identified *r-ḥnt* as Lahun in an earlier article, but did not make the connection between *mr-wr* and Moeris at first because of his translation of *mr-wr* as *š-wr*.[50] In his next article, written twenty years later (by which time the study of ancient Egypt and the language had both moved forward considerably), he set out specifically to address the issue of Moeris in the light of new evidence and brought together all the Classical references, the Fayum Papyrus, and new material from Gurob and Edfu (all Ptolemaic). By this time it was obviously established that *mr-wr* was Moeris.[51] In 1929 Caton Thompson and Gardner fittingly opened an article entitled "Recent Work on the Problem of Lake Moeris" with the sentence, "It has been said that whoever works in the Faiyum is sooner or later drawn into the problem of Lake Moeris."[52] Their work in the northern regions of the Fayum had enabled them to shed better light on the geology of the region, and they presented their theories on the changing levels of the lake based on those results, which they then updated in 1937.[53]

It was not until 1943 that the issue of the name was addressed again, by eminent British philologist Sir Alan Gardiner, who wrote principally in the light of a great deal of new evidence found in the fifty years since Brugsch's work—not only a wealth of Ptolemaic and Roman papyri but also the Wilbour Papyrus and documents from Gurob. Gardiner, with his co-author Harold Bell, was concerned with what seemed a peculiar name. If *mr-wr* translated as 'Great Lake,' then Herodotus's Lake of Moeris was a tautology: lake of the Great Lake. However, they concluded that the word *ḥnt* clearly referred to a body of water, not a canal/river, and that *mr-wr* was a place name. They were able to establish that during the Ptolemaic/Roman period, *ḥnt n mr-wr* (Henet of Mer-wer) was a feature of the Fayum landscape around which towns were placed. In the papyri they studied, the towns were described as being north or south of the *ḥnt n mr-wr*. Gardiner and Bell also decided that *mr-wr* was the town-site at Madinat al-Gurob. Following a theory developed by Griffith in a study of demotic papyri, they concluded that *mr-wr* actually should translate as

'Great Canal' and that the town of Gurob had been named after the Bahr Yusuf river or at least a branch running close by the town.[54]

The notion that *ḥnt n mr-wr* in the account of Herodotus translates as the lake of Mer-wer (or Lake of Moeris) has been contested. Eugene Cruz-Uribe (1992) first posed the idea that *ḥnt n mr-wr* was actually a canal that acted as an administrative border in the Fayum and that the phrase 'the canal' was extended to all the canals of the Fayum.[55] Later, Katelijn Vandorpe (2004) stated unequivocally that at least as early the Ptolemaic Period but probably even since the Middle Kingdom, *ḥnt n mr-wr* was a canal—most likely the Bahr Yusuf.[56]

The biggest issue affecting all the ideas about Moeris/Mer-wer is the simple fact that the use of the name *mr-wr* or *ḥnt n mr-wr* must surely have changed over time. The dramatic transformation of the landscape of the Fayum under Ptolemy I or II in the third century BC has never really been considered as a factor affecting the use of the name. That transformation surely affected the way this name was used, not least because it would have affected every watercourse and lake/pool in the region. It is abundantly clear in the layout of the preserved copies of the Fayum Papyrus that the *ḥnt* was a canal or river, not the lake. However, the writing of the name strongly implies that it was a body of water, a pool or lake. The word Henet is represented with a hieroglyph of a hand holding a small 'pool':

 *pr.f m ḥnt m š.f* 'He comes out from the Henet in his Lake' (Fayum papyrus line 491).[57]

The difficulty in dealing with this document is the fact that it mixes contemporary Greek and Roman ideas about Egyptian religious ideology with far more ancient notions, which the scribes and priests responsible for creating the document may well not have fully comprehended. The key issue to be borne in mind is that at the time the Book of Fayum was compiled, the region had undergone major alterations, so that the landscape and hydrology were completely different to the landscape of the ancient pharaonic or even more recent Persian periods. The Book of Fayum reflects a landscape transformed even since the time of Herodotus, and it is probably fair to say that the priests responsible for drawing up this document were faced with as many difficulties in untangling the religious geography or sacred landscape of the Fayum as we seem to face today with untangling the ideas of Lake Moeris.

The translation of the term *ḥnt* has been revised from the standard Faulkner dictionary definition 'swampy lake,'[58] to 'watercourse' in the more recent *Ägyptisches Wörterbuch* I and II.[59] In the latter, the distinction between *mr* (canal) and *ḥnt* (watercourse) is clearly made. Unfortunately this possibly acts to confuse the issue of the *ḥnt* of *mr-wr* even more. It would be reasonable to say that the name *ḥnt n mr-wr* refers to a watercourse near the town *mr-wr*, which was named after a large canal. These observations do not actually help with understanding how Herodotus came to describe the *ḥnt* of *mr-wr* as a large lake or expanse of water. The word Herodotus uses is 'lake,' which has always been believed to correspond to the Coptic word for lake, which in turn is believed to have its root in ancient Egyptian *ḥnt*. Μοίρις vocalizes as Moeris and has long been accepted as the Greek version of the ancient Egyptian *mr-wr*. If Herodotus was being 'guided' around the Fayum, the locals would not have described the Fayum lake as the *ḥnt* of *mr-wr* if that was the name given to the Bahr Yusuf river or a major canal. While the central area of land in the Fayum may have later been referred to as the *ḥnt* (if, as Cruz-Uribe hypothesizes, the entire network of canals was described as the *ḥnt*), at the time Herodotus visited that was certainly not the case, because the lack of managed irrigation at that time meant the entire region was flooded.

Herodotus's belief that the region had been transformed by Amenemhat III is perhaps connected to confusion regarding the name of that pharaoh. The full name of this pharaoh was Nimaatre Amenemhat (*n-mꜣꜥt-rꜥ—ꜣmn-m-hꜣt*). In Greek this became Marres—Μάρης or Μάρρης—which could potentially be misvocalized as Moeris.[60] In many translations the king responsible for transforming the Fayum is named Moeris.

The sheer number of possibilities for interpreting Herodotus's account, and the many convoluted ways in which the names have both changed and been transmitted, make it impossible to state with any certainty the chain of history relating to this place name. What we can be sure of is that Herodotus visited the region (presuming he did) at the time of flood, when the majority of the landscape was covered with a large expanse of water that he believed was a lake. Possibilities for how he came upon the name Lake Moeris (or lake of Moeris) are that he inquired about the origin of the lake and was told it was created by the pharaoh Nimaatre/Marres/Moeris, or was told the name of the canal/river that fed the lake, namely the *ḥnt mr-wr*, which to his ear sounded like λίμνη Μάρης, or Lake Moeris. Alternatively, he might have inquired about the name of the lake, and to the locals his Greek word for lake—λίμνη—sounded like *ḥnt*, and so they thought he was asking about the *ḥnt* (the watercourse), which was of course known as the *ḥnt* of *mr-wr*. One other possibility is of course that by the time he visited the name λίμνη Μάρης was already in use by local Greek priests who themselves had 'transformed' *ḥnt mr-wr* into Lake Moeris.

The Labyrinth 'Problem'

The earliest European account of the Fayum containing any mention of the Labyrinth is that of Father Johann Vansleb (dated 1672–73, see Chapter Six), who was clearly using the account of Pliny as his 'guidebook' for his trip.[61] At this time the temple of Qasr Qarun was believed to be the Labyrinth, which is unsurprising given the undoubtedly labyrinthine internal architecture of that temple. It was the famous explorer–archaeologist Giovanni Belzoni who first questioned this notion, but he did not name Hawara as the site of the Labyrinth. Just a few years later, in 1825, when British orientalist Edward William Lane visited the region, he stated that "the Pyramid of Häwa'rah and the adjacent remains are considered by some modern travellers, as the relics of the famous Labyrinth."[62] There seems to be no account in which the matter is discussed or debated, so it is impossible to know how this change of mind took place. The Labyrinth 'problem' has attracted only slightly less attention than the Lake Moeris issue, partly due to the fact that since 1825 there has been no question about its location being Hawara. Instead, the problem has been to 'find' the remains of the amazing edifice described by Herodotus (then Strabo, Pliny, and others).

Several early teams made surveys of the area in which the Labyrinth was believed to be in the early nineteenth century, but the mid-nineteenth century Prussian expedition led by Lepsius undertook more detailed work, which is still relied upon as an accurate record of the remains at the site at that date.[63] Petrie's excavations in the late nineteenth and early twentieth century did not really add to the Labyrinth debate, other than his hypothetical reconstructions based on the known early remains and Herodotus's description. Various reconstructions of the Hawara Labyrinth temple have been proposed by different people, based on various sources of evidence and using different approaches and methods, most notably Eric Uphill,[64] and the striking visual conceptions by a team connected to the Petrie Museum in London.[65] Ultimately, the remains at the site are far too scanty to give any real idea of the form of the temple as it was in the Middle Kingdom, what it looked like at the time of Herodotus, or how it might have evolved in the Ptolemaic Period.

Unraveling Herodotus's Vision

The many misconceptions arising from interpretations of Herodotus's *Histories* have led to a loss of appreciation of the continuity of the Fayum theology through time. What Herodotus reported about the lake and the Labyrinth may have been a misunderstanding of the Fayum creation story by his guide, or it may have been Herodotus's misunderstanding of what he was told, but the roots of his ideas that the lake was man-made, that water flowed in and out of the region, and that there was a tunnel leading away from the lake underground do seem to lie in the stories about the sacred landscape of the Fayum in which the gods dug the lake and the sun god traveled through the region during the day and then back through the lake at night. It is possible even that his account of the magnificent Labyrinth temple was influenced by the belief that the entire Fayum landscape was a temple of Sobek.

The perception of the Fayum that Herodotus presented is of an imagined landscape. In order to create a good story, he did not convey the reality of his experience but rather what he understood from his guides. His stories were based on observation, but then elaborated on in order to entertain his listeners and readers. Conforming to the poetic style, Moeris was set up as a pseudohero who achieved deeds of epic proportions. Herodotus was almost certainly in awe of these two wonders. The temple he named the Labyrinth, probably in order to provide a familiar point of reference to his audience, was possibly the largest temple he visited, and he probably saw the lake during the impressive flood season. He aimed to amaze his audience, so his descriptions of the lake and the Labyrinth were exuberant and exaggerated. His perception of the Fayum was that it was the direct result of the greatness of one pharaoh, and that the lake and the Labyrinth, being the physical manifestations of that greatness, needed celebrating. The fact that the lake and the Labyrinth became the foci and the obsession of later travelers and writers is principally a result of traditions in education and the reliance on Herodotus as a primary source. Only recently, with the 2013 publication of the Book of Fayum, has there been any recognition that Herodotus's account might be linked to the Fayum theology.[66] Because the Book of Fayum was not fully translated and easily available until the end of the twentieth century,[67] the long-running issues with interpreting just what Herodotus meant can only now begin to be resolved.

Ptolemaic Egypt (332–32 BC)

Following the first Persian Period, the rule of Egypt was not held continuously either by Egyptians or by one foreign state until the conquest by Alexander the Great in 332 BC. From the end of the Twenty-seventh Dynasty (359 BC), for around sixteen years, the country had a brief period of independence from Persia. In 343 BC the Persian forces succeeded in retaking Egypt, but the country was still far from stable and Alexander, with Macedonian forces, was able to exploit anti-Persian sentiments in Egypt when he invaded in 332 BC.[68]

After the death of Alexander in 323 BC, the newly named Alexandria became the capital of Egypt and showpiece of the Ptolemaic Dynasty in the Hellenistic world. It was the place for scholars, not least because of the library established there, and it became the heart of scholarship and scientific learning during the third and second centuries BC. The established Egyptian elite seems to have had good relations with the new Macedonian–Ptolemaic rulers, and the Ptolemies made great efforts to Egyptianize themselves. Some of the best preserved temples in Egypt at Edfu, Esna, Kom Ombo, and Dendera were built in the Egyptian style by the Greek rulers. Greek culture was prevalent in Egypt; many aspects of it were well known in Egypt prior to the Ptolemies due to immigration since the mid-seventh century BC.[69]

Over 30 percent of the Greco–Roman papyri that have been found in Egypt are from the Fayum.[70] As a result of this wealth of texts, a great deal is known about Ptolemaic and Roman administration, and more is known about the Fayum than about any other region in this period of Egyptian history.[71] The majority of Greco–Roman sites in the Fayum were first explored during the late eighteenth and early nineteenth centuries AD, when the region underwent a new phase of land reclamation under Muhammad 'Ali. This work renewed the abandoned Ptolemaic irrigation systems, expanding the habitable land back to its late-first-millennium extent and revealing the 'lost' Ptolemaic settlements that had been engulfed by desert sands. The sites contained rich archives of papyri, which started coming to light as the sites were exploited for mudbricks (used as fertiliser in a practice known as *sebakh* digging).[72]

As many new settlements had been founded by the reign of Ptolemy II Philadelphus (285–46 BC), it is thought by most scholars that the transformation of the Fayum began during the rule of Ptolemy I Soter (305–285 BC). By the reign of Ptolemy III Euergetes I (246–21 BC), the inhabitable and agricultural land of the region had expanded from 400 to 1,500 square kilometers. The scale of this reclamation project cannot be underestimated. Massive dams must have been constructed at the entrance to the region (a harbor is attested at Ptolemais Hormou [Lahun; see plate 12]). The waters of (what is now known as) the Bahr Yusuf were channeled through major new canals running around the periphery of the region, redirecting water in a highly managed system to allow the central region of the Fayum to dry out. This facilitated habitation and cultivation, while also drawing waters out to the edges of the region and massively expanding the areas available for agriculture.[73] The remnants of some of these canals used to be visible on aerial photographs, and cultivation plots were once visible around the towns of Philadelphia, Theadelphia, Euhemeria, Philoteris, and Dionysias.[74] Evidence for specific parts of this engineering project can be found in the so-called Petrie Papyri, which come from burials at Gurob in which mummy cases were manufactured using old papyri, known as cartonnage. The cartonnage can be 'dismantled' to access the papyri, and the material from Gurob included the archives of an engineer named Kleon who was responsible for overseeing parts of the new irrigation systems.[75] It is likely that the size of the early Ptolemaic lake and cultivation area closely resembled the region as it was following the phase of land (re)reclamation undertaken by Muhammad 'Ali in the early nineteenth century.

Contrary to the generally idyllic image of the Fayum found in Classical geographic and historical works, during the Ptolemaic and Roman periods the region was probably in a constant state of tension due to the precarious nature of the irrigation works. Numerous papyri attest to the scale of labor required to maintain the canals, and the fact that the region no longer experienced wide-scale flooding meant that the land became increasingly saline, and thus increasingly infertile.[76] There is direct evidence of some of the problems in the Fayum irrigation in the Kerkeosiris papyrus archive from Tebtunis.[77]

The development of agriculture, settlements, temples, and new administration in the Fayum region played a major role in the Ptolemaic government. In a relatively short time, existing settlements expanded and new ones were founded due to a major increase in the population. The administrative divisions of the Fayum were organized into regions known as merides, and within these were smaller districts known as nomarchies, with even smaller areas of new land of ten thousand auroras (2,756.25 hectares), managed by *myriarouroi*. The expansion of the settlement network in the region probably followed the creation of new canals as land became available. Evidence in administrative papyri suggests that the first new settlements appeared in the eastern parts of the region, then the south, and finally the west. This roughly equates to the new administrative districts, which are thought to have been named after their earliest governors: Herakleides, Polemon, and Themistos. The majority of new Greek settlers in the Fayum were *clerucs*, soldiers who had been gifted land in the region as compensation for their services. In 276 BC Ptolemy II Philopater renamed the region after his sister wife: the Fayum became the Arsinoite nome.[78]

Early in the Ptolemaic period Shedet was renamed Crocodilopolis, then Arsinoë. By the late second century BC (116 BC) it was again renamed, as Ptolemais Euergetes, in honor of the deceased Ptolemy VII.[79] The city must have been redeveloped, and it was surely a hub of administration and temple activities, but virtually nothing remains of the Ptolemaic or Roman city. The earliest European travelers to the Fayum recorded that Madinat al-Fayum was built on the ruins of ancient Arsinoë and that there were many 'relics' in the city.[80] Lepsius visited the site during his survey in 1843, making some very small excavations, but the first archaeological record of the site (known as Kiman Faris) is a map made by Schweinfurth in 1887, which shows just the last remnants of temple ruins with a small area of (probably Roman, Byzantine, and medieval Islamic) settlement remains covering an area of around 2.4 by 2.2 square kilometers. The site was explored by Jean-Jacques Rifaud in the late 1920s, but during the 1960s–70s the town underwent a major expansion and all but five small areas of archaeological remains were destroyed.[81] Today, Fayum University occupies the land that was once the main Sobek temple area; a small area of blocks is visible from the university hotel windows.

Alongside this undoubtedly dramatic period of transformation of the physical landscape, there was an equally spectacular transformation of the sacred landscape. The new rulers began a program of major temple building across Egypt, including in the Fayum. Ptolemy I founded a new temple on the site of an older one at Tebtunis (Umm al-Burigat) in the southern Fayum,[82] but it was Ptolemy II who initiated a wide-scale scheme of temple construction and expansion. The Sobek temple at Crocodilopolis (then renamed Arsinoë) was replaced, a small shrine was built at Theadelphia, and a temple was founded at Bacchias. The temple to Renenutet and Sobek at Dja (Madinat Madi) was significantly enlarged, and there is evidence of early Ptolemaic foundations at other sites in the Fayum, for example at

Karanis.[83] There are extensive archaeological remains of the new settlement system, but as is the case with the pharaonic evidence, the surviving sites are all located around the peripheries of the region. This is principally due to the fact that possibly as early as the fifth and certainly in the sixth to seventh centuries AD the irrigation systems fell into almost total disrepair, stranding the sites in the desert and ensuring their preservation and protection from damage by the continued occupation and expanded agriculture that caused the loss of almost all Ptolemaic and Roman remains in the central parts of the Fayum.

The majority of the sites now known in the region were first uncovered during the late eighteenth century reestablishment of the irrigation systems, as mentioned above. Many were recorded by Jomard during the Napoleonic expedition to Egypt of 1798–1801. Lepsius then recorded and explored several sites during his 1843 survey of the region (Madinat al-Fayum, Lahun, Hawara, Soknopaios Nesos, Dionysias), and Petrie surveyed twenty sites in 1890, going on to excavate the Ptolemaic and Roman cemeteries at Hawara and Gurob (as well as pharaonic remains at those sites

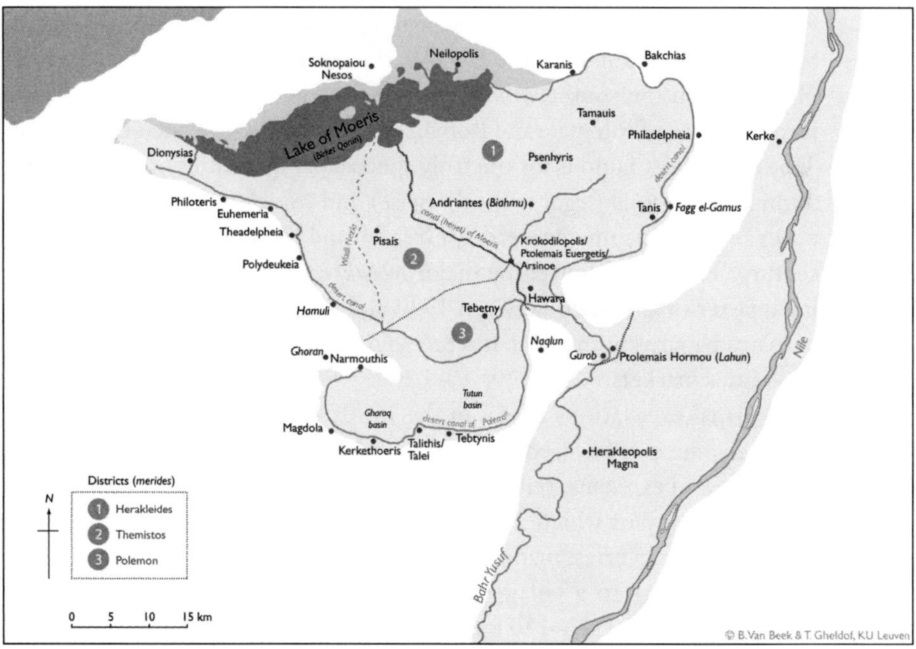

10. Map of Greco-Roman towns in the Fayum, after B. Van Beek and T. Geldhof, KU Leuven, Trismegistos Project. *Reproduced by permission of the Trismegistos Project.*

and at Lahun). Grenfell, Hogarth, and Hunt followed Petrie, spurred by his spectacular finds of papyrus archives. They explored sixteen Ptolemaic and Roman sites around the edges of the region in 1895. As their goal was the recovery of more documents, their methods were less than rigorous, and they abandoned many sites certain they had been thoroughly looted, only for papyri to show up in later, more careful excavations.[84] Since then many missions have worked and continue to work in the region, at Ptolemaic and Roman sites, increasingly less focused on recovering papyri and more dedicated to recording aspects of the settlement archaeology of the region and the architecture of the temples. The best introduction to the archaeology of Greco–Roman Fayum and history of explorations is the work by Paola Davoli.[85] The list of sites located across the region is increasingly large, and there have been several very complex investigations dedicated to determining the probable location of many of the 'lost' settlements known only from papyri.[86] A major project at the University of Leuven hosts a large database of the Fayum towns and papyri, including detailed maps.[87]

The New Landscape

Ptolemy I (305–285 BC) founded a temple dedicated to a new form of Sobek—Soknebtunis—at the Twelfth Dynasty site of Umm al-Burigat (Tebtunis) on the southernmost edge of the Fayum. The town flourished throughout the Ptolemaic and Roman periods and into the medieval period. Tebtunis is most famous for the truly spectacular quantities of papyri found during excavations (legal and otherwise) and *sebakh* digging. The earliest major finds of documents were by Grenfell and Hunt in the early twentieth century. This was followed by major *sebbakhin* destruction of the residential quarter of the town between 1920 and 1930, leading to the discovery of many papyrus archives that were sold on the European and American antiquities markets.

Formal excavations began in the 1930s and have been running continuously since 1988. Led by Italian and French teams, the excavations have revealed extensive remains of buildings, but above all, large numbers of papyri, many of which are still awaiting publication. One of the most significant discoveries, made in 1900, was a collection of discarded documents belonging to a village scribe named Menches, dating to the late second century BC (120–110 BC, reigns of Ptolemy VIII–IX). The contents relate to administration of a small village called Kerkeosiris, and local land surveys.[88] These provide a wonderful glimpse into the complexities

11. Google Earth image of Tebtunis.

and nitty-gritty of everyday life at this time in the region. One of the most unexpected pieces of information gleaned from this 'archive' is the fact that Fayum land was not actually deemed to be especially productive. The price of land was low and far less land was privately owned than in the Nile Valley, hinting again at lower-quality land. This has to be considered with caution, however, because while the papyrus archives from the Fayum are undoubtedly rich, they are very patchy, giving highly detailed insights into small areas. At Kerkeosiris in 118 BC only around six percent of land was unsuitable for cultivation.[89]

Archaeological work at Bacchias (Kom Umm al-Atl) has yielded important papyrus archives concerning the administration of the temples in that town. It was founded at least by the third century BC (possibly much earlier) and occupied for at least seven hundred years. The first exploration of the site was by Petrie during his Fayum seasons in the late nineteenth century, although he did little more than note the existence of the site and the approximate date based on surface scatters of ceramics. Grenfell and Hunt also spent time here searching (with some success) for papyri in 1896. They recorded the remains of the temple of Soknobkonneus.[90] The papyri found at the site were almost all Greek. Italian archaeologists working at the site since 1993 have proven that this is one of the best preserved archaeological sites in the region. They have

12. Google Earth image of Bacchias.

carefully recorded the remains of several temples and noted large areas of housing (approximately seven hundred dwellings) as well as administrative and storage facilities across two distinct mounds (or *koms*) covering an area of 600 by 700 meters.[91] Their work was focused on the temple precincts (at least five temples are known), and a complex sequence of successive construction and rebuilding throughout the Ptolemaic and into the Roman period was clearly evident.[92] The team recovered more Greek papyrus fragments and ostraca, with a few examples of Demotic texts. In total they have recovered 222 texts, adding to the 93 found by Grenfell and Hunt and 33 known documents from illegal explorations.[93]

The village of Philadelphia (Kom al-Kharaba al-Kebir) on the northeastern edge of the region was established by Ptolemy II and is the site of the discovery of the Zenon papyrus archive that contains transactions and management relating to a large tract of land here (270–30 BC). The town was occupied until at least the fifth century AD. Early excavations at the site by a German team led by F. Zucker in 1908–10 showed that at that time the settlement was still in a good state of preservation, but their consequent publication sadly does not shed much light on any details of their work. In fact the published sketch plan was actually made much later, in 1925 by Borchardt.[94] By the time this plan was made, the site had undergone heavy *sebbakhin* destruction, which led to the discovery

13. Google Earth image of Dimai.

of the important Zenon Papyri archive in around 1914. When Borchardt planned the ruins in 1925, there was still a significant area of town remains, but since then the site has been severely damaged. The cemeteries of the town are now the focus of new excavations, led by Basem Gehad for the Ministry of Antiquities.[95] The papyri attest to the presence of various temples, storage facilities, administrative offices, bath-houses, and possibly a theater. The presence of a fortification wall hints that this town was probably acting as a border control point for goods and people.[96] The Zenon archive is a collection of around two thousand letters covering fifty years, written to Zenon, a resident of Philadelphia. Following the death of his sister-wife Arsinoë, Ptolemy II Philadelphus appointed Apollonius as his 'right-hand man,' granting him royal patronage that came with many privileges, including the estate of the 'Ten Thousand Auroras' in the Fayum. He assigned Zenon to work for Apollonius. In 256 BC Zenon was placed in charge of the estate in the Fayum. In this archive is clear evidence of the increasing pressures to increase the productivity of the Fayum lands, and the systems for clearing and irrigating the land are set out in detail.[97]

The site of Soknopaios Nesos (Dimeh/Dimai/Dimay) lies on a ridge above the northern shore of the lake, and was also founded by Ptolemy II, probably to act as a desert trade station. The town was occupied into

14. The temple and enclosure walls, Dimai. *Photograph by R. Neil Hewison.*

the fourth century AD, but like so many sites it seems to have declined and been abandoned by the fifth century AD. The majority of the remains date to the second to first centuries BC, including houses, public buildings, bath-houses, and two temples dedicated to 'Sobek Lord of the Island,' as well as cemeteries (Ptolemaic and Roman) that held both human and crocodile mummies.[98] The site has always attracted attention because of the presence of extensive archaeological remains, including a massive mud-brick temenos wall that dominates views of the site. Most early travelers visited Dimai, including Vansleb, Pococke, Belzoni, and John Gardner Wilkinson. The site was recorded by the French and Prussian survey missions, and also Petrie. It was briefly excavated by Grenfell and Hunt, Zucker, and Ahmad Kamal at the beginning of the twentieth century and the University of Michigan worked at the site briefly, conducting the first stratigraphic excavations.

Since 2001 Dimai has been excavated by an Italian team from the Universities of Lecce and Bologna.[99] The Italian mission recognized that the site had not experienced the effects of *sebbakhin* as much as other Fayum towns, and a comparison between their surveys and the older plans of

Wilkinson, or Lepsius,[100] shows that little of the site has been lost since it was first mapped. The town was home to a major complex dedicated to Soknopaios, located in a large temenos area. It had a paved dromos (wide central roadway) 6 meters wide leading directly into the temple, which essentially divided the town into two parts. On both sides of the dromos are extensive remains of the settlement, covering a total area of 640 by 320 meters.[101] At least twenty buildings have been identified in the temenos area, including three temples, one of which may have been founded during the Ptolemaic Period, but the remains generally date to the Roman Period.[102] The papyri from Dimai reveal a great deal about the organization of temple activities, including lists of names of personnel, activities of people associated with the temple, and accounting of income and expenditure of temple goods.[103]

One of the most visited Ptolemaic sites in the Fayum is the temple at Dionysias (Qasr Qarun; see plate 13). At one time this temple was thought to be the Labyrinth of Herodotus, and it is easy to understand why, as the temple architecture is undoubtedly labyrinthine. The problem is, of course, that this temple did not exist when Herodotus was said to be in Egypt. The temple is dedicated to a form of Sobek/Souchos and contains a bewildering array of storage rooms on several levels either side of the main central rooms, as well as underground spaces and an upper level spanning

15. Google Earth image of Qasr Qarun.

16. Google Earth image of Theadelphia.

the full temple roof. Around the temple are the remains of a large town including housing bath-houses and workshops as well as a fortress.[104] The first archaeological mission at this site was a French–Swiss collaboration between Jacques Schwartz and Henry Wild in 1946, and two seasons of excavation took place in 1948 and 1950.[105] The mission conducted a general survey of the area, producing a basic map of visible remains, including traces of a canal running south toward Madinat Watfa (Philoteris) and on to Madinat Madi. The remains cover an area of around 800 by 400 meters, but very little of the ancient town was recorded, as much of the site had suffered badly from *sebbakhin* quarrying. The town is attested in papyri from the third century BC and the last dated document is correspondence of Abinnaeus circa AD 350, but the town is known to have been occupied until the fifth century AD. The temple lies in the center of the archaeological area, with settlement remains spread around to the south and west and the fortress to the west on the edge of the site. What was interpreted as a possible processional way/road runs from the temple to the east, with a smaller kiosk/temple at the eastern end. In a small 'island' of ruins to the south of the temple, the French–Swiss mission excavated several well-preserved dwellings, and others to the west of the temple. Based on comparisons to other Roman forts, the fortress, which was around 94 by 80 meters, has been dated to the reign of Diocletian.[106]

To the east of Qasr Qarun are the remnants of the third to fourth century AD village of Theadelphia (Kharabet Ihrit), discovered by Grenfell and Hunt in 1898–99. The first formal archaeological work took place here in 1902, led by Otto Rubensohn, whose excavations were the first in the houses of the Ptolemaic town. His goal was to find papyri, but he uncovered both housing and temples. The site was also explored by Gustave Lefebvre in 1908, and by Evaristo Breccia in 1913–14, who discovered the remains of a further temple (now in the Alexandria museum), the Bubasteon, and a crocodile cemetery.[107] At its height, Theadelphia seems to have been one of the larger villages in the Fayum, with 1,736 hectares of land. This was almost double the amount of agricultural land average for Egypt at the time (827 hectares), surpassed only by Karanis (3,390 hectares) and Philadelphia (at least 2,756 hectares). Theadelphia yielded exceptionally large quantities of papyri, and one of the largest private archives from Roman Egypt was found here: in total, the archive of Heroninos consists of over a thousand texts.[108]

The southern part of the Fayum has two natural basins, Gharaq and Tutun. This area was naturally flooded by the annual inundation, and waters then flowed through the al-Wadi drain out into the lake. During the early Ptolemaic Period an enormous dike/wall was constructed across the northern part of these basins to prevent the waters from flowing into the main lake, holding them in the basin area in order to create new expanses of cultivatable land. Following these major hydrological works, a large permanent lake was created in at least the Gharaq basin and a large number of small villages were established on the shores of the lake: Magdola, Maraka, Kom al-Khamsim, and Madinat al-Ghuran.[109]

The Twelfth Dynasty temple of Renenutet and Sobek at Madinat Madi (ancient Dja) on the northern edge of the Gharaq basin had lain empty since the end of the New Kingdom, but during the early Ptolemaic period the town and temple were revived and expanded considerably (see figure 7 and plates 14 and 15). The ancient Middle Kingdom temple was restored and became the core of a new temple of Sobek/Renenutet. The sacred lake was expanded and the area was enclosed with a wall. The full extent of temple and town remains at this site are not yet known, but to date, the remains of a really very large temple have been uncovered, including a long dromos (processional way) with two kiosks, lined with several pairs of lion statues, and many service buildings either side, two courts/portals, and a pylon behind the core temple with a large altar courtyard. This site was excavated throughout the twentieth century, primarily by Italian teams. The earliest excavations at the site were undertaken by Pierre Jouguet in 1900–1902. During the 1930s excavations were led by Achille Vogliano, who uncovered the Middle Kingdom remains at the site. Work continued in the 1960s (University of Milan), and since 1978 the work has been led by a team from the University of Pisa. The team from Pisa have uncovered a further temple at Madinat Madi to the east of the main Sobek/Renenutet temple, which, due to the discovery of over thirty unhatched crocodile eggs containing foetuses in various stages of development, is believed to have been the sacred-crocodile nursery. The Ptolemaic name for the town was Narmouthis, which means 'town of Thermouthis,' Thermouthis being a form of Renenutet. The Ptolemaic town remains are overlain by later Roman buildings.[110]

Discoveries of third century BC administrative documents in mummy cartonnage in cemeteries at Madinat al-Gurob suggest a reoccupation of the old palace town of *mr-wr* during the early Ptolemaic Period.[111] The archive from Gurob comprises the official correspondence of two chief engineers, Kleon and Tehodorus, in charge of the maintenance of irrigation in the Fayum and stone cutting in Fayum quarries.[112] Discovered by Petrie in 1889, the papyri had been reused as mummy cartonnage in burials at Gurob. The texts date to 264–37 BC. The publication of these documents by John Pentland Mahaffy between 1891 and 1895 (as the 'Petrie Papyri') remains the principal resource, as the reinvestigation of the archive conducted by Bart Van Beek in the early 2000s has yet to appear in print.[113]

The Middle Kingdom pyramid of Hawara became a center of attention in the Fayum during the Ptolemaic Period, and, thanks to both Herodotus and Petrie, it has become the most famous site in the region. Possibly due to its already established fame, and the fact that Amenemhat III (known as Premares or Marres) had a cult dedicated to him in the Fayum by the Ptolemies, Hawara became the principal burial ground for the inhabitants of Crocodilopolis/Arsinoë, and people from as far away as Alexandria chose to be buried close to the pyramid of Amenemhat III. A village was established here to support the massive funerary industry, occupied by priests and necropolis workers and their families. The Ptolemaic cemetery contained cartonnage coffins, some of which were made using the papyrus archives of four families of undertakers working at Hawara. This is undoubtedly a historically valuable discovery, but it is the Roman cemetery that is far better known due to the discovery, by Petrie, of the painted mummy portraits.[114] A huge amount of detail regarding the lives of people in the village at Hawara can be reconstructed from papyri and remains of material culture, housing, and burials—illustrated best in the exhaustive study by Uytterhoeven.[117]

During the second half of the second century BC the Ptolemaic Empire started to become less stable. In-fighting meant that there was no clear sole ruler of Egypt, and in 169 BC the Seleucid king Antiochos IV planned to conquer the country.[116] It was only due to the support of Rome that this was prevented. Roman intervention had been increasing in the eastern Mediterranean, and Roman interest was growing. This was not restricted to a political level, as 'tourism' by elite Romans began to be more commonplace. There is, in particular, one record of a trip to the Fayum by a Roman senator, Lucius Memmius.

Papyrus Tebtunis I.33: Letter from Hermias to Horos, Dated 5 March 112 BC

This letter, dating to the (first) reign of Ptolemy IX, contains instructions for the organization of a trip to "see the sights" in the Arsinoite nome, and provides insight into the impact of the account of Herodotus on tourism in the region. It appears to be the only preserved account of any such trip in the Fayum (Tebtunis) papyrus archives.

> Hermias to Horos, greeting. Appended is a copy of the letter to Asklepiades. Take care that its instructions are followed. Good-bye. The fifth year, Xandikos 17, Mecheir 17. To Asklepiades. Lucius Memmius, a Roman senator, who occupies a position of great dignity and honor, is making the voyage from Alexandria to the Arsinoite nome to see the sights. Let him be received with special magnificence, and take care that at the proper spots the chambers be prepared and the landing-places to them be got ready, and that the gifts of hospitality below written be presented to him at the landing-place, and that the furniture of the chamber, the customary tit-bits for Petesouchos and the crocodiles, the necessaries for the view of the Labyrinth, and the offerings and sacrifices be provided; in general take the greatest pains in everything that the visitor may be satisfied, and display the utmost zeal. [here the papyrus breaks off][117]

This letter illustrates the early effect of Herodotus's account. The crocodiles, and most importantly the Labyrinth, had already become part of a standard 'tourist' trail in Egypt. In order to impress a Roman of some status, it was important that his trip to the Fayum be as smooth and as entertaining as possible. The Labyrinth was perceived to be the most impressive monument in the region, and it is notable that none of the 'newer' Ptolemaic temples were considered worth visiting, although it is impossible to know if longer trips included visits to other sites. It may be safe to presume that this trip was a short one, and that the senator in question would simply travel to Crocodilopolis and be taken on a short sight-seeing trip. The ancient heritage of the region and the curiosity of seeing the crocodiles seem to have been considered more worthy of the attentions of an important visitor than their 'own' Ptolemaic culture—the many impressive temples to Sobek.

A more modern example provides greater understanding of this phenomenon. A tourist to Egypt will undoubtedly visit the Pyramids, and perhaps the eighth-century mosque of Ibn Tulun or the mosque of Muhammad 'Ali at the citadel, but the likelihood of making a trip to visit one of the fantastically impressive new mosques in (for example) Sheikh Zayed, Sixth of October City, or New Cairo is less than slender. Only a tourist in their 'home' nation would be likely to make a special trip to see a new sacred building (temple, church, synagogue, mosque). Only the most spectacular new buildings, such as the Burj Khalifa in Dubai, are considered worth visiting by a foreign tourist.

Early Roman Egypt (First Century AD)

In 80 BC when Ptolemy IX Soter died without an heir, the Romans chose the next (Ptolemaic) ruler, Ptolemy XII. Although he managed to secure independence from Roman rule via bribery and negotiation, Egypt was essentially under Roman control. In 59 BC one of the most infamous and well-known episodes in history started to unfold when Cleopatra VII (daughter of Ptolemy XII) ascended to the throne of Egypt. Despite the best efforts of her brother Ptolemy XIII, with the support of Julius Caesar she managed to hold this position. Following the murder of Caesar in 44 BC Cleopatra famously turned to Mark Anthony for support, eventually marrying him, but by then Octavian (Caesar's adopted son) had declared war. His defeat of Mark Anthony and Cleopatra triggered the double suicide of the couple in Alexandria in 30 BC. There was a brief power struggle between Octavian and Cleopatra's brother Ptolemy XIII, which Octavian won, beginning true Roman rule as the first Roman emperor in 30 BC, renamed Augustus Caesar.[118]

Roman interest in Egypt had been growing for a long time, as evidenced by the account of the visit of Lucius Memmius to the Fayum in 112 BC. Following the Persian and Greek rulers, the new Roman rulers continued the tradition of Egyptianizing their images, building new temples, and taking Egyptian titles. They retained major aspects of the administration, and other than the highest-ranking officials the government consisted of Greek and Egyptian personnel. Greek remained the predominant language, over Latin. The people of Egypt retained many Hellenistic traditions. As with Ptolemaic Egypt, due to the wealth of papyrological finds from the region, evidence of Roman Egypt is weighted heavily toward the Fayum and surrounding area. Many of the Greek papyri from the Fayum date to the Roman period.[119]

During the final years of the Ptolemaic Dynasty, the Fayum irrigation systems had fallen into disrepair, and it is highly likely that during the early years of Roman imperial rule the hydrology of the Fayum had to be reestablished in order to maximize the agricultural productivity of the region. Egypt was the granary of the empire, and the Fayum was the granary of Egypt, making it one of the most important regions of the country and indeed the empire.[120] While some Romans expressed disdain for the Egyptian worship of animals, others were happy to participate in it, and the crocodiles of the Fayum remained a popular attraction.[121]

Diodorus Siculus (c.90 – after 30 BC)

At the same time that Cleopatra came to the throne (59 BC), during the chaotic and turbulent transition from the Roman Republic to the Roman Empire in the final years of the Ptolemaic Period, the Greek–Sicilian writer Diodorus Siculus visited Egypt prior to beginning work on his important historical account. The only information known about the life of Diodorus is found within his own works; he is in fact never referred to by any other historian. He grew up in the Sicilian town of Agyrium, and lived in Rome until 30 BC.[122] During his lifetime the Mediterranean had come almost totally under Roman control, and Egypt was essentially a Roman protectorate. One of Diodorus's goals was to collate a history of all the countries under Roman rule. He claims to have visited all the nations of Europe and Asia, but there is no evidence to suggest he ever did this.[123]

Diodorus's work took thirty years to compose and originally consisted of forty books, of which only fifteen are preserved in their entirety while the remainder exist only in fragments. The majority of his work is a compilation of other works—he named his own work *Library of History*—and many of the original sources are now lost, making this a very valuable account. He makes it clear from the outset that he wanted to produce a universal history from the beginning of mankind to his time, with the firm belief that the events of the past educate the men of the present.[124] Studies of the work of Diodorus have not always been especially positive, and indeed for a long time he was either overlooked or considered unworthy of the attention of modern scholarship. His contribution to history is seen by some as an (often flawed) act of preservation of historical tradition, not creation. As a result, the majority of studies of his works have focused on attempting to ascertain and discover his sources rather than valuing his work for its contribution to the writing of history in its own right.[125]

Although nothing is known of his education, it is clear that like most writers of his time Diodorus was familiar with the works of Homer and Euripides, both of whom he cites with caution, trying to expose the reality of the events they described using literary terms. He was also familiar with the major philosophers, including Pythagoras, Plato, Aristotle, the Epicurians, and the Stoics. Unlike many Greek historians, he placed value on recording a large number of myths, acknowledging that while myths made historical research extremely difficult by confusing chronologies, they should never be totally excluded as they play a role in history.[126] Diodorus's work presents a set of beliefs about history that represent first century BC thinking. He understood the value of inquiry and exerted caution, without rigidly adhering to one school of thought.[127]

The earliest manuscript copy of the work is Codex Vindobonensis 79, dating to the eleventh century. The first printed publication was a translation into Latin of books One through Four in 1472, by Poggio Bracciolini. The first English edition was by George Booth in 1700.[128] The structure of *Library of History* is regional. Book One covers Egyptian history, Book Two encompasses India, Assyria, Arabia, and Scythia, Book Three covers Ethiopia, Africa, and Atlantis, Book Four changes focus slightly to discuss Greek gods, Book Five covers the western Greeks, and books Six through Ten (incomplete) cover the years from the Trojan war to 480 BC.[129]

In Book One, Moeris is first introduced as being the twelfth ruler in line after Uchoreus:[130]

> Twelve generations after the king just named, Moeris succeeded to the throne of Egypt and built in Memphis itself the north propylaea, which

> far surpasses the others in magnificence, while ten schoeni above the city he excavated a lake which was remarkable for its utility and an undertaking of incredible magnitude. For its circumference, they say, is three thousand six hundred stades and its depth in most parts fifty fathoms; what man, accordingly, in trying to estimate the magnitude of the work, would not reasonably inquire how many myriads of men labouring for how many years were required for its completion? And as for the utility of this lake and its contribution to the welfare of all the inhabitants of Egypt, as well as for the ingenuity of the king, no man may praise them highly enough to do justice to the truth.[131]

In Chapter Sixty-one he discusses King Marrus/Mendes, who "did build himself a tomb known as the Labyrinth."[132] In Chapter Sixty-five he tells the story of the twelve kings who constructed a tomb to commemorate their union: "For selecting a site at the entrance to Lake Moeris in Libya they constructed their tomb of the finest stone . . . ; and in the carvings and, indeed, in all the workmanship they left nothing wherein succeeding rulers could excel them."[133] It is not explicit at all that this tomb and the Labyrinth are one and the same monument. In Chapter Eighty-four he describes the worship of sacred animals, including "the crocodile of the Lake of Moeris,"[134] and in Chapter Eighty-nine he describes the reason for this worship:

> The security of the country is ensured, not only by the river, but to a much greater degree by the crocodiles in it; that for this reason the robbers that infest both Arabia and Libya do not dare to swim across the Nile, because they fear the beasts, whose number is very great.[135]

He gives a second reason for the worship of crocodiles:

> For some say that once one of the early kings whose name was Menas, being pursued by his own dogs, came in his flight to the Lake of Moeris, as it is called, where, strange as it may seem, a crocodile took him on his back and carried him to the other side. Wishing to show his gratitude to the beast for saving him, he founded a city near the place and named it City of the Crocodiles; and he commanded the natives of the region to worship these animals as gods and dedicated the lake to them for their sustenance; and in that place he also constructed his own tomb, erecting a pyramid with four sides, and built the Labyrinth which is admired by many.[136]

The story about King Menas and the crocodile of the Fayum is possibly one of the most explicit examples of 'tour guide imagination' found in any of the Classical sources about the Fayum. The situation is easily envisaged: Diodorus asked why the crocodiles are worshiped and was given an entertaining answer. Diodorus's account generally follows that of Herodotus, which is natural given his methodology of collating known works. Although he did live in Egypt, it is not known whether he visited the Fayum. It seems plausible that, having read about the wonders of the Fayum in Herodotus's work, he inquired further regarding the lake, the Labyrinth, and the crocodiles and was provided with answers that were somewhat fantastical in their content. His perception was shaped entirely by that of Herodotus and so was essentially imaginary.

Diodorus had no conception of the realities of the landscape, and his focus was entirely set on recording the ancient history of the region, not recording the present state of the land, people, or administration. As a result, the contemporary landscape, both sacred (the many temples) and secular (the critical importance of upkeep of irrigation), were not a part of his vision when compiling this account, although, somewhat ironically, it was relatively recent interventions in the landscape that created the lake he saw. He considered only the ancient monuments and modern attractions, and he only knew about those mentioned by Herodotus: the Labyrinth, the crocodiles, and the lake, which was of course not the lake seen by Herodotus. Diodorus can be considered to be the first writer participating in the perpetuation of the Herodotean tradition of 'facts' about the Fayum.

Strabo (c.64 BC—c. AD 23)

Strabo is thought to have been born into an influential, wealthy, aristocratic Greek family in Amasia in Pontus and well educated in the Classical Hellenistic tradition. Certainly, his teachers nurtured his admiration of Homer, philosophy, and geography. He traveled to Rome some time before the death of Caesar in 44 BC and made a trip to Egypt around 26/24 BC, accompanying the Egyptian governor Aelius Gallus as a member of his entourage. In Egypt he traveled to Alexandria, Heliopolis, Memphis, the Herakleopolite/Arsinoite nome, including the Labyrinth and the lake, and as far south as Thebes and Philae. It is possible that his name, which is Roman not Greek, is one he adopted or was given by Gallus.[137] It is probable that Strabo worked on his geographical account for around twenty years. It was published before his death in AD 21/23, and was therefore composed during the very earliest turbulent years of the empire in Egypt under Augustus and Tiberius. Strabo's work reflects his interests and beliefs. As a geographer he fell into the school of descriptive, not scientific, geographers, and as a philosopher he had Stoic tendencies.[138] Greek philosophy during the Hellenistic period developed into two opposing schools, Epicurian and Stoic: the Epicurians believed that life was beyond the control of external forces, while the Stoics believed that life was the result of an all-powerful 'Reason' *(Logos)* and that the structure of the world followed a rational plan, which if studied could be understood and directed.[139] Strabo was influenced by Homer, Polybius, Eratosthenes, and Hipparchus (a mathematical/scientific geographer), and he was well aware of all the major historians, geographers, and philosophers. He considered Herodotus's account to be foolish and held views more in line with Thucydides, that myth had to be either rejected or rationalized. He believed that the factual roots of these myths had to be sought out, acknowledging that myth was an excellent didactic tool as it was pleasing to read and thus stimulated curiosity and encouraged learning.[140]

Strabo lived an almost dual cultural life between the Greek and Roman worlds, but based on his education his thinking was Hellenistic. He held that the Greeks were superior in all but politics to the Romans as they were the more ancient people. Although he did not refrain from criticizing the Romans, he did respect them, and to a certain extent it can be seen that he was writing his account for a Roman audience.[141] His identity as a Stoic philosopher meant that he aimed to provide enough information on the wonders he encountered to enable others to "marvel at nothing," as they would know so much that nothing could ever astound them.[142] This work is sometimes considered to be the greatest Greek geographical work ever written, and the fact that it was composed during a period of major cultural exchange between the Greek and Roman worlds at the beginning of the Roman Empire makes it invaluable for the study of the history, culture, and philosophy of that time.[143]

The earliest preserved fragments of Strabo's *Geography* are predominantly papyrus scraps from Oxyrhynchus dating from the second to third centuries AD.[144] There is one version of the *Geography* from which all others are considered to be copied. The oldest existing copies date to the end of the tenth century: the Epitome Vaticana and Codex Parisianus 1397 (tenth-century Greek translation of Latin text). The earliest translation into Latin was by Guarinus Veronensis, a holograph of which, dated 1458, is held in the Bodleian library in Oxford, after which date it was revised and republished numerous times throughout the sixteenth century. The earliest published edition of the *Geography* appeared in 1516, produced in Venice by Aldus, which was swiftly followed by other editions in the sixteenth century.[145] The *Geography* consists of seventeen books, beginning with a definition of the study of geography. Book Two discusses the mathematics of geography, and in Book Three the regional survey begins with the Iberian peninsula. The final book covers Africa.

Egypt first appears in Book One of Strabo's *Geography*. Lake Moeris is first mentioned in a section describing the propositions made by Strabo to explain the beach shells found in deserts across the world. Egypt was, he says, formerly covered by a sea that linked the Mediterranean to the Red Sea. When the sea retreated, the lakes were left behind, which explained the fact that the beaches of Lake Moeris resemble sea beaches more than river banks.[146] In Book Seventeen Strabo describes the monuments and wonders of Egypt. Chapter Four, dedicated to the description of the Nile, includes a brief mention of the Arsinoite nome:

> The river [Nile] flows in a straight course about 40,000 stadia through only one channel, except . . . where the river is diverted to a greater extent than usual by a canal into a large lake or a territory which it can water, as, for instance, in the case of the canal which waters the Arsinoe Nome and Lake Moeris.[147]

Chapter Thirty-five includes the Fayum, or the Arsinoite and Herakleote nomes.[148] Strabo stated that the Herakleote nome lay on a large island that cut across the canal that ran toward Libya into the Arsinoite nome:

> This Nome is the most noteworthy of all in respect to its appearance, its fertility, and its material development, for it alone is planted with olive trees that are large and full grown and bear fine fruit, and it would also produce good olive oil if the olives were carefully gathered. But since they neglect this matter although they make much oil it has a very bad smell. . . . And it produces wine in no small quantity, as well as grain, pulse and the other seed-plants in very great varieties. It also contains the wonderful Lake of Moeris, which is an open sea in size and like a sea in colour; and its shores, also, resemble those of a sea.[149]

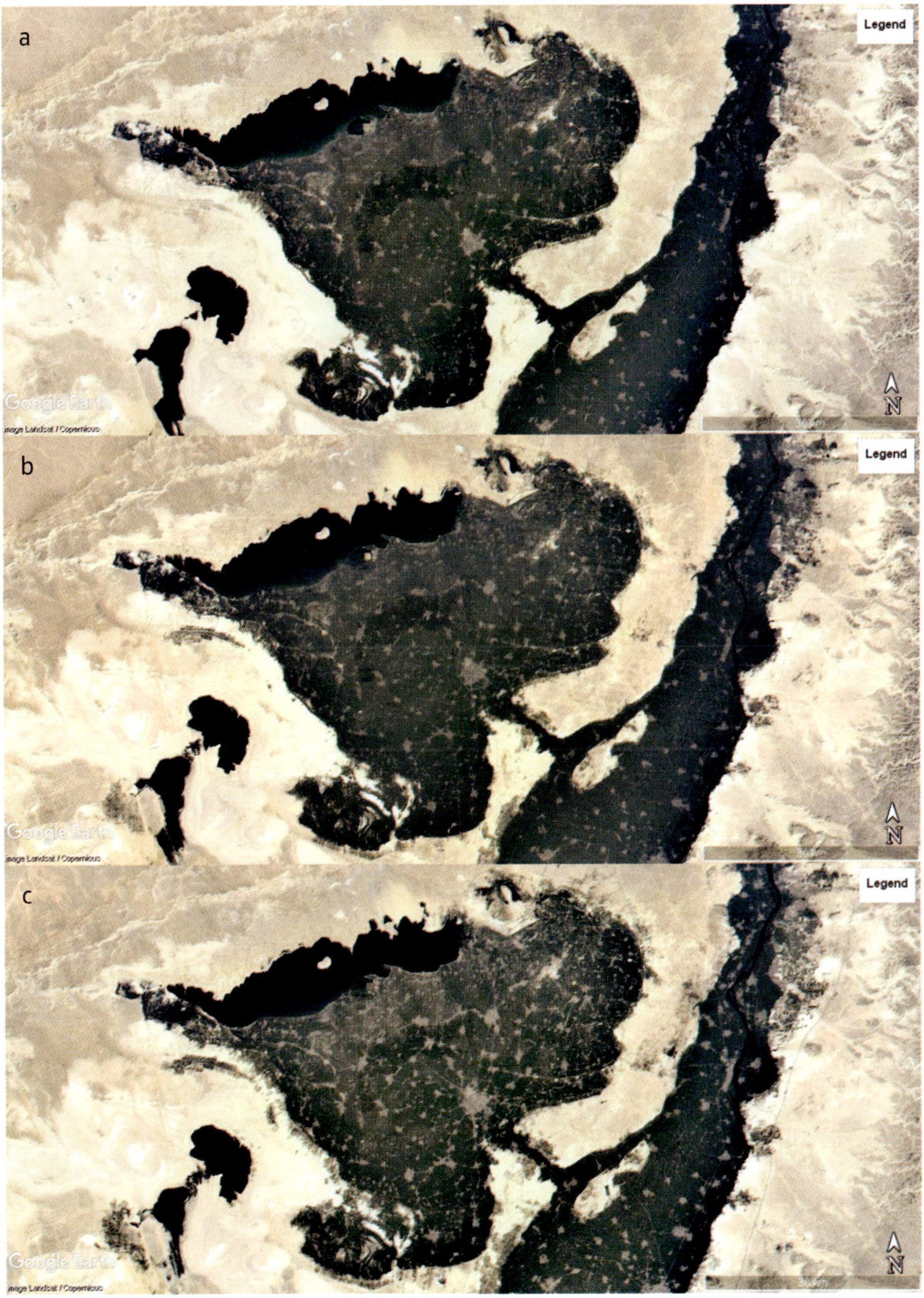

1a. Google Earth image of the Fayum, 1996.
1b. Google Earth image of the Fayum, 2006.
1c. Google Earth image of the Fayum, 2016.

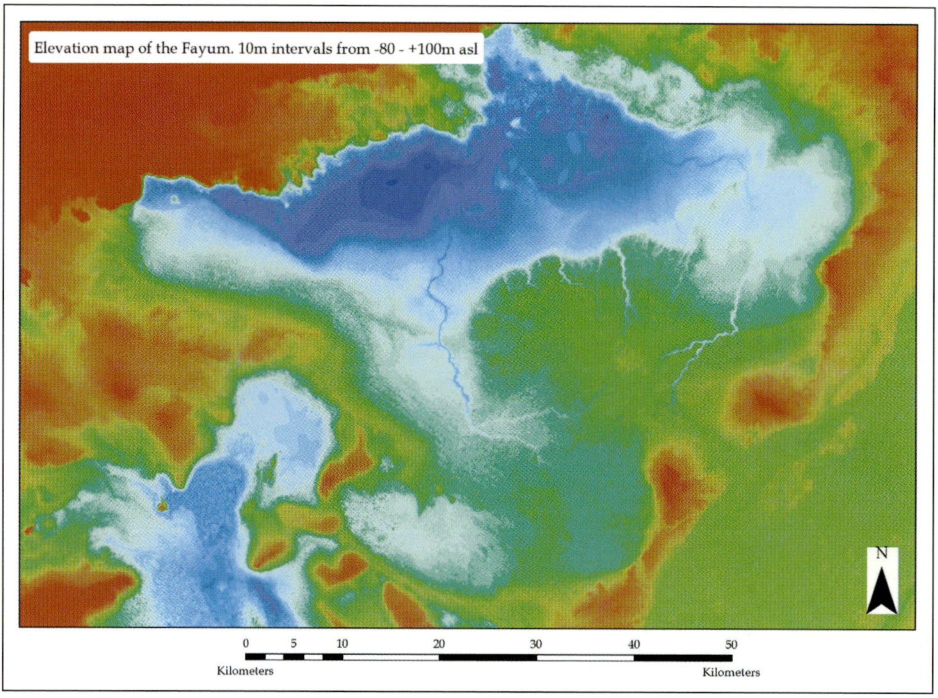

2. GIS Elevation map of Fayum.

3. Google Earth map of principal Fayum sites.

4. Block from Hawara, Petrie Museum UC14794. *Reproduced by permission of the Petrie Museum London.*

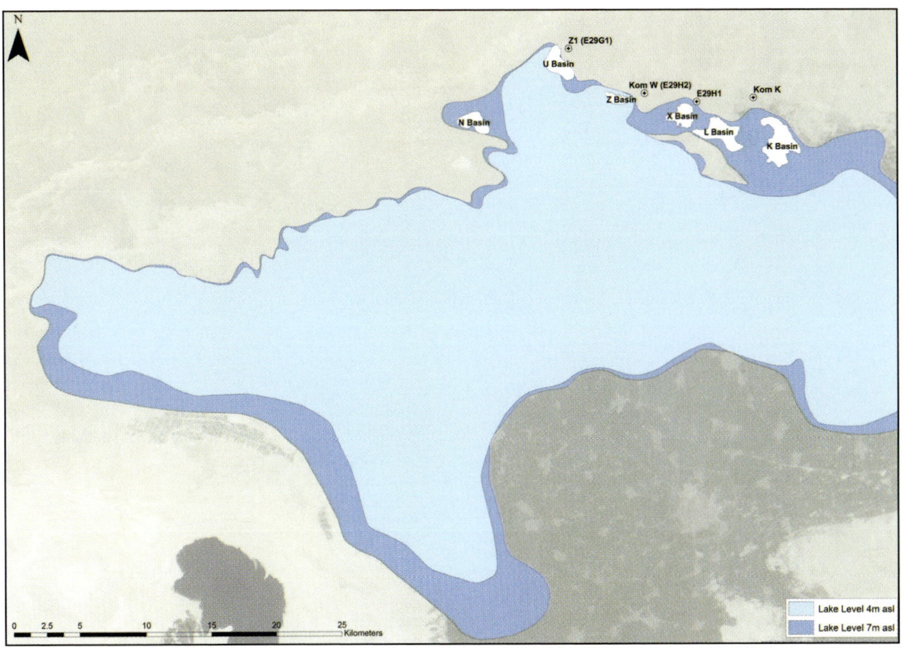

5. Map of the northern Fayum lake basins. *From S. Holdaway and W. Wendrich 2017, reproduced by permission of the Cotsen Institute of Archaeology Press.*

6. Fragments of inscription from Giza Mastaba G2150, Ka-nefer. Museum of Fine Arts, Boston. *Photograph by Claire J. Malleson/Pier Paolo Raffa.*

7. Kahun town. *Photograph by Claire J. Malleson/Pier Paolo Raffa.*

8. Biahmu Pedestal, 2006. *Photograph by Claire J. Malleson/Pier Paolo Raffa.*

9. Hawara Pyramid, 2006. *Photograph by Claire J. Malleson/Pier Paolo Raffa.*

12. The Lahun dike, 2017. *Photograph by Claire J. Malleson/Pier Paolo Raffa.*

13. Qasr Qarun temple. *Photograph by Claire J. Malleson/Pier Paolo Raffa.*

14. The Ptolemaic temple at Madinat Madi. *Photograph by Claire J. Malleson/Pier Paolo Raffa.*

15. The dromos at Madinat Madi. *Photograph by Claire J. Malleson/Pier Paolo Raffa.*

16. Fayum portrait,
Petrie Museum UC19609.
Reproduced by permission of the Petrie Museum, London.

17. Fayum portrait,
Petrie Museum UC19613.
Reproduced by permission of the Petrie Museum, London.

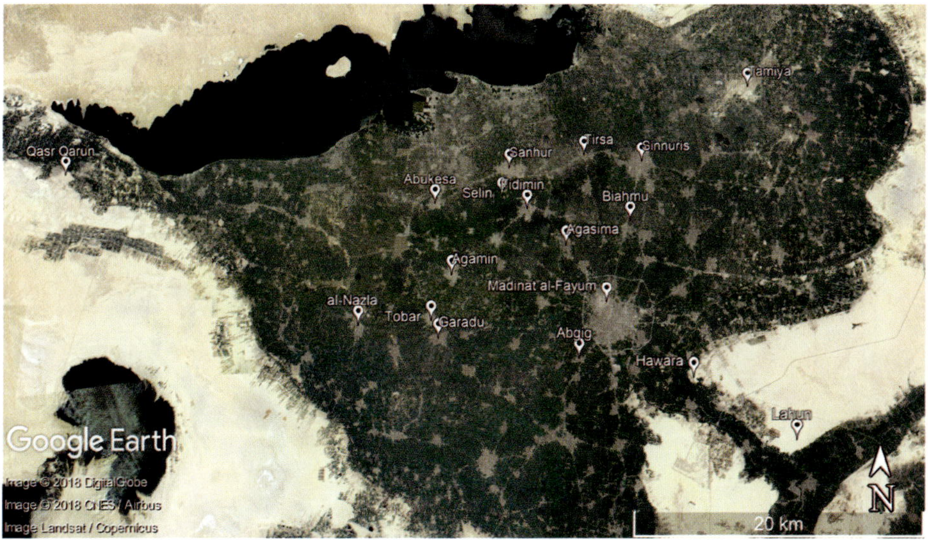

18. Google Earth map of locations mentioned by European travelers.

19. Fishing boats on Birkat Qarun, 2006. *Photograph by Claire J. Malleson/Pier Paolo Raffa.*

20. Crimson sunset over Birkat Qarun, 2006. *Photograph by Claire J. Malleson/Pier Paolo Raffa.*

21. Postcard of painting by Jean-Léon Gérôme, Madinat al-Fayum, 1868.

In Chapter Thirty-seven Strabo returns to describing Lake Moeris:

> Be this as it may, the Lake of Moeris, on account of its size and depth, is sufficient to bear the flood-tides at the risings of the Nile and not overflow into the inhabited and planted parts, and then in the retirement of the river, to return the excess water to the river by the same canal at each of the two mouths and both itself and the canal, to keep back an amount remaining that will be useful for irrigation. While these conditions are the work of nature, yet locks have been placed at both mouths of the canal by which the engineers regulate both the inflow and the outflow of the water. In addition to the things mentioned, this Nome has the Labyrinth, which is a work comparable to the pyramids and near it, the tomb of the King who built the Labyrinth. Near the entrance to the canal, and on proceeding thence about thirty or forty stadia, one comes to a flat trapezium-shaped place, which has a village, and also a great palace composed of many palaces—as many in number as there were Nomes in earlier times; for this is the number of courts, surrounded by colonnades, continuous with one another, all in a single row and along one wall, the structure being as it were a long wall with courts in front of it; and the roads leading into them are exactly opposite the wall. In front of the entrances are crypts, as it were, which are long and numerous and have winding passages communicating with one another, so that no stranger can find his way either into any court or out of it without a guide.[150]

The entire building was constructed of monumental slabs of stone supported by twenty-seven monolithic pillars. At one end of the building was the pyramid–tomb of Imandes, the king who built it.[151] Chapter Thirty-eight continues the description of the Fayum:

> Sailing along shore for a distance of one hundred stadia, one comes to the city of Arsinoê, which in earlier times was called Crocodeilonpolis; for the people in this Nome hold very great honour of the crocodile, and there is a sacred one there which is kept fed by itself in a lake, and is tame to the priests.[152]

The chapter continues with a description of how the tame crocodile, named Suchus, was fed by the priests to entertain any foreigners who came to visit.

His group was taken to the lake by a priest, who then fed the crocodile meat and honeyed wine. When more foreign visitors arrived, the priests chased after the crocodile to feed it again. In Chapter Forty-two, Strabo briefly mentions that Lake Moeris is in one of the three Libyan oases.[153]

The account of Strabo stands out as the only classical account that can be said to describe an experience of the Fayum. His description is detailed, but he does not provide any dimensions for the lake, simply stating that it resembled a sea and could contain all the flood waters. He describes the location of Hawara relatively precisely: near to the first entrance to the canal and a "village of trapezium shape." Overall, this is perhaps the most realistic and detailed Classical account of the Fayum, which is likely to be a result of his direct contact with the region. It seems probable that Strabo only included the Labyrinth as it had become an established element of the Fayum narrative and to omit this feature may have encouraged criticism. When he visited the Fayum he would have been taken to the site of the Labyrinth and given a tour, as it was an expected part of the Fayum tour, and it was a major part of his Fayum experience. As with the Islamic accounts, in this description the canal and locks are the most significant features of the landscape, which is fertile and rich in produce. His description really does speak of direct contact: it is clearly a personal perception as he independently describes the lake as resembling a sea. The fact that he does not employ numbers to convey a sense of the size of the lake or Labyrinth is one factor that makes this account seem plausible as an eyewitness account.

Unlike Herodotus, for whom he had little respect, Strabo does not seem to have considered reporting any local legends or tales. He conveys his own perception of the landscape, which was rich and abundant, fertile, and productive. The major aspect of the interventions of man in this landscape was the canal that regulated the irrigation. He does not consider the lake to be man-made or mention the 'pyramids' in the lake. This is probably because the Biahmu colossi (thought to be what Herodotus believed to be pyramids) had been nowhere near the lake since the early Ptolemaic irrigation systems were established. This is the one real eyewitness Classical account, and the experienced perception it reveals shows that the idea of the region changed little from this time until the ninth century, when Islamic scholars began traveling in the region. It is worth noting, once again, the total absence of mentions of any of the temples or the many large and important towns. The productivity of the region is considered to be one of the outstanding features of the Fayum, and yet the fact that a staggering landscape transformation had been initiated by Ptolemy I seems either to have already been forgotten or to not have been considered interesting enough. Temporalizing the landscape—making it more ancient—made it far more interesting.

Tacitus (AD c. 56–c.120)

In AD 19, during the earliest years of the Roman period in Egypt, Germanicus (commander-in-chief of Germany) was moved to a commission in the east by his uncle Emperor Tiberius.[154] He was accompanied by Marcus Silanus and Lucius Norbanus. They set out with the express desire to visit Egypt and its antiquities and to inspect the province, about which there were some concerns.[155] What is more, Germanicus traveled despite the fact that as a Roman he had no permission from the emperor to be there. He was thus breaking the ban on senatorial visits and further exacerbating the declining relationship he had with his uncle, and causing political upset in Rome.[156] The ban on travel to Egypt was due to the fragility of rule there; it was feared that a powerful senator might try to take control of this important Roman province.[157] Details of the trip are recorded in *The Annals* of Tacitus (II.61). While he was in Egypt Germanicus visited Thebes and "the lake hollowed out of the earth to be a receptacle for the Nile's overflow"—the Fayum lake—as well as Elephantine and Aswan.[158] There is one other piece of evidence for this trip, P.Oxy 2435, which seems to record the arrival of Germanicus in Alexandria.[159] This brief reference to the Fayum underscores that the lake was perceived to be a man-made phenomenon, and therefore an antiquity and worthy of visiting. It highlights the fact that the 'man-made' landscape of the Fayum continued to be a tourist attraction because it was evidence of the 'epic' deeds of ancient rulers.

Pomponius Mela (?–c. AD 45)

Pomponius Mela was the author of the earliest known Latin geographical work, *The Chorography* (sometimes known as *The Cosmographie*). Very little is known about his life, and what is known derives from within his own work. He was born in Tingetera (in modern Spain) and wrote his account during the reign of Claudius (AD 41–54). His work was published circa AD 44. His primary interest lay not in the description of monuments or human achievements but in (what would now be seen as) anthropological curiosities and natural/supernatural phenomena. Pliny listed nine works of Pomponius Mela in his *Natural History*, but only the four geographical texts are known. In his work Pomponius Mela explicitly stated that he perceived the world as a puzzle. People and places were puzzling and hard to understand, and his aim was to describe as much as possible. He drew all his information from existing works and maps (Homer, Strabo, Herodotus, Posodonius, Eratosthenes, Polybius, Artemidorus). John Romer describes his account as an "armchair travelogue."[160] The work may have been accompanied by a map; however, the pre-fourteenth-century manuscripts that were circulating in France contain no maps.[161]

There are at least 121 manuscript copies of Pomponius Mela's work and 150 printed editions, highlighting the popularity of his work. *The Chorography* was consulted by many scholars in the third and fifth centuries AD. The work was heavily used by Pliny the Elder as well as several other Classical scholars. The principal manuscript on which all modern editions are based is a ninth-century copy, Vaticanus Latinus 4929, which is a copy of a fifth-century manuscript that is now lost. This document was moved around Europe from one collection/library to another, and several copies were made of it. From these copies around 117 more were made during and after the fifteenth century. Only three other pre-medieval copies survive. The principal edition dates to 1471, and the first English translation was published in the sixteenth century (British Museum MS London Hargreaves 399).[162]

Egypt appears in Book One. After describing the borders of the country from Elephantine to the Delta and various natural phenomena (fauna), Pomponius Mela introduces the Pyramids and Moeris in Chapter Fifty-five. Moeris, "once a plain, now a lake accommodating a circumference of 20 miles, is deeper than necessary to sail in heavy freighters." In Chapter Fifty-six he notes:

> The Labyrinth is a work of Psammetichus; it embraces a thousand homes and twelve palaces within its continuous enceinte. It is built of marble and roofed and has one passageway down into it, but almost countless paths inside; many confusing paths turn back on themselves this way and that, but extend in both directions with a continuous winding and with porticos that are often circular, with these paths promptly making one circle on top of others, and with the cone of a circle promptly bending back as far as it had advanced, the labyrinth is puzzling with its long yet solvable, wandering paths.[163]

The account continues with descriptions of burial and mourning customs and of animal cults, and a section discussing the Egyptian sense of history.

Romer considers Pomponius Mela's description of the Labyrinth to be an "emblematic" statement in *The Chorography* because it sums up the entire work. He notes that the description is layered with literary meaning. For Pomponius Mela the world is a puzzle, and the Labyrinth represents that puzzle.[164] This description of the Labyrinth appears to be based on that of Strabo. Either this is Pomponius Mela's own interpretation of what Strabo wrote, having not fully understood Strabo's description, or the principal manuscript, Vat. Lat. 4929, contains copyist errors. The concept of the continuous winding paths stacked one on top of another with a 'cone' turning back upon itself seems implausible. However, as Romer suggests, this description is probably a literary device, not a description of a monument.

More importantly, Pomponius Mela states that Moeris was once a plain and is now a lake. This description seems to imply that the region did not always contain a lake, and that the lake that existed in his time bore the name of the region. While not many conclusions can be drawn from one brief sentence, this mention of a plain that was somehow transformed into a lake has some similarities with the later medieval Islamic folk tales of Joseph transforming the region from a marshy plain into an inhabitable area. Although their accounts are close to the truth—the region being drained of water for cultivation, rather than a (dry) plain having a lake dug into it—the underlying implication perpetuated the Herodotean tradition that the landscape was transformed and that the lake had not always existed. It is worth noting that Pomponius Mela does not attribute this work to anyone specific, but does name the creator of the Labyrinth.

Pliny (the Elder) (AD 23/24–79)

Pliny the Elder's nephew, Pliny the Younger, recorded a great deal of detail about his uncle's life and working methods, and it is through the letters of Pliny the Younger that we know so much about Pliny the Elder. He was born in Comum in northern Italy in AD 23 or 24, during the reign of Emperor Tiberius, and died 'in the name of curiosity'—when he went to view the eruption of Vesuvius he was asphyxiated by its gases. He was a wealthy man and held several major army/civil service posts, serving in Germany during the reign of Nero (AD 54–68). He was a prolific writer and produced a history of the German Wars, a biography of Pomponius

Secundus, and works on grammar and rhetoric. His *Natural History* was completed in AD 77, and was dedicated to Titus.[165]

The *Natural History* was created principally through reading and note-taking, working with a large team of scribes. Pliny's work is to a great extent more a reflection of literary tradition than of his own personal perceptions. Essentially it is an accumulation of knowledge he gleaned from every extant account, and could have been produced entirely inside a library, but he did also attempt to observe and experience phenomena, places, and people himself. He asserted his dependence on written sources, stating that he had read two thousand books by a thousand authors about twenty thousand things, which was very probably a way of illustrating the superiority of his work over all others. However, he always credited his sources, as he believed that information was a commodity. He felt that he was honored by being freely given the information, so it was his duty to credit the original author. This is a reflection of the Roman ideal of sharing wealth: the most significant demonstration of your greatness was measured by your generosity, not by your personal accumulation of wealth.[166]

The work can ultimately be seen as a symbol of the power of Rome. It was only the commercial, military, and political power of the Roman Empire that made the book possible, and because knowledge is a commodity the production of the book meant that all the knowledge it contained became the intellectual property of Rome. By this time Rome was already nostalgic for its past glories, and Pliny gives the impression that he was determined to collate and present as much information as he could before it was lost. Like all writers, he wanted to astonish and astound readers, employing both fact and myth, and he set the boundaries for what was normal by employing extreme comparisons of people, places, and phenomena.[167] There are many manuscript copies of Pliny's texts,[168] but the first printed publication of the *Natural History* was produced in Venice by Johannes de Spira in 1469, followed not long after by Joannes Baptista Palmarius in 1499.[169]

Pliny set out the contents and sources of his work in Book One. Book Two covers mathematics and the physical description of the world; books Three to Six cover geography and ethnography; Book Seven covers anthropology and physiology; books Eight to Eleven cover zoology; books Twelve to Twenty-seven cover botany and agriculture; books Twenty-eight to Thirty-two cover pharmacology; and finally books Thirty-three to Thirty-seven cover mineralogy and stone-/metal-working. The account of Egypt starts in Book Five, Chapter Nine. Pliny describes the borders and names the nomes from south to north:

> There are two nomes called the Arsinoite; these and the Memphite extend to the apex of the Delta, adjacent to which on the side of Africa are the two Oasite nomes. Certain authorities alter some out of these names and substitute other nomes, for instance the Heropolite and Crocodilopolite. Between the Arsinoite and Memphite nomes there was once a lake measuring 250, or according to Mucianus's account 450, miles round, and 250 feet deep, an artificial sheet of water, called Lake of Moeris after the king who made it. Its site is 62 miles from Memphis the former citadel.[170]

In Chapter Eleven he lists the past glories of Egypt and names some of the principal cities and their notable monuments. This list includes "Arsinoe's Town and Memphis already mentioned, between which and the Arsinoite district on the Libyan side are the towers called pyramids, and on Lake Moeris the Labyrinth, in the construction of which no timber was used with the masonry."[171]

Given the wealth of material Pliny must have consulted, his account can be read as a synopsis of what was 'known' about the Fayum region at this time. The landscape of the region seems to have been condensed to such a degree that only the lake and the Labyrinth are considered. Elsewhere in the work Pliny considers aspects of the landscape of Egypt (mountains and rivers, as well as man-made interventions such as canals and bridges) to be famous, and in need of description. However, despite the fact that he had most likely consulted the work of Strabo (only he mentions the lack of wood used in the construction of the Labyrinth), who does describe the locks in the region, Pliny does not discuss the canal, the locks, and the dams at Lahun or the multitude of rivers and bridges in the Fayum.

The perception of the Fayum landscape conveyed by Pliny is very much based on the perceptions of others, which were in origin largely derived from Herodotus. His perception was thus entirely constructed within his imagination. He cannot have had any real vision of what the landscape of the region looked like, if in fact he even perceived the region as we know it. He describes the lake and pyramids as being located between Memphis and Arsinoë, and the Labyrinth as being by the lake. Nothing about this conjures up any idea of an irrigated oasis-like landscape. He makes no mention of the fertility of the region, or of any contemporary features such as towns and temples. Pliny's perception of the Fayum landscape is a distillation of the perceptions of Herodotus, and he continues the tradition that had already been passed down via several writers. The landscape had 'become' the ancient man-made wonders—the lake and the Labyrinth—neither of which held any significance other than the fact that they represented the constructions of the past.

(Claudius) Ptolemy (AD c.100–c.170)

The geographer Ptolemy lived in (or near) Alexandria throughout his career, which spanned the mid-120s to the 140s, during the reigns of Hadrian (AD 117–38) and Antoninus (AD 138–61). There is some evidence to suggest that he was born in Ptolemais Hermiou in Upper Egypt. He came from a Greek or Hellenized family that had been granted Roman citizenship. The fact that he lived in Alexandria indicates that he would have had access to the Library, but other than the suggestion that he may have been a student of Theon there is no evidence of what kind of education he had. His first work, the *Almagest* (this modern name is derived from the Arabic translation), is a study of astronomical observations and geographical calculations. This work was the dominant influence in theoretical astronomy for 1,500 years, until the sixteenth century. The oldest preserved copies are Arabic translations dating to the ninth century, and the text became known in Western Europe via a Latin translation by Gerard of Cremona dating to 1175.[172] Ptolemy himself states in the text that a great deal of the basic work on his second work, the *Geography*, was drawn from an earlier (now lost) geographical work by Marinos of Tyre.[173]

The *Geography* is preserved in fifty-three Greek manuscripts, all dating from around or after AD 1300 and seeming to derive from one (lost) original. Many of these copies show signs of having been altered and edited.[174] The oldest preserved version of the tables is the Arabic revision by Muhammad ibn al-Khwarizmi, which dates to the early ninth century. This is based on an earlier but now lost Arabic translation. It was not widely available until the fourteenth century, when Byzantine Greek copies were made (c.1406 by Jacobus Angelus). It was translated into Latin during the fifteenth century. The text was first printed in 1533 in Germany.[175] The *Geography* is divided into eight books. Book One is a theoretical outline of how to draw maps, and books Two to Seven are a catalog of places. Finally, Book Eight acts as an atlas containing maps accompanied by instructions for their construction. There is some debate as to whether the maps occurred in the original manuscripts or were later additions, but there are essentially two versions of the maps. The first set consists of twenty-six regional maps in Book Eight, while the second version consists of sixty-four regional maps distributed throughout the text.[176] The work lists towns and locations with coordinates based on Ptolemy's geographical calculations. Egypt is presented in Book Four, Chapter Five. Moeridis (Moeris) occurs in the list of lakes, towns listed as being near Moeridis are Bacchis and Dionysias, while Herakleopolis is listed as an island. The Arsinoite nome appears, as do Arsinoë and the naval station Ptolemais, which are listed as towns within it.[177]

Ptolemy's work is purely geographical, but he still had to choose which towns to include. This is the first and only Classical account in which any contemporary aspects of the Fayum landscape are included. Arsinoë was the principal town of the region and Ptolemais was a naval base. Bacchias and Dionysias were the locations of Greco–Roman temples in the region, but not the only ones, thus the inclusion of just these two must indicate their premier importance over and above the other temples in the region. The simple fact that they are included here is notable. While this account cannot really provide any insights into the perception of the Fayum that Ptolemy had, his work undoubtedly provided firm foundations for later Islamic geography and cartography, and gave the location of Lake Moeris, a detail used by later travelers.

The Later Roman Fayum (Second–Fourth Centuries AD)

Some of the most evident changes made by the Romans in Egypt were to the central administration systems, most particularly a reorganization of the districts. The question of the division of the Fayum into different districts is particularly confusing, but it seems that until AD 60 the region was administered as one nome, after which it appears to have been divided into three. From AD 136/137, it was administered as two nomes.[178] Within the initial nome, the split into three *merides*—Herakleides, Polemon, and Themistos—was maintained. Based on the abundant textual evidence, scholars have recorded that *tꜣ-ḥn.t-(n-)mr-wr*, the Henet of Moeris, formed the border between the northern *meris* of Herakleides and the southern *merides* of Polemon and Themistos. However, they generally also conclude that the Henet of Moeris was the Bahr Yusuf.[179] There is one problem with this assumption: the Bahr Yusuf ends in the eastern part of the region at the capital (Madinat al-Fayum/Arsinoë/Crocodilopolis/Ptolemais Euergetes). The irrigation system had fallen into disrepair, but during the early years of the Roman Period the canals were repaired and the system was once again maintained.

The Fayum was critical to the Roman Empire. As the most productive agricultural region in Egypt, it was the focus of Roman irrigation works. During the rule of Nero a major building scheme took place in the Fayum, with temple construction works at Karanis in the northeast, Dimai on the northern shores of the lake, and Qasr Qarun in the southwest. During the second century AD, under the reign of Marcus Aurelius (AD 161–80) a second, northern temple was built at Karanis.[180] Some of the temples at Bacchias date to the Roman Period and, generally speaking, during the imperial Roman period all the settlements in the Fayum expanded and population density increased.[181]

The inhabitants of the capital (Madinat al-Fayum) continued to be buried in the cemetery at Hawara, and it was in these Roman burials that some of the most spectacular works of ancient art were found, the so-called 'Fayum Portraits' (see plates 16 and 17). These wonderful images were found in relatively rough graves, but it is thought that they were displayed in homes until all remaining immediate family also passed away, at which point bodies were moved and were buried very simply.[182] The images are astonishing, often truly life-like portraits, many obviously painted during the lives of the individuals. Painted usually in wax on wood (a technique known as encaustic painting), they were inserted into the wrappings above the face of a mummy. Confusingly, they are almost purely Greek/Hellenistic in style, but are of Roman individuals. It is clear that the artists in Alexandria retained their skills and styles and that their works were highly valued.[183] Of the thousands of mummies excavated by Petrie at Hawara, only a very small percentage (about 2 percent) included a portrait, and they certainly were only possible for the richest members of society. The portraits show that these individuals wanted to have non-idealized images of themselves, suggesting that their values were less 'Egyptian.' The images are certainly very different to the standardized form of traditional and less 'personal' Egyptian art.[184] The Fayum is not the only place in which these images have been found, but by far the overwhelming majority does come from the Hawara cemeteries.

Karanis is the best preserved and largest Roman site in the Fayum, covering 60 hectares in total. The site was first explored by Grenfell, Hogarth, and Hunt in 1895 during their Fayum survey and search for papyri. They concluded that the site was almost totally looted, and that quarrying for *sebakh* was legal and conducted on an almost industrial scale (up to 200 cubic meters per day) into the 1920s. Papyri from Karanis continued to appear on the market. Excavations started again in 1924, run by the University of Michigan (until 1935). They continued from 2005, led by Willeke Wendrich of the University of California Los Angeles as part of a broader Fayum project.[185] Many of the artifacts uncovered by the University of Michigan excavations were exported to the United States (following the division of finds) and are held in the Kelsey Museum of Archaeology in Ann Arbor. These materials and the rich archives of excavation records were the subject of two recent exhibitions, in 1983 and 2011–12.[186] The work undertaken by the University of Michigan was exceptional, and the teams' detailed recording has meant that Karanis is still the best understood site in the Fayum. Exceptionally, for the time, the team collected large quantities of the plant remains preserved in the settlement. The plants include stored crops such as barley, safflower, and peas, as well as numerous other plants, including radish, acacia, persea, flax, castor oil, chickpeas, dates, peaches, walnuts, hazelnuts, doum palm, lupin beans, garlic, nigella, chufa, and lentils.[187] The town certainly had Ptolemaic foundations, but very little remains of the earlier phases. The Roman town was clearly prosperous and there were remains of

17. Google Earth image of Karanis.

bath-houses, temples, palaces, vast storage and food-processing facilities, and hundreds of houses,[188] although sadly little of this is preserved today. The temple built for Nero was dedicated also to a form of Sobek.

It is the location of Karanis on the northern edge of the region that indicates its likely purpose as the principal 'border' town for entry into and exit from the region for people and vast quantities of goods (particularly grain) at the height of the Fayum's agricultural productivity. Almost all publications referring to Karanis state that by the fourth century AD the site was in decline, and that it was abandoned during the fifth century, but recent work is questioning this. Previous conclusions were based on the lack of documentary evidence of any occupation at the site after the fourth century, and many references to the troubled irrigation systems. Evidence from ceramics analyses, however, points to a different conclusion. Since the Kelsey Museum excavations took place, the study of Egyptian Greco–Roman ceramics has advanced considerably, and new work shows that there is a considerable number of imported goods in the Karanis assemblage that date to the sixth century AD, suggesting not only continued occupation of the town but also occupation by people who could afford 'luxury' goods.[189]

At Dionysias (Qasr Qarun) the remains of an early fourth-century AD fortress were discovered during excavations by Schwartz in 1948–50. The fortress housed the 'Ala V Praelectorum (a Roman cavalry unit) and has been dated to the reign of Diocletian. It was built to control desert trade routes.[190] The site of Madinat Madi (Narmouthis/Dja) continued to be an important town and temple until the end of the third century AD, and during the fourth and fifth centuries the strategic location of the town on the southern edge of the region became important. A fortified camp was built on the eastern edge of Narmouthis to house the soldiers of the Cohors IV Numidarum.[191] This camp was uncovered in 2006–2007 by an Italian mission, and thousands of ostraca were discovered containing records of temple activities that have added a great deal to our understanding of the day-to-day functioning of Roman temples in Egypt.[192]

Despite the fact that Latin had been chosen as the principal language of the Roman state, Greek continued to be used in education and by the elite. This was due partly to the Roman aim of mastering the language and knowledge of the Greek Classical scholars. Early Roman politicians (such as Cato the Elder, second century BC) made use of Greek rhetoric in their speeches. An interest in producing geographical works was developing in Rome, driven by the expanding empire—Julius Caesar and Nepos (work now lost) being the primary exponents.[193] Throughout Roman rule in Egypt, Greek authors continued to be copied, and Homer remained popular. Roman papyri from Oxyrhynchus attest to a healthy trade in Greek literature. Evidence suggests that Roman schooling included the Greek classics, and that Alexandria remained the primary center of scholarship.[194]

Christianity in Egypt and Coptic Traditions (First–Seventh Centuries AD)

By the first century AD a Jewish community was well established in Alexandria. Tradition states that a Christian community was also founded there, within the Jewish quarter, in around AD 41–43 by Saint Mark. There is really no evidence of Christian activities in Egypt until much later, in the third century, but it is thought that Jews from Palestine were traveling to Alexandria, bringing Judaism with them. As was the case across the Roman Empire, the Christians in Egypt suffered persecution under Roman emperors for many generations. The community was primarily Greek and generally restricted to Alexandria until the late second century, after which there is some evidence of churches elsewhere in predominantly Greek centers at Oxyrhynchus, Antinoopolis, and Panopolis. A few Egyptians did convert, but as the teaching was in Greek, very few were able to understand or engage with this new religion.[195]

What is now recognized as a distinctly Egyptian form of Christianity and the appearance of the new Coptic language can be dated to the reign of Diocletian, and may have occurred in response to the persecutions instigated during his reign. The Copts take year one of his reign as year one of their calendar (AD 284), and this period is known as the 'Era of the Martyrs.' With the death of Diocletian came the beginning of the conversion of Rome to Christianity under Constantine (AD 306–37), whose mother was Christian, and Christianity spread rapidly through Egypt, primarily due to the fact that preaching was now conducted in Egyptian rather than Greek. Constantine also moved the capital of the empire from Rome to Byzantium and founded a new city, Constantinople (modern Istanbul). As soon as this happened, however, the Christian Church started to fracture and disputes over moral conduct, theology, and doctrine led to divisions and in-fighting.[196] The word Copt derives from the Greek word for Egyptians, which is an indication of the fact that during the fifth century Egyptian Christianity developed its own discrete nature, different from the original Greek Christianity, practiced by native Egyptians, and conducted in the distinct Coptic language.

The Coptic Period is also known as Late Antique Egypt, or Byzantine Egypt (a reflection of the fact that in 527 Emperor Justinian founded a new ruling dynasty, named after the original name of Constantinople), but strictly speaking the Christian era in Egypt began before the Byzantine period. The Coptic Period therefore overlaps with the Roman Period, in effect beginning in the third century. One of the most distinctive aspects of Coptic Christianity was the founding of the first monasteries. Monasticism was born in Egypt, and is still active today. It was in those monasteries and their libraries that some of the most important Christian documents were written and preserved. Several gospels are only known via the preserved copies found there.[197] The Fayum was home to several monasteries, but despite the vast quantities of papyri found in the region there is amazingly little information about its Coptic communities. Most of the documents are copies of gospels and other religious works. Four main monasteries are known: al-Hammuli, Naqlun, Qalamun, and Tebtunis (Tutun). There is little evidence of distinctly Roman culture in the Fayum after the fifth century. The Roman Empire had already begun to fracture at the end of the fourth century, and in the early seventh century Persian forces were gaining momentum. Egypt was occupied from 616 until 629, and in 642, ten years after the death of the Prophet Muhammad, Egypt was invaded by Arab troops led by 'Amr ibn al-'As.[198]

A Landscape Transformed

There are several key observations that can be made about the Classical Greek and Latin texts. The truly 'epic' deeds of the early Ptolemaic settlers in the Fayum—the spectacular transformation of the region from relatively uninhabitable and unproductive land into a dense network of settlements with a complex system of canals that facilitated large-scale agriculture—were almost totally overlooked, ignored, and unappreciated and were clearly never deemed worthy of acknowledging. The other massive transformation in the region—the development of a major new sacred landscape represented by numerous Greco–Roman temples—also played no part in their perception of the landscape. This is almost certainly due to the fact that these texts were principally historical, and regardless of the fact that some were written long after the temples were 'new,' the antique monuments of the pharaohs were their primary interest.

The gap in time between Herodotus and Diodorus Siculus is around 465 years. By the time Diodorus wrote his account, the 'new' Fayum landscape was around two hundred years old, so it is perhaps unsurprising that there was no longer any sense of transformation. It is plausible that while a memory that this landscape had not always been irrigated, cultivated, or inhabited so densely remained in cultural traditions, the details of who transformed the landscape were forgotten. Despite the fact that almost every aspect of the Fayum—sacred and secular landscape, population, economy, and culture—utterly changed after Herodotus created his record, the perception of later scholars changed very little. They perpetuated the traditions of Herodotus. There is no hint in the post-Herodotus accounts that the landscape, especially the lake, was any different to the one he witnessed. Herodotus had described a great lake, and they saw a great lake. Just as many thousands of people today question the age of the pyramids and the Sphinx, asserting in some instances that the Sphinx is over ten thousand years old, somehow 'needing' the monuments to be more ancient than they are, these writers perhaps needed the constructed wonders of the Fayum landscape to be more ancient than they were.

The classical perception of the Fayum was overwhelmingly temporalized. This imagined landscape of the past was perceived to be have been made by humans, and was dominated by two monuments, the lake and the Labyrinth. The influence of Herodotus is apparent from the outset. Despite major temple construction activities and significant alterations to the irrigation works that reshaped the landscape of the Fayum after his visit, it is his perception of the Fayum landscape that persisted and was transmitted by subsequent scholars. The Greco–Roman sacred landscape of temples dedicated to forms of Sobek does not seem to have had any impact on perceptions of the Fayum, even for Strabo, who, unlike many others, actually visited the region.

5

Legendary Landscape: Medieval Islamic Accounts (AD 860–1442)

> There is no country in the world that has been reduced and cultivated by Divine Revelation but this. There is not upon earth a less and yet a more fertile province, nor one that abounds in all sorts of good things or is better furnished with rivers.[1]
>
> —Murtada (early twelfth century AD)

> Among the provinces of Egypt you find the province of Fayum which is made up of 360 villages, a number the same as the number of days in the year. All of the villages are always irrigated with a sufficient quantity of water. If one year the Nile is insufficient each village provides for one day the needs of Egypt. There is nowhere in the world a land like this province which is built with divine inspiration, nor so precious, nor more abundant in goods, nor more criss-crossed with canals. When one compares the canals of Fayum with those of Basra and Damascus the advantage stays with the first.[2]
>
> —Maqrizi (fourteenth century AD)

One of the most enduring perceptions of the Fayum landscape that was first recorded in Islamic works is one shared by visitors to the region today, over a thousand years later. The image of the region appearing on the horizon as a welcome scene at the end of a hard journey across the desert is striking, and is only slightly diminished in the twenty-first century by the urban expansion of Cairo. In later European accounts that describe this image, it appears to play a large part in forming the exceptionally positive perceptions of the entire region, its fertility and abundance seeming to be enhanced by the aridness of the desert that had to be crossed to arrive at it. The travelers who visited the region and were sources for Islamic geographers must have communicated this sense of awe, the perception of great abundance and fertility and an air of divinity, akin perhaps to the Garden of Eden concept in Judeo-Christian and Muslim beliefs, infusing accounts of the region with this feeling.

The earliest Islamic accounts, which focus on physical geography, grew out of the study of Ptolemy's *Geography*. The works of what is known as the 'Iraqi school' are the most purely geographical of all the geographical texts produced by the Islamic scholars. Later texts are considerably different in their nature, as either pure mathematical studies of the shape and size of the Earth or studies of human geography. The monuments mentioned are provided with no real context, no explanations are given for them, and no historical relevance is attached to them. It seems probable that in most cases these scholars did not actually visit all the locations they mention. They were creating political/economic works that were based on other scholarly works, providing information in a very specific format about very specific phenomena. The landscape was viewed purely as an object on which towns and a few monuments were placed and in which crops were grown. It is not 'peopled' beyond the names occurring in folk traditions, which are given no personalities. The landscape was something to be measured and classified, divided up and managed. These scholars were describing the blank sheet onto which the values and culture of their own society were being inscribed.

One point of particular interest is the occurrence of a name for the Fayum lake and/or one of the canals: Aqna and Tenhamet/Benhamet. These names do not appear earlier in any form, and the current name of the lake—Birkat Qarun—never appears. Another issue is the total omission of any mention of the crocodile cults in the region. It seems likely that this aspect of the Fayum was deliberately overlooked as it was so overtly non-Muslim.

The medieval Islamic perception of the region was of course influenced by the intentions of the writers and their own need to familiarize and establish 'ownership' of the landscape by associating it with familiar characters from the Qur'an, placing the region firmly within the Islamic Empire/realm. The physical aspects of the landscape they recorded were all man-made elements placed upon the landscape: the irrigation (because it was responsible for productivity and therefore taxes) and some of the monuments, namely the Greco–Roman temples of the northern shores, as well as the dams on the eastern side of the region. The lake is only referred to occasionally as the lakes of Aqna and Tenhamet. There seems to be no acknowledgment of the existence of the lake in the majority of the accounts, and it is perhaps incredible to note that there are no tales or traditions specifically relating to the lake. Considering the focus on the lake in pharaonic sources, the ancient names for the region that overwhelmingly refer to the lake, and the apparent fascination with the lake held by Classical scholars, it is extraordinary that the medieval Islamic scholars paid so little attention to it. Any memories of the association of crocodiles with the region appear to have been totally forgotten, yet the stories that refer to the Fayum having been created to house the pharaoh's daughter and to the existence of fertile females and royal women in the region strongly hint at a latent memory of the presence of the royal 'harem' palace at Madinat al-Gurob. The perceptions found in these accounts reveal a long history of changing traditions and ideas confused with ancient cultural memories.

The earliest 'Western' studies of the medieval Islamic historical and geographical works were undertaken by (principally French) orientalists and philologists in the nineteenth century, primarily looking at the language itself: medieval Persian or Arabic. The works were valued for the insights they provided into the early Islamic state, medieval Islamic history, and medieval science, and for their contribution to Western understanding of the early Islamic faith. Certain genres became the focus of interest for specific groups of scholars, including mathematics, astrology, astronomy, geography, cartography, and history. Simultaneously, during the early to mid-nineteenth century, Egyptology as we understand it today became established. Egypt was more accessible to Europeans after the invasion of Napoleon in 1798, and during the late nineteenth century the Service des Antiquités was founded. There was initially interest in the value that some of the Arabic and Persian material had for Egyptologists. Maspero, the second head of the Antiquities Service, studied the French translation of the anonymous *Akhbar al-zaman (l'Abrégé des Merveilles)*,[3] acknowledging the value of the work for Egyptologists. Evidence of his wider knowledge of Islamic works is apparent in his noting that many passages were borrowed or copied from al-Mas'udi, Maqrizi, and Murtada. This interest was, however, only briefly held within Egyptology, and only rarely since Maspero have Egyptologists considered these texts. A summary of the few works that have considered medieval sources is presented by El Daly, and includes Penny Wilson and David Jeffreys, but the full list is not long.[4]

Early History (AD 642–Ninth Century)

After the death of the Prophet Muhammad his followers continued the jihad he had begun, eventually conquering a large empire covering Iran, Iraq, Syria, Palestine, Jordan, parts of India, Egypt, parts of northwest Africa, and Spain. The conquest of Egypt took place in AD 642 / AH 21, twenty-one years after the first pilgrimage of the Prophet, during the rule of the second caliph, 'Umar, led by 'Amr ibn al-'As. It is highly likely that the conquest of Egypt made very little difference to most native Egyptians and that the new Islamic influences only affected those living in Fustat (Cairo) at that time.

Around the same time, the authorized version of the Qur'an was first compiled, during the rule of the third caliph, 'Uthman, in AD 644.[5] Islamic historical writing was based on a tradition of inquiry developed by the Hadith scholars (Hadith are sayings of the Prophet) and their need to provide *isnads* (the chain of authority responsible for transmitting a speech from one person to the next). The earliest histories were accounts of the life of the Prophet. Two schools of writing existed, sometimes overlapping: those who adhered to *isnads* and written accounts, and those who included folkloric elements as well.[6] Accounts of Islamic conquests in different regions were motivated in part by juridical needs, namely establishing the laws and constitution of the new empire.[7]

One of the first regional accounts of the conquest is also the first known written account of Egypt by any Islamic scholar: the account of the conquest of Egypt, written by Ibn 'Abd al-Hakam in the mid- to late ninth century.

Ibn 'Abd al-Hakam (c.798–871)

Abu al-Qasim 'Abd al-Rahman ibn 'Abdullah ibn 'Abd al-Hakam is a well-known early Egyptian historian who was born in Fustat.[8] His work, *Futuh Misr* (The Conquest of Egypt), is the earliest surviving account of the Muslim conquest of Egypt, and he was among the earliest Arab historians compiling written accounts of the Islamic world.[9] The text is preserved in four manuscripts held in Paris (two manuscripts dating to 1190 and 1375), London (twelfth-century manuscript), and Leiden (dating to 1566). They all appear to derive from one specific copy made of his manuscript, created by the scribal teacher Ibn Qubayd.[10] The exact date of the original composition is unknown. Ibn 'Abd al-Hakam came from a family of legal scholars in Fustat.[11] His sources were oral—*rawis* (poets)—and writers such as Ibn Lahi'a and Ibn Bukayr (both Egyptian) whose works are unrecorded elsewhere, as well as his own father.[12] He used the same methods as the Hadith scholars, authenticating the tales he gathered by recording *isnads* (the chain of names of people from whom information has come).[13] This account of the conquest of Egypt is particularly significant because almost all later historians relied on it, rarely adding additional information.[14]

The manuscripts have never been fully translated into any one language. Charles Torrey edited the text of the London manuscript, providing an introduction in English in 1932, having previously translated the section on Egypt in 1901, which covers the events in Egypt and North Africa after the defeat of Alexandria, the principal seat of government in Egypt, by ʻAmr ibn al-ʻAs in AD 642. According to this account, following the conquest of Alexandria the next region of Egypt to be conquered was the Fayum. Ibn ʻAbd al-Hakam gave several different versions of these events. The first tells that for one year the region was unknown, until a man came and told ʻAmr of its existence, at which point he dispatched someone to search for it. After some time and a journey through al-Majaba (the great desert), "the cultivated fields of the Fayum burst on their view" and the region fell to the Muslims without resistance.[15] The second version records that Malik ibn Naʻima was exploring al-Majaba when he came across the cultivated fields of the Fayum. He returned to tell ʻAmr. The third story tells that the region was discovered by Rabiʻa ibn Hubaysh while he was traveling north to ʻAmr from Upper Egypt.[16]

Within *Futuh Misr* Ibn ʻAbd al-Hakam also discussed what could be termed a 'creation story' of the Fayum:[17]

> The story is of Joseph being under test when he got old (envious courtiers asked Pharaoh to test Joseph's ability). Joseph had to drain water in the Fayoum depression which was a swampy marsh land, first, before digging up a canal to bring Nile fresh water to irrigate it. He managed to do so in 70 days and when Pharaoh came to visit he was astonished at this vast achievement and said "*this is the work of a thousand days*" [18] (alf youm) so it was named al-Fayoum. Joseph asked Pharaoh to bring from each village in Egypt, a family to settle in Fayoum and build a new village this creating a number of villages equal to all the villages in Egypt. When each family finished building and settling their own new village, water was allocated to them, and the Fayum flourished.

This is, in essence, what the Ptolemaic irrigation engineers had done.

This legend about the Fayum is found again later in the history of al-Mas'udi, after which it is repeated in almost all accounts of Egypt. It is interesting that this tale or creation legend of Joseph seems to have existed in the very earliest written account of Egypt, an account based on local poets' stories and religious tradition. This first recorded description of the region highlights one notable aspect of the way in which the landscape of the region was perceived: that it is in some respect deemed to be hidden. The implication is that people had to actively search for the region, either by crossing the desert from the north or in one instance by traveling west from the Nile. This could be an indication that the Fayum was perceived to be somehow outside the accepted landscape of Egypt, outside the Nile Valley and the Delta. This seems hard to understand from a modern perspective, as the Cartesian view given to us in maps is so familiar that it is hard to conceive of a perception of landscape with no cartographic information available. The fact that one part of the account refers to entering from the east is important, as this is never reflected in later medieval Islamic views of the Fayum landscape. The view of the Fayum is always from the north.

This account was compiled by Ibn 'Abd al-Hakam primarily to aid the construction and confirmation of Islamic law. Although he is considered Egyptian, he would undoubtedly have had a very strong Arab/Islamic identity. His background in a family of legal scholars means that he would have been a part of the elite Muslim society of Fustat, and it is probable that he perceived himself as Muslim first and foremost, with his Egyptian identity coming second. The fact that the history, culture, and geography of Egypt were unknown to these scholars implies that a certain amount of psychological distance between the culture of this country and their own culture was unavoidable. They did not describe anything about Egypt as being 'known.' This particular story of the prophet Joseph in the Fayum would have felt familiar, but it does not exist in the Qur'an, so was accepted as a detail of history regarding this nation. Thus, the perception of the landscape of the Fayum from this earliest account is that it is 'different,' even to someone who grew up in Egypt. It is unfamiliar and needs explanation. It had to be discovered by the conquerors and brought under their control. The landscape was made familiar through the story of Joseph, setting it in a context that was appreciable by these Islamic scholars. The story provided an Islamic identity for this Fayum.

Although there is no description of the physical landscape in this account, other than a mention of the cultivated fields, the account shows that the Fayum was viewed as an entity separate from Egypt. It is an obvious assumption that the story grew in the Fayum among Coptic inhabitants, who found a way to adapt the local 'pagan' tradition, and that it was then passed on. The oral tradition—though rooted in the region and transmitted by the inhabitants who engaged with the landscape of the Fayum on a daily basis—was clearly based in the past. This was not a landscape they actually experienced; it was something imagined. This temporal distance probably provided a large measure of respectability to the accounts as they were transmitted.

The Early Abbasid Empire (Ninth–Tenth Centuries)

At the inception of the Abbasid Empire (750–969) in Egypt, the majority of the country was still Coptic Christian. Islam and Arab culture were largely confined socially to the ruling classes and regionally to the north in Fustat and Alexandria. Until 809 Egypt was ruled by the local Arab elite, but after the breakdown of the Islamic Empire, triggered by the death of Harun al-Rashid, Egypt was ruled by outsiders from Baghdad.[19] For many years at the beginning of the ninth century, the leadership of Egypt was in turmoil and the government of Egypt in disarray, with the local Arab leaders gradually losing power to Turkish military forces until the establishment of Ahmad ibn Tulun as ruler in 868.[20]

Despite the political uncertainties, during the Abbasid Empire there was a great flourishing of learning. Indeed, the early ninth century is considered by many to have been the height of scientific discovery and literary creativity in Islamic history. The seventh Abbasid caliph, al-Ma'mun (812–33), is usually thought to have been the instigator of this movement.[21] He is considered the most educated and knowledgeable of the Abbasid caliphs. He founded the Bayt al-Hikma (House of Wisdom) in Baghdad and actively encouraged the Mu'tazili point of view.[22] He is also rumored to have managed to break into the Great Pyramid at Giza—the tunnel via which tourists enter the chambers is still known as Ma'mun's Passage. During this period, in what has been termed the 'translation movement,' many (now lost) Greek works were translated into Arabic, the most important being the *Geography* and *Almagest* of Ptolemy. Greek geographical works, particularly mathematical geography and astronomy, had a major influence on the thinking of early Islamic geographers on many things, most particularly the measurements of the Earth. During the rule of al-Ma'mun a map was created that attracted great fame at the time. No copy of the map is preserved and very little is known about it, other than unclear descriptions of it by al-Mas'udi and al-Zuhri.[23] The earliest known geographic work is that of al-Khwarizmi. While this work does not include a reference to the Fayum, it was the foundation of all later works and therefore is important to consider.

Khwarizmi (b. before 800, d. after 850)

Abu Ja'far Muhammad ibn Musa al-Khwarizmi is the earliest known author of a work in the genre in which most books were titled *Kitab surat al-ard* (Book of the Picture of the Earth). They consisted of lists of placenames and their locations with basic descriptions. Little is known of his biography, but it is thought that he worked at the court of al-Ma'mun in Baghdad as an astronomer, and at the Bayt al-Hikma. He also wrote many important mathematical and astronomical works which were translated into Latin during the twelfth century. The availability of these major texts in Latin triggered the 'birth' of European algebra.[24]

His geographical work—*Kitab surat al-ard*—is generally considered to be a translation/revision of the *Geography* of Ptolemy into Arabic.[25] Like the *Geography*, the work consists primarily of tables of placenames and major topographical features, such as rivers and mountains, with coordinates. It is thought to have been written in about 830,[26] and is now preserved in one (incomplete) copy dating to 1037 compiled in Baghdad, held currently in Strasbourg, the manuscript having been discovered in the nineteenth century in Cairo.[27] Khwarizmi's work is thought to have been written with a cartographic output in mind and the manuscript does include copies of four maps, but these are all deemed to be additions by the eleventh-century copyist.[28] However, despite probably not having been created by Khwarizmi, the maps are considered to be the oldest preserved Islamic maps.[29] The map of the Nile in this manuscript does not include the Fayum at all, and his account does not mention the Fayum, which is interesting given the fact that the Fayum does appear in the *Geography* of Ptolemy.

The 'Iraqi' School of Geography (Ninth–Tenth Centuries)

Following on from this first written geography of the Islamic Empire, a distinctive 'school' of scholars emerged in the mid-ninth century known as the Iraqi school, Iranian school, or Classical school. The scientific aspect of geography developed into its own genre, and from that a more 'human' geography developed, which combined geography with history and economics.[30] Much of the motivation for the new genre came from a need to record information about different regions in order to efficiently run the government of the expanding empire.[31] During the ninth century the Abbasid Empire was weakened by a civil war following the death of Harun al-Rashid (809), which allowed the local governor Ahmad ibn Tulun to form a breakaway Islamic state in Egypt in 868.[32] The short-lived Tulunid period (868–905) was largely peaceful. Ibn Tulun constructed a new city next to Fustat, including a mosque that is still preserved in its entirety—the oldest mosque standing in Cairo today. The era ended with the occupation of Egypt by an Abbasid army in 905.[33] A new form of literature developed, known now as *adab*. The real meaning and scope of *adab* is hard to define, but in historical and geographical works it generally refers to an overtly literary approach to writing, and a focus on 'man,' his humanity, and the environment in which he lives.[34] The members of the Iraqi school of geography included Ibn Khurradadhbih, al-Ya'qubi, al-Mas'udi, al-Hamadani, Ibn Rusta, and Qudama, not all of whom included the Fayum in their accounts.

Ibn Khurradadhbih (c.820–c.912)

Abu al-Qasim 'Ubayd Allah ibn 'Abdullah ibn Khurradadhbih was a well-educated member of a well-to-do family. A member of the inner circle of the Abbasid caliph al-Mu'tamid, he was chief of postal routes and intelligence in Baghdad, a job that entailed much travel. According to al-Muqaddasi he was also a vizier and personal friend of the caliph.[35] Ibn Khurradadhbih's *Kitab al-masalik wa-l-mamalik* (The Book of Routes and Provinces) is not completely preserved, but it is thought that the first edition was written in 846–47 (pre-Tulunid), the second in 885–86 (post-Tulunid).[36] Two copies of the same edition of this work are held in the Bodleian Library (dated 1232) and Constantinople (undated) and were translated from Persian into French and published by Charles Barbier de Meynard in 1865. This work is considered the earliest example of true Islamic literary geography, not simply a translation of Ptolemy. It was used a great deal by later scholars. For this reason Ibn Khurradadhbih is considered the 'father' of the genre.[37] Other members of the Iraqi school wrote works with the same title and format. The work is a fusion of information from Ptolemy's *Geography* and (Persian) Islamic traditions.[38] It takes the form of lists of postal and pilgrimage routes through the Islamic

Empire and a little beyond.[39] The little we have of Ibn Khurradadhbih's biography is known to us primarily through al-Mas'udi.[40] Ibn Khurradadhbih is believed to have written up to eight texts on varied subjects, including cookery and music, of which only three survive.[41]

Alongside the placenames and itineraries in the book are some anecdotal notes, poetry, and historical information. It is the earliest preserved Islamic geographic text to mention so many different regions of Egypt. Ibn Khurradadhbih mentions both the Fayum and Ahnas (*nn-nsw*/Herakleopolis Magna/Ihnasya al-Madina).[42] Although he provides no information about the landscape of the Fayum, the work is a crucial link in the chain of information about the region. While influenced by al-Khwarizmi and the Greek tradition, Ibn Khurradadhbih adopted a different method of dividing the world, following his 'native' Persian tradition. His work could be deemed more overtly political and economic, as he was listing routes taken by merchants around the Islamic Empire. Interestingly, he did not list the produce of the regions but rather the 'marvels,' in a manner that could be considered reminiscent of the Greco–Roman tradition of listing the marvels of a nation. Madinat al-Fayum receives a listing, but the region is not specifically mentioned. No 'marvels' are mentioned for any city outside Fustat or Alexandria. It seems likely that the information Ibn Khurradadhbih included was gathered by asking locals about towns in Egypt. This is the first mention of the Fayum in any 'geographical' work, and the text formed the basis for many works both in this genre and others.

Al-Ya'qubi (d. c.905)

Unlike other members of the Iraqi school, Abu al-'Abbas Ahmad ibn Ja'far ibn Wahb ibn Wadih al-Ya'qubi is known to have been part-Egyptian, rather than Persian. His great-grandfather was the governor of Egypt during the reign of the Abbasid caliph al-Mahdi in 779.[43] Ya'qubi lived most of his life in Iran and Iraq but settled in Egypt soon after 870 and died there.[44] He wrote several books, including *Tarikh*, a treatise on history, and *Kitab al-buldan* (Book of the Countries), of which only part survives.[45] He completed *Kitab al-buldan* while living in Egypt in 891, during the reign of the Abbasid caliph al-Mu'tamid. The work is considered to be a geography based partly on knowledge he gained while working in administration.[46] *Kitab al-buldan* was translated and published in 1937 by Gaston Wiet based on editions of the Arabic text published by Michael Jan de Goeje (in 1860) and Gautier Juynboll (in 1892).[47]

This work is thought to have been written for the service of the Abbasid state. It provides a list of countries and their capitals, economy, and condition for the use of the government.[48] As this work was written with an economic and political intent, *Kitab al-buldan* is furnished with considerably more information about the different towns and regions than the surviving text of Ibn Khurradadhbih, particularly regarding the produce and products of the different countries. Ya'qubi traveled a lot, gathering historical information assiduously, and states that whenever he met a man from a distant country he questioned him about the name of the leader, the capital, the agriculture, the people, and the religion and verified this with other accounts where possible.[49] He also noted the Islamic conqueror, the caliphs, methods of taxation, names of capitals, the regions dependent on each town, distances from one country to another, and descriptions of mountains, plains, watercourses, and the climate.

In his list of locations in Upper Egypt, unlike Ibn Khurradadhbih, Ya'qubi includes at least one comment about most places. He mentioned Memphis as being the ruins of the ancient capital, residence of the pharaohs, and that the Fayum region was celebrated for its abundant prosperity, corn, and linen.[50] The work represents a development in Islamic geography. Ya'qubi built on the work of his predecessor, taking the format of the lists of towns and locations and supplementing it with additional information. He seems to have been far more diligent about collecting information than Ibn Khurradadhbih, thus his work is far richer in detail. This is the earliest Islamic record of the fertile and abundant Fayum landscape, and because the work of Ya'qubi was utilized a great deal, the region continued to be described in these terms by many later scholars.

Al-Mas'udi (c.893–956)

Abu'l-Hasan 'Ali ibn al-Husayn al-Mas'udi wrote the first edition of the historical/geographical work *Kitab muruj al-dhahab wa ma'adin al-jawahir* (Book of Meadows of Gold and Mines of Gems)[51] in 943 while living in Egypt.[52] The work is an abridged version (and the only surviving edition) of his book *Kitab akhbar al-zaman wa-man abadahu al-hadathan min al-umam al-madiya wa-l-ajyal al-khaliya wa-l-mamalik al-dathira* (Book of the History of Ages and of the Ravages which Time Has Wrought upon Past Nations, Ancient Generations, and Desolate Kingdoms).[53] He revised *Kitab muruj* in 947 and then just before his death in Fustat in October 956.[54]

Al-Mas'udi was born in Baghdad and his family was able to trace their origins to a well-known companion of the Prophet Muhammad—Ibn Mas'ud.[55] He was a prolific writer but only *Kitab muruj* and *Kitab al-tanbih wa-l-ishraf* (composed 955–56) survive.[56] The earliest version of *Kitab muruj* that does survive is preserved in a manuscript dating to 1283,[57] which was translated in its entirety into French in 1861–77 by de Meynard (*Les Prairies d'Or*—updated by Pellat in 1962–65), having been partially translated first into English by Sprenger in 1841. The book is a historical work, which does include geographical information, most of which he appears to have personally verified—not relying on other people's accounts.[58] *Al-Tanbih* is thought to have been the last work composed by al-Mas'udi, and is essentially an updated and corrected abridged review of all his earlier works.[59]

Al-Mas'udi was apparently not particularly well respected by his contemporaries. He was aware of this, but made it clear in his writing that he believed they were jealous of his knowledge.[60] In modern scholarship he is well regarded as an exponent of human geography, and much has been written about his travels and works.[61] His is considered to be both the best and the last of the works of the Iraqi school of geographers, and he is viewed by some as one of the greatest travelers of his time, a very descriptive writer and highly reflective throughout.[62] Like Ya'qubi, but to a far greater extent, his style can be classified as *adab*—as noted above, a form of writing regarded for its literary qualities as well as its content, and intended to entertain the reader—aspects of which are apparent in his work.[63] The work differs in many ways from that of the earlier Iraqi school and, in fact, should probably not be classified as part of any specific genre or school. It stands alone in style and content, and represents a major development in Islamic geographical/historical writing.

Al-Mas'udi studied the *Geography* of Ptolemy, including the presentation of the material by Khwarizmi, and works by earlier members of the Iraqi school, especially Ibn Khurradadhbih, but also Farghani, and Battani.[64] He was aware of the Ma'mun map and the Balkhi school of geographers, but he seems not to have drawn on their ideas at all.[65] He was heavily influenced by works of Greek and Islamic philosophers, such as Aristotle, al-Jahiz, and al-Kindi, as well as Islamic historians such as Ibn 'Abd al-Hakam.[66] However, al-Mas'udi was explicit in his belief that his predecessors were not always right.[67] This may well be a reflection of the fact that he was writing during a time of controversy/revolution ('ancients' versus 'moderns') in historical writing.[68] While he gathered much of the information for his writings by studying other scholars, he then criticized their works, attempting to back up his comments and correct their errors with information gathered during his extensive travels. This approach of gathering first-hand knowledge was clearly important to him.[69] Al-Mas'udi's work reflects, and was heavily influenced by, his theological and political viewpoints, and it is generally thought that he favored the Mu'tazili spirit of enquiry. This belief was fundamental to his work, and the idea that the physical nature of land—environment, ecology, landscape—affected all aspects of life, shaping people both physically and culturally, is apparent in his approach to the landscape.

Although Egypt (and the Islamic Empire) was politically unstable due to the growing strength of the Fatimids,[70] al-Mas'udi's work is clearly a part of the tenth century flourishing of the arts and sciences. The influences on al-Mas'udi were considerably different to the influences on any of the earlier geographers/historians. His work sits far apart from that of his predecessors both in content and style. It also sits far apart from that of his contemporaries; as a historian he cannot really be classified as a member of either the Iraqi school or the Balkhi school. He spent a considerable amount of time in Egypt and studied a large variety of earlier written works in different genres. His theological beliefs underpinned his approach to enquiry and study, and as a result he was inquisitive and extremely thorough. Most important, his approach to the landscape was holistic. The fact that his beliefs drew him to see the landscape as having great influence on people and society means that his landscapes are exceptionally vivid, rich, and carefully considered. His conception of the human–land relationship was critical to his understanding of culture and society.

In *Kitab muruj* it is Chapter Thirty-one that refers to the history of Egypt, the Nile, the 'curiosities,' the history of its kings, and other details, while Chapter Thirty-two covers Alexandria and Chapter Thirty-three the Sudan. Because al-Mas'udi lived in Egypt for a while, it is thought that he gained most of his knowledge about the country via oral tradition from Egyptians,[71] rather than simply relying on other scholars' accounts, although he clearly consulted those accounts as well. Overall, the richness of his work has to be attributed to the combination of his beliefs, extensive research, and easy access to local knowledge. Al-Mas'udi begins by introducing mentions of Egypt in the Qur'an—stories about Joseph and Moses.[72] He describes the flooding of the Nile Valley[73] and briefly outlines some aspects of human geography as told by a 'sage.'[74] This is followed by a discussion of the differing beliefs regarding the source of the Nile, and the history and locations of Nilometers and 'gardens' along the banks of the river.[75]

The Fayum and 'al-Menha' canal (clearly placed in the Fayum in this account) are included among the seven major canals of Egypt.[76] They were, he says, cut by Joseph, son of Jacob, on the orders of Pharaoh al-Rayyan ibn al-Walid. This occurred because the pharaoh was satisfied with Joseph's explanation of his dream of cows and grains and entrusted him with administrative offices. God caused Joseph to ask to be placed at the head of the stores of Egypt, as he was wise and scientific (al-Mas'udi notes that there was some disagreement among scholars regarding the reasons why the 'infidel' pharaoh would follow the instructions of Joseph).[77] Al-Mas'udi records that the canals in the elevated areas were named *matati* by the inhabitants, and that Joseph created the region in a basin and funneled the water from Upper Egypt. The waters surrounded the region on almost all sides, creating an island, the full details of which, he says, could be found in another work. Al-Mas'udi concludes by noting that the origin of the name of the region was 'one thousand days'—alf youm (then there is a lacuna in the text).[78]

Part of the text relates a story about how in 873 Ibn Tulun (the ruler of Egypt) heard of a Copt aged 130 years living in Upper Egypt who was a great scholar and knew much about the history of Egypt. Ibn Tulun summoned him and questioned him.[79] Tarif Khalidi (1975) considers this 'ancient Copt' story to be a literary device intended to highlight the great temporal and cultural distance between contemporary Egypt and ancient Egypt,[80] but there is nothing to suggest that al-Mas'udi in any way questioned the account. His acceptance of facts that he was unable to corroborate is not totally out of character: where he had no conflicting reports and no reason to question information, he accepted it with little question.

The ancient Copt told a story of how the lake of Tinnis and Damietta used to be unique in Egypt because they had the most fertile soil. They were covered in gardens, palm trees, vineyards, cultivation, and trees. The only other similar place was the Fayum, which was rich and abundant in an infinite variety of fruits and aromatic plants.[81] The Copt and Ibn Tulun discussed the Fayum, al-Menha, and the dam of Lahun, and the Copt entered into a lengthy account about the Fayum. He stated that a young girl had settled in the region, which then, as a result, became cultivated. The lock of Lahun did not exist; the water entered the region at the time of the Nile flood via al-Menha canal near Damuna. It was said that the lock was constructed much later, by Joseph under the reign of Pharaoh al-'Aziz. Joseph was also responsible for the system of canals and irrigation in the region. He described the bridge of 'Yusufi,' as well as a column found in the center of the region. This column was considered one of the marvels of the world, tall, with very deep foundations. On several occasions people tried to find its base but failed because of the water level.[82] He then discussed the lock of Lahun, the water falling into al-Menha from it, and the openings in the dam, some of which had water flowing through them and some of which were no longer visible. The base of the dam was in a basin between al-Qubbatayn and Lahun, near the 'steps.' The ancient Copt stated that the water entering the region was controlled by the lock, and that the dam had been carefully built to control the quantity of water needed for the region. He said that the lock of Lahun was a remarkable building, which had survived the ravages of time, and that many people in the region believed that Joseph was responsible for its construction. He concluded by saying that the many rulers of the country had been attracted by the celebrity of the dam and always visited it.[83]

While al-Mas'udi provided a detailed account of the landscape of Egypt based on both experience and knowledge gleaned from other works, his section on the Fayum reveals a very temporalized perception of the landscape. The history of Joseph and the 'ancient Copt' story legitimize his account by framing it with respected and trusted sources. There is also the fact that he places the telling of this story in the past, during the reign of Ibn Tulun. The description of the Fayum in the account cannot be considered contemporary with the writing of the account. Al-Mas'udi recounts what the landscape was once like, in the past—not the distant past, but before living memory. He also provides a different opening to the creation story, involving a young girl. This story clearly places the creation of the region before Joseph, as Joseph comes along later to build the dam at Lahun and the irrigation canals. Thus, the root of this creation appears to be neither Qur'anic nor Biblical and might even perhaps originate in the Fayum creation theology, in which the Fayum is the embodiment of the Mother Goddess. In this version of events, the Fayum is actually, therefore, less divine than it is in the earlier version of the story that he provides at the beginning of his account of the region. It is only certain aspects (principally the lock/dam at Lahun) that were created by the prophet; he had no part in the clearance or initial regeneration of the fertility/productivity of the Fayum.

Al-Mas'udi mentions the event found in both the Qur'an and the Bible that led to Joseph becoming a leader in Egypt: the dream interpretation (Qur'an Sura 12:43–56 and Bible, 41:1–41). The details of the creation activities are more standard, following the account of Ibn 'Abd al-Hakam, but the description of what the landscape looked like includes an interesting detail: the Fayum (probably referring to the central town) was like an island, surrounded on all sides by water. This may be an indication that al-Mas'udi visited Madinat al-Fayum during the inundation and had first-hand experience of what the Fayum landscape looked like when it was flooded. But it also may be something he was told.

Al-Mas'udi presents more than one Fayum landscape. He was able to assimilate the 'real' physical geography into the 'imagined' geography of religious tradition. The physical landscape of the region is a part of history, not just a platform on which events occur. It is imbued with religious meaning. Yet it is not truly divine, as the region as a whole was created through the presence of the female figure. It was the intervention of the prophet Joseph, guided by God, which then led to the development of the irrigation. This landscape is an example of how humans, with the assistance of divine forces, can overcome nature and reshape the landscape for the benefit of mankind, making it fertile and productive—a common theme in ancient Egyptian religion. The fact that al-Mas'udi also recorded a story about the presence of a female figure in the Fayum is highly significant, as it hints at the possibility that there was a memory in the region of both the ancient Egyptian religious tradition and the 'harem' palace town of Gurob. There is a distinct difference between this account, in which the region became fertile due to the presence of the girl and then Joseph created the irrigation, and the accounts that place Joseph at the center of the story as the creator of the fertile landscape.

Akhbar al-zaman (Chronicles of Time)

It is generally agreed that this anonymous historical work, frequently attributed to al-Mas'udi, but also attributed to Ibn Wasif Shah[84] was written in the tenth century.[85] The work was translated and published by Bernard Carra de Vaux in 1898 as *l'Abrégé des Merveilles* (reprinted 1984). It has two parts: the first consists of accounts of creation and the ancient history of Biblical characters such as Adam and Noah, while the second is dedicated to the history of ancient Egypt. The second part covers priests of Egypt, kings before the Flood, kings after the Flood, the pharaoh of Abraham, the

Amalécite dynasty (Hyksos), the pharaoh of Joseph, and the pharaoh of Moses.[86] A copy of the text is preserved in several manuscripts in the Bibliothéque Nationale of Paris, the oldest of which dates to 1477. This work was used later by Maqrizi, who borrowed entire passages.[87]

Chapter Ten of this work is dedicated to the pharaoh of Joseph, al-Walid, and his son al-Rayyan, known to the Copts as Nehrâous.[88] The Fayum story is told late in the chapter, with the author reporting that Joseph 'desiccated' the Fayum for the daughter of the king.[89] In this version of the story it is the age and ability of the pharaoh that is questioned, not Joseph. In later versions Joseph is the one being questioned. Joseph tells the pharaoh of the doubts of his people, and Pharaoh Nehrâous is unconcerned but tells Joseph that he wishes to give a certain region to his daughter, a region that is currently ponds and marshes. He wants to divert the water and make the country habitable and fertile, and sets Joseph the task of finding the best way to achieve this. Joseph goes to the region and drives out the waters, regulating the watercourses, filling the depressions, and transforming the land that becomes known as the Fayum, achieving the task in a very short space of time.[90] Nehrâous is also credited with the cutting of the Menha canal and the construction of Lahun (no details are given).[91]

The Fayum in this account is clearly placed in the possession of the pharaoh's daughter, and is recreated for her by Joseph at the will of the pharaoh. The story maintains Joseph as the principal character of the creation, and retains the idea of the connection to royal women. The perception here is that the Fayum was created under orders from a pharaoh by a prophet and therefore is part of the Qur'anic/Biblical landscape of Egypt. It was not created for or populated by the people of Egypt (as it is in the account of Ibn 'Abd al-Hakam), but was created for the sole use of the daughter of the pharaoh. This significantly alters the resulting perception of the region. The landscape was inhabited by one royal woman rather than ordinary Egyptians; it is a landscape that is privately owned, and the implication is perhaps that it is not part of the landscape of Egypt but separate and apart.

This work describes only the creation of the Fayum, which of course cannot have been experienced by the author or any inhabitant of the region. The (contemporary) rich fertility of the region is perceived to be a result of the imagined semidivine creation, but the details of how Joseph drained the region clearly reflect some knowledge of the Ptolemaic transformation of the Fayum landscape. The landscape is imbued with meaning, and there are strong undertones of the fertility having a distinctly female nature. The landscape is also perceived to be somehow apart from Egypt, not created in the same way or by the same hands, or for the same people. Traditions and events are intertwined here, with the Fayum being the embodiment of a female figure, the region being 'man-made' by a divine figure, and the canals being cut to drain the waters and create agricultural and habitable land. This perception is a true palimpsest of ideas about this landscape.

The Balkhi School of Geography (Tenth Century)

In 909 the Fatimids started to seize control of the Islamic Empire, and by 969 the rulers of Egypt had ceded to them.[92] A new garrison town was founded northeast of Fustat, known as al-Qahira, al-Azhar mosque was built, and Egypt became the ruling seat of the Fatimid Empire, although most of the population of Egypt outside Cairo and Alexandria was still Coptic. During this period, Egypt's prosperity grew as it became a crossroads of international trade and a key source of gold and wool, cotton, and linen fabrics through the Near East and into Europe. The caliphs in Egypt gained some supremacy over those in Baghdad, and Egypt now 'fed' the holy cities.[93]

During the transitional period from Abbasid to Fatimid rule, a new school of geographers emerged. These scholars were far more concerned with cartography than the members of the Iraqi school, and in general their works contain less historical information. The founder of the 'school' was Abu Zayd Ahmad ibn Sahl al-Balkhi (850–934), from Balkh in Khurasan, northeast Iran, on whose (now lost) work these scholars based their own works. Al-Balkhi's *Taqwim al-buldan* (or *Suwar al-aqalim*) is thought to have been a text accompanying twenty-one maps covering the tenth-century Islamic (Abbasid) Empire.[94] Balkhi himself was a student of the philosopher al-Kindi, and although early in his life he was liberal and connected to the Mu'tazila, he seems to have gone against this and sought to react against the liberal thinking of his teacher al-Kindi and the Iraqi school of geography. Later in life he stuck firmly to his more orthodox beliefs, writing several highly regarded books on religious subjects. His geography had clear religious undertones.[95] He wrote the *Taqwim* in about 920, and the distinguishing features of the work seem to be its restriction to the Islamic world and the use of a new system of dividing the world, following neither the Persian nor the Ptolemaic traditions.[96]

The texts of the Balkhi school are often difficult to distinguish from each other, particularly as the preserved manuscripts do not always contain the name of the original author, and sometimes even have the wrong name on them.[97] The sets of maps are consistent: all depict the same twenty regions.[98] If in different styles, the most consistent is the depiction of the Persian provinces.[99] The origin of the maps may lie in the postal routes found earlier in the *Masalik wa-l-mamalik* texts of geographers such as Ibn Khurradadhbih. Istakhri's work has this same name. These geographers seem unconcerned by any of the preoccupations with true geographic or mathematical projections of other contemporary Islamic scholars.[100] The maps, it seems, are simply a way of visually representing the lands and routes they then describe.

The works of the Balkhi school have none of the poetic nature of the *adab* genre, but are furnished with more geographical detail than the earliest works of Ibn Khurradadhbih or al-Khwarizmi—most notably the cartographic element. The texts are limited to the places marked on the maps and lack the 'eyewitness account' feel. It is worth noting that at least two of these scholars are thought to have been closely allied with the rising Fatimid powers.

Al-Istakhri (d. c.961)

Little is known about the life of this important member of the Balkhi geographic school, Abu Ishaq Ibrahim ibn Muhammad al-Farisi al-Istakhri, sometimes known as al-Farisi.[101] The one well-known fact is that he did at some point meet Ibn Hawkal.[102] It is thought that he came from Persia, was Sunni, and may have worked in some kind of administrative/financial capacity for the rulers of Persia.[103] Istakhri's text *Kitab al-masalik wa-l-mamalik* (The Book of Routes and Provinces) is believed by most scholars to be a revised edition of the (now lost) text of the same name by al-Balkhi.[104] There are thirty-four different copies of this text, primarily in Persian, the oldest preserved copy being a manuscript dating to 1173 that was published in 1839 and translated into German in 1845 (Mordtmann *Das Buch der Länder*). The date of the original creation of the text is thought to be c.930–50.[105] Study of the various manuscripts has led scholars to the conclusion that there were two editions of the text, with slightly different maps. The later text is considered to be more complete and seems more refined.[106] His work is based on a combination of personal experience and second-hand accounts,[107] but he did not travel to Egypt, thus his information on the Fayum is all second-hand.

Egypt, in the text translated by Andreas Mordtmann (1845), is described as covering the area between the Red Sea and the desert behind the oases, from the Mediterranean Sea to Nubia. In Egypt al-Istakhri lists thirty-four locations. He describes Fustat, including the two principal mosques built by 'Amr ibn al-'As and Ibn Tulun. He briefly describes the Nile flood and notes that the Fayum was the only place in Egypt that had an alternative source of water. He refers to the Joseph story, stating that it was said that Joseph had a canal dug there and that it was lined with stones and called Lahun. His description includes some details that are clearly myth, such as stories about turtles shaped like dolphins that gave people nightmares.[108]

Given the lack of written description of the region in this account, it seems appropriate to turn to an analysis of the maps. Istakhri himself certainly placed emphasis on maps, and the cartographic element of this entire group of works is considered to be essential.[109] It seems likely that the cartographic activities of these scholars were linked to their politics. If they were Fatimid agents, it is quite possible that the maps were tools of the growing new power. The significant differences between their works and those of their contemporaries in the Iraqi school may also be easily explained. Sayyid Maqbul Ahmad considers that the developments were a conscious move away from mapping the known world toward overtly Islamic mapping of just the Islamic Empire.[110] It is possible that these Fatimid sympathizers were mapping what they hoped would become Fatimid territory. Johannes Henrik Kramers suggests that the difference derives from the nationality of the writers, and that they took their format from earlier Iranian maps or postal lists from Sassanid times.[111] Another factor that probably influenced the Iranian focus of the works is that both Balkhi and Istakhri were patronized by the Samanid rulers of Persia.[112]

These scholars had no interest in the scientific side of cartography, as the maps are not meant to be accurate representations of countries, pay no attention to projections, and do not conform to any scale. While they are considered to be the focus of the work, with the text being supplementary, the maps lost importance in later works. In the work of Ibn Hawkal, there is no doubt that the maps play a secondary role to the text. The maps are geometric images, showing the principal locations and their relationship to major geographical phenomena, such as rivers. The listings and cartographic elements represent an administrative need to record and manage a region. The accompanying description provides the backdrop, the landscape onto which man has placed himself. The creation legend of Joseph is presented as such—"it is said that Joseph dug a canal there"—and does not imply that this is the reality of the landscape. The account quite clearly distinguishes two aspects of the landscape. The temporally distant, imagined, 'created' landscape is the setting in which the reality of the experienced landscape is placed. The landscape that can be engaged with and experienced is there to be recorded and mapped and brought into the controlled, known, and familiar environment.

Ibn Hawkal (d. 988)

Abu al-Qasim Muhammad ibn Hawkal traveled a great deal—so much in fact that it is believed that he must have worked as either a merchant or a missionary. He began thirty years of travel in 943, passing through Egypt in 955. He was a Fatimid sympathizer and a member of the 'Balkhi School' of geographers, and wrote three editions of a book entitled *Kitab surat al-ard* or *Kitab al-masalik wa-l-mamalik* in 967, 977, and 988.[113] It is clear from the dedications that the three editions were written for different patrons.[114] His work closely resembles that of al-Istakhri—whether it is considered to be a revision of his text or plagiarism is a matter of debate—but it is known that he did meet al-Istakhri, and was requested by him to revise some maps.[115]

It is sometimes considered that Ibn Hawkal was the first of the Balkhi school to create a complete geographical text rather than simply a commentary on the set of maps.[116] Indeed, his text is far more extensive than that of al-Istakhri, and although it is known that he did create maps himself it seems that the descriptions took precedence.[117] It is known that he studied the works of al-Jayhani (now lost), Ibn Khurradadhbih, and Qudama, as well as the *Geography* of Ptolemy, and he also referred to Ibn 'Abd al-Hakam.[118] His work was utilized by many later scholars, including the anonymous author of *Hudud al-'alam*, Muqaddasi, Yaqut, Abu al-Fida, and Maqrizi.[119]

The text is preserved in nine manuscripts, the oldest of which is also one of the oldest preserved manuscripts of any of the Islamic geographers or historians. The document, held in Istanbul and dated to 1086, is a copy of the first edition of his work dated to 973, with almost complete text and all twenty-one maps.[120] There are three recognized 'editions' of the Ibn Hawkal account: Ibn Hawkal I, II, and III. Ibn Hawkal II has the most complete text but no maps, and Ibn Hawkal III has the most complete set of maps.[121] The manuscripts of Ibn Hawkal II are held in Leiden and Oxford.[122] Most transcribed editions and translations are based on these manuscripts. The Oxford manuscript has no date, while the Leiden copy dates to 1325.[123] Ibn Hawkal III contains two different versions of the map of Egypt, the second of which bears a striking resemblance to the map found in the manuscript of Ibn Khurradadhbih.

Several of Ibn Hawkal's regional maps show development from those of al-Istakhri: Egypt is represented in far greater detail. The two versions of his map of Egypt (in I and III) also differ from each other: the third edition map is more angular and perhaps less detailed and informative. Unlike al-Istakhri, Ibn Hawkal represents the Delta in great detail, not simply a semicircle containing the islands of Tinnis and Damietta but a network of rivers/canals. The Fayum is present, represented by a river channel running in a semicircle from Ashmunayn to just south of Fustat, and a river running off this, west, to a circular 'lake' surrounded by a mountain chain to the west and north. It is an accurate, if geometric, representation of the region. This work was translated into French in 1925 by Kramers and Wiet from the Ibn Hawkal II text, with a few additions from the manuscript of Ibn Hawkal III, which, unlike the second edition, contains maps (reproduced in the translation).

After a description of the maps and lists of the locations in them, Ibn Hawkal describes Egypt as a land that had great revenues in its ancient past but in recent times became less productive. He discusses the Fayum in a section covering aspects of cultivation and irrigation, stating that the town of Fayum, in the region of the same name, was the only town in Egypt not affected by the rising of the Nile. The town of Fayum was divided into two areas, and it was said that the prophet Joseph created a course for a canal along which the Nile waters could constantly run into the region, consolidating it with stones and naming it Lahun.[124] Ibn Hawkal mentions the Fayum again later in the text, noting that there were many large towns there that were renowned for their weaving.[125] He states that the Fayum was dependent on the canal of Lahun and that the town had many advantages. They grew many fruits and other products and the air was not bad, although the town did not offer any comfort to visitors. The principal product was rice. Around the outside of the region were beautiful antique monuments. The region had the same name as its administrative center. What follows seems to be the first reference to a monument that is also referred to in the works of al-Idrisi and al-Maqrizi: a 'distantly ancient' large wall enclosing the region and all the towns in it, named the 'Wall of the Old Woman,' which Ibn Hawkal notes was (in the tenth century) almost entirely engulfed by sands.[126] One particular point of interest here is that he 'notes' the large wall and is the first to make any mention of ancient monuments around the region, which suggests that he did in fact visit the region.

Not only did Ibn Hawkal map the Delta in detail, he also included the Bahr Yusuf. In both versions of the map he depicts the loop of river from Ashmunayn to Atfih and the Bahr Yusuf is marked, but unnamed, coming off the loop at Lahun. Adjacent to the bulb at the end of the river—presumably the lake—is written: "Here is the Lake of Aqna and Tenhamet, it has a length of 2 days, in the middle of the mountains and the yellow sand. During the winter, one can see birds in numbers not found anywhere else."[127]

The development from the cartography of al-Istakhri to that of Ibn Hawkal is extraordinary, and the detail in which Egypt is depicted is remarkable. The lake, named the lake of Aqna and Tenhamet, is not mentioned in any account prior to this one, and it is impossible to know from where the name derives. Even if this map is from a much later copy of the text (a manuscript dating to 1445), it is still possibly the earliest map of the region, and it provides the medieval names given to the Fayum lake(s), which actually never appear in other Islamic historical accounts of the region. The lack of any overt descriptions of the fertility of the region and the inclusion of descriptions of monuments indicate that this account presents a more personal experience of the landscape of the Fayum. Ibn Hawkal does mention the legends of the prophet Joseph with regard to the creation of the main canal and the dam at Lahun, but that story is clearly derived directly from the account of al-Istakhri and the element of the young/royal girl is missing. The only mention of women in the stories is in relation to the ancient wall he claims to have seen: the 'Wall of the Old Woman.' Even though he discusses the monuments, he does not then imbue the landscape with any sense of history or antiquity.

Al-Muqaddasi (c.945–1000)

Shams al-Din Abu 'Abdallah Muhammad ibn Ahmad ibn Abi Bakr al-Banna' al-Muqaddasi is known to Islamic scholars as al-Bashshari, and as 'the man from Jerusalem.'[128] He was born in Jerusalem to a family of architects, and his paternal grandfather worked for Ibn Tulun. He lived an itinerant life working as a traveling merchant and may, like Ibn Hawkal, have been an agent of the Fatimid rulers of Egypt. Two editions of his work *Ahsan al-taqasim* are preserved in four manuscripts, two of which are very recent (nineteenth-century) copies and two of which date to the thirteenth and fifteenth centuries. The two editions were written for two different patrons, the Samanids in 985 and the Fatimids of Egypt in 988.[129]

Muqaddasi's work is considered the culmination of the Balkhi school geographies, as it is more structured and methodical than that of his predecessors and possibly heavily influenced by his own experiences of travel. Netton states that Muqaddasi's work originally contained no maps, but the existing copies of the text do contain copies of al-Istakhri maps.[130] However, in the translation of the surviving thirteenth-century copy of the 985 version of *Ahsan al-taqasim*, the text states that "the maps in which we have portrayed the countries" were the result of studying other maps. In the section about Egypt, it states: "Herewith is an outline and representation of it."[131] Gerald Tibbetts concludes that Muqaddasi's maps were considerably less important than the text and that he certainly based his maps on those of al-Istakhri, with some edits. The maps are generally less detailed, particularly those of Persian provinces and the Mediterranean.[132]

From the outset Muqaddasi makes it clear that his work is a deliberate attempt to preserve his own name, and that he considers the existing accounts of the regions of Islam to be deficient. He states that he searched extensively for similar works in many libraries and collections and that the only works he found to study were those of al-Jayhani, al-Balkhi, and al-Hamadani, as well as al-Jahiz and Ibn Khurradadhbih,[133] although it is likely that the version of al-Balkhi he saw was the revision by al-Istakhri.[134] He consciously tried to be as original as possible, avoiding plagiarism, and his account does have a notably different style to those of his predecessors.

His description of Egypt begins with a brief introduction on the importance of Egypt within Islam, mentioning Joseph, Moses, and the escape of Mary to Egypt with Jesus. He notes only towns with mosques, ignoring the many villages in the countryside, as they were inhabited by Copts. The town of Fayum is counted in the Upper Egyptian district (al-Sa'id). His description seems to follow the route he may well have taken as a merchant entering from Palestine: first he describes Farama (north Sinai), then several Delta villages, and Alexandria and Fustat.[135] He notes that the Fayum was an important place with fields of the finest rice and cotton of an inferior quality: "It has a number of rich villages that are called al-Jawhariyyat."[136]

In the discussion on aspects of the Nile, Muqaddasi states that in the past the Nile did not reach the Fayum so the people complained to Joseph, who then built a great dam with glass ducts. The dam held the water in, the land was irrigated, and the Fayum became the most watered area in Egypt. They had rice farms and high taxes due to their large revenues. Sometimes during the flood the water flowed over the dam, carrying with it boats that then capsized. He also mentions that the water in the Fayum was "unhealthy because it flows over the rice fields."[137] Muqaddasi is the only geographer of the Balkhi school to make any mention of the now familiar Joseph story. The details are significantly different from those in the more overtly historical accounts (for example, al-Mas'udi), but the essence—that it was Joseph who irrigated the region—is still present.

Muqaddasi was the last of the Balkhi school geographers. His description of the Fayum is relatively brief. The fact that they had good revenues and high taxes might be an indication that the region had not yet fallen into decline, yet he does not say anything about the region being abundant or especially fertile. He presents the story of Joseph in a matter-of-fact manner, not as a creation legend but as an important part of the history of the region—it was due to the creation of the dam at Lahun by Joseph that the landscape became managed. As with the accounts of the other members of the Balkhi school, this account essentially presents a perception of a managed and 'present' landscape. The landscape is an aspect of Egypt that contributes to the economy of the country. The landscape is measurable and definable; it is classifiable. Aspects of the landscape were man-made and those man-made elements could be easily ascribed to those who created them. The walls, ancient monuments (of Ibn Hawkal), the dam, and the canal all sat within this measured, present, and 'real' landscape. They held no special significance, other than their contribution to the economy (for example, the dam enabling the region to become irrigated, allowing agriculture). The landscapes of this group of writers were undeniably less romanticized and viewed far more clinically than those of writers who aimed to include more historical information or who aimed to entertain readers.

Late Fatimid Period (Eleventh–Twelfth Centuries)

The flood of scholarly investigation into human geography and history tailed off during the later Fatimid era. Only a few works are known from this time, although it should be noted that there were significant advances in geographical knowledge.[138] The most notable scholar from this period is al-Biruni (973–1050), who studied both Greek and Islamic science (but not geography or history) and wrote 138 works, many of which are considered to have been ground-breaking.[139] Egypt's dominance in the Islamic Empire waned in this period, as severe famine and shortages followed by epidemics (the result of repeatedly low inundation levels) caused major economic instability.[140]

Al-Idrisi (1100–65)

Also known as al-Sharif al-Idrisi, Abu 'Abdallah Muhammad ibn Muhammad ibn 'Abdallah ibn Idris al-'Ali bi-Amr Allah al-Idrisi completed *Nuzhat al-mushtaq fi ikhtiraq al-afaq* (Book of Pleasant Journeys into Faraway Lands), also known as *Kitab Rujar* or *al-Kitab al-rujari* (The Book of Roger), in 1154. He was commissioned to make a book to accompany a map of the world by Norman King Roger II of Sicily (1130–54). It is believed he was being groomed by the king to become a puppet ruler of North Africa.[141] Idrisi was born in Ceuta to an old ruling family and started traveling as a young man, visiting Europe (England) and North Africa, as well as Asia Minor. Despite becoming one of the best known Islamic geographers as a result of the translation of his Arabic text into Latin in 1619, his work was shunned by contemporary Islamic scholars because of his connections to a Christian king.[142] While he was aware of the work of the Balkhi school (he refers to Ibn Hawkal, and his world map is based on al-Istakhri and Ibn Hawkal), he followed al-Khwarizmi and Ibn Khurradadhbih, and introduced some major innovations.[143]

Tenth-century Sicily, under the rule of Roger II, had a good relationship with Fatimid Egypt. Roger II was recognized by scholars as being knowledgeable regarding sciences, and the Norman kings patronized the Islamic scientific arts.[144] Roger II had aspirations to empire, and this work was commissioned in order for him to know the details of 'his lands' so that he could "master them with a definite knowledge."[145] King Roger initially wanted an accurate world map, and over fifteen years Idrisi collected information from scholars, which culminated in the creation of an engraved silver map.[146] The book *Nuzhat al-mushtaq* was written by Idrisi to accompany this map and explain what could not be included in the map regarding the socioeconomic and cultural conditions of different countries. It is widely regarded to be the most advanced and detailed world geography of any medieval Islamic scholar. The original silver map is (perhaps unsurprisingly) lost, but a small copy accompanies one of the manuscripts.[147] During this time Sicily was a melting-pot of medieval European and Arab–Islamic cultures, and the work of Idrisi contributed greatly to geographical knowledge in both cultures.[148] The text is preserved in ten manuscripts, with varying selections of maps attached/preserved. The oldest copy dates to 1300, and the book has only been fully translated once (into French) by Pierre-Amedée Jaubert in 1836–40 (reprinted in 1975).

At the beginning of *Nuzhat al-mushtaq* Idrisi lists the works he consulted but found to be lacking in precise and detailed information. The scholars he names include al-Mas'udi, al-Jayhani, Ibn Khurradadhbih, al-Baghdadi, al-Ya'qubi, and Claudius Ptolemy. To rectify this situation he gathered educated travelers who had visited the regions and questioned them, only including the information if it agreed with other accounts.[149] In the section on Egypt he discusses the canal of al-Menha, which flowed north to al-Bahnasa/Oxyrhynchus and then on to Ahnas and the Fayum, where it discharged its waters into the "lakes of Akna and Tihmat."[150] He notes that the Fayum was two days' journey to the west from Misr (Cairo), and that the (main) town was large and surrounded by orchards, gardens, and cultivated fields and built on the banks of the river of Lahun, which was created by Joseph. He states that the region was fertile and abundant in fruits and cereals as well as rice, and that the air was good. He also mentions that both in the Fayum town and around the area were the remains of large monuments, as well as the foot of a wall that was visible surrounding the entire region.[151]

Idrisi then recounts the Joseph story, with more detail and elaboration than is found in any previous version:

> As Joseph became old the king desired to relieve him of some of his affairs. His family [Joseph's] had grown large. The king gave them the territory of the Fayum, which was a marsh, with water, rushes and roses, things which displeased the king because the lake was near where he lived. Joseph went to Soul where he cut the canal known as Manhi as far as Lahun. Then he built the dam of Lahun with large and small stones of lime, bricks and shells like a tall wall, with a door at the top and in the middle. He cut a canal to Fayum from the east and another to the west which passed outside the Fayum, called Tenhemet. This took a few days. Then he cleared the roses and plants, the rushes and tamarisks, after which the water could flow to the Nile—this is how the water gets to Lahun. Then he cut a canal from Lahun to Fayum. The waters entered the region and it

> became like a sheet of water. This took 70 days, when it was finished the king exclaimed that it was a work of one thousand days; this is how the region got its name. Later Joseph built 85 villages, one for each of his family members and allocated water for the irrigation of the lands and for drinking.[152]

The first part of this description is of the landscape of Idrisi's time. He describes certain features of the town and the produce of the region. He describes monuments that could be seen in the town and the remains of a large wall, presumably ancient, around the region. This is the landscape of his time, the evidence and remains of man's activities within the landscape. He then adopts an alternative perception: that it was created by the prophet for a specific purpose.

It seems plausible to suggest that his version of the Joseph/Fayum story is an amalgamation of what he had read and the accounts brought back to him by merchant travelers. The story has a few details not found earlier and a few alterations—an inevitable development of oral transmission. For example, the name Tenhamet is linked to a canal not a lake. Joseph is not asked to recreate the Fayum by the pharaoh but rather given the region to house his family, although there is an implication that the pharaoh asks him to 'clean it up.' The details regarding the practicalities of how he reirrigated the region are new additions to the story and provide specific geographic detail. There is the detail of the region appearing to be entirely flooded—as it "appeared like a sheet of water"—much like the creation of Lake Moeris, based on a time when the entire region was a lake. The number of villages differs from other versions of the story: here it is eighty-five, bearing no connotations of being able to provide food for all of Egypt, but suggesting that each of the villages housed a different branch of Joseph's family.

As with the story in the anonymous *Akhbar al-zaman* account, the Fayum here is distanced from Egypt. The landscape is shaped by Joseph for his family; it belongs to him and not to Egypt. This part of the story may well have been shaped by the fact that Idrisi would have been familiar with the Bible, not just the Qur'an, as he lived in a Christian nation.

This work could be viewed differently to earlier accounts, given that both the influences on the author and his background are significantly different. His motive for creating the account was in some ways similar to that for the earlier *Masalik wa-l-mamalik* accounts: a record of the nations and their towns, rivers, and produce. And in some ways his style reflects those accounts: it covers each geographical area in order, detailing various aspects of the geography and society in each area. But his account combines that record with cartography, and therefore could be considered a typical account created by a nation with the aim to later 'own' Egypt—mapping the country makes it controllable and manageable. It could thus be analyzed in much the same way as the *Description de l'Égypte*, which has been described as an example of the way in which intellectual ownership derived from detailed fact-gathering is followed by publication, leading to attempted conquest and physical ownership of the land.[153] Idrisi does not seem to have traveled to regions to gather additional information to add to that which he gained from the earlier sources he consulted, but he did obtain stories from people who had been there, giving his account the feel of 'experienced' landscape.

Essentially, the landscape of the Fayum is entirely imaginary to Idrisi, as there is little evidence that he went to the region or even Egypt. He is describing a landscape that is known to him only through literature, cartography, and second-hand oral transmission of tales. He knew certain 'facts' about the physical landscape and some elements of the history of the region. However, he did have a clear perception of the region as being part of the Biblical/Qur'anic landscape of Egypt, making it untouchable and temporally distant. In his account he manages to make the mental leap from the real landscape to the imagined ancient landscape with no problems—they existed as one. The layers of the palimpsest landscape had become even more intertwined by this point, so his account blends the Joseph tradition with the far older Herodotus tradition, both of which are versions of the Fayum creation theology, either misunderstood or deliberately adapted.

Ayyubid Period (Twelfth–Thirteenth Centuries)

After a long period of political instability and struggle between different factions (Ayyubid, Fatimid, and Abbasid), Salah al-Din al-Ayyubi took power in Egypt from a severely weakened Fatimid caliphate in 1171. He later constructed the Citadel outside the Abbasid capital, Fustat.[154] During this era, the Ayyubid rulers were generally mostly concerned with protecting the Islamic Empire from the Crusaders, but they also, to some extent, started to alter both the physical (architecture) and political nature of Egypt to fit into line with Syrian practises.[155] During the Ayyubid period (1171–1250) a genre of writing appeared that was more akin to travel journalism than the earlier geographic accounts.

Al-Murtada (1154–1237)

Al-Murtada ibn al-'Afif ibn Hatim ibn Muslim al-Maqdisi al-Shafi'i, also known as Murtadi son of Gaphiphe, is thought to have been born in the Sharqiya province of Egypt to a family from Jerusalem. He trained under scholars in Alexandria, Cairo, and Damascus.[156] The Bibliothèque Mazarine possessed a manuscript copy (dated 1584, now lost) of his work on Egypt that was translated and published by Pierre Vattier in 1666 and then translated from French to English in 1672 by John Davies of Kidwelly.[157] This work was used a great deal by later writers, who borrowed entire tracts and anonymously incorporated this work into their own.[158] Gaston Wiet[159] suggests that Murtada consulted the works of Ibn 'Abd al-Hakam and al-Quda'i, as well as of a historian named Jawwani. He also notes that some consider this work to be an extract lifted from a work by Ibn Wasif Shah.[160] Regarding the reliability of the sources, Murtada himself notes (regarding the stories about the Ark of Noah) that "others say these stories were invented for pleasure's sake, and that they are not of faith, as having no grounds."[161] Despite the difficulties of relying on this text, due to the loss of the original manuscript and the lack of accuracy in the translation, it does fit well into the pattern of development of the stories about the Fayum in historical works. The detail it contains clearly places it after al-Mas'udi, and it is obvious that the work was the basis for much of the account produced by Maqrizi.

The author first introduces the Fayum via the Joseph story, citing the "Histories of Egypt" by Chasan son of Ismael the Sarrabian. The tale in the book recounts that the author 'heard' that the land of the Fayum (alphiom) was governed by the prophet Joseph, who divided it into 360 villages (under command from God)—as many as the days in a year. This ensured that if the Nile failed, each village could supply Egypt for one day. Murtada writes, "There is no country in the world that has been reduced and cultivated by Divine Revelation but this. There is not upon earth a less and yet a more fertile province, nor one that abounds in all sorts of good things or is better furnished with rivers."[162] The author then compares the rivers of the Fayum to those of Basra and Damascus, concluding that the Fayum is better.[163] The account becomes a little confused and the following section seems to imply that nobody was able to account correctly for all the rivers and channels in the region. Following this, the narrator (Chasan son of Ismael the Sarrabian, via Murtada) relates that when Mamunus (Caliph al-Ma'mun) went to Egypt, he sent for chieftains and learned men of the country, among them one named Abulseriphus and one named Suguidus son of Gaphrius, whom he questioned about the advantages of Egypt. Suguidus "made him a large discourse," and Abulseriphus recounted that after God placed the affairs of the Fayum into the hands of Joseph, given him supremacy over it, and ordered the inhabitants to serve him, Joseph caused 360 great farms to be cultivated—as many as there are days in the year—so that the village of each farm could furnish Egypt with one day's sustenance. Joseph did this by revelation from the Lord.[164]

According to Hasam the son of Isaac, Joseph was highly favored by Pharaoh Rayan, and by the time he reached a hundred years of age the other courtiers were jealous of his closeness to the pharaoh and his power. The courtiers spoke with the pharaoh and condemned Joseph as old and weakening in knowledge, wisdom, judgment, and beauty. The pharaoh did not like to hear this and disapproved of them; they feared to say any more, but after two years they renewed their attack. The pharaoh asked them to suggest a challenge with which he could test Joseph. At that time the Fayum was known as 'Geouna' and served only as a 'sewer' for Upper Egypt, so the courtiers decided this should be the challenge. Joseph was to be commanded to clear the waters and create a new province that could provide new revenue. The pharaoh took this challenge to Joseph, saying, "You know how dear such a daughter of mine is to me, and you see it is time I should assign her some place where she may be mistress, and whereof the revenues may be sufficient to maintain her."[165] The pharaoh suggests Geouna as the new province because "that land is neither too near, nor at too great a distance, and there is no coming in to it of any side unless it be through the desert and dangerous places; the case will be the same with her; none can come near her on any side, but through the desert and dangerous places."[166] Also, the Fayum is in the middle of Egypt as Egypt is in the middle of other countries; one cannot get into Egypt without crossing a desert and dangerous places.

The king asked Joseph to perform the task as soon as possible. Joseph completed the task as inspired by God, who commanded him to cut three channels: one from Upper Egypt, an eastern channel, and a western channel. Joseph cut the Manhi channel from Ashmunayn to Lahun, then the channel of the Fayum, the eastern channel, and another near it named Benhamet, then the western channel that draws the waters from the desert of Benhamet to the west. By these means he emptied the water out of Geouna. He then had workers cut down the reeds and tamarisk from the region, allowing it to become pure and clean. The Nile water rose, entered the Manhi channel, flowed to Lahun, and then turned into the Fayum. The king came with his courtiers to see this, and all were astonished by Joseph's wisdom and invention. The king inquired how long it had taken, and when told seventy days he turned to his courtiers and remarked that no one could have done it in a thousand days. This is how the region became known as al-Fayum (alphiom, alf youm, 'one thousand days' in Arabic).[167] Once again, the description of cutting canals appears to reflect the reality of the Ptolemaic irrigation works but no acknowledgment of those rulers.

The author then relates a different version of the story, from Fesidus the son of Gbebibus. God made Joseph the master of Egypt after he was thirty years old, and after forty years of governing the Egyptians questioned his prudence and judgment. They suggested he test himself by choosing an area of barren fields and useless ground to cultivate. If he succeeded he would regain his place in government. Joseph chose the Fayum. He brought a channel of water from the Nile, named Manhi, so that the water of the Nile could flow over all the land of the Fayum. Joseph succeeded, with the help of God and many workers, and continued to govern, 130 years in total.[168]

A third story, also from Hasam the son of Isaac, continues the tale. After completing the work in Fayum, Joseph said to Pharaoh Rayan that the king had not seen all that he could achieve. Joseph told the king and his courtiers that he would place a family of every city in Egypt into the Fayum to build towns for themselves. There would be as many villages in the Fayum as there were in Egypt, and he would provide them with sufficient water for their lands via aqueducts, so that each village would have neither too much nor too little water. The pharaoh replied by saying that this creation would be the 'Kingdom of Heaven.' Joseph then began this enterprise, assigning the limits of each village. The first village was named Betiana, and the pharaoh's daughter lived there. He had channels dug and bridges built, and then allotted land and water. This was the beginning of geometry, a discipline previously unknown in Egypt, which Joseph was taught by the Lord. Joseph was also credited with being the first to measure the flood of the Nile and with the construction of the Nilometer at Memphis.[169]

No other medieval account places so much meaning on the landscape of the Fayum as this one. The Fayum landscape is clearly given great religious meaning: it has been altered and recreated by 'divine revelation,' by Joseph with the assistance of God, more than any other place on Earth. It is also considered to be the most fertile and well-irrigated land—attributes one might expect from such a divine landscape.

It is clear that this landscape is perceived to be both hidden and separate. It is not a part of Egypt, and can only be reached with some difficulty. This strongly suggests that at the point of origin of this story, the Fayum was not considered approachable via the Nile Valley from Beni Suef. The view of and route to the Fayum was from the north, from Cairo, the location and home of the writers, *rawis*, scholars, and houses of learning (including mosques). From here the journey to the Fayum was across the desert. The entrance to the region was not, as we perceive it today (through appreciation of maps), via the Bahr Yusuf near Beni Suef and Lahun. Before the construction of the modern asphalt road, the desert route would naturally have been more dangerous, possibly with the potential for 'bandits' but certainly with the dangers of getting lost, running out of water, and being dependent on the time of year, hot weather, or sandstorms. This perception relates only to the physical landscape of the region—it is seen as physically distant and separate, but still very much as a part of Egypt.

Joseph undertakes the task and is assisted/directed by God, thus again the Fayum is believed to be a semidivine landscape made hospitable by man—order versus chaos. The description of the canals can be mapped easily. The main stretch of the Bahr Yusuf is named the Manhi canal, and from Lahun to the Fayum it is named the canal of Fayum. The third channel Joseph is instructed to cut may refer to one of the two main natural channels that run to the north and eventually into the lake. The name Benhamet is almost certainly a mishearing/-spelling/-transcription of Tenhamet, which was the name given to one of the channels by Idrisi, but to one of the lakes by Ibn Hawkal.

This set of tales about the Fayum provides a rich palimpsest of perceptions of the landscape, and a memory of the realities of the Ptolemaic transformation. The landscape is physically distant and hard to reach, but an integrated part of Egypt. It was uninhabitable, but with the intervention of God, acting through his prophet Joseph, under the command of the pharaoh, it became managed and cultivated. This is a purely imagined landscape, a mythological one, but the story explains the physical characteristics of the region, as does any other creation legend. As a historical work, it contains less information regarding the state of the region at the time, but Murtada's perception of the region is heavily influenced by the traditional stories. He does not mention any of the monuments or their history. His landscape is entirely dominated by the legends surrounding the semidivine creation of the irrigation of the Fayum. Murtada imbues the landscape with meaning and only perceives the ancient imagined landscape.

Al-Nabulsi (1192–1261)

'Uthman ibn Ibrahim al-Nabulsi came from a Palestinian (Nablus) family that emigrated to Egypt. His father was a judge. Nabulsi enjoyed a successful career under Sultan al-Kamil working in administration, during which time he wrote several works. He had risen through the ranks, occupying posts in Fustat, the Delta, and Upper Egypt under the particular favor of the sultan, who was keen for him to become a leader in his state.[170] He was appointed governor of the Fayum in 1243, a position he held for two years, during which he wrote *Tarikh al-Fayum wa-biladihi* (History of the Fayum and Its Places), an extensive report on the entire region. His aim was to outline how to rebuild the failing infrastructure and return the area to its ancient prosperity.[171] The impression Nabulsi gives in his work is that although he was honored to hold such a post, he was not totally happy with his position in the Fayum, which might go some way toward explaining his vehement attacks on the nature of the Fayumis. The work was edited and published (but not translated) by Bernhard Moritz in 1899, who had been given access to a copy of the text dated to 1447, probably deriving from the personal library of a director of the Imprimerie Nationale (Bulaq).[172] A second copy was held (at that time) in the Aya Sofia library of Istanbul. The work remains largely untranslated.

Nabulsi, despite having a negative opinion of the inhabitants of the Fayum, appreciated the natural landscape, commenting on its beauty and likening it to paradise.[173] His work was divided into ten chapters: 'General description of the region,' 'Characteristics,' 'Climate,' 'Why water stands regularly in the canals although the tributaries from the Nile are lacking,' 'Inhabitants (Bedouins and sedentary population),' 'The changes of the lake and its causes; the alluvial lands and its laborious and costly cultivation,' 'Alphabetic register of place names,' 'List of the main and minor mosques, churches, and monasteries,' 'General description (property values, etc.),' and 'Description of the places and their agricultural production.'

The final chapter with descriptions of all the places in the region is by far the largest section, forming most of the book, as the initial nine chapters are all relatively brief. His list of places is extensive, including 198 localities. He discusses the fact that many people were forced to move from their homes to new villages for a variety of reasons, one being the need to be close to the shoreline of the lake, which was receding.[174] The irrigation of the region was one of his primary concerns, principally the degradation of the ancient systems. The Manhi canal, which supplied the region with water, was, he believed, the creation of Joseph (the prophet). The Bahr Yusuf was another canal, linked to and fed from the Nile by the Manhi canal. All the tributaries that watered the region derived from the Bahr Yusuf or the Fayum canal, and were either fed naturally or via a water wheel.[175] This is the earliest mention of the name Bahr Yusuf, and given the popularity of the Joseph creation story, it is perhaps unsurprising that the river finally took on his name. By Nabulsi's time the two major canals that ran north and south from the western end of the Bahr Yusuf in the western district of Madinat al-Fayum (and ran into opposite ends of the lake) had almost entirely silted up. This was, he believed, a direct result of lack of maintenance. Along the ends of these two canals, where no water flowed at all, were dozens of deserted villages.

In order to prevent the Bahr Yusuf from silting up, two walls had been constructed in the Manhi canal near Lahun that prevented sand and waste flowing from the Nile into the region. As these walls were not functioning, two drain-off channels had been dug from the Bahr Yusuf to draw the silt and waste away. These also failed to work, and Nabulsi had his engineers try several other methods to restore the flow of the water into the region. The most significant element in the irrigation works of the region was still the Lahun dam. It stretched 417.18 meters and was 8.10 meters high and 8.64 meters wide, running from the canal to the desert either side of the Manhi canal.[176] For each town, Nabulsi summarizes its primary agricultural resources, mosques, and churches, noting which canal supplied the water and the distance from Madinat al-Fayum. He also notes some of the antiquities, namely the dam and pyramid at Lahun and the colossi at Biahmu.[177]

This account is one of the most detailed inventories of the irrigation and population of the Fayum. It was compiled purely for administrative purposes and is therefore perhaps more objective than other accounts. In many ways Nabulsi's listing of distances is reminiscent of the books of routes and provinces of earlier geographic works. Although Nabulsi recorded the Joseph legend, he believed it to be a fact of history. Joseph's works were a significant element in the irrigation of the region, and Nabulsi was seeking to return the region to its former prosperity, most likely so that the ruling sultans could levy higher taxes on the inhabitants. It is unclear if Nabulsi made any reference to the former abundance and richness of the region.

The implication is that this abundance was what he was hoping to achieve by restoring the irrigation of the region.

Overall, Nabulsi's perception of the region was rather negative. However, he clearly did find the landscape itself to hold some value, and beauty. He seems to have separated the landscape from the people, and from their interventions in the landscape. The irrigation was imposed on the landscape in order for the people to reap more value from the land. The past landscape was the desired landscape, and his perception of the landscape he experienced was basically negative. The past landscape was richer and more populated, more productive and pleasant. He believed it was the fault of the inhabitants of his time that the interventions made by their more worthy predecessors had fallen into disrepair, leading to a negative impact on the natural landscape. His perception of that past landscape was perhaps imbued with some sense of the imagined and idealized landscape, but he did not place any real meaning in the landscape as such—he just maintained the belief that it had been better. This attitude that the local inhabitants were incompetent and had let the land fall into disrepair is mirrored in the later European attitude toward native Egyptians and their perceived mistreatment of and lack of respect for the pharaonic monuments. Nabulsi felt that the land itself was a monument, a remnant of people's activities in the past, and the work of a divinely inspired prophet. The interventions that had shaped the landscape were works to be celebrated, and by letting the irrigation fall into disrepair the modern inhabitants were failing to respect the work of God and Joseph. He did focus on recording the experienced landscape, the aspects of the landscape that could be measured and accounted for, exploited, and adapted, in much the same way that the earlier geographers had done during the early stages of the expansion of the Islamic Empire.

Mamluk Period (Thirteenth–Sixteenth Centuries)

The Mamluks—slave-soldiers—played a crucial role in the armies of the Islamic Empire from as early as the Abbasid period, but it was the death of the Ayyubid sultan Najm al-Din in 1249 during the invasion of Egypt by Louis IX that led to their rise to power in Egypt in 1251–53 (Syria in 1260). During this period (1250–1517) the Islamic power base moved out of Baghdad to Cairo. These 'new' previously enslaved rulers proved themselves, upheld their legitimacy to rule, and maintained their status through their success on the battlefield and by placing a shadow Abbasid caliph on the 'throne' in Cairo.[178]

Al-Maqrizi (1364– 1442)

Taqi al-Din Abu al-'Abbas Ahmad ibn 'Ali ibn 'Abd al-Qadir al-Maqrizi came from a well-to-do family and was well educated—Ibn Khaldun was among his teachers. He worked as a judge, imam, Hadith professor, and administrator and traveled to Damascus and Mecca. He gave up his career to write full-time and produced over two hundred works, including the well-known *Kitab al-mawa'iz wa-l-i'tibar bi-dhikr al-khitat wa-l-athar* (Book of Advice from and Observations on the History of the Regions and Monuments, abbreviated as *Khitat*).[179] The work is published in French, but scholars acknowledge that these publications contain many errors.[180] Quatrèmere de Quincy studied but did not publish this work. His notes are held in Munich and were studied and published in part by Urbain Bouriant as an introduction to the French translation. The work, usually translated in French as *Description de l'Égypte*, is principally a very detailed account of Cairo, with descriptions of monuments and the history of the city. The rest of Egypt is also covered but with considerably less detail and accuracy.[181] One of the earlier translators of the work, Quatremère, notes that many of the fables Maqrizi recounts are more likely to derive from Coptic Christian sources than Muslim Egyptians, and he found it hard to understand why the medieval Islamic Egyptian historians failed to use any of the Classical Greek histories of Egypt.[182]

Chapters Eighty-two through Eighty-four cover the Fayum. Chapter Eighty-two opens with the statement that the Fayum was the 'spillway' of the Nile waters, which was cultivated by the prophet Joseph when he was governor of Egypt. Maqrizi furnishes his account with lengthy records of stories and historical tales.

After being vizier to the pharaoh for thirty years, Joseph was relieved of his duties. He asked why this was and the pharaoh replied that he was not unhappy with Joseph but that his father had told him never to keep a vizier for more than thirty years. Joseph asked for some land for his family, and the pharaoh allowed him to choose as he pleased. He marched into the desert and arrived at the Fayum, where there was a mountain and a plain extending from the mountain to the river. He examined the water of the river and recognized that the Nile covered all that country. He pierced the mountain and made the water pass through, which then spread into the Fayum and irrigated the soil. On the two sides of the water he raised up 360 villages, after the number of days in a year, and filled them with grain from the harvests he collected. When the Nile shrank and food shortages occurred in Egypt, he sold the produce of each village of the Fayum. This way he had his turn as leader of Egypt. The fortune of Joseph became immense as his riches accumulated, and a while later the pharaoh took him back as vizier, a job he held until his death.[183]

Maqrizi then retold the second version of the Joseph story, which is found in Murtada's work, involving the pharaoh's daughter. The one difference is that the name given for the Fayum is al-Goubah (the pit) not Geouna, although this could be a copyist's error or a result of transliteration of Arabic script. The description of the channels Joseph cut is slightly more lucid, but still hard to follow:

> Joseph put the workers to work and cut al-Menha which left the Nile a little south of Ashmunayn and went as far as Lahun. He ordered the masons to cut al-Lahun and he cut the canal of Fayum which is the eastern canal, and another canal which passed to Benhamet one of the western villages of Fayum. The water left the eastern canal and spilled into the Nile, the water that left by the western canal spilled into the desert of Benhamet to the west; he did not leave any water in al-Goubah.[184]

After this, Maqrizi repeats Murtada's third story with a few small differences in the details.[185] Maqrizi notes that the author, Yazid ibn Abu Nabib, commented on passages in the Bible, that the pharaoh ordered the Israelites to make bricks to build Pithom and Ramses. Maqrizi notes that one author commented that these cities must be Fayum and Houf-Ramses. At the time of al-Rayyan ibn al-Walid, Jacob and his children entered Egypt—73 people in total—and Joseph gave them fertile and prosperous land between Ain Shams and Farma (Farama?). The rest of the chapter simply recounts other stories of Joseph.[186]

Chapter Eighty-three is titled 'What has been said about Fayum, its canals, and villages.' Maqrizi drew on works of many other scholars, including al-Mas'udi, al-Ya'qubi, Murtada, al-Quda'i, and Ibn Radwan, and retold the familiar accounts of the Fayum being 'created' by Joseph, with 360 villages to supply water to Egypt, and Joseph building the dam at Lahun. He included some details not preserved elsewhere, including that the account of Ibn Radwan noted that the region stored the waters of the Nile, and that the inhabitants were able to sow more than one crop per year. When the water was released it changed the color of the Nile waters, which was most remarkable at the height of summer at Saft and Nahia. This situation was said to be detrimental to the inhabitants of the region, and when the wind blew from the south the people in Fustat said it was good that the Fayum was some distance away. The implication is that the region smelled bad.[187]

Maqrizi quotes a book titled *Guide for the Science of Taxes*, in which the Fayum was given a favorable report. It was beautiful and easily cultivated, although some of the region lay fallow as it had been abandoned and engulfed by sands. He states that he saw a 'table' by Abu Ishaq Ibrahim ibn Ja'far ibn al-Hani ibn Ishaq in which the neglected canals of the province and the villages on the banks were 'inscribed.'[188] This table is likely to be a register of the irrigation management of the region, the water used by each village, and the regulation of the dams, used to calculate taxes due. It had a date of May–June 1031. Maqrizi's account of this table is confused, and it is hard to decipher exactly what is going on. He starts with the 'great canal of Fayum.' The water is taken into this canal from a small branch of the Nile named al-Menha at the 'stone of Joseph.' The branch is below the canal, close to a mountain named 'siege of the sorcerer' in the province of Ashmunayn.[189] Maqrizi closes the chapter with this statement: "I have summarized the names of the villages reported in the register because most of them are in ruins."[190]

Chapter Eighty-four is a short account of the conquest of the Fayum and the revenues from the region. Maqrizi repeats the account of Ibn 'Abd al-Hakam and quotes an account of al-Kindi known as the 'Merits of Egypt.'[191]

> Among the provinces of Egypt you find the province of Fayum which is made up of 360 villages, a number the same as the number of days in the year. All of the villages are always irrigated with a sufficient quantity of water. If one year the Nile is insufficient each village provides for one day the needs of Egypt. There is nowhere in the world a land like this province which is built with divine inspiration, nor so precious, nor more abundant in goods, nor more criss-crossed with canals. When one compares the canals of Fayum with those of Basra and Damascus the advantage stays with the first. A great number of intelligent and educated people seek what are the revenues and riches of the Fayum but they have considered it so much that they have abandoned their searching. One does not make an account of the lands in this province, as none belong to any Muslims, nor to any of their tributants, and one can also find rich and poor people, and seventy categories of these lands.[192]

The mix of traditions in this account is a real reflection of the 'Chinese whispers' effect. Over time, so many different versions of the Fayum creation story grew out of tradition and cultural memory that all the stories were confused and mixed together. Maqrizi's perception of the Fayum is almost entirely that of the imagined landscape. As a historian he recounts the familiar legend of Joseph and thus imbues the landscape with richness and abundance. He does mention some of the 'monuments' of the region and recounts what he read in the irrigation tables, which could be considered a record of the administered, managed, experienced landscape, but even here he attributes some sense of history to the works by attributing them to Joseph. He places these actions in the past, providing temporal distance between the major works and the contemporary landscape, thus imbuing those actions with meaning and placing them within the imagined landscape.

Continued Traditions

The tradition that attributes the creation of the Fayum to Joseph was clearly still strong in the region during the twelfth century. The twelfth-century Jewish traveler Benjamin of Tudela records that the Muslims of the Fayum told him the story of Joseph,[193] which strengthens the argument that the story was rooted in local oral tradition. In fact, the story is told to this day. Fayumis today attribute the creation of the region to Joseph (saying that it is 'just a story'), but the circumstances of the creation tale they tell are very different. They say that Joseph was traveling from Upper to Lower Egypt on a donkey when he fell asleep. The donkey walked to the Fayum and the imprints left by the donkey's hoofs became joined and filled with water, creating the Bahr Yusuf. I was also told that Joseph dug the ground to make the Fayum area, but that the lake was made by Qarun. At Madinat al-Gurob there is a story told that may well be almost as old, as it provides some background for the name of the mountain noted by Maqrizi, Siege of the Sorcerer. The story is confused but essentially the characters involved include a royal woman living at Madinat al-Gurob and a jealous lover who was a sorcerer. The conclusion of the story is the sorcerer lifting up and folding the mountain and desert to cover the queen and her court.

Any discussion of the root of the Joseph creation myth can only be conjecture. The story must derive from unrecorded oral traditions and tales. The first written record of it is in the account of Ibn 'Abd al-Hakam. During the Arab conquest of Egypt and for some time after, the Fayum was home to notably large Coptic and Jewish populations. Peter Holt attributes the myth to the presence of an ancient Jewish settlement in the Fayum, and a possible Islamized Jewish shrine.[194] An important Jewish scholar, Saadia Gaon, bears the epithet 'al-Fayumi' as he was born in Madinat al-Fayum (in 892). This epithet is 'ha-Pithomi' in Hebrew, pointing to the fact that Hebrew tradition considered Fayum to be the biblical Pithom.[195] Benjamin of Tudela records in a letter from Cairo: "Fayum, which is Pithom. . . . This is the native district of R. Saadia ben Joseph, gaon of Sura; it contains about 20 Jews."[196] There is also an unavoidably close resemblance between the Hebrew Pithom and the Coptic Pa-yum[197]—ideas that were exploited by Frederick Cope Whitehouse in the late nineteenth century (see Chapter Six). It is quite possible that the story derived from one of the many Coptic monasteries or communities in the region, when the Christian inhabitants adapted the local 'pagan' beliefs to fit with Christian doctrine.

6

Explored Landscape: Western Accounts (Seventeenth–Nineteenth Centuries)

> Lake Moeris had been to me, through the greater part of my life, a fabulous lake, exactly like those waters described in the 'Arabian Nights,' abounding with blue fishes, and dragged by nets of fishermen. It had now emerged from the region of myths and fables into the category of real existences. It was the genius of Herodotus that had invested that dreamy lake with so much beauty and fascination for me.[1]
>
> —James Augustus St. John (1853)

> The province is a delicious place, by reason of its essentially gentle and primitive character, its biblical inhabitants, and the wildness of its vegetation wherever man's hand has not meddled with it. It is a true terrestrial paradise, in which pastoral peoples have succeeded each other, all whose efforts have been confined to the culture of their fields. They were the real civilisers of Egypt—those intelligent rustics of the universe, who wanted nothing to aid their progress but the laws of nature seconded by the toil of man.[2]
>
> —Paul Marie Lenoir (1873)

It has been argued that early modern European interest in the ancient Egyptian past began in Italy during the Renaissance (fourteenth century) when obelisks removed from Egypt by the first-century emperors were rediscovered in Rome.[3] Post-Crusade travel to Egypt was usually undertaken by those on pilgrimage to the Holy Land or traders visiting Alexandria.[4] During the Renaissance the educated classes increasingly began to value familiarity with and understanding of Latin classics as a mark of social status. The first Greek grammar book was produced by Roger Bacon in the thirteenth century, but it was not until the fifteenth century that there was any real interest in the work of Greek scholars. The desire to read Greek authors referred to in the Latin works eventually led to the translation of many Greek works into Latin during the early years of the Renaissance. In 1457 Pope Nicholas V, who established the collection of manuscripts in the Vatican library, ordered translations of Herodotus, Strabo, and Ptolemy. The early fifteenth century saw the first European collecting missions to the Near East in search of new manuscripts for the study of Classical and Biblical texts.[5]

The invention of the printing press in the late fifteenth century led to a huge increase in the availability of classical works, and the study of both Greek and Latin texts (and the Bible) flourished. The fashion of traveling to collect manuscripts almost certainly increased the desire to gain access to more of the Classical geographical works and to glean information on the countries to which the collectors were heading. While traveling, scholars encountered local (oral) folklore, which at that time was accorded similar importance to the Classical texts.[6] There can be no real doubt that the early Renaissance travelers to Egypt held this view as the stories included in many of the early European accounts display a blend of Classical and local oral folklore traditions. The epic nature of events and the heroic deeds of the characters in the stories captured the imaginations of both the travelers and the readers of their accounts.

During the sixteenth and seventeenth centuries Classical scholarship became firmly established in universities across Europe. Any gentleman of 'learning' was expected to be able to read and appreciate Greek and Latin Classics. Educated men visited Egypt to see the country described by Herodotus, Diodorus, Pliny, and Strabo. From the sixteenth century onward, European travelers started to visit Egypt in increasingly large numbers. Their ideas about the landscape of Egypt were based on the Classical sources available to them, and to a certain extent they divorced the unfamiliar modern Egypt of the Mamluks from the ancient Egypt of the pharaohs, which had been made 'familiar' to them by those Classical accounts. Modern Egypt was a place that, in their eyes, needed transforming, while ancient Egypt needed studying. Their perception of the Fayum was frequently shaped by their ideas about the Labyrinth and Lake Moeris of Herodotus, and more often than not they visited the region explicitly to see those monuments.

Over time, perceptions of the Fayum landscape gradually became inextricably linked with Herodotus's description of the lake and the Labyrinth. His account eventually dominated all discussion of the region and its monuments. The earliest writers made reference to the works of Islamic authors, legends of Joseph, and local tales about Qarun, but by the mid-nineteenth century these were all but forgotten. The apparently authoritative account of studies of the Fayum written by Brown in 1892 included only passing reference to the Islamic accounts. From the outset, there was a focus on traveling through the region to visit the monuments, and until orientalism and romantic poetry started to have an influence on travel literature the landscapes in which the monuments were found hardly received a passing reference. In the minds of these writers, the contemporary landscape had nothing to do with ancient Egypt.

One of the earliest pilgrim travel accounts to include the Fayum is by traveler Père Antonius Gonzales. He noted that Arsinoë was otherwise known as Crocodilopolis and was where crocodiles were worshiped. Nearby was a great lake with a huge crocodile living in it. He also noted the large numbers of vines near the town named Fayum.[7] One writer mentioned the Bahr Yusuf, saying that when the Nile was flooding it was possible to go to the Fayum via a canal, and that Fayum was "good for grapes."[8] The early account by English traveler Henry Blount seems to indicate that he traveled to the Fayum, but he may have been recounting information gleaned from other accounts rather than his own experiences. He says he went to Egypt in the 1630s, and reported that he traveled fifteen miles from the river to see some great ruins he hoped were those of the Labyrinth built by the twelve kings in Moeris.[9] See plate 18 for the locations of places visited by European scholars/travelers.

Seventeenth-Century Scholarship

Under the reign of Louis XIV, seventeenth-century France was a place where cultural achievements, including literature, were perceived to be of great importance.[10] The tradition of pilgrimage travel to the 'Orient' continued and many seventeenth-century accounts are little more than itineraries of the Holy Land. Some of the travelers did begin to emphasize the adventurous nature of their explorations, while others placed great importance on recording their observations.[11] Interest in the sciences was increasing and the study of Classics was seen to be a scientific discipline. The Académie Royale des Inscriptions et Médailles was founded in Paris in 1663, with members specializing in history and antiquity.[12]

In England during the early seventeenth century the archbishop of Canterbury and vice-chancellor of Oxford University, William Laud, began to encourage the acquisition of 'eastern' manuscripts for the newly founded Bodleian Library. He established a chair of Arabic, and the first professor in the post was Edward Pococke.[13] Scholars such as John Greaves and John Locke also began to study these Islamic manuscripts, believing that they held lost secrets of astronomy, geometry, and other sciences. Manuscripts were collected from Italy, Istanbul, and Egypt. Pococke in particular advanced English orientalist studies by translating many classical Arabic texts into Latin. The first Arabic–Latin dictionary was printed/published in 1613.[14]

The seventeenth century also saw a significant increase in the exploration of Egypt and the beginning of serious collecting of 'curiosities.'[15] The ruling classes and nobility were 'rediscovering' the Classical world and building collections of natural and scientific curiosities, as well as art and artifacts. This was facilitated by easier means of travel. Collecting became a way of establishing one's own identity, status, and wealth, and place in society, and for the more industrial classes a way of asserting one's rising social rank and financial standing.[16] Egypt at this time was nominally under Ottoman rule, but the power was generally in the hands of the Mamluk beys.[17]

The foremost English traveler to the Near East and Egypt in the seventeenth century was George Sandys, whose account was first published in 1615, titled *A Relation of a Journey Begun an. Dom. 1610*. Sandys was the son of the archbishop of York and had been educated at Oxford University. He began his travels in 1610, going through Europe to the Levant and arriving in Egypt in 1611. He was the first European writer to set his account in a geographical/historical framework and include direct quotes from the Classics.[18] He did not go to the Fayum or make any reference to the region in his account, despite discussing Herodotus, Pliny, and Strabo.[19] However, his account was widely read and for some time was the only contemporary account available to travelers in Egypt. Sandys's works are known to have influenced many later literary figures, including John Dryden, Alexander Pope, and John Milton.[20]

Père Johann M. Vansleb (1635–79)

Father Vansleb (or Vansleben) was born in 1635 near Erfurt in Germany, the son of a Lutheran pastor. He was well educated, studied languages, and worked on a dictionary of Ethiopian for notable German Ethiopic scholar Hiob Ludolf. As a consequence he was employed by the Duke of

Saxe-Gotha to make an expedition to Ethiopia in 1663–64.[21] He did not reach Ethiopia, but instead remained in Egypt for one year, producing an account of his trip in Italian, *Relazione dello Stato Presente dell'Egitto*, printed in 1671.[22] On returning to Europe he went to Rome, where he entered the Dominican order in 1666. He then traveled to Paris in 1670, where he was introduced to Jean-Baptiste Colbert, the minister of finance under Louis XIV and a major patron of French orientalism in the seventeenth century, who was particularly interested in developing French commercial interests in the Levant.[23] Colbert decided that Vansleb's knowledge of both the languages and the people of the Orient made him an ideal candidate to send to the Levant in search of manuscripts and other treasures.[24] In 1672–73 Vansleb made his second trip to Egypt, the account of which was published in French in 1677 as *Nouvelle Relation en Forme de Journal d'un Voyage Fait en Égypte en 1672 et 1673*, and translated into English in 1678 as *The Present State of Egypt: Or a New Relation of a Late Voyage into that Kingdom*. Colbert was not satisfied with Vansleb's results, and after a third trip refused to reimburse his expenses. Vansleb died in 1679 "miserable and discouraged," having never reached Ethiopia.[25]

Vansleb had a good command of Arabic, both spoken and written, which gave him a major advantage over many other travelers. He was familiar with the Classical scholars and contemporary European travelers (specifically naming Jean de Thévenot), and he had also clearly studied medieval Islamic works. Maqrizi is referred to many times in his account, and he refers to Ibn Bitar (presumably Ibn Battuta), Ibn 'Abd al-Hakam, George le Mekkin, and a writer whom he describes as being famous among the Copts: Abulbaracas.[26]

During his second visit to Egypt, Vansleb made a specific trip to the Fayum. He states that the province had always been considered "one of the best regions of Egypt" and that for that reason he had a great desire to travel there.[27] In this account, Vansleb describes Madinat al-Fayum, also known as Madinat Fares. Built partially on the denuded ruins of the ancient Arsinoë, the town was considered to have once been one of the greatest cities in Egypt. According to a legend Vansleb was told, the city was destroyed by cats with firebrands tied to their tails sent in by 'the enemies,' which reduced it to ashes.[28] He made note of the many antiquities in the town, such as capitals and pillars of broken 'marble,' and recorded that most houses appeared to have something 'remarkable' in them. He mentions that the town was walled, and that there was an artificial channel which cut through the town from east to west known as both the river of Joseph and the channel of Manhi. This channel, he says, began three days south of the Fayum at 'Tarut Isscerif' (Dairut al-Sharif) and ran into the lake named Birket al-Kern.[29]

Vansleb was told that in 'ancient' times the region had 365 villages and towns, but he notes that only 62 still existed, the remainder having been swallowed up by the lake or destroyed by the "tyranny of the governors." It is tempting to consider this piece of information—the former existence of 365 villages in the Fayum—evidence of the continued presence of the Coptic/Islamic Joseph legends in local oral tradition. Vansleb comments that the region was very cut up by river channels, all of which derived from Joseph's river, and that only the great number of bridges made travel about the region possible. These (mud-brick) bridges were said to have been built in the time of the pharaohs. Local Copts told Vansleb that they had been built by the Israelites.[30]

Vansleb traveled to Fidimin and visited Biahmu to see "the body of a great statue of a giant of a red stone without head or arms standing on a base," which was situated behind the village in a broad road. He found that the locals had no traditions about it and that nothing was written about it in the histories. The locals simply called it the 'statue of pharaoh.' The base was square, constructed of giant stones 2.5 feet wide and 10 feet long. Nearby were five other bases with no statues attached, arranged in a 'demicircle.'[31] The village was named Agiasma, or 'fountain of holy water,' and on each Holy Thursday many Christians used to come to drink from this fountain. The five other bases in a 'demicircle' around it are probably the second pedestal that had no statue and the corners of the enclosure. It is unlikely that there were ever five other monumental pedestals (there has never been any evidence to suggest the presence of more than two), and even more unlikely that they were in a semicircle, as that is a very un-pharaonic architectural style.

On his way back to Madinat al-Fayum on this trip, Vansleb detoured to visit the 'needle' (obelisk) of 'Bibig' (Abgig). The obelisk was on the ground, with no base, in the middle of a cornfield, with no buildings nearby. He says it was 6 feet by 4 feet wide and very tall, with no sharp point at the top, covered in hieroglyphic signs divided into ranks that were much eroded and covered in white bird dung.[32] Vansleb had no doubt that the lake was the famous Lake Moeris of Pliny, with the famous castle of the vizier Caron (Qasr Qarun) at its western end. The lake received all its waters from the region during the floods, and from the river of Joseph.[33] The opposite shores of the lake were flanked by sand deserts in which, he was told, were many ruins of ancient towns, particularly Temeh of Lions (Dimai) and the monastery of Deir Abu Lifa. The Labyrinth lay at the western end of the lake, said by Pliny to have been built without using any wood. Qarun, Vansleb says, was a famous lord in the histories of the Arabs who was believed to be buried at Qasr Qarun with his treasure, which was kept in place by terrible talismans. The castle had 365 chambers in which a man would get lost. Vansleb desired to travel to see this, but was warned against it as it was considered too dangerous; the danger apparently lay in the jealous guarding of the treasures by the local 'Moors.'[34]

Vansleb tried to visit Hawara but the pyramid was in a sandy wilderness and hard to reach. His group traveled through the dried-up course of the Bahr bila-Ma' but was unable to cross the ditch of the river of Joseph, having to view the pyramid (which appeared "more like a pile of dust") from a distance. Vansleb comments that around the pyramid were "wells of mummies." On the return to Madinat al-Fayum his group traveled back through the dry riverbed, passing the ruins of an ancient town and a very ancient bridge. He notes that the pyramid of Lahun was said by Arab historians to have been built by Joseph, and refers the reader to Maqrizi.[35]

Vansleb's account is primarily descriptive. His main interests were the ancient sites, as he was on a mission to gather manuscripts, although he makes no direct mention of this in his account. Since there were no contemporary accounts available to guide him around the region, as existing accounts did not include the Fayum, he had to rely totally on the guidance of locals and Classical/Islamic accounts. He names several Islamic authors and it is possible that he had also read the French translation of the account of Murtada, produced in 1666. Being one of the more detailed accounts, it would have provided him with a good deal of useful information.

The fact that Vansleb mentions nearly all the major pharaonic ruins—Biahmu, Abgig, Qasr Qarun, Hawara, Lahun, and sites on the northern shores of the lake—is interesting because no 'real' monuments are mentioned in either the Classical or Islamic accounts. He clearly asked to visit ancient sites and ruins, and it seems that the locals were well aware of nearly all the ancient Egyptian remains in their region. There were obviously still many tales regarding Joseph alive in the region. Not only was the creation of the river attributed to him, but also several other works, such as bridges. It seems likely that the locals may well have attributed anything 'ancient' to Joseph or the pharaohs. The reference to the channel of Manhi/Menha is one of the last to appear in a written account. Despite appearing regularly in the Islamic accounts, this name died out, virtually falling out of use in the region by the time of Vansleb's visit. Even in his account there is a notable difference in the description of it: in the Islamic accounts the Bahr Manha runs to the Fayum and the Bahr Yusuf runs into Madinat al-Fayum, while in his account the watercourse is named the Bahr Manha/Bahr Yusuf. He was clearly uncertain about which river/canal was named what. This account does include the first reference to a legend of Qarun. Although this story appears in the Qur'an, it does not appear in any of the medieval Islamic geographies or histories, which begs the question of how this specific legend began.

Vansleb had no reason to be particularly interested in the landscape. He was not interested in contemporary Egyptian culture and so had no motive to record land use or productivity. The one aspect of the landscape he does note is the waterways he had to negotiate in order to travel about. He was interested in the monuments as potentially good locations for collecting, but at this time these monuments were essentially incomprehensible curiosities. The only 'knowledge' available to explain their function or purpose derived from Classical accounts, and none of those accounts mention any of the sites he visited.

Vansleb attributed equal value to the Classical accounts, the Islamic accounts, and the local stories. Man-made elements of the landscape were easily attributed to both Joseph and the pharaonic inhabitants, given that he understood Moeris to be ancient Egyptian. He would have had no conception of ancient chronology, nor any sense of ancient Egyptian history. He viewed the monuments simply as ancient works, with no specific idea of who created them, when, or for what purpose. At this time the Pyramids at Giza and the obelisks of Heliopolis were the only antiquities that had ever attracted any real attention, and very few travelers had ever ventured up the Nile. Vansleb described what he saw, not what he wanted to see, and this is an account about antiquities. Vansleb's Fayum landscape consisted of standing monuments and the physical remains of human intervention in the landscape.

Paul Lucas (1664–1737)

Paul Lucas was a doctor, naturalist, merchant, and antiquarian born in Rouen, France. It is possible that his desire to travel was inspired by his father, a merchant who traded in precious stones.[36] On his first trip to Egypt he was not traveling for religious purposes or as an employee of the French state; instead, he had a personal goal to make a description of Egypt from Cairo to the cataracts—an exceptionally ambitious aim for that time. He was also interested in antiquities and did some collecting for the state, but he was never fully financed and so must have done some trading during his travels to support himself. He was certainly not personally wealthy and thus was probably not simply traveling in order to make his name known as a great explorer.[37] There can be no doubt, however, that he had a great passion for travel and was first and foremost an adventurer.

There is some question over the authorship of the publications, as it is thought that successive editors were essentially ghost-writing for Lucas based on his journals. Lucas made three voyages to Egypt, in 1699–1703, 1704–08, and from May 1714 to November 1717.[38] Each journey was published (in 1704, 1712, and 1719 respectively) and more recently republished with forewords by Henri Duranton.[39] From the outset Lucas wanted to visit the Fayum. On his first trip he was unable to get there, but during his second and third voyages he was able to make trips to the Fayum. His second trip was specifically commissioned by the state for collecting, possibly due to the fact that he returned to France after his first (personally financed) trip with 'curiosities' that he presented to Louis XV.[40]

The Second Voyage (1704–08)

Paul Lucas was attracted to the Fayum by the fame of its fertility. His familiarity with Islamic accounts is apparent from his noting that "according to Arab historians" the Fayum was "separated from Egypt, as Egypt was separated from the world, by deserts and sea."[41] He also repeated the story of 'Amr ibn al-'As's discovery of the region. Lucas described the region as "a plain surrounded on all sides by mountains."[42] He considered the Fayum to be home to the finest ancient monuments and antiquities (the canals being included as antiquities), which he said were believed to be the works of the prophet Joseph by oriental historians. He stated that Madinat al-Fayum was built on one side of the ruins of ancient Arsinoë and that the canal on which he traveled to the region, which passed through the city, was named the Bahr Yusuf—no mention any more of the Menha canal. The city was filled with bridges and there were many traces of ancient monuments such as marble and granite columns, capitals, and pedestals. The region had exceptionally fertile soil and the Fayumis were able to cultivate many fruits. He attributed its name, al-Fayum, to the fact that Joseph had taken a thousand days—alf youm—to complete his work.[43]

On his first, shorter trip to the Fayum (the second voyage), Lucas visited the obelisk of Abgig and the village of Fidimin, in which he said he could see many carved and broken stones. He appears to have also visited some catacombs near Sinnuris.[44] He spent some time in Sinnuris and spoke with a local sheikh who told him several stories, one of which Lucas presented in full, in a similar story-telling style to that found in the medieval Islamic histories. The story was a legend of Qarun and began in pharaonic times in a nearby town that was a residence for the pharaohs. A lady of the town who was unable to become pregnant saw the fertility of the animals around her and flew into a rage blaming the gods for her predicament. She heard a voice that proclaimed she would have a son named Qarun who would become great, like a pharaoh. She did indeed give birth to a son, whom she named Qarun. However, Qarun was malicious and greedy. He conceived a plot to become rich by camping in the place where people came to pass across the lake with the bodies of the dead for burial and demanding a fee, stating that this was an order from the king. He carried out this plan for several years, but was finally discovered when he failed to recognize the king and tried to demand payment from him. Qarun was sent for by the pharaoh and cleverly extricated himself from his situation by claiming that he was collecting the money in order to enrich the pharaoh's coffers. The king then made Qarun a vizier and gave him a palace. Qarun was credited with inventing taxation, and became so rich that he eventually killed the king and took the throne himself.[45]

Lucas was told that the castle of Qarun had more than four hundred chambers, and it was believed that anyone who entered it would be lost and unable to leave. The Fayumis gave him a reason for this superstition: the palace was filled with treasures and guarded by powerful talismans that killed all those who were bold enough to enter it.[46] Lucas was annoyed not to be able to enter the 'castle,' although he did note that it appeared to be very large. On his return to Madinat al-Fayum from the lake, he passed Biahmu, where a 'giant stone statue' could be seen. The statue, which the people of the region called 'statue of the pharaoh' was mutilated, with no head or arms, but it sat on a large pedestal. He reported that nearby were five other pedestals in a semicircle, smaller than the former and without statues. This is almost certainly simply a case of Lucas repeating Vansleb's account. En route back to Cairo, he traveled along the canal, from which he observed brick roads and a bridge of ten arches, as well as two pyramids.[47]

One other tale Lucas gathered was apparently the most frequently told history of the region at the time, which does not actually appear in any of the (available) Islamic accounts:

> A king of Egypt was going to conquer Ethiopia, he remained 20 years on that expedition. During the time there the vizier usurped the kingdom of which he had the regency, persuaded that the king would never return. However, apprehensive in case the king did return he took precautions in case the king reappeared as conqueror. To this end he had the marsh of Fayum cleared, and had many towns built, and fortified one, not only with the usual methods but also with the protection of talismans. The king did return and the usurper was forced to retire to that town, but as nobody dared to attack it the Pharaoh was forced to hand the region over to the vizier/usurper.[48]

The Third Voyage (1714–17)

On his third voyage to Egypt, Lucas was determined to visit what he believed to be the Labyrinth at Qasr Qarun. On arrival at the Fayum lake in February 1717, he asked two fishermen to conduct him to the island in the lake, on which he believed there to be 'most curious' things, perhaps the debris of the pyramids about which Herodotus had written—a fairly logical assumption. Lucas noted that Herodotus considered the lake to be the most admirable monument in all of Egypt, which, along with the canal, was the work of an ancient king, and that the Labyrinth was the most beautiful monument in Egypt. Lucas discussed the dimensions of the lake as provided by Herodotus and made profuse statements of admiration regarding the skill of the ancient engineers who created the region's irrigation system.[49]

During this trip to the lake arrangements had been made for him to be introduced to the sheikh of the village closest to Qasr Qarun, where he was provided with thirty men for protection against armed robbers known to be in the region. During the journey he was told "a thousand" tales about the region, Qarun featuring in many of them. He was told that Qarun, master of the region and its three thousand villages, was so malicious that he used his magic to turn the region into the most sterile and desertified region of Egypt. He first enchanted a great flood to the region, then made a large wind blow that covered the region with sand. Lucas understood these tales to be fables, but felt that it was his job as a traveler to return accounts of the traditions of the lands he visited and that many scholars found some underlying truth in these tales. Lucas questioned the idea that the region was ever abandoned, convinced by the various ruins he saw on his journeys that it must have always been habitable. As his expedition advanced on its way toward Qasr Qarun, Lucas noted that there were considerable remains of ancient towns in the desert areas. As they approached they were hit by another sand and rain storm, which some people, he said, would conclude was the protection enchantments in effect.[50]

They eventually arrived, Lucas noting (correctly) that no modern voyager had entered that monument. He did what so many early travelers did and left his name on the monument (see Figure 18). His belief that Qasr Qarun was the Labyrinth was bolstered by his understanding that Herodotus and Pliny had placed it close to ancient Arsinoë, which, in the context of Egypt as a whole, it is. He noted that near the monument were many fallen blocks, and described the temple in great detail, listing every pylon and court, counting 150 chambers in total, many of which he had to crawl on his belly to enter. When comparing this Labyrinth to the one on Crete, he stated that the Egyptian Labyrinth was far larger and more varied. He was told by an "old Arab" that it used to be possible to enter underground chambers. He decided that he could not question Herodotus regarding the function of the Labyrinth as a place of worship for ancient kings and crocodiles, and he attributed the differences in the ancient descriptions to the inherently confusing nature of the monument and the fact that each scholar had chosen to describe the elements he personally found most interesting—very insightful.[51]

Lucas chose to sleep in the temple, and after a mildly eventful night he searched all around the area, concluding that the amount of ruins nearby must indicate that the monument had previously been considerably larger. The group set off in order for Lucas to make a return visit to the lake. He examined the island in the lake with his telescope, and was told by his guides that they had been there and seen many monuments on it, such as ruins of temples, tombs, and many large stones, as well as figures

18. Lucas graffiti in Qasr Qarun. *Photograph by Claire J. Malleson/Pier Paolo Raffa.*

of men, women, and animals—stories obviously fabricated to entertain their customer. None of them knew of the pyramids (of Herodotus) and after inspection Lucas concluded that the island appeared to be nothing more than a rock, but a rock made by the king who created the lake. He departed the Fayum taking the road to Beni Suef, passing the pyramid of 'Davara' (Hawara). He observed that when the river overflowed, the waters passed under the bridge before spreading into the countryside. He was certain that the bridge was an ancient work with the same date as the canal of Joseph.[52]

There is another section in the publication on Lucas's third voyage dedicated to descriptions of several different areas of Egypt, including the Fayum. He notes, and repeats, that the Fayum was the most fertile and most populated region of Egypt, producing fine linen and large quantities of many varieties of fruits. The region "started" at Laon (Lahun), near the canal of Joseph, and the deserts of Libya were its western limit. The province contained 360 villages. The canal, called the river of Joseph, derived from the Nile and was the source of the fertility of the region. Near the region was a small area filled with "an infinity" of palms, producing the best dates in Egypt. The capital of the province was al-Fayum, which was large and well populated and built on the ruins of ancient Arsinoë. It was still possible to see many antiquities in the town.[53]

By the time of Lucas's trip oriental studies were becoming more established, and he refers at least once to the opinions of 'oriental scholars' in his account. There was more reference material available to him before he traveled than there had been to earlier scholars, including not only better access to Classical materials but also more contemporary travel accounts. Although the focus of his account was the antiquities in the region, he also discussed the produce of the region and is one of the only Western writers to have recorded contemporary local stories in detail. There is a real sense of adventure and exploration in Lucas's lengthy and vivid account of his trip to Qasr Qarun. His approach to the region is representative of early orientalist approaches. He was interested in both the antiquities and 'modern' culture, taking a more anthropological approach. Lucas's account blends the earlier approach of the medieval Islamic scholars (whom he had read), who focused on gathering stories about histories, with the more Westernized approach to an archaeological landscape in which the primary focus was on the description of the monuments and validation of older accounts.

It is not clear if Lucas actually visited all the monuments he described. His account of Biahmu is essentially identical to that of Vansleb, but his descriptions of Fidimin, Sinnuris, and Abgig are original and he probably did spend time in each of those places. During his first trip to the region he gathered several local stories, but in contrast to the Islamic accounts the legends he recorded all associated one character, Qarun, rather than the creation of the region set within the Joseph story. Once again, more layers were added to the traditions about the Fayum landscape. It is likely that his professed personal interest in Qasr Qarun meant that he asked many people about the temple and therefore gathered many stories about Qarun. As was the case with Herodotus, and continues to be the case today, when he asked locals about ancient monuments they provided him with entertaining 'histories,' which he recounted to entertain his own audience in order perhaps to secure future funding for his explorations. The one key point to note is that even in these Qarun myths, the region is associated with a residence of the pharaoh and the presence of a (royal) woman connected with divine conception. Essentially this Fayum creation story is an elaborate version of the Qur'anic morality story of Qarun (or Korah, 28:72–83), presented with a local twist placing the events in the region.

The purpose of Lucas's visit brought him more into contact with locals, and with the stories that revolved around the shaping of the landscape. In some respects he describes two different landscapes: the Classical one, which is represented by the monuments to which he traveled, and the one he encountered along the way, which was the landscape magically shaped and protected by legendary ancient kings. The monuments invited exploration and recording, and had somehow to be reconciled with the classical descriptions. They were objects to be studied. He experienced the monumental landscape, which was divorced from the present by the fact that these were such ancient works, but also divorced from the surrounding land. The ancient landscape full of history needed to be conjured up via stories and fables; it could not be directly experienced as it no longer existed. These stories only partly related to the monuments. This temporalization of the landscape became a dominant theme in travel accounts over the next century,[54] though it had in essence been in place since the earliest creation stories were recorded. This ancient landscape was one which Lucas and later travelers sought to experience. He imbued the landscape with meaning; fables, legends, and tales provided explanations for aspects of the landscape and the monuments. He possibly related to the monuments, which were familiar and 'belonged' to his own Western/Classical history. Perhaps far more than any later traveler, Lucas accepted the local stories, attributing to them as much value as to the Classical Greco–Roman sources. Perhaps he trusted the stories more because he trusted them to have roots in the Qur'an, a text he respected as being scholarly.

The Eighteenth Century: Enlightenment and Collectors

A number of factors began to have great effect on European travel and travel writing in the eighteenth century. The Industrial Revolution facilitated the means to travel and was the backdrop for the reactionary picturesque movement in the arts. The perceived destruction of the natural unsullied landscape and 'invasion' by factories led to the formation of ideas still held today: that the natural landscape is the purest form of beauty. The eighteenth-century Enlightenment movement saw rationalism come to the fore, the search for the empirical truth was the basis of science, and the past was seen to hold clues for the advancement of nations in the future.[55]

European travelers in the eighteenth century increasingly began to 'temporalize' the landscape of the countries they visited, viewing them as antique lands rather than acknowledging the reality of the modern landscape. As the number of published works steadily increased, accounts become more literary and more subjective because their authors felt they needed to be entertaining in order to maintain a readership. By the end of the eighteenth century travel writing was the most popular form of literature after theology. Accounts were published at more affordable prices and available to the general public in popular periodicals. By collecting and recording their observations of artifacts, monuments, plants, animals, traditions, and the landscape in its physical form, and by taking these observations 'home' in books, people were taking possession of the culture. Equally, by psychologically closing the physical distance between countries, the 'other' landscape became almost familiar. Romanticism played an important role in the creation of these accounts, providing the writers with a mechanism to temporalize the landscape, to discuss it as an antique land—once glorious, now faded.[56]

Fueling the exotic image of the Near East at the start of the eighteenth century was the publication of the *Arabian Nights* in translation (Antoine Galland, 1704–17), which instantly became hugely popular. One task undertaken by travelers to the Near East was to authenticate the stories in the tales, and they traveled hoping to encounter the scenes the book depicted.[57] The people involved in collecting 'curiosities'—both those who funded it and those who traveled abroad to obtain the objects—began to develop a group identity. Two major groups with interests in ancient Egypt were formed in the early eighteenth century: the Society of Antiquities (founded 1707) in London and the Académie des Inscriptions et Belle Lettres (founded 1701) in Paris. The very first Egyptian Society was founded in London in 1741. These collectors began displaying their antiquities in part to share these resources, in part to demonstrate their own wealth and status to the largest audience possible, and museums were 'born.' The first publicly funded museum in Britain was founded in 1753, with a large collection of Egyptian antiquities bequeathed to the British government by Sir Hans Sloane (1660–1753). This became the British Museum, which opened to the public in 1759.[58]

The work of the philosopher John Locke (1632–1704) had a great influence on literature of this period. While Locke wrote many works on politics, it was his *Essay Concerning Human Understanding* (1690) that had the most impact on thinking of the time.[59] In the essay Locke supports the notion that all intelligence is acquired through experiences. He argues that at birth the mind is a blank canvas and that the primary sense through which knowledge is gained is vision. He repeatedly uses the metaphor of a picture to describe the way in which abstract ideas, memories, are held in the brain—ideas as pictures.

Locke's ideas were promoted by Joseph Addison, the founder of *The Spectator*, in which some of the most influential literary criticism and philosophical writings of the time were published. Addison himself wrote many articles on *Paradise Lost*, and importantly he wrote an account of his travels in Italy. But in *The Spectator* (June–November 1712) he wrote about the pleasures of the imagination, a topic of great concern in eighteenth-century philosophy. It was in these works that he referenced Locke.[60] Addison discussed the idea that natural objects—elements of the landscape—are among those that have the sense of a 'rude magnificence,' which can invoke a sense of happiness, amusement, or awe in man. Vast expanses of desert or water, or huge mountains, are sublime and created by God in order for man to fully appreciate His divine nature and to provide sources of happiness for man.[61] Addison promotes Locke's ideas about vision being the primary sense and the concept of 'pictures' as metaphors for the imagination, proposing that:

> we cannot have a single image . . . that did not make its first entrance by sight; we have the power of retaining, altering and compounding those images which we have once received, into all varieties of picture and vision that are most agreeable to the imagination; for by that faculty a man in a dungeon is capable of entertaining himself with scenes and landskips more beautiful than any that can be found in the whole compass of nature.[62]

These ideas can be considered part of the 'picturesque' movement, in which landscape painters and romantic poets sought to capture beauty, pleasure, and a sense of paradise in the depiction of nature. At this time, writers were coming to terms with great advances in science, which required a reevaluation of the cosmos and our place in nature.[63] The Grand Tour of Europe had placed the educated classes in the middle of landscapes they struggled to describe. The wild ruggedness of mountains seemed to have more in common with concepts of earthly Eden as found in *Paradise Lost*, and it was artists and poets who captured this sense of beauty. As travel in the Near East and Egypt expanded, even more landscapes of beauty were encountered. Indeed, Addison's vast expanses of desert were there to be experienced. Ruins were considered to be a part of this natural, wild paradise.[64]

Richard Pococke (1704–65)

Reverend Richard Pococke (later bishop of Meath, Ireland; not a direct relation of Edward Pococke, the seventeenth century orientalist), grew up in Southampton and studied at Oxford University, after which he had an easy ascension through the ranks of the church.[65] Pococke traveled to

Egypt in 1737–38 and was a member of the short-lived Egyptian Society founded by William Stukeley in 1741 to promote "Egyptian and other ancient learning."[66] His two-volume publication, *A Description of the East, and Some Other Countries 1743–45*, is considered by some to be the most authoritative and comprehensive English account of Egypt of the eighteenth century. It contains some of the earliest detailed records of many archaeological sites in Egypt. His account was designed primarily to impart information on both the antiquities and modern Egypt and is, to some extent, a catalog of curiosities. He was persuaded to include some description of his experiences by friends in order to render the book more popular.[67] In the preface, Pococke states that his initial plan was to make a record of ancient architecture in the style of Joseph Addison's influential book *Remarks on Several Parts of Italy* (1705), but that he then decided also to make an account of modern Egypt and its Turkish government. One of his main objectives was to check the Classical accounts of the monuments and topography of Egypt.[68]

Pococke traveled to the Fayum in February 1737, when the smaller canals were dry, via Mit Rahina and Dahshur to Tamiya. (See plate 18 for map of towns mentioned by European travelers.) From there his group traveled to Sinnuris, where he said they were "in the province of Arsinoë; the most beautiful place in Egypt according to Strabo."[69] The group continued to Biahmu where Pococke thought that there must have been a considerable ancient city or large buildings. To the north of the village there were ruins either side of the road that he "found" to be pyramids, called "al-harem Biahmu" by the locals. This is the only account in which these are pyramids named by the locals, and it is possible either that the local name was the root of Herodotus's misunderstanding or that so many travelers had asked to see the 'pyramids' near Biahmu that the locals began to refer to them as pyramids. It is also important to recognize that Pococke records that they were on either side of the road, more obviously forming the 'entrance' to the heart of the region than they do today. The party arrived at al-Fayum, passed through the "heaps" of ancient Arsinoë, and entered the city from the north. Pococke explored the ruins of Arsinoë, which according to Strabo were once known as the city of crocodiles, the animals being bred in the lake (twelve miles away). He conjectured that the city was about four miles in circumference, with a canal on each side. He repeated the King Menes story of Diodorus and noted many canals and brick bridges all around the ancient city.[70]

Pococke visited the obelisk at Abgig, carefully recording the decoration on it. Close to Nesle (al-Nazla) he could see, at a distance, the ruins of two 'castles,' 'Casr Cophou' and 'Casr Cobal,' although which sites he could see is hard to know. To the west he could see a hill, shaped like a pyramid, and named 'al-harem Medaiah al-Hebgad' by the locals. At a great distance from there he could see the ruins of the Labyrinth (Qasr Qarun), surrounded by "heaps of ruins" and many stones "as if there had been some great building there." It was known locally, he recalls, as the town of Caroon and seemed to have had great breadth from east to west, extending north to the lake. Pococke quotes Diodorus, Strabo, and Pomponius Mela on the subject of the Labyrinth. He did visit it, recording the visible ruins of the 'main' building and noting that this site was now known as Qasr Qarun. Pococke encountered some difficulties in verifying the measurements (of the Labyrinth) of Strabo and Herodotus with those he found at Qasr Qarun, but like Lucas he concluded that the ancient authors must have been confused. Pococke also notes the different dimensions of the lake recorded by various authors (Diodorus, Pomponius Mela).[71]

In his account, Pococke discusses Herodotus's account of the creation of the lake, and questions the notion that the water ran into the lake for six months and out for six months. He also notes that some accounts stated that the lake was designed to prevent the river from overflowing too much. He decided that this outflow of the Nile must have been via the valley of Bahr Belame (al-Bahr bila-Ma', 'the river without water') into the sea, as the valley extended from the west end of the lake as far as the sea. Quite how he 'knew' this is difficult to imagine. When sufficient water had been let out, the valley was blocked, thus creating the lake. Afterward, at some point, the canal into the lake became blocked and the lake dried up, giving rise to the stories about the area once having been a plain or fields. Then, Moeris opened up the blockage, installed floodgates, and in some areas increased the depth of the lake, during which time the lake was considerably smaller. Pococke considered this to be the root of the legend that the lake was created by Moeris.[72]

Like Lucas, Pococke connected the island in the lake with the remains of Herodotus's pyramids. He could also see buildings to the north of the lake and was told that the building he thought to be ancient ruins was the monastery of Deir al-Harakatilmi. Pococke mentions the traditions surrounding Qarun, stating that Qarun was a king with many treasures. He then discusses the story that he controlled transport across the lake to the burials on the island. He notes that Diodorus recorded the ceremony of transporting bodies across water at Memphis, thinking that perhaps the lake here might have had the same function.[73] Traveling on from Qasr Qarun the party continued back to Nesle, through Tobhar, on to Sanhur, and back to al-Fayum. While at Nesle Pococke asked to be taken to the two great pyramids of 'Davara,' which he could see ten to twelve miles south of al-Fayum. As they were on the wrong side of the canal he was unable to visit them. He was told that they were made of unburned brick, and that one of them was built with three stories of arched niches. Pococke departed the Fayum via Tamiya to Dahshur and Cairo.[74]

Pococke visited the Fayum in order to describe the region and its monuments. He was a classically educated gentleman of his age, prepared for a career in the Church, who had the means to travel and make a name for himself by engaging in scholarly activities. His focus was entirely on validating the Classical accounts via rational scientific explanation. Although he makes no reference to other accounts of Egypt, he is likely to have at least read some of the most important accounts of earlier European travelers. He accepted the ruinous state of the ancient capital at Madinat al-Fayum, but like other travelers he was not particularly interested in exploring it any further. Knowing the location seems to have been enough, although he is the only European traveler to make any mention of crocodiles.

Some of the landscape Pococke passed through between monuments is included in his accounts, but in a very matter-of-fact manner, recording crops or soil types. He described the major rivers and canals but, again, only in order to create a record of their condition. There is no implication that they were significant ancient works. The only exception is the canal that supplied the lake, because its creation by Moeris appeared in the Classical accounts. He makes one mention of the stories about Qarun, and suggests that they were derived from the description by Diodorus of the transport of bodies across the water at Memphis[75]—thus totally invalidating the indigenous Coptic/Islamic story.

His description is highly representative of the beginnings of Egyptology: gathering information, recording locations and descriptions of monuments, and focusing totally on the antiquities. He saw the landscape merely as a backdrop in which the ancient monuments were located. His landscape consisted of a series of monuments that held importance because they had been described by the Classical authors.

The Beginning of the Great Explorations

The French Revolution and the Napoleonic Wars changed the face of politics and culture across Europe. Napoleon's invasion of Egypt was driven in part by his desire to threaten Britain's interests in the East, and he deliberately set out to emulate Alexander the Great. He brought savants with him to explore and record every aspect of Egyptian society, including the antiquities.[76] One of the aims of the resulting publication, *Description de l'Égypte* (1809–28), was to 'reconstruct Egypt.' In it, the landscape was reordered by translating the 'chaos' of Arabic placenames into Latin script. The chaos of the ruined monuments was brought under control through reconstruction drawings and detailed measurements.[77] The *Description* has been a focus of renewed interest in recent years. Various studies have highlighted not only the political aims and effects of the publication, but also the effect it had on the study of Egypt and Egyptology. Anne Godlewska (1995) adopts an approach taken from cartographical studies and advocated by Brian Harley, arguing that the maps were representative of new approaches to imperialism. They represent a focus on scientific fact and demonstrate the way in which the French sought to take control of Egypt's heritage by rationalizing, recording, and representing it within their own formats.[78] Andrew Bednarski (2005) analyzes the reception of the *Description* in Great Britain in the early nineteenth century. He concludes that despite the seemingly ubiquitous nature of this work, it was in fact relatively inaccessible to British audiences. He argues that it was actually the works of Belzoni and Wilkinson that played a major role in popularizing images of Egypt and shaping early British Egyptology.[79]

The images of landscapes in the *Description* exclude all elements of modern Egypt. The images of monuments are usually surrounded by landscapes, but a landscape that is devoid of any contemporary elements. Many of the topographic maps suggest a high level of accuracy, despite the fact that very little precise information had been gathered.[80] Outside the publication of the *Description*, the French savants studied earlier works about Egypt and presented their own discussions of these materials, sometimes gathering all accounts of a location and then presenting and discussing this information in light of their work on the ground in Egypt.[81] It was probably in this vein that Jomard (1812) published his treatise on Lake Moeris.[82] Usually these sources were the Classical scholars. Very occasionally Arab scholars were discussed, but in the spirit of Enlightenment and dispelling of myth, during the colonial era the collection of local knowledge and folklore was specifically avoided.[83]

During the Napoleonic Wars (1799–1815) the focus of antiquarian travel changed from being a personal undertaking to a national one, meaning that missions were state-sponsored and run in the name of national prestige. New literary fashions reflected the perceived closeness of Europe to Egypt and a perception that the ancient Classical cultures were the root of modern European culture. Egypt came to be seen as a European antique land.[84] It was viewed as a colony, and therefore Egyptians were treated as subjects. The attitude toward the country was similar to that regarding other African nations, or India. Interest in 'ancient' Egypt was growing for several reasons. Accounts like that of Pococke, for instance, had piqued interest in ancient Egyptian art and architecture, but the intense competition between Britain and France to dominate Egypt at the start of the nineteenth century also often manifested itself in battles over antiquities—most notably the Rosetta Stone. Egyptian antiquities were voraciously collected as curiosities and wonders of the Biblical and Classical roots of European civilization.[85]

At the end of this period, in 1807, Muhammad 'Ali expelled the European armies and established Ottoman rule over Egypt. The country stabilized, and he set about modernizing the nation and taking advantage of trade with Europe. One major project was the development of the canal irrigation system of Egypt still found today,[86] including the reestablishment of the Fayum irrigation system. This stability encouraged a flood of European travelers to Egypt, including antiquarians and collectors, among them British Consul Henry Salt and French Consul Bernadino Drovetti, who continued the Anglo–French rivalry over antiquities. Even more than previously, Europe could now 'own' Egypt via the antiquities that were transported to museums and collections in huge numbers—a move Muhammad 'Ali allowed as a trade-off for increasing economic and diplomatic advantages.[87] His work on the hydrology of the Fayum transformed the region once again. The irrigation system had fallen into total disrepair and the habitable area of land had shrunk considerably, but the work Muhammad 'Ali instigated meant that the Fayum lands reached again the Ptolemaic extent. As a result, those sites around the outskirts of the region were 'discovered.'

Throughout the sixteenth and seventeenth centuries, collecting antiquities had been seen as a means of establishing oneself in society and thus preserving one's name for posterity. Increasingly in the eighteenth century it became a way of enhancing the image of one's country, with individuals seeking to promote themselves as great nationalists by developing collections for their nation. Private collections continued to be formed, but were often sold or donated to the new national collections that emerged. As a result, the first exhibition of Egyptian antiquities in the newly founded British Museum was in 1759, while the Louvre opened in 1792. Antiquities and ancient history were no longer the sole property of the educated wealthy elite.[88] Ancient sites had been excavated (rather than just plundered) in Italy since the early eighteenth century at Herculaneum and Pompeii, but prior to the French invasion of Egypt, Italy and Greece had been the only countries from which collectors could obtain objects.[89] After 1798 the borders of Egypt were open for antiquarians and collectors to easily obtain Egyptian antiquities.

The inability to read the ancient scripts and language or to comprehend the history of Egypt ensured that an air of mystery surrounded Egyptian antiquities for some time. This created two perceptions of Egypt, as a source of fantastic objects for collections and as a romanticized and mystical ancient culture. Despite the fact that hieroglyphs were not translated until 1825, however, a gradual unraveling of the perceived mysteries of Egypt started to lend a more scholarly air to studies of ancient Egypt. This was due in part to the travelers to Egypt who published first-hand accounts of the monuments.[90] By the nineteenth century those who traveled to Egypt specifically to study the remains no longer all saw themselves solely as antiquarians or collectors; they were gathering materials for the study of the ancient history. The discipline of archaeology started to appear as a profession, rather than just a hobby. Egyptian archaeology was taught in the Collège de France in Cairo.[91] However, philology still took precedence over archaeology as a means to learn about the ancient past.

Edme Jomard (1777–1862)

One key figure in the creation of the *Description de l'Égypte* was Edme François Jomard, who is credited with writing and editing much of the final work. He also published a small volume on Lake Moeris. Jomard, son of a silk merchant, was a member of Napoleon's Institut d'Égypte in Egypt. In fact, by 1859 he was the only surviving member of the mission.[92] His 1812 account of the Fayum, *Mémoire sur le Lac de Moeris Comparé au Lac du Fayoum*, was the first real study of the Lake Moeris 'problem.' Before his work was published, people simply accepted that the Fayum lake (Birkat Qarun) was Lake Moeris, and indeed the region did match the coordinates found in the 'map' of Ptolemy. Jomard was clearly acquainted with the accounts of Vansleb, Lucas, and Pococke. The great advantages Jomard had over his predecessors were that he had been a part of the first real survey expedition and not a lone traveler, and that by the time he wrote this account he had the *Description de l'Égypte* map (produced by Jean Baptiste Bourguignon d'Anville) available to him.

Notably, Jomard clearly states that the Bahr Yusuf ran up to Lahun, where a branch turned into the Fayum under a bridge and the main 'river of Joseph' continued north. He notes that the branch running into the Fayum was named Bahr Yusuf, and indeed he states that this branch turned north in Madinat al-Fayum toward Tamiya, where it joined the lake, with a second branch leaving the main river three kilometers after Hawara, which ran west past Nazla into the lake. Both branches (now known as al-Wadi and al-Bats drains) were clearly ancient as they ran through deep ravines, over a hundred meters wide and up to ten meters deep at origin, becoming considerably smaller (only about six meters wide) close to the lake.[93]

When considering Lake Moeris, Jomard begins by stating that the ancient accounts were undoubtedly somewhat exaggerated. He remarks that Herodotus had not only been confused about different terms for distances in different languages, but had also wanted to convey a sense of the 'marvelous' in his account. It was apparent to Jomard that the size of the lake had varied a great deal, and he notes the visible 'high water' line. One of the biggest problems he felt needed addressing was the fact that Herodotus described a lake that had its greatest length from north to south, which was not the case for Birkat Qarun. He explains this by concluding that the general line of the Libyan mountains is north to south, and thus that Herodotus probably just assumed this was the natural border of the lake.[94]

Jomard was aware that Herodotus visited Egypt during the Persian period, and that it was likely that the irrigation of the region was in disrepair at that time. Later, at least during the Roman period, the irrigation system was better maintained. He attempted to trace as many different accounts of the lake as he could and presented them chronologically, concluding that since the time of Augustus the irrigation had been so neglected that the original Lake Moeris had shrunk to the far smaller Birkat Qarun.[95] On the issue of whether the lake was artificial, he is fairly clear that although people simply accepted the statement of Herodotus that it was artificial, this was clearly preposterous given the size of the basin. He proposes that 'Moeris' cut the branch of the Nile known as the Bahr Yusuf and linked the Nile waters to the two ravines in the Fayum.[96]

Jomard's account became one of the foundations for all later studies of the issue of Lake Moeris and the physical form of the Fayum landscape.

Giovanni Belzoni (1778–1823)

The 'Great' Giovanni Battista Belzoni was the son of a barber from Padua, Italy, who became one of the first great archaeologist–explorers of Egypt. He had a very varied early life, first studying hydraulics in Rome, followed by a brief career in the Church. In 1803 he worked at Sadler's Wells theater in London as a performing 'strongman' before becoming a full-time showman, often performing in 'oriental' dress.[97] In 1815 he went to Egypt in search of work as an engineer on the advice of an agent of Muhammad 'Ali whom he met in Malta. He soon met the French–Italian (ex-)French consul/collector Bernadino Drovetti, who was to become his arch rival in Egypt. British Consul Henry Salt employed Belzoni to collect antiquities for him. Belzoni transported many antiquities to England and discovered several important monuments, including the tombs of Seti I and Ay.[98] He has been greatly criticized for his methods, as he carved his name into many monuments and statues and damaged several tombs. But in comparison to his contemporaries, primarily Drovetti, and his predecessors, he is generally respected for the care he took to preserve sites and monuments.[99]

Belzoni's account, *Narrative of the Operations and Recent Discoveries within the Pyramids, Temples, Tombs and Excavations in Egypt and Nubia* (1820), is invaluable to Egyptologists as he recorded both the state of the monuments and his work in great detail. It was a highly popular account, which conveys (in a way that was unusually sympathetic for his time) his relationships with the local Egyptians.[100] He was, and still is, seen as an exceptional 'character.' Belzoni's previous career as a strongman, his choice to adopt local dress and observe local customs, and his behavior and long-standing public rivalry with Drovetti all contributed to his larger-than-life persona.

Belzoni visited the Fayum in 1819, while en route to the western oases. He considered the Fayum relatively unexplored and stated that he made efforts to visit all the known sites. After traveling to Beni Suef from Alexandria, his group stopped for the night close to the Lahun pyramid. Belzoni explored the pyramid environs and climbed to the top of it, noting that from there both Hawara and Madinat al-Fayum were visible, as was the valley entrance into the region. The group then moved on to Hawara, where Belzoni noted that the ruins of banks and dikes surrounding an area of six hundred square feet was probably the site of an ancient town, of which only a few blocks of stone and some brickwork remained. On the south side were the "remains of an Egyptian temple which must have been most magnificent"—although no mention is made of this being the possible location of the Labyrinth.[101]

On arrival in Madinat al-Fayum Belzoni arranged a trip to the lake. During the journey his group passed over the ruins of Arsinoë, arriving at Sinnuris in the evening. The following morning they proceeded toward the lake and Belzoni wrote that the mountains on the north side appeared to be sterile and 'awful.' The lake, which they reached at noon, appeared to be deserted. He compared the boat that appeared to take them across the lake to the mythical boat of Baris, or boat of Charon, which conveyed passengers to the land of the dead in Classical Greek mythology, likening the ferryman to Charon himself. The scene that greeted them on the far side of the lake appears to have evoked some emotion in Belzoni, and he launched into a highly romantic description of the landscape.[102]

> The scene here was beautiful—the silence of the night, the beams of radiant moon shining on the still water of the lake, the solitude of the place, the sight of our boat, the group of fishermen, the temple, which bears the name of Old Charon, a little way off, put me in mind of the Lake Acheron, the boat Baris and the old ferryman of the Styx. I perceived this was the very spot where the poets originated the fable of the passage of the souls over the river of Oblivion. Nothing could be more pleasing to my imagination than being so near Elysium, perhaps on the very Elysium itself. . . . I wish that I had been a poet, that I might sing in verse the beautiful ideas and sensations I felt on that occasion. I thought that night one of the happiest in my life, and myself out of the reach of evil mortals. Happy in the Elysian fields, I feared not the malice and treacherous arts of envy, jealousy, spite, revenge, nor the thousand other snares of man.[103]

After this poetic interlude, Belzoni returned to his usual matter-of-fact recounting of events. They rose early and returned to the boat to continue west to Qasr Qarun—the Labyrinth—which he observed to be in the middle of the ruins of a great city. After exploring the area he concluded that it could not be the site of the Labyrinth of Herodotus, as there were no remains anywhere that even slightly resembled his description of that monument. Belzoni determined that he would try to find the remains of a town he had seen marked on maps on the northern edge of the lake. He was told by the boatmen that there was nothing to be seen but some old houses and a tall wall, which was of course exactly what Belzoni was looking for. On arrival at some ruins on the northern edge of the lake he concluded them to be those of a Greek town, probably Bacchus (Bacchias), which he "had observed in some maps of ancient authors." He spent some time exploring and partially excavating areas of a town, which was called Dinay (Dimai) by the locals.[104]

Belzoni traveled to the island in the lake and back through the region, noting several areas of ruins along the route. He sought in vain the remains of the Labyrinth that according to Pliny were situated on the west side of the lake, and although he found many fragments of pink granite and other monumental remains in the region he found nothing he considered to be significant enough to be the ruins of the Labyrinth. He considered the possibility that the Labyrinth had been either totally engulfed by sand or flooded by the lake.[105] At Fidimin he managed to satisfy himself with a more conclusive answer to this question. He noted that the town was on a large mound and was clearly built on ruins. The full name of the town was 'Fedmin el Kunois'—Fidimin of the Churches—and he was told by the (Coptic) inhabitants that in ancient times there had been three hundred churches on that spot that fell into ruin and were subsequently built over by the new Muslim inhabitants. Belzoni pondered briefly the possibility that this story could invite modern travelers to think that this was the location of the Labyrinth, that the number three hundred could suggest the three thousand chambers of the Labyrinth of Herodotus. He examined the cut of the canal through the town, knowing that the remains of those three hundred churches should be visible (he was of the understanding that the canal was less than two hundred years old), and found no remains. He was thus certain that this spot was probably not the location of the Labyrinth, but that it cannot have been far away because of the large number of stone fragments clearly deriving from a large monument in the area.[106]

The group continued its journey "through beautiful country" back to Madinat al-Fayum. The following morning Belzoni went to visit the ruins of Arsinoë. He observed many fragments of granite statues and granite columns and large quantities of bricks. Based on the damage to all the remains he saw, he thought that the town must have been destroyed by fire. This small 'fact' hints at the possibility that he had been told the story recounted by Vansleb. He could see that much of the new town of Madinat al-Fayum appeared to be built out of ancient ruins, as fragments were visible throughout the town. He visited Abgig, but stated that so much had already been said about the obelisk that he would not report anything.[107] From Madinat al-Fayum he set out on his journey west to Siwa Oasis.

The most significant passage in this account is the one in which Belzoni conjures up the image of the Elysian fields, as it is the first time a writer really imbues the Fayum landscape with 'romantic' meaning. His imagery is primarily that of Greek and Roman legends. The use of the Elysian fields as a metaphor for paradise was not uncommon in eighteenth-century literature. Belzoni confused (or blended) Greek and Islamic mythology here, referring to Qasr Qarun as the temple of Charon (he then later names it Cassar el-Haron), and, perhaps understandably, confused the Qarun ferryman myth with that of the Greek/Roman mythological ferryman character Charon. His imagery derives primarily from Homer's *Odyssey* (Book Eleven) and Virgil's *Aeneid* (Book Six), naming the people and places associated with the passage to the afterlife in popular Greek and Roman folklore, including Charon the ferryman, the River Styx, Lake Acheron, and the Elysian fields.[108] The myth he recounts blends together these images from the Classics with aspects of the Qarun myth—ferrying of the deceased to the afterlife across a lake for money—and it seems plausible that he was told the Qarun myth then chose to retell it using more socially accepted and familiar Classical imagery. This also brought the Charon/Qarun story into the Classical European past, instead of the 'foreign' Islamic past. Although Belzoni was not a Classically educated gentleman of his age, he was well aware of the need to appear to be educated in order to be accepted into the realms of the men he mixed with—those who sponsored him.[109]

Belzoni's approach to the monuments was driven by his need to 'find' the Fayum of Herodotus, and he was the first writer to assert the fact that Qasr Qarun was not the location of the Labyrinth. The ruins around the region he recorded were monuments he examined in case they were the ruins of the Labyrinth. However, he was so focused on his self-imposed task that he did not even visit Biahmu or Abgig, as he knew they could not be the Labyrinth. His note that they were passing through "beautiful country" is the earliest reference to the fertility of the Fidimin area, which appealed hugely to the sensibilities of many later travelers. Belzoni's perception of the Fayum landscape was shaped entirely by the account of Herodotus and the paradise imagery of Classical mythology. He temporalized the landscape and employed Classical images and language to describe what he 'saw,' implying that he was somehow experiencing the ancient past by being in this landscape. The use of the familiar Greek and Latin myths and histories to describe the Fayum helped to 'claim' this ancient landscape as part of a European heritage.

The Age of Orientalism

The London arrival of the bust of Rameses II, famously removed from the Ramesseum by Belzoni in 1816, played a large part in developing the romantic image of Egypt in the early nineteenth century. Belzoni's great exhibition was the cause of a surge in interest in ancient Egypt. The bust was the subject of the popular and hugely influential Shelley sonnet "Ozymandias" (1818). The foundations for the scholarly discipline of orientalism had been set in France in the late eighteenth century by Silvestre de Sacy. De Sacy established orientalism as a formal discipline and trained generations of academics in 'oriental' languages: Persian, Arabic, and Turkish. Philology was considered to be a cutting-edge science.[110] Many geographical, historical, and mathematical works by medieval Islamic scholars were translated and studied during the nineteenth century, and this scholarly fascination with the 'Orient' was reflected in the arts, in the romantic movement. To some extent, these scholars began to view medieval Islamic heritage in the same way they viewed ancient Egyptian civilization, as once great and now decayed. The Ottoman Empire was seen to be the force responsible for destroying the classical Islamic culture of the eighth to the tenth centuries, which produced great scholarly works. It was the works of this 'classical' period that were the focus of the work of orientalist scholars.[111]

The nineteenth-century orientalist movement can be viewed in different ways. For some, Western fascination with and, in many cases, colonization of 'oriental' nations, eastern and Arab, can only be understood as part of a period in which all 'non-white' societies were thought to be inferior and less 'civilized.' Any interest in or study of customs, traditions, and history of those countries was undertaken with a view to appreciating and promoting the superiority of Western society. However, this view of the orientalist movement is simplistic. While the underlying culture and sensibilities of the era undoubtedly affected the way in which Europeans perceived and interacted with people in Africa and the Near, Middle, and Far East (or perhaps more appropriately, in Western Asia), many of these scholars genuinely felt that the traditions of the people they chose to live with and the societies they engaged with and studied, were in many ways superior to Western/European society. Whichever way one thinks about the opinions and outlook of orientalist scholars, there can be no doubt that they were deeply fascinated with many aspects of both ancient and modern society in the 'East,' and Egypt was one of the most popular places for travel and study by these scholars.

The early nineteenth century was also a period of great change in the natural sciences. The revolutionary work of scholars such as Charles Lyell, Jean-Baptiste Lamarck, and Charles Darwin was dramatically changing ideas about the human past. These advances played a major role in the development of archaeology as a distinct professional and academic discipline as it is understood today. But in the study of the Classical Greek, Roman, and Egyptian empires, art and architecture remained the focus. Work by various scholars on the translation of hieroglyphs transformed the study of ancient Egypt. Once the script was deciphered, the principal task of the Egyptologist working in Egypt was the recording of inscriptions on monuments. Many of the most eminent 'explorer' Egyptologists in Egypt during the early nineteenth century knew each other well, and frequently met or collaborated. Many chose to live in Egypt as anonymously as possible, adopting local Ottoman (Turkish) dress and customs.

Linant de Bellefonds (1799–1883)

Born in Lorient, Brittany, Louis Maurice Adolphe Linant de Bellefonds grew up in a relatively privileged position as the son of a naval officer (his maternal grandfather was a general), and was therefore able to obtain a good education, especially in mathematics and art. He joined the Navy aged only fifteen, but by age eighteen had been recruited as a replacement for an artist on a scholarly expedition to the Near East, aboard *La Cléopâtre*, led by Louis de Forbin, the director of the National Museums of France. The mission arrived in Egypt in 1818 and Linant de Bellefonds decided to stay on, traveling extensively throughout Egypt, Sudan, and Arabia until 1831. His decision to settle in Cairo was due to new employment as an engineer for Muhammad 'Ali, who made him chief of works in 1873. Linant de Bellefonds died in Cairo in 1883.[112]

Early in his career Linant de Bellefonds worked for William Bankes as a draftsman on expeditions to the second cataract (with Belzoni and Salt) and in the Sudan. His first visit to the Fayum was in 1821, and on the basis of his observations during that trip and further research he was commissioned to 'find' Lake Moeris in order to restore it. He published a small volume entitled *Mémoires sur le Lac Moeris* in 1843, which formed the basis of an extended chapter in his book *Mémoires sur les Principaux Travaux d'Utilité Publique Executés en Égypte depuis la Plus Haute Antiquité jusqu'*à *Nos Jours* (1872–73).

Linant de Bellefonds agreed with Jomard's earlier conclusion that Lake Moeris was located in the Fayum, but was unconvinced that Birkat Qarun was the same lake as Lake Moeris. His discussion follows the usual method of recounting the Classical accounts of the lake and then comparing them with his observations in the Fayum. He concludes that the ancient Lake Moeris must have been situated in the northeastern portion of the region, based on his 'discovery' of the dike running close to the Bahr bila-Ma' ('river without water').[113] The Bahr bila-Ma' is referred to by different travelers but it is difficult to know if they all refer to the same wadi. Some locate it to the north of the lake, running north to the Mediterranean, and some identify what is now known as the al-Bats drain as the 'Bahr Belame.'

In common with Jomard, the account of the Fayum by Linant de Bellefonds differs in character to that of other European travelers. He was not aiming to entertain his readers but to inform them, and he considered himself first and foremost a scientist, an engineer, rather than an explorer, Egyptologist, or writer. But it was his work, and his theories, that vexed later scholars, especially Frederick Cope Whitehouse. Linant de Bellefonds's perception of the Fayum revolved entirely around the nature of the lake, and to a great extent his notion of the region was shaped by the Classical accounts. It is clear that he was actively seeking ways to restore the Fayum to the region described by Herodotus, that is, its ancient form. While his account may not shed any particular light on changing perceptions of the Fayum landscape, it does typify the attitude of so many of the increasing numbers of explorer–archaeologists in Egypt at that time. It is devoid of emotion toward the landscape due to the fact that these scholars were engaged in either recording the ancient monuments or running projects to 'improve' it.

Edward William Lane (1801–76)

The heartland of oriental studies during the nineteenth century was France, but one of the foremost oriental scholars of the early to mid-nineteenth century was the Briton Edward William Lane. His father, Theophilus, was an officer in the Royal Marines, later becoming an honorary canon attached to

Hereford Cathedral. His mother Sophia was the favorite niece of the artist Thomas Gainsborough, which probably played a part in the strong artistic inclinations she passed on to her fourth son. Lane had a solid education in Classics, Greek, Latin, French, art, and mathematics, but despite his scholarly disposition never attended university. Instead, he became an engraver.[114]

It was not long before Lane developed an intense passion for the study of ancient Egypt, and despite having no formal training set out to establish himself as an authority.[115] He went on to become the foremost European scholar of modern Egypt of his time. He taught himself Arabic, becoming fluent enough to produce significant translations of classical Arabic works, and was the first person to write an ethnographic study of Egypt. From the outset he was interested in both modern and ancient Egypt, and his work is still invaluable to Egyptology today. His *Description of Egypt* was only published in 2000, yet it would have been his first publication had the project been seen through to the end. It was the publishers' preference for *Manners and Customs of the Modern Egyptians* (1836), Lane's most successful publication, that prevented *Description of Egypt* from being published in his lifetime. Had *Description of Egypt* been published when written, it would have become one of the most important early Egyptological works.[116]

Lane was a highly focused individual and a deeply serious scholar, but also very perceptive and sensitive. He wanted to immerse himself in the culture of Egypt, and although he never formally converted to Islam many of his Egyptian friends believed he had done so because he was totally at ease practicing traditional prayers in a mosque. He was clearly a most personable young man and became a close friend and colleague of many of the European men who were busily exploring, surveying, and recording monuments in Egypt in the wake of the Napoleonic expedition, including Linant de Bellefonds, Robert Hay, James Burton, Henry Salt, and John Gardner Wilkinson. He was often asked to join expeditions due to his keen observation skills and attention to detail.[117]

The manuscripts he produced (in three editions) and his journals are held in the Bodleian, the Griffith Institute, and the British Library. His book was initially intended to be a four-volume set covering all his experiences in Egypt, as well as the history of Islamic Egypt, an account of the career of Muhammad 'Ali, and sections on aspects of life in Egypt. With each edition the parts covering modern Egypt grew, and the second draft contained a chapter entitled "Manners and Customs of the Moos'lim Egyptians."[118] It was this second manuscript that he submitted to the publishers, which stimulated them to suggest that the sections on modern Egypt and on his observations of antiquities be split into two separate books. He first worked on the *Description of Egypt*, producing a third draft of the book, which was due to contain a large number of illustrations and maps in three volumes of text and five volumes of plates. He returned to Egypt and worked on his account of modern Egypt, which was published without delay in 1836.[119] As time passed the *Description* became impossible to publish. Other authors such as Wilkinson had produced similar works and literary fashions had changed, so Lane turned to his translations and worked on a dictionary. He traveled to Egypt once again, with his sister Sophia Lane-Poole and her family. Sophia's son Stuart went on to become an Egyptologist and one of the founding members of the Egypt Exploration Fund (1882), while her other son Stanley became an orientalist.[120]

Lane's interest in Egypt is thought to have been inspired in the 1820s by Belzoni's 'Egyptian Hall' exhibition and the publication of his *Narrative of Operations*. Unlike many of his contemporaries, Lane became fascinated with modern Egypt and Arabic, not ancient Egypt and hieroglyphs (although he did retain some interest in antiquities). Like so many nineteenth-century city dwellers, his poor respiratory health meant that he was advised to spend time in a different climate, and he was given the chance to fulfill his ambitions to travel to Egypt through the assistance of a benefactor. In 1825 he set out for Alexandria via Malta, where he met Linant de Bellefonds.[121] On arrival in Cairo he immediately adopted local dress—Turkish, not Egyptian—which provided him with a means of ingratiating himself with the ruling classes (it was perhaps also a way of emulating his hero Belzoni). As he wanted to avoid being recognized as a European in order to properly immerse himself in Egyptian culture (and avoid 'Franks,' or Westerners, who were not popular and whom he generally disliked), he adopted an Arabic name, Mansur, and was soon fluent in Arabic. He avoided the Europeans in Cairo, except a few who also adopted Egyptian dress and customs.[122] His trips up the Nile provided him with a wealth of new experiences and insight into the lives of most Egyptians living in small rural towns. He described all aspects of their lives, making many illustrations using a camera lucida as he traveled, and provided a magnificent snapshot of the socioeconomic situation of individual villages.[123] Lane studied Arabic manuscripts, especially the *Khitat* of Maqrizi and the *'Aja'ib al-athar* of al-Jabarti, both of which provided him with much valuable historical information.[123]

Lane traveled up the Nile twice in order to see the antiquities, visiting all the major archaeological sites and recording them in great detail. This was a time of rapid growth in Egyptology, as Champollion had just made his breakthrough in deciphering the hieroglyphic script, yet comparatively little was known about the history of ancient Egypt. Lane, along with his contemporaries and colleagues (Hay, Burton, Wilkinson, and Linant de Bellefonds), was still working almost in the dark with regard to reading any of the inscriptions he so carefully recorded.

Chapter Nineteen of *Description of Egypt* covers the Fayum, which Lane visited during his second voyage up the Nile (the first trip began in March 1826 and lasted over seven months, but he did not go to the Fayum during that trip). His journey began from Beni Suef on June 26, 1827, and he was accompanying Robert Hay, with whom he had a good relationship.[125] From higher desert above the fields, they had a good view of the Lahun pyramid, the village of Lahun, and the village of Hawwarat al-Lahun, the pyramid and village of Hawara being obscured by trees. They passed over the dry bed of the canal of Bahr Yusuf and camped for the night by the 'new' bridge over the branch of the canal that ran to al-Fayum from Hawwarat al-Lahun. He states that the Greek port of the Arsinoë nome, Ptolemais (Eugertes), was situated at this village. Interestingly, he is the only person to ever mention this in an account of the region. At Lahun he noted the ancient dike running from the village to the pyramid. From the top of the pyramid he had an excellent view of the surrounding landscape: "Its verdure had a particularly pleasing appearance, contrasted with the glaring tracts of desert which hem it on either side."[126]

In his account Lane reflects on the matter of Lake Moeris, concluding that the artificial lake / wide section of canal found just before the entrance to the valley was the only body of water in the region that could possibly be the ancient lake, as Birkat Qarun was clearly natural and Lake Moeris was a man-made lake. This man-made lake served as a holding reservoir to prevent the natural Lake Qarun from flooding at times of exceptionally high flood and to hold water for times of low flood. He considered that, in order to fit with the dimensions of Lake Moeris provided by Herodotus, this artificial lake may have extended as far south as Herakleopolis.[127]

Regarding the issue of the Labyrinth, he notes that most modern travelers considered Hawara to be the site of that ancient monument. The group continued from Hawara, forded the Bahr Yusuf, and cut across the cultivated area to Madinat al-Fayum. At this point Lane notes that their heightened expectations of the fertility and verdure of the region had been disappointed, partly due to the fact that this was the dry season. He reports that the Egyptians believed Madinat al-Fayum to have been founded by Joseph. Lane was not impressed with the town, which he considered inferior to other chief towns along the Nile Valley. He notes, however, that the region to the northwest, between the town and the lake, was "the most fertile and abundant region in Egypt." The houses and mosques were partially constructed from the remains of the ancient town of Arsinoë, and there were extensive mounds of rubbish that included fragments of granite, stone, bricks, pottery, and glass to the north of the town at the site of the ancient capital.[128]

Lane paid a visit to the obelisk of Abgig. He observed that the village there was situated on high mounds and "more naked" than most Egyptian villages due to the lack of palm trees around it. One mile away from the village, the obelisk was to be found lying on the ground broken into two pieces. On a second visit to the obelisk the following day to record it in more detail, he searched for any other remains nearby. Finding nothing, not even any mounds, he concluded that successive inundations must have buried any other remains in the area. Their journey continued the next day toward the lake, passing several villages. The country in this area was thickly covered in palm groves and gardens.[129] He writes that as they approached the lake it appeared to be "like a broad river, of a deep blue colour, bounded by sandy mountains on the other side."[130]

The lake, he says, resembled a sea in magnitude, color, and the nature of its shores, and he could see the ruins of Dimai on the opposite shore as well as the ruins of Qasr Qarun to the far west. During his trip on the lake he recalled the vivid description of the boatman provided by Belzoni, but noted that the legends originated from nearby Memphis, not from the Fayum, as there were no burial grounds to the north of the lake.[131] Lane felt that "there was nothing of beauty in the surrounding scenery; low yellow mountains on the northern side, with bushes stretching along the shore, bound the prospect in that direction; and on the southern side is a barren expanse of sand and rock."[132] At this point he must have been nearing the western end of the lake, as by the afternoon they had landed and started to walk to Qasr Qarun.

On the short two-mile walk to the temple he noted the remains of trees and vines, concluding that there must have been a village with fields nearby at some point in the past, when the inundation spread farther from the lake. He also discovered that not far beneath the sand there was richer, dark soil. The advancement in Egyptological knowledge meant that he was able to state that the temple had the aspect of an ancient Egyptian temple, but dated from the time of the Romans. The group was delayed for some time waiting for water, and for the rest of his life Lane blamed the brackish water they eventually found and some unripe cucumbers he ate that day for the fact that he soon then developed an uncomfortable case of dysentery and opthalmia, from which he did not fully recover for the duration of his trip to Egypt. He returned to Madinat al-Fayum, crossing another ancient branch of "the artificial Lake Moeris" and an area strewn with fragments of granite, stone, and pottery, as well as two ruined "pyramids." From there he returned to the valley and continued his journey south.[133]

Lane was a true orientalist, and worked in a way that would be considered ethnographical today. He immersed himself in the culture in order to observe and record aspects of society. The many details of village names he included in the account of the Fayum reflect his genuine interest in rural life in Egypt. He made great efforts to correctly record place names. He studied the major Arabic accounts of Egypt, but does not refer to them in his descriptions of places. In fact, except for one brief reference to Herodotus, he does not refer to the accounts of any Classical, Arab, or other scholars at all. This lack of acknowledgment of earlier sources is unusual for the time, but it has to be remembered that the text is taken from a draft of his account. He may well have intended to add the references to a later edition.

Throughout his description of the Fayum, Lane repeatedly refers to views, across the landscape to monuments and across land from monuments. These descriptions of the landscape have considerable romantic undertones, and his appreciation of different landscapes is apparent. He valued green fertile cultivation areas, but loathed the desert. He was disappointed with the landscape, however, and had obviously hoped to experience the exceptional and impressive fertility described by other travelers to the region. This demonstrates how expectations shape a person's perception of the region. Lane's perception was that the Fayum was not actually especially rich or spectacular and that other travelers had probably just found ways to experience the landscape of Strabo. They sought any small element of that famed fertility and described it using the most romantic and entertaining language possible. It is also possible that this reflects the fact that he spent considerably more time exploring the villages of the Nile Valley than other travelers. He was possibly more immune to the perceived beauty of the Fayum because he really took the time to observe the rural landscape, instead of viewing it through rose-tinted glasses that obscured the local rural life in favor of the antiquities or the exotic beauty of the land. Earlier accounts described the region as exceptionally lush and beautiful, which he believed it would be, but because he was viewing the landscape more thoroughly he saw what was there, not what he wanted to see.

Lane does present a far more accurate and detailed account of the monuments and landscape of the Fayum. He visited the Lahun pyramid and dam and Hawara, which he accepted as the location of the Labyrinth. He also visited Madinat al-Fayum, Abgig, Dimai, Qasr Qarun, and Biahmu, and presented far more observations about any potential antiquities in the landscape than his predecessors. He did consider the monuments within their landscape, noting the fact that Abgig village was located on mounds, although there were no mounds near the obelisk itself. He noted the remains of trees near Qasr Qarun, suggesting that there must have been cultivation and a village nearby in the past. Lane perceived the landscape itself to be ancient. He associated the monuments with the landscape and looked for signs of antiquity in the landscape, not just the monuments. He placed much more value on the land itself, and unlike earlier travelers he was not simply moving from one monument to the next and relating interesting events of the journey. Rather, he attempted to capture the nature of the entire society, which included the land in which people lived. To him the landscape was not simply the background on which monuments happened to be placed, it was the land in which they existed, and the landscape was as antique as the remains themselves. By closely observing contemporary life in Egypt he must have become aware of the reciprocal relationship between the people and the land.

Lane's account was written to inform his readers about the state of Egypt and the state of its monuments. While he inescapably had preconceptions about the region deriving from earlier accounts and a belief in the truth of the Classics, he does reveal a broader appreciation of the landscape than previous visitors to the region. The fact that he was one of the foremost scholars of Arabic yet failed to make any reference to descriptions of the region in Islamic accounts most probably reflects the attitudes of the era. Although he studied these works, he probably still did not place as much value on them as he placed on the Classics. His expectation was that he would encounter the imagined landscape of the Classical authors or of the ancient Egyptians; however, his perception was dominated by the landscape he experienced.

Romantic Poets

In the early nineteenth century the Romantic movement was growing, and imagery of the 'Orient' was becoming a staple literary and artistic theme. The poet Lord Byron's publisher, for example, encouraged him to use oriental imagery to increase the saleability of his works.[134] Ideas about 'imagination' from seventeenth-century philosophy were still current and debated by the romantic poets. Samuel Coleridge, among others, believed that poets should be philosophers, and to that end he strove to define 'imagination' and 'fancy.'[135] In essence he believed that imagination is deeper and transforms the writer; it was what he believed the poet should strive for, while fancy is more frivolous. One aspect of romantic travel writing was an attempt to capture the ideal image of the perceived freedom and simplicity of the past.[136] For this reason the orientalist image of the simple life of the Bedouin appealed to several Romantic poets. It was in contrast to their perceptions of the Ottoman ruling classes, as the Ottoman Empire was seen to be smothering the more sublime and ancient local cultures.[137] Inextricably tied into orientalist ideas, this poetry conjured up images of the landscape that idealized the past.

James Augustus St. John (1795–1875)

Born James John in Camarthenshire to a family of modest means, St. John was self-taught in many subjects, including philosophy. He changed his name several times and followed a career in politics and journalism, including working as assistant editor to James Silk Buckingham at the *Oriental Herald and Colonial Review*.[138] He spent some years traveling in Europe before going to Egypt in 1832. St. John has a long list of publications to his name. He wrote poetry under the pseudonyms of Bion and Horace Gywnne, but was not particularly successful. He produced several travel accounts, including *Egypt and Mohammed Ali or Travels in the Valley of the Nile* (1834; a more traditional account) and *Isis: An Egyptian Pilgrimage* (1853; a more personal account written for his daughter). He also wrote *There and Back Again in Search of Beauty* (1853), which primarily follows his travels across Europe. He authored many political, historical, and literary works, including a biography of Walter Raleigh, a study of Milton, an edited volume of the works of Locke, and *The Lives of Celebrated Travellers* (1837).

With poem titles such as "Anticipation of Spring" (1824) and "Hymn to Minerva" (1825), it cannot be doubted that St. John was a Romantic poet. Before going to Egypt he wrote several poems about the 'Orient,' including "The Wild Ass of the Desert" (1824) and "The Hospitality of the Bedouins" (1824), and two full-length compositions, "Abdallah, an Oriental Tale" (as Horace Gwynne, 1824) and "The Adventures of Firooz" (1825).[139] The oriental literature and poetry of the time—particularly, the popularity of the *Arabian Nights* in the mid-nineteenth century—was so prolific and popular that he was able to write a vivid poem about the 'East' without ever having set foot there. The most dominant theme in his work is the cycle of nature, which he used to reflect on the hardships of life. St. John aligned himself with Byron in several ways. His poetry reveals a dislike of tyranny, and he clearly loathed the wealthy. In *Riches* (1824) he muses on the idea that a wealthy man cannot experience the simplicity and beauty of nature. He debates the notion of the corruption of man by society and the idea of freedom from social constraints—ideas derived from the earlier philosophers John Locke and Thomas Hobbes,[140] whom he studied. He did on one occasion debate philosophy in poetry (*On the Stoic Philosophy*, 1825).

Poems such as "Hymn to Minerva" were clearly a reflection of the preoccupation with Classical imagery found in John Keats's "Ode to a Grecian Urn." Classical mythology was certainly a major theme in his poetry, and he regularly invoked that imagery in his poems on other subjects. Like many Romantic poets, he was self-reflective in his poems. "On My Grey Hairs" (1825) reflects his concern with ideas of youth, and "Lines Written during Illness" (1824) suggests he may have rather romantically wished to align himself with Wordsworth. He considered the idea of fancy as defined by Coleridge and Locke, and seems to have felt that the loss of fancy was a bad thing. He clearly was in favor of fancy as a medium of aesthetic expression, which is apparent in his account of the Fayum.

Egypt and Mohammed Ali or Travels in the Valley of the Nile was presented as a journal based on the notes he took in Egypt.[141] *Isis* (1853) is less formal, more like a letter than a traditional travel account, and contains far more information about the events of his trip. But the earlier account does contain more description and more poetry, as St. John went to the Fayum for the express purpose of seeing Lake Moeris.[142] By this point in his life he had given up publishing poetry, but had quite clearly not given up being a poet. In many ways this account could be read as a full-length poem about travels in Egypt. His language throughout is imbued with strong romantic sentiment:

> Fields and copses steeped in dew—which trickling over the leaves and grass, glittered like diamonds in the sun—and sprinkled with delicate wild flowers, involuntarily recalled to remembrance the enthusiastic descriptions of poetry, and that golden age of impassioned innocence, "When love was liberty, and Nature law."[143]

He was openly revolted by the local Egyptians and at one point remarked: "To the traveller, in a climate so warm and delightful as that of Egypt, the Golden Age, so long as he keeps the inhabitants out of sight, is no fable."[144] This one sentence more than any other perhaps honestly reflects his opinion of Egypt, his desire to experience ancient Egypt, and his general fear or distrust of Islamic and Arab culture.

St. John set off for the Fayum during a sandstorm in March 1832. After a journey south across the desert, his group reached the Fayum: "At length, late in the day, we discovered, on the edge of the horizon, the tops of the palm trees, extending in one dark line from west to east, as far as the eye could reach, and marking the northern boundary of that celebrated and beautiful oasis—for such is the Fayum."[145] He continues this description with more poetic lines, deciding that the cultivated area was, in essence, feminine in nature (thus implying that the desert, with its wildness and grandeur, must be masculine).

> If the desert has its charms,—and charms not a few it has,—those green and fertile spots, which its burning sands encompass like an ocean, are, in a different way, no less attractive. To the former belongs wildness, grandeur, sublimity; qualities that powerfully stir up the energies of the soul, and nerve it for exertion and strife;—to the latter whatever is soft, and soothing, and lovely; or, to sum up all agreeable qualities in one word, all that is feminine, in nature. The desert therefore, can only please certain temperaments, and in certain moods of mind; but those landscapes on which heaven has showered down the principles of beauty and fertility, where the earth is filled with abundance, and the air with fragrance, must delight, like woman, at all times, by awakening those poetical and impassioned assertions that constitute the elements of the most perfect enjoyment.[146]

During his search for antiquities, St. John came upon a view that stimulated his imagination: "I caught the first glimpse of Lake Moeris, magnificently stretching away from east to west, crimsoned all over by the setting sun, and glittering like a sea of molten amethyst,"[147] a phenomenon that can still be experienced at sunset on the lake on some days (see plate 20; see also plate 19 in relation to the following paragraph). In *Isis* he elaborated on this point:

> Lake Moeris had been to me, through the greater part of my life, a fabulous lake, exactly like those waters described in the 'Arabian Nights', abounding with blue fishes, and dragged by nets of fishermen. . . . It had now emerged from the region of myths and fables into the category of real existences. . . . It was the genius of Herodotus that had invested that dreamy lake with so much beauty and fascination for me.[148]

His journey toward the lake inspired more poetic descriptions:

> We occasionally, in riding along, caught hasty glimpses of the calm shining surface of the lake, with the sterile crags and wide wastes of sand which form its northern shore. Never at any point of my life . . . did I derive, from the presence of mere inanimate objects, a delight so perfect, so capable of absorbing the thoughts and filling the whole mind, so replete with poetic enjoyment, so intense and rapturous as I experienced during this morning's ride. The landscape appeared to comprehend every element of interest and beauty: a plain of unrivalled richness and fertility, exhibiting each various shade of verdure, intersected by streams of water, sprinkled with tufted groves, disclosing between their foliage the rural village, and the towering minaret; beyond these the artificial sea of Moeris, quivering and glittering in the sun; and, in the distance, forming the majestic back-ground of the picture, a range of rocky mountains, of commanding elevation, arid, frowning, desolate, but invested with an air of gloomy grandeur highly congenial to the state of mind in which I viewed them. . . . History and fable had united in peopling the spot with numerous interesting reminiscences.[149]

At Sinnuris he attracted the attention of the locals, who believed that he had come to remove the gold that was hidden in the shores of the lake. They thought that the book he was reading would cause the ground to open and draw hidden treasure to the surface, something they claimed had been done by a famous magician who visited the region some years before. To calm the locals, St. John closed his books and went for a walk, but unfortunately he chose to walk around the tombs, which caused them to believe that he might actually be a ghoul or vampire, as these were the only beings who would roam about a cemetery.[150] The journey continued to Sanhur, from where St. John could see the lake, which now seemed even grander: "It seemed to have been created for the purpose of awakening in the mind the spirit of poetry . . . the Lake . . . which, on the morning of our visit, glittered in the sun like a sea of molten silver."[151]

St. John did make a note regarding the fable of the name of the lake, Birkat Qarun, mentioning both Belzoni and Pococke, the treasure of Qarun, and that it could be thought by some that the Greek fable of Charon and the Labyrinth derive from this location. As they left Sanhur, he noted that "the general features of the landscape were here exceedingly beautiful, every turn of the path-way presenting a new vista, between woods and copses, over fields exquisitely green, and ending, perhaps with the prospect of some distant village."[152]

St. John noted that local tradition stated that Fidimin was the location of the Labyrinth, but that this actually reflected the presence of three hundred Coptic churches. It was possible, he considered, that Fidimin lay on top of some ancient remains, as the mounds of rubble that surrounded every Egyptian village were notably large here.[153] The group did not stay long in Madinat al-Fayum, although St. John did note that it was supposed to be the site of ancient Crocodilopolis. He remarked briefly on the mounds of rubbish containing fragments of columns and bricks. The group traveled on to Hawara, "where the French . . . place the site of the Labyrinth."[154] Between the canal and the pyramid he noted large mounds that resembled a town overwhelmed by the sand. There was a "small plain" close to the monument that he supposed to have been the site of "some great edifice," as it was covered with fragments of columns of white marble, and blue and red granite. They climbed up the pyramid, enjoying views of much of the region from the top.[155]

They moved on to Lahun, where St. John mentioned one story he heard, apparently told by 'Herodotus of King Asychis,' who had built a brick pyramid with mud drawn from the bottom of a lake. If this lake was Moeris, then the pyramid in question could be Lahun. The group then headed east for Beni Suef and left the Fayum.[156]

It is impossible to analyze this work without taking into consideration the fact that St. John was widely read. His edition of the works of Locke reveals his opinion of what he aspired to be:

> A Great Man arises and occupies himself with the study of nature; he reads, he inquires, he investigates, he meditates; his ideas and opinions under the influence of the peculiar conformation of mind which we designate character. . . . When this process is completed, men smitten by the thirst of knowledge, ardent, enthusiastic, approaching within the sphere of the philosophers influence, are attracted towards him and become his disciples.[157]

Despite the fact that St. John did not publish works on writers until after his trip to Egypt (Locke in 1854 and Milton in 1848), he had already studied the works of the ancient Greek and Latin Classics; the philosophers Plato, Aristotle, and the Stoics; the poets Milton and Byron; orientalist writers Pococke, Belzoni, and Denon; and philosophers Bacon, Descartes, Hobbes, Leibnitz, Malebranchs, Hume, and Berkeley.

In *Isis* it is apparent that despite his horror of the locals, St. John did in fact have great respect for the people he encountered. His disgust really only related to his romanticized ideal of the ancient past of Egypt. This is a rather typical 'Western' phenomenon. Although people may not want to admit to it, many tourists and travelers to Egypt even now do not necessarily hold the general population or culture of Egypt in high regard and disapprove of the fact that the modern culture appears to blot out the ancient, while simultaneously loving and greatly respecting Egyptians they know personally. When he was encountering people he imagined to be strong 'simple' Bedouins or important local leaders, he was fascinated by their lives and annoyed with the Franks' treatment of them. He was told the Qarun treasure story by the men who approached him in Sinnuris, but, despite the fact that he spent a lot of time with locals, he perhaps did not go out of his way to enquire about the area, as he makes no mention of the Joseph stories.

Despite his romantic notions about the past, St. John seems to have been relatively unconcerned with the monuments in the region. The fact that he was in the vicinity of Lake Moeris was of greater importance. Every aspect of the landscape filled him with pleasure; each view he encountered lived up to his heightened expectations. His preconceived ideas about the ideal images of the sublime nature of the desert, the beauty of the simple life of the Bedouin, and the exquisite splendor of the lake were brought to life during his travels. His descriptions of the lake are all romantic, and there is no debate about the academic issues that concerned so many other travelers. While he described the land he traveled through, he also devoted a great deal of the work to describing his perceptions and his experience of the landscape. His perception of the landscape itself, however, is so overwhelmed with his expectations and imagination that it is hard to discern how much of what he wrote was written to impress the reader. For St. John the landscape was imbued with ancient history and meaning. He certainly temporalized it, and was irritated if anything occurred to shake him out of his romantic reveries of 'being' in the ancient landscape of Moeris, but the monuments themselves do not really feature in his romantic vision. Despite the fact that this account is a record of St. John's experience of the region, there can be no doubt that his perception was of the landscape he had imagined and expected. Any experiences that did not fit into his perception of the ideal, fertile, ancient, imagined landscape were brushed aside.

Paul Lenoir (1843–81)

Nothing is known about Paul Marie Lenoir other than that he visited Egypt in 1856 as a member of a group of French orientalist artists that included the influential Romantic orientalist artist Jean-Léon Gérôme, of whom he was a student (see plate 21).[158] Lenoir's account was first published in French as *Le Fayoum, le Sinaï et Pétra: Expédition dans la Moyenne Égypte et l'Arabie Pétrée* in 1872, then translated and published in English in 1873.

The trip was undertaken "to look out for subjects to paint for pictures and to paint them. We did not pretend to see everything, but we wished to see thoroughly, and to paint the truth of everything we were to see."[159]

Lenoir and his party traveled to the Fayum from Dahshur, arriving at Tamiya: "This wide Oasis is a charming landscape, framed in a broad golden line, which bounds it on every side. It is an island of verdure in a vast expanse of desert."[160] They moved on to Sinnuris, which Lenoir describes as clearly being on a mound and having the appearance of a fortress. He states that during the inundation all the land around would become flooded, forming an immense lake.[161] The group then headed toward Madinat al-Fayum, and Lenoir describes the region around the canal of Joseph as having the most extraordinary vegetation. They came out of this "rich forest" onto a branch of the canal, which he says was one of the most important works in Egypt, to which various legends were attached regarding its construction and Biblical origin.[162] They arrived in Madinat al-Fayum, then immediately set off again back toward the west to Fidimin, which they visited as they believed it "preserved a rare and curious stamp of primitiveness," because it was generally neglected by travelers.[163]

The party followed the route of the canal of Joseph, through "vast savannahs of vegetation" and "woods, where Robinson Crusoe might have believed himself to be in his island," and where "enormous grasses and lianas stretched from side to side."[164] They continued ascending until they were above the surrounding countryside on a plateau, bounded by "an immense precipice" with a stream below, down to which they descended to find themselves at "the picturesque entry of the village of Fidémine."[165] Lenoir observes that at times the small stream probably became a torrent, as he could see uprooted palms and tumbled rocks. The group pitched their tents near a group of trees: "It was a virgin forest."[166] They then continued their journey into the village, with Lenoir noting, "We plunged into labyrinths of rocks, parasites, aloes and palm-trees, where only serpents could get about freely."[167] Their escorts headed off into this "jungle" to hunt.[168]

The group returned to Madinat al-Fayum to explore it properly. Lenoir describes the canal (Joseph's) as immense, noting the debate about whether it was natural or man-made (by Joseph). The region, he says, acted as a reservoir for the country, holding excess water and reserving it for years of drought, with ancient dikes visible all over the province. He disagrees with the idea that the lake was man-made and discusses the fact that the name of Moeris was debatable. The works in the Fayum, he knew, were attributed to Amenemhat III, and the name of the region derived from the word 'marsh'—Phaioum.[169]

They spent quite some time in Madinat al-Fayum, and made several further trips around the region, during which Lenoir says they found that "the extraordinary fertility of this portion of the province surpasses all that we could have imagined." He describes agricultural processes, noting the ease of cultivating anything in the Fayum. He remarks that "everything in this wonderful country seems like a dream,"[170] because "the fellah [farmer] scratches the ground with a match," while "we" use steam machines.[171] He concludes by stating:

> We were about to quit this living page from the book of Genesis, to plunge into the turmoil of the sticky and restless world which has already invaded Cairo, and undertaken, by dint of steam and electricity to change the scene from that of the Thousand and One Nights, to a copy of the Boulevard Malesherbes and the Rue Tronchet.[172]

With a few more final poetic lines Lenoir describes the group's departure from the Fayum by train to Cairo.

Lenoir was clearly indulging all his fantasies of the Orient. His imagery is of the sensual oriental Biblical Eden, filled with serpents, virginal, and richly fertile. The 'simple life' of the 'fellah,' who used no machinery to farm but toiled manually in tune with nature, appealed to him, as did the seemingly primitive nature of the landscape. He presents new ideas of exotic landscape, likening the Fidimin valley 'forest' to something from *Robinson Crusoe*. His description of this part of the region is exceptionally exaggerated in places. Nothing is mediocre; everything he saw he describes in excessively positive or overly negative terms. He was painting a picture of the region in terms that might be familiar to readers of fictional adventure/travel literature.

Lenoir's observation that the flooded area around Sinnuris appeared to be an 'immense lake' is most revealing. His use of those specific words almost echoes Herodotus and, given that his account does not appear to have been shaped by Classical accounts in any way, this one remark perhaps shows just how the 'myth' of the enormous lake of Herodotus came into being. The fact that he makes no reference to Herodotus at all could possibly have been a conscious attempt to distance himself from academia. He did not want to appear to be anything other than an artist inspired only by his observations, and so he felt no need for academic validation. More so than perhaps any other writer, Lenoir turns the Fayum into an exotic, sensuous, vividly fertile landscape. This language is very much of its time, and he needed to employ a sense of heightened reality to ensure that his trip was perceived to be adventurous, exciting, and otherworldly. Not just anyone could experience this particular landscape; he was ideally placed to fully appreciate this rich encounter due to his education and experience as an artist, and he had the skills to communicate his perception to others. By making the landscape seem so luxurious, he was upholding the myth of the Orient, and went as far as to say it was in fact like Eden, a Biblical paradise, unspoiled by modern industrial advances, untamed and largely untouched by the human hand. His saw the Fayum landscape through a veil of sensual romantic orientalist imagery, and he indulged his desire to imbue himself into this "living page from the book of Genesis."

The End of Exploration: The Beginning of Archaeology and Tourism

By the mid-nineteenth century some of the most influential French accounts of the Orient had been written, including Alphonse de Lamartine's *Voyage en Orient* (first published in 1835) and Gérard de Nerval's *Voyage en Orient* (first published in 1851). These authors reflect that the age of adventure and experience of the 'unknown' Orient was over. Industrialization, railways, and steam ships meant easier travel, more and more people had access to the countries of the Orient, and there was a plethora of writings about all the countries of the East, which removed any real mysterious romance from the experience.[173] As a result, the form and nature of travel writing was changing. Formal guidebooks for travelers—now usually considered tourists—started to appear in the mid-nineteenth century. In Britain John Murray started producing 'handbook' travel guides in 1836. The first *Handbook of Egypt* (1847) was a revised edition of Wilkinson's *Modern Egypt and Thebes*,[174] the book that Murray chose to publish instead of Lane's *Description*. The scholar–travelers, the orientalist specialists on the country, its people, customs, sights, and monuments who had gathered the material for the guide, took a backseat, and the publishers became the authorities.[175] Academic Egyptology and archaeological work began in earnest in the later nineteenth century. Writing about Egypt naturally took on a new form: reports and publications on work at sites, translations of texts, and studies of the history, religion, and culture of ancient Egypt. The Fayum was the focus of some of the earliest serious archaeological work in Egypt, by Flinders Petrie.

William Flinders Petrie (1853–1942)

Sir William Matthew Flinders Petrie is one of the most important figures in the history of Egyptology. He conducted surveys and excavations across Egypt, at virtually every major site and many smaller sites, between 1880 and 1924. He is perhaps most famous for his innovative methods of excavation and for developing sequence-dating for ceramics, as well as his undeniably unique temperament and behavior. His father William was a scientist, and his parents raised him (in the main) in his father's religion

(Exclusive Brethren) rather than his mother's more mainstream Christian faith. Flinders received no formal education until he was twenty-four, instead training with various home tutors and teaching himself when he could. He developed an interest in archaeological survey work at a young age, and in 1874 he and his father began the first accurate measurements of Stonehenge, a project they completed in 1877. Between 1875 and 1880 he conducted surveys of many British monuments, developing exceptional survey skills and a keen eye for measurements.[176]

Petrie became increasingly fascinated with the idea that different ancient societies had developed their own systems of measurement and would therefore each have had their own standard units of measure. In order to investigate this idea, he began measuring aspects of different ancient monuments, stones, and statues, including Egyptian, Assyrian, Greek, Roman, Phoenician, and oriental artifacts in the British Museum. In 1877 he published his first book, *Inductive Metrology, or the Recovery of Ancient Measurements from the Monuments*. Meanwhile, Petrie and his father had both become involved with the work of Charles Piazzi Smyth, an old family friend. Piazzi Smyth was convinced that the Great Pyramid of Giza contained secrets, coded in the dimensions of the monument, and therefore accurate survey was critical to unlocking this ancient wisdom. Piazzi Smyth had conceived the notion of the pyramid-inch, which he believed to be an ancient Egyptian standard of measure. The result of this connection, Petrie's fascination with ancient measurements, and his aptitude for and love of archaeological survey was that in December 1880 Petrie undertook his first expedition to Egypt in order to conduct an accurate survey of the Great Pyramid.[177]

This was the beginning of Petrie's long association with the archaeology of Egypt. During his first trip, in January 1881, the director of the Egyptian Antiquities Service, Auguste Mariette, passed away. Mariette had delivered an impassioned lecture not long before his death about the urgent need for the exploration and protection of Egyptian antiquities, and it was not clear who might take his mantle. Mariette himself had directed work at hundreds of sites in Egypt, and was aware that it needed someone with as much passion and energy as he had in order to save the sites and obtain information before it was lost. Gaston Maspero was appointed successor to Mariette in the service, but it could be argued that Petrie was the person who took on the role of exploring and investigating as many sites as possible in Egypt, with a sense of great urgency.[178]

Petrie's work in Egypt was initially supported financially through the efforts of Amelia Edwards and the Egypt Exploration Fund she set up. Petrie's increasing frustration with the management of the fund and the methods and attitudes of the other benefactors (Edouard Naville and Francis Llewellyn Griffith) led to his departure from that organization and need for alternative financial support. Edwards remained a stalwart supporter of Petrie despite this rift and introduced him to wealthy Manchester merchant Jesse Haworth, whose fascination with the potential to discover Biblical archaeological remains in Egypt meant he was happy to finance Petrie in return for a split of the finds. Around the same time Petrie met Martin Kennard, a keen collector who was also happy to support him in return for a portion of the antiquities.[179]

Petrie's work in the Fayum coincided with this new sponsorship by Kennard and Haworth. His first season there was in 1888. Petrie had spent some time in the Fayum in 1882, assisting Cope Whitehouse with a survey of the region, and had visited Biahmu and Hawara.[180] But in 1888 his decision to work in the Fayum was more by accident than design:

> On applying last autumn to M. Grebaut to have some place named for my excavations, he decided on allotting the Fayum province to me: it was not being worked by anyone else—the department of antiquities not having touched it for a quarter of a century—and it was a district containing many interesting problems.[181]

Prior to beginning work in the region Petrie conducted a survey of the existing publications, and the introduction to his first report on work in the Fayum summarizes what was known at the time:

> At the opposite end of the ruins [at Madinat al-Fayum], towards the north, is the great temple enclosure of the old Egyptian town. Before its name of Arsinoe, the city had obtained the name of Crocodilopolis, from the worship of the sacred crocodiles maintained there; and still earlier it was known as Shed—meaning, apparently that which is saved, cut out, delivered or extracted, referring to the district being reclaimed from the great lake. The whole province was known as Tashe, "the land of the lake," and whatever may have been the mistakes of historians about Lake Moeris there is no doubt that the lake was the main feature of the district. So many opinions have been broached

> about Lake Moeris that an account of antiquities in the Fayum without mentioning it would seem impossible. . . . . This then, was the state in which the great engineering monarchs of Egypt found the province;—a basin full of overflow Nile water, replenished at each inundation through a marshy shallow inlet. Amenemhat I is the earliest king of whom we have any evidence in the Fayum. He appears to have reclaimed the site of the capital, Shed, "the separated" or "extracted" and thus he established "the land of the lake."[182]

In 1888 Petrie began work first in Madinat al-Fayum, then moved to Biahmu and finished the season in Hawara. At Biahmu Petrie succeeded in identifying the 'true' nature of Herodotus's 'pyramids' in the lake. He recovered not only a fragment inscribed with the cartouche of Amenemhat III but also sufficient carved fragments to conclude that colossi had once surmounted the two pedestals. He was able to surmise that Herodotus had viewed these colossi across inundation water.[183] From Biahmu he moved on to work in Hawara, where he soon found the intact Roman cemeteries in which the mummies were decorated with the life-like portraits. He concluded that the remains recorded by Lepsius were of a very late date and could not possibly be the ruins of the famous Labyrinth.[184] Before finishing the season at Hawara, he paid a short visit to Madinet al-Gurob to determine its potential for excavations.[185] In 1889 he resumed work in Hawara, but became aware that he should turn his attention to Kahun sooner than planned:

> Within a fortnight of beginning I heard that a German was intending to occupy Illahun where I was going myself. As this person was quite ignorant of archaeology and was allowed to dig simply for the sake of plunder, I could not tolerate his ruining the results of such an important site. And as his power of working in the Fayum was exactly the same as my own—a permission from the Government—I had to occupy the ground at once if it was to be saved.[186]

Petrie's primary focus at Lahun was exploration of the pyramid, but he soon became aware of an area close to the pyramid at which there were Twelfth Dynasty ceramics and a great deal of 'domestic' items. He correctly identified it as a town associated with the pyramid. He instigated a highly systematic program of clearing the town house by house, room by room, to recover as many artifacts as possible and obtain a clear plan of the settlement. During that season he also began work at Madinat al-Gurob, where he found some obviously high-elite tombs of the New Kingdom and a number of Ptolemaic burials. He noticed that the cartonnage mummy cases were constructed using old papyri and that they could be deconstructed easily, allowing the study of the recycled documents—the so-called Petrie Papyri.[187] Petrie continued working at Gurob and Kahun the following season (1889–90), somewhat regrettably employing Walter Hughes-Hughes to oversee the work at Gurob. Not only did Hughes-Hughes treat the workmen with contempt, he also did a terrible job and kept barely any records, none of which now survive. Petrie was so frustrated he left Hughes-Hughes to his own devices, which unfortunately now means that what was possibly the one good window of opportunity for thorough archaeological exploration at Gurob was essentially wasted. In 1892 Petrie's long-term supporter Amelia Edwards passed away and in her will endowed a chair of Egyptian archaeology and philology at University College London. Petrie was appointed to this professorship, the terms of which ensured he still had sufficient time to continue his archaeological work in Egypt.[188] He then turned his attention elsewhere in Egypt, but returned to Gurob in 1904 while he was working at Ihnasya and the nearby cemetery at Sedment to the east of the Fayum. He continued his work in Hawara in 1910–11 and at Lahun in 1913–14, and in 1919–20 he once again resumed work in Gurob. His work in the Fayum thus spanned almost his entire career in Egypt (1880–1924). Since Petrie, only a few small investigations have taken place at Madinat al-Fayum, Hawara, Kahun, and Gurob, with surveys to corroborate his results and minor new excavations. No further work has ever taken place at Biahmu. This makes Petrie's work at those four sites the foundation of any study of the archaeology of the eastern Fayum region. The division of artifacts from his earliest excavation in the region ensured that all the material not left in Egypt was divided between his two sponsors, Haworth and Kennard. Haworth subsequently donated his share to the University Museum in Manchester, much of which is on display there now.

Frederick Cope Whitehouse (1842–1911)

The work of this lawyer-turned-engineer and Egyptologist does not really fit into the genre of travel writing explored in this chapter, but his contribution to the Lake Moeris debate was significant because of the volume of writing he produced on the issue. He seems to have been almost obsessed with demonstrating the extent of his research, quite possibly because he was engaged in research in a field dominated by so many huge characters, such as Brugsch and Wilkinson, who all had far more tangible credentials than he did, and so he clung to his theories with dogged determination.

Born in New York in 1842, the son of the eminent Protestant Episcopal bishop of Illinois, the Reverend Henry J. Whitehouse, Frederick Cope Whitehouse passed his bar exam in 1871 and soon became a successful lawyer. He was a member of many 'learned societies' and in his obituary in the *New York Times*, dated 19 November 1911, Cope Whitehouse was described as an Egyptologist[189] due to the vast number of articles and notes he published as a result of his research into the Fayum and Lake Moeris and his 'discovery' of Wadi al-Rayan. He had sufficient wealth to support his research and travel, and perhaps the innate confidence of someone who is free from financial concerns. Reports from a lecture he gave in 1884 show that he was an entertaining speaker, engaging, well-spoken, and convincing: "He is of exceedingly nervous temperament and great refinement of manner. He looks like a scholar, and evidently is an accomplished gentleman."[190]

None of his publications gives any real clue as to what drew Cope Whitehouse into his work in Egypt. His upbringing in such a religious family almost certainly played a part in at least some of the research he conducted, revealed in a theory he developed to prove that the Fayum was the land of Goshen of the Bible (Genesis 45–47). The earliest record of a lecture given by him is in a self-published paper, "The Topography of the Pyramids and Their Connection with the Bahr Yusuf, Labyrinth, Moeris and the Sphinx," based on a lecture given in York (UK) in September 1881. It suggests that he had already conducted fieldwork (survey) and certainly a great deal of research on the issue of Lake Moeris.[191] Over twelve years he published around thirty papers on issues connected to Fayum irrigation, both its history and potential for future development. He was exceptionally well-versed in the state of Egyptology at that time and familiar with the most important scholars and their work. He was acquainted with Petrie, with whom he conducted a survey in the Fayum.

Cope Whitehouse's publications reveal something of his character. Somewhat extravagant in language, his earlier reports are full of flamboyant phrases detailing the lengths he went to in the process of his research:

> In placing on the table maps, diagrams, field notes, and quotations, my purpose is to show that not only had a certain amount of general preparation enabled me to take advantage of the opportunity of personal observation, but that no such effort has been spared, either in the examination of such standard and accessible works such as those of Bunsen, Birch, Brugsch, Linant, Lepsius, Perring, Rawlinson, Vyse and Wilkinson, but also authorities cited have been re-examined, the original passages in the Arabian and Jewish writers consulted, the valuable notes or monographs of De Sacy and the French *savans* compared, and benefit derived from consideration of the various translations of the Egyptian part of the Pentateuch.[192]

This first report actually barely mentions Lake Moeris or the Labyrinth, focusing almost entirely on a summary of the pyramids in the Giza/Saqqara/Dahshur area.

In 1882 Cope Whitehouse was accompanied by Petrie on what seems to have been his second survey mission (he makes reference to previous trips, but there is no real account of these).[193] The two had met 'by accident' at Giza on 20 March, the day before Cope Whitehouse was due to depart alone for the Fayum, and Petrie agreed to accompany him on what was his first trip to the Fayum. They mapped the northern desert areas (the so-called Wadi Fadhi, probably Umm al-Sawan or Widan al-Faras), then returned to Saqqara where they were joined by a Mr. Ellis, an artist and engineer. The next mission was a week-long survey around the perimeter of the region in search of the Labyrinth and any other ancient remains. Cope Whitehouse met up with Petrie once again at the lake and they traveled to Madinat al-Fayum via Abgig and Biahmu, then headed to the Gharaq basin and on to the Wadi al-Rayan, which he was afterward credited with 'discovering.' The result of this mission was a map of the Fayum with several elevations carefully marked.[194] It is interesting to note that their relationship clearly ended here. Petrie seems to have fallen out with most other scholars who investigated the Fayum landscape, especially Gertrude Caton Thompson, whom he initially supported.

Most of Cope Whitehouse's early papers summarize all the existing theories, then present his own ideas deriving from his extensive reading and survey work. He regularly asserted that he consulted all available sources, Coptic, Greek, Arabic, and Hebrew, and always compared his results with the work of Linant de Bellefonds and Jomard, as well as every other map or survey he could lay his hands on.[195] He first proposed his idea that the Wadi al-Rayan might have been a reservoir associated with the Nile flood in the Fayum, or might perhaps be utilized as such in the future.[196]

Based on his extensive mapping and reading, he concluded that the Fayum, Gharaq, and Rayan basins had all been almost permanently flooded until the fifth century BC. The surveys all revealed silt layers far away from the cultivated areas, especially in the southern part of the Fayum—evidence of a far larger lake than existed in his time. He hypothesized that the northern area of the Fayum basin must have been drained to allow for the extensive cultivation of the Ptolemaic period. It was in this article that he also first seriously addressed ideas he had about the Labyrinth and the land of Goshen. In a somewhat grand leap of understanding, he came to the conclusion that the Greek notion of a Labyrinth and the Minotaur came from Egyptian mythology born in the Fayum. It was this line of thought that led him to the Arabic stories in which the prophet Joseph was known as the founder of the Fayum, which he then connected with the land of Goshen, given to the Hebrews in Egypt by Joseph.[197]

Cope Whitehouse's ideas about the land of Goshen were not very well received by mainstream Classicists, although he asserted that major Egyptologists did agree with him. The reason was probably that at the time it was beginning to be thought that the eastern Delta was the home of the Biblical cities of Rammeses and Pithom (both in the land of Goshen). Several increasingly frustrated reports reveal what seems to have become a rather bitter dispute, concluding with an open attack on the credentials of the Egypt Exploration Fund in which Cope Whitehouse wrote that "the Fund has become the laughing-stock of scientific circles."[198] The Islamic traditions concerning Joseph provided him with ample ammunition for his arguments, and he attempted to draw a parallel between the name Fayum and Pithom. Further survey work undertaken in 1883 served to cement his resolve to make his point, and, bolstered by the apparent support of many eminent Egyptological scholars (he always ensured he noted exactly who agreed with him to back up the validity of his assertions), he continued this argument for quite some time.[199]

Cope Whitehouse was making his arguments about the Fayum being the land of Goshen principally on the basis of his research into medieval Islamic writing, which, as noted in Chapter Five, attributes the creation of the region to Joseph, after whom the river was named. Cope Whitehouse's extensive use of these sources was highly unusual for this time: Arabic and

Persian histories and geographies of Egypt were rarely considered to be of any value by Egyptologists or Biblical historians. He in fact placed as much value on these sources, primarily al-Mas'udi and Murtada,[200] as he did on the Classical scholars. His extensive knowledge of the Bible, Torah, and Qur'an, as well as his familiarity with the Book of Fayum, certainly added depth to his research. His interpretations and etymological leaps of faith did sometimes stretch the realms of possibility: linking Pithom to Fayum is not unreasonable, but claiming that Moeris actually came from Mary based on the fact that the Fayum papyrus depicts a female as the personification of the Fayum lake is somewhat far-fetched even for him.[201]

Having revised his thoughts about Moeris a little, Cope Whitehouse's reports eventually contained a map showing Birkat Qarun with Lake Moeris to the south in the Wadi al-Rayan, although it is apparent that he believed the ancient Lake Moeris had in fact been an agglomeration of the two. He mentions almost in passing that restoring this ancient lake (in the Wadi al-Rayan) would provide a reservoir and relieve the pressure and devastation caused by high floods.[202] This idea was taken seriously by the (British and Egyptian) authorities in Egypt as the matter of controlling the Nile became increasingly important. A series of reports were published in *Engineering* outlining the process of ascertaining the possibility of controlling the floods via an outlet into the Wadi al-Rayan.[203] The idea was eventually abandoned as it did not help Upper Egypt at all, and the final result was that in 1902 the Aswan (low) Dam was completed, following research and planning by the British hydrological engineer Sir William Willcocks. However, in the 1960s Cope Whitehouse's vision was realized and Wadi al-Rayan was indeed flooded. It is now home to a very popular protected nature reserve. Cope Whitehouse may have learned that just beyond his beloved Wadi al-Rayan lay the Wadi al-Hitan, which has fossilized remains of mangroves and pre-whale species. It was discovered in 1902–03, but his final publication seems to have been in 1893, in which he presented one final note on the Book of Fayum.[204]

Despite his often flamboyant language in transcripts of his lectures, Cope Whitehouse does not really reveal what he thought about the landscape of the Fayum. He makes no comment on the nature of the Fayum or the people he encountered there. He repeats the statements found in the Classical and medieval Islamic accounts about the region being fertile, but offers no opinions of his own. He clearly believed the landscape to have been created by Joseph and inhabited by the family of Jacob, and for that reason he may have placed some meaning in the landscape. He obviously saw the landscape as the product of the most incredible engineering feat in history. What is perhaps most interesting about him is his unwavering faith in his belief that the Fayum was the land of Goshen, that Wadi al-Rayan had been a part of the ancient Lake Moeris, and that Bahr Yusuf was the work of the prophet Joseph. The importance he gave to the medieval Islamic sources was extraordinary for his time, and may well have been at the root of his ongoing dispute with some characters in mainstream Egyptology, as those sources were so clearly dismissed by most scholars. It is regrettable, however, that he never saw his vision of flooding the Wadi al-Rayan realized in his lifetime, and that his 'discovery' and extensive survey work, which no doubt provided the foundations for future engineers engaged in that project, have been all but forgotten.

7

Ten Thousand Years of Archaeology, Texts, and Traditions

Perceptions of the Fayum landscape are varied and layered; they are a palimpsest of ideas shaped by the natural forms of the land, the human interventions into the land, the monuments placed on/in the landscape, and the ways in which the Fayum was thought about and written about. Several themes have persisted through time. These perceptions are the ones that could be said to be free from time and place, and hold true for most landscapes on the earth at most points in time: that the fertile landscape is feminine, and that the desert is masculine, powerful, and dangerous. This is not only found in many of the Western travel accounts but is also very explicit in the Book of Fayum, in which the river and its fertile banks were deemed to be the embodiment of the mother goddess, the inundation was deemed to be the embodiment of Osiris, the landscape itself as a whole was thought of as a temple of Sobek (who was a form of Horus), and the desert was the embodiment of the enemy of Osiris, Seth.

Any study of a landscape naturally reveals aspects of the relationship between people and their land. The interventions into the landscape—in the case of the Fayum the huge irrigation projects, and the monuments—could be said to be manifestations of people's beliefs. The decision to build any monument, funerary or cultic, reveals not only collectively held beliefs about the afterlife, spirituality, or religion, but also a complex process of decision-making, administration, and aspects of their knowledge about land, geology, materials, and engineering. The Fayum lake is the only major inland lake in Egypt, and probably the only lake that ancient Egyptians ever encountered; the significance of this lake is thus quite understandable.

The monuments of the Fayum, broadly speaking, date to two well-defined and culturally very different time periods—the Middle Kingdom and the Greco–Roman Period, and actually the foundation of the majority of the monuments dates to a relatively short span within each period—the reign of

Amenemhat III and the reign of Ptolemy II. The investment in the region made by these rulers attests a belief that the region was rich with valuable resources, and that the landscape was sacred and important to their place on the throne. But the perception that the Fayum was an area rich with resources is apparent from the earliest phases in the history of the region. From the Epipalaeolithic c.7000 BC people started living along the shores of the vast lake filling most of the Fayum basin. They were drawn to the region for the resources—wild plant foods and animals/fish, and access to materials for making tools. Formal agriculture—deliberate cultivation of crops—appears at sites in the region around 5500 BC, indicating that people had decided to settle on a more permanent basis in the region. From the beginning of the pharaonic period, as early as 3000 BC, the cult of the crocodile god was established, and later in the Old Kingdom the Fayum was clearly still perceived to be a landscape rich with resources; it was named 'Southern Lake'—probably meaning the lake region south (upstream) of the primary administrative 'central place' of the 'state' organization.

Early kings of the Middle Kingdom developed an increasingly close association with the Fayum. The earliest evidence of a temple of any size in the region is the few remains that may come from a Sobek temple of Amenemhat I in Shedet (Madinat al-Fayum). The lack of evidence for a temple of the Old Kingdom is unsurprising, given the fact that there are no remains of any cult temple of that period in Egypt—only funerary monuments survive. For this reason, if there had been a major cult temple of Sobek in Shedet at this time it would have been one of the earliest of its kind. The earliest (probably) in-situ monument is the so-called obelisk of Senwosret I found originally at Abgig, which very clearly symbolically displays his desire to connect himself to the Fayum as legitimization of his reign. The choice of location for this monument may not be a coincidence. The village in which the obelisk was found lies at the head of one of the two main channels running from the principal river/watercourse (the Bahr Yusuf) toward the lake (Birkat Qarun). The al-Wadi and al-Bats drains are deep ravines that were almost certainly major and very visible dominating elements of the natural landscape before the irrigation works of the third century BC, and before the region became densely populated. It could be speculated even that there may have been a partner obelisk at the head of the second ravine, to the north.

The Pyramid of Senwosret II at Lahun, and the establishment of the town adjacent to the valley temple demonstrates an even deeper desire to link to the Fayum. This is the most southerly traditional Egyptian pyramid complex, and as is the case with many of these monuments, the exact location was to some extent determined by geology. The Egyptian architects were well versed in pyramid construction by this date, and while each one is architecturally different, as they continually adapted their engineering skills, attempting to perfect construction methods and reduce expenditure, the foundations on which the pyramids were built were carefully planned and considered. The Lahun pyramid is mudbrick, but the core is the natural bedrock, and it seems likely that this natural outcrop may well have been a factor in the choice of this location, but the fact that the pyramid lies close to the Bahr Yusuf, and the later evidence that this area of the region was named *r-ḥnt* (mouth of the channel) has to be significant. As with the obelisk—this monument is a sign of the importance of the watercourses in the Fayum.

The reign of Amenemhat III can be seen as the pinnacle of royal engagement with the Fayum landscape. The Hawara funerary monument also lies close to the principal waterway (Bahr Yusuf), but is also far 'deeper' into the Fayum and is located on what was probably the closest possible point to the cult center at Shedet while remaining in the desert on stable grounds. The monument at Biahmu was built on what was then the edge of the 'lake,' possibly designed to be flooded annually (as was the case at nearby *nn-nsw* / Herakleopolis (Ihnasya al-Madina) in the temple of Herishef), and may well have acted as a symbolic entrance to the habitable parts of the region (which at that date was just a relatively small area around Shedet (Madinat al-Fayum)). If the belief that the Fayum itself was the embodiment of a temple of Sobek was already active at this date, the two colossi may well symbolize the entrance to the 'temple of the Fayum.' During the Middle Kingdom the form of Egyptian temples was gradually taking shape, and the first stone-built cult temples appear in this period. By the New Kingdom it was not unusual for mortuary and cult temples to have colossi at the entrance, the Colossi of Memnon at the temple of Amenhotep III being the most monumental examples. The colossi of Biahmu not only represent the earliest examples of truly monumental stone sculpture in Egypt (excepting the Sphinx), but may well be precursors to standard elements of New Kingdom temples. There can be no doubt that that Book of Fayum contains many very old beliefs about the Fayum landscape, and the idea that the Fayum landscape was the embodiment of a temple of Sobek may well have found its one physical manifestation in these monuments.

The smaller monuments in the south of the region are likely to have been linked to each other in some way; the temple of Renenutet and Sobek at Dja (Madinat Madi), the tombs of the officials at Kom Khelwa to the east, and possibly also a temple at Tebtunis clearly indicate that the southern edge of the region was inhabited. This activity may be linked to the older First Intermediate Period activities at *nn-nsw* (Herakleopolis) and Sedment; it is impossible to know, but it is not outside the realms of probability that the southern edge of the region was exploited by the ruling kings of that earlier period, who were based just outside the Fayum 'proper' along the edge of the Nile Valley to the east of the southern Fayum.

The monuments in the region attest the significance of elements of the Fayum landscape, but the name given to the region as a whole reveals the perception that it was the 'Lake Land.' It is the only place inland in Egypt that has ever had a lake of any significant size; Egypt is a land of rivers and so the lake must have seemed a truly amazing phenomenon. During the Middle Kingdom there was a real flourishing of literary activities, and many popular tales found in later copies were composed in this time. The literature which mentions the Fayum maintains the perception of a rich, pleasurable, fertile lake landscape, in which there was a royal palace, and the many inscriptions dedicated by priests and officials attest the importance of the cult of Sobek/Sobek Shedty in Shedet/the Lake Land. The text which reveals the most detailed information about their beliefs that the landscape of the Fayum was sacred, the birthplace of Sobek, inhabited by the gods, is the hymn dedicated to the crocodile god Sobek as Horus in the Lake Land. This hymn quite clearly outlines the Fayum creation theology, which is found in the much later Book of Fayum.

The tradition upheld the belief that the God (Sobek/Horus) 'traveled' across the lake land (*tꜣ-š*) and the 'Great Green' (*wꜣḏ-wr*)—probably meaning the region as a whole and then specifically the Lake, which here is probably an embodiment of the life-giving waters of the afterlife. In the Book of Fayum this journey is made by the sun god Ra, during the night, to rise again in the morning in the *ḥnt*. He enters the Lake (*š*) via the *r-ḥnt* (mouth of the *ḥnt*)—in the Book of Fayum it is explicitly stated that the God (Sobek/Horus) is born into the lake out of the mother goddess Mehet-weret, the embodiment of the *ḥnt*—so it seems likely that this is what is implied earlier in this Middle Kingdom text.

The daily cycle of sunrise in the east, and sunset in the west was mirrored in the Fayum landscape. The main waterway (*ḥnt*) comes through the hills in the east, floods into the land of the Lake (*tꜣ-š*) and rests in the main Lake (*š* or *wꜣḏ-wr*) in the west—the sun appears to set into the lake each day in the Fayum. The fact that they then believed the sun to travel back through the night from the west to rise in the east gave rise to the idea—in the Fayum—that the sun then travelled back through the waters of the lake, through the Lake Land into the waterway in the night to repeat this journey again. Additionally, it is easy to draw a parallel between the passage of the waters from the waterway through the Lake Land and then into the open expanse of the lake with the passage of birth—through a channel into the open expanse of the world. The God (Sobek/Horus/Ra) traveled from the entrance of the region to the Lake, then back again, each day—a tradition that quite possible gave rise to a misunderstanding thousands of years later when Greek writers recorded that the waters of the Fayum flowed into the lake for half the year, and back out for the other half.

Whether or not Amenemhat III engaged in any hydrological engineering projects in the region at this date has to be questioned. It cannot be totally ruled out, but the idea that he somehow transformed the landscape via hydrological engineering and canals and engaged in major land reclamation projects has more foundations in traditions and tales than it does in archaeology. If the pharaohs of the Middle Kingdom had mastered this kind of work it seems unlikely that it would not have been employed elsewhere in Egypt, or at least maintained in the Fayum during the New Kingdom. The fact that he was so revered in the region following his death probably reflected his investment into the region, into the landscape, with construction projects, and he may have made some attempts to 'tame' the landscape with increased agriculture, but, there is no evidence for any major hydrological engineering in Egypt at this date anywhere. Water, in particular the annual flood, was managed, but there were no canals as such, and dams may well have been constructed but their effectiveness is questionable.

The almost total absence of any evidence for a temple building/reconstruction program in the Fayum during the New Kingdom is astonishing. Given the major impact that the ambitious program of Rameses II had elsewhere in Egypt including all the peripheral regions, the presence of only a small number of remains from his reign in the region is very perplexing; certainly, the Greco-Roman period activities may well have simply obliterated what was there, but given the fact that at Madinat Madi they incorporated the Middle Kingdom temple into their new extended temple it seems unlikely that they would have destroyed earlier remains here. But the region was certainly still very important. The earlier New Kingdom palace and temple at *mr-wr* (Madinat al-Gurob) is strong evidence for continued engagement with the Fayum region; once again, the location reveals a deep connection to the primary waterway via the name *mr-wr*. The fact that some people felt very strong ties to the Fayum landscape is revealed in the collection of artifacts and the tomb associated with the Sobekhotep family of governors.

The Ramesside Wilbour papyrus attests that the Fayum was a very active agricultural region, with many shrines, temple personnel, and a network of officials, including the still-active (it seems) palace of *mr-wr* at Madinat el-Gurob. This document gives the first clear insight into their mental 'map' of the Fayum landscape. The place names are almost all associated with the waterways; *mr-wr*—was in existence from the early New Kingdom as a palace close to the Bahr Yusuf at the eastern end of the principal channel/waterway; *wp-š*—encompassed the entire area around this eastern region where the channel cuts through the chain of hills west of the Nile valley; *š*—the Lake, and/or town named after the Lake; *ḥnt*—probably the main waterway/channel; and possibly *pꜣ-ym*—this might be the name for the main Fayum lake.

Clearly, the perception of the Fayum landscape was shaped by the waterways, and the bulk of their activities and interventions into the landscape via the construction of funerary monuments focused along and around the one main waterway—the Bahr Yusuf. This might well be a reflection of deeply rooted subconscious habits and traditions—life in Egypt centered along the Nile River and its banks, so it is perhaps unsurprising that activities in the Fayum centered along the one major river of the region. And just as during the pharaonic period activities in the Delta were probably far more diffused in hundreds of small rural settlements with just a few major centers, the 'Delta' of the Fayum in the center of the region was home to just one main central place at Shedet which acted primarily as the principal cult center for Sobek and Sobek Shedty—the Patron God of the Fayum.

The changing names for the region, the primary waterway and the lake also reveal a great deal about perceptions of the landscape. While the two primary names for the imagined and experienced landscapes of the pharaonic period are very clear—*tꜣ-š* and *š-rsi*—other names do appear. The name *pꜣ-ym*, found in the Wilbour Papyrus is somewhat confusing, and does not appear again until far later in history. Herodotus did not actually name the region at all; he simply referred to the area around Lake Moeris (*ḫnt mr-wr*). In the Islamic records of the region, it is already named al-Fayum, but they say it was previously known as el-Geouna (the sewer). This less-than-positive name may well have been simply a way of emphasizing how marvelous the work of Joseph had been, transforming 'the sewer' into the amazing fertile land of the Fayum. The name al-Fayum is explained as having been given to the region as a result of Joseph having taken 1000 days (in Arabic *alf youm*) to transform the region.

It is not obvious if the lake was actually named in the pharaonic period. The name *š*, lake, appears early on, but in many cases it is clear that this refers to a specific town in the region. In the overtly religious documents the name *w3ḏ-wr* is given to a body of water within the region, in the landscape of the gods.

By the time Herodotus visited the Fayum, Egypt was a very different place; the traditional Egyptian pharaohs were already a distant memory of an era five hundred years earlier, the form of religion had changed, and previously strongly held beliefs were diluted with ideas from other cultures. However, traditions surrounding the Fayum landscape were still active. While there is no earlier evidence, the account of Herodotus may well reveal that the structured system of beliefs about the sacred landscape of the Fayum which is explicit in the Hymns to Sobek had been upheld, and then maintained and recorded again in the far later Book of Fayum. His statements that the priests told him the region was dug by hand might reflect the Fayum creation myth in which the gods created the landscape themselves. As mentioned earlier, the belief that Sobek/Horus/Ra traveled in one direction during the day and through the water in the night may well have given rise to statements by later writers that the waters flowed in one direction for part of the time and then back again, but the description of a tunnel running from the lake toward the west might well also derive from a misunderstanding of this aspect of the Fayum theology—the 'tunnel' he thought they described might have actually been them telling him about the passage of the god through the night.

From the moment his account first became a guide for visitors to the region, the landscape took on new and very different meanings to all who went there. The fact that he thought that the priests meant the region was 'man-made' imbued the Fayum landscape with new meaning. His description of what was probably the remains of the mortuary temple of Amenemhat III at Hawara transformed this monument into something entirely different: it was no longer an Egyptian temple, it was the Labyrinth, an enigma, and one of the most spectacular achievements of the ancient Egyptians. The Fayum landscape became an embodiment of Herodotus's perception, and it was his perception that became the foundation, and the core of almost every other account of the region. It is only through a full appreciation of the transmission of traditions that it is possible to understand that in actual fact Herodotus did learn about the true nature of the sacred landscape of the Fayum. It was his misunderstandings and the terms he used, followed by the loss of those ancient ideas when the Egyptian language died, compounded with modern preconceived ideas that led to the situation in which people believed everything he had described were aspects of the physical form of the landscape.

For thousands of years now the Fayum landscape has been perceived (by outsiders) to be the landscape of the Lake and the Labyrinth, and the ancient Egyptian beliefs have been generally lost. But that is not only a consequence of the impact of Herodotus's account; it is a consequence of history, as mentioned briefly above. The loss of ability to read any Egyptian documents or inscriptions meant that ancient Egyptian beliefs were also lost. Egypt was famed in the Greek and Roman worlds for the richness of its antiquities and the fertility of its land, which became symbols of political prowess and power. While the medieval Islamic scholars did what they could, they never succeeded in translating ancient Egyptian scripts, so ancient Egyptian culture and beliefs remained a mystery. The only accessible histories of Egypt that might have helped explain those monuments to early European pilgrims were oral traditions of the inhabitants of Egypt (Christian Copts), the Bible, and accounts in Greek and Latin (sometimes translated into Arabic or Persian).

The beginnings of exploration in Egypt, which formed the roots of Egyptology, took place at a time when the language of ancient Egypt was still utterly incomprehensible, and the medieval Islamic documents that held records of the Coptic versions of the Fayum creation theology were unavailable and generally unknown to most Westerners, so they still relied almost exclusively on the Classical Greek and Latin accounts for their appreciation of Egyptian history and explanation of the remains. This of course meant that Herodotus's (mis-)perception of the Fayum landscape perpetuated for millennia despite the truly spectacular hydrological achievements of the early Ptolemaic engineers and the total transformation of the landscape not only in the form of hundreds of square kilometers of new land but also the development of the monumental manifestation of the sacred landscape with many temples and the recording of the creation mythology. Even when advances in scholarship meant that the chronology of Egypt was better understood, nobody ever really appreciated the fact that the physical landscape of the Fayum could not possibly be the landscape recorded by Herodotus, and the nuances of his perception of the sacred landscape were lost on them as they never made the link to the older Egyptian versions of the creation mythology in the Hymn to Sobek. Even when they acknowledged that his perception was not of the real landscape but of something he imagined based on misunderstood snippets of information, people persisted in trying to 'find' the lake and the Labyrinth.

From almost the earliest point in the Ptolemaic period the Fayum was invested in heavily. Ptolemy I clearly decided he wanted another area in which to vastly expand the agricultural output of Egypt, and perhaps wanted somewhere not too far distant from Alexandria with 'new' lands (not owned by Egyptians) to parcel out as compensation to soldiers. The hydrological project of cutting canals in order to drain the Fayum lands and manage the water was carefully planned from the outset, and once this was underway and functioning, land became available for cultivation, and construction of dwellings and villages for the new inhabitants. Any inhabited area also needed temples, clergy, and administrative centres, and these soon also appeared. The Ptolemies generally respected long-standing Egyptian traditions, and no doubt the teams undertaking the irrigation works in the region encountered crocodiles as they moved into the wetter, marshier lands and drained them, so the adoption of the crocodile cult is unsurprising. Their relationship to the existing monuments is unclear. At Madinat Madi they expanded the existing Middle Kingdom temple, but what happened in Shedet is essentially unknown as so little has ever been found there, and the lack of any work at Biahmu is a little perplexing. What is also astonishing is that the famed Labyrinth seems to have been allowed to vanish. By the Roman Period the temple must have been all but totally destroyed, because a town had been built on the site.

The Fayum became both a tourist attraction and an agricultural goldmine during the Roman Period, but the landscape was not significantly altered. The irrigation of the Ptolemies was generally maintained, but the land was not as productive as it was anticipated to be. The high taxes reflect that expectations were high, but there is ample evidence that the drained land was far too saline to allow for easy agriculture. The Fayum also became a valuable outpost for overlooking desert trade; forts on the western edges attest the importance of this role played by the region in the Roman Period. The beliefs about the sacred landscape of the Fayum were recorded in the Book of Fayum, temple cults were clearly maintained, and the sacred crocodiles became popular tourist attractions, but the perception of the landscape in the minds of visitors was the landscape of Herodotus—the priests clearly were unable to convey the older beliefs to those visitors. Despite the fact that the Labyrinth no longer existed, it was still celebrated as a great monument, and the lake Herodotus saw also no longer existed as it had, thanks to the irrigation works—but was still usually reported in the way he had done.

The decline of Roman control in Egypt and the rise in Christianity that led into the Coptic Period naturally led to changes in perceptions of the Fayum landscape. Christianity has a long history and tradition of assimilating existing 'pagan' beliefs, and adapting them to fit Christian theology. In Egypt, the most obvious example is the way in which images of Isis nursing Horus were reused as images of Mary with Jesus. The Fayum became an important center of Coptic Christianity, and the Fayum creation myth was adapted to fit their beliefs—attributing the creation of the region to the prophet Joseph. Despite the wealth of Coptic texts from the Fayum, there is no contemporary record of this new story; it was recorded only by the medieval Islamic scholars, to whom the tradition probably felt very 'acceptable,' due to the fact that Joseph was also recognized as a prophet in the Qur'an.

There are several details in some versions of the tale that are especially interesting and may well reflect not only the ancient traditional belief of the Fayum having been created by the hand of gods, but also some historical realities. The details of the tales vary, but in one version Joseph is said to have drained the Fayum in order for the king's daughter to have somewhere to live that was safe. This story appears to reveal a cultural memory of the region having been home to royal women, and that the land had been drained to make it habitable—as opposed to having been cut out to allow the lake to form, which reveals memories of the Ptolemaic irrigation projects. The story also shows that the desert was perceived to be a threat (which of course it was—and still is); in this case it was a threat to those who might want to harm her, and thus was actually protecting her, as opposed to the older creation myth in which the desert was perceived to be Seth, the enemy of the floods of Osiris which were carried in via the channel that embodied the mother goddess, and thus the desert was a threat to the safety of the Fayum. In other versions Joseph is said to have been challenged to drain the Fayum of waters in order to prove his wisdom and abilities to the pharaoh; he then populated the region with his families. This could possibly recall the way in which the Fayum was reclaimed and then parcels of land were given to Greek mercenaries by the Ptolemies. The palimpsest of intertwined perceptions about the Fayum landscape became especially rich in this time.

The medieval Islamic scholars, geographers, and historians who visited the Fayum encountered Coptic Egypt, and thus, when they visited the Fayum they encountered the Coptic 'creation' traditions and tales. The scholars engaging in recording history were initially recording the history of the Islamic conquests, but even that writing seems to have been affected by the traditions of the region. The earliest recorded account of the Fayum's 'discovery' by 'Amr Ibn al-'As has such remarkably strong parallels with the Coptic tales of the Fayum being only accessible via a dangerous desert crossing that it has to have been influenced by the earlier accounts. What this tradition does reveal is that the Fayum was viewed 'upside-down.' Looking at a map, the 'entrance' to the Fayum is naturally placed at the Lahun–Hawara divide, where the channel cuts through the western hills and floods into the Fayum basin toward the lake. However, if Cartesian images are put aside and Egypt is viewed from the perspective of central administrative organizations in Alexandria, Cairo (Fustat), or Memphis then the natural route to the Fayum is across the desert from Giza/Saqqara, and the 'entrance' lies on the northern edge in the region of Karanis. The fact that the current main highway route to the Fayum from Cairo runs from Giza is no coincidence.

By the time the earliest European visitors arrived in the Fayum, any real comprehension of ancient Egyptian language, history, and religion was essentially totally lost. They relied upon the sources they did have, which were sources they valued as worthy and scholarly—Latin and Greek accounts, and the Bible. In these, the Fayum landscape consisted of the (man-made) lake, the Labyrinth, and the mysterious pyramids in the lake; the waters were thought to flow in and out of the region, and Herodotus had described a tunnel leading away from the lake. The earliest travelers did encounter and accept the idea that the main watercourse had been created by Joseph, but their primary interest lay in finding the landscape of Herodotus, and this desire was upheld and pursued by early

Egyptologists. As information started to become available, hieroglyphs were translated and ancient Egyptian history and religion gradually began to be unraveled; Herodotus started to be questioned, the irrigation system was reinstated, and new sites were discovered along with thousands of papyri revealing the details of Ptolemaic and Roman life in the Fayum. Despite the fact that so many of these accounts conveyed a perception that the Fayum landscape was far from ideal, many travelers saw themselves as explorers and adventurers, and wanted to find the ancient landscapes described as being so lush and rich. Their romantic ideals allowed them to inhabit a perception of the ancient landscape, and once again the Fayum landscape was imbued with new layers of meaning; it became feminine and fertile, and steeped in history.

The ancient Egyptian perception of the Fayum sacred landscape was preserved in Roman copies of a Ptolemaic book (the Book of Fayum), and a misinterpretation of that tradition dominated Classical scholarly accounts of the region—with some added embellishments. Coptic tradition went unrecorded at the time, but existing beliefs were adapted to fit Christian theology, and incorporated far older cultural memories. Islamic writers recorded the Coptic traditions because they fitted Muslim beliefs. European travelers had no access to any older knowledge, other than Greek and Latin accounts, and paid no respect to Muslim traditions—thus reviving the far older misinterpreted ideas about the Fayum landscape they found in the accounts of the Classical scholars. They wove in ideas from Classical Greek mythology, romanticizing the landscape, imbuing it with more meaning and adding layers to the palimpsest of perceptions. With the full spectrum of the history of perceptions of the Fayum landscape now revealed, it is clear that the Fayum was always considered to have been created by divine and sacred powers—be it the gods, God, or divine humans. The landscape itself naturally inspired the earliest beliefs, but the major human interventions into the landscape did not significantly change the root of the ideas—the Fayum landscape was 'created,' and that creation needed explaining.

The physical form of the Fayum landscape played a significant role in shaping the perceptions of the region. The large lake, the raised, fertile, central zone, the network of rivers, and the surrounding desert created a commonly held perception of the Fayum as the landscape of a lake, and of rich, productive, fertile land. The natural environment—an ideal habitat for crocodiles—led to the creation of the crocodile cult in the region.

The crocodile cult was manifested in the sacred landscape of temples, the physical form of which (the choice of locations of temples) was shaped by the natural environment; almost all the temples are on the desert edges, with the exception of the center of the cult—at Shedet—which was placed on the highest ground of the region. The lake and the remains of ancient Egyptian monuments were the subjects of the folklore of the region, and as such became monumentalized in the account of Herodotus, who attributed the creation of these features to an epic and ancient hero and believed the Fayum landscape to be a man-made phenomenon. The fertility of the region and the network of canals attracted the attentions of the Ptolemaic rulers, who reshaped the physical form of the landscape, as well as developing the sacred landscape through their continued dedication to the crocodile cult. This major intervention into the landscape was remembered later, in the medieval period, but the knowledge of who had created the landscape was lost, and thus was attributed to a more familiar name—Joseph—and the image of the Fayum as being a man-made landscape was upheld.

Folklore attributed the creation of the fertile Fayum landscape to this ancient heroic character, and there was a vestige of memory of some of the ancient inhabitants (of the royal palace at Gurob), found in the medieval stories about ancient women dwelling in the region. The landscape continued to be perceived as being rich, feminine, and fertile—despite the fact that the irrigation, agriculture, and population were declining. When the European travelers arrived their perceptions had already been shaped by their expectation of an ancient landscape of a lake, a great 'Labyrinth' temple, and a crocodile cult. Despite their focus on this landscape, which was only physically present at the peripheries of the region, their perceptions were affected by their experience of the central zone of the region, which in turn both upheld and fueled their romantic ideals of a lush, fertile landscape. Their perceptions of this aspect of the Fayum landscape were shaped by images from contemporary Romantic idealism, the notion of the exotic Orient, and their connection to the Classical authors.

The perception of the Fayum landscape has, throughout history, been both imagined and experienced. The imagined and the experienced perceptions of the landscape have both been shaped by the physical form of the landscape, which shapes folklore attached to that landscape. That folklore in turn contributed toward shaping the physical form of the landscape. Thus the imagined and the experienced landscapes of the Fayum are inextricably tied to one another through archaeology, texts, and traditions.

Notes

Timeline

1. (Shirai 2010, 44–51).
2. (Shirai 2010, 44–51).
3. (Shirai 2010, 44–51).

Chapter 1

1. Brown 1892, 5.
2. Hewison 2008, 1.
3. Hewison 2008, 2–4.
4. Dumont and el-Shabrawy 2009.
5. Hassan and Tassie 2006.
6. Brugsch 1872; Brown 1892; Brugsch 1892, 1893; Caton Thompson and Gardner 1929; Caton Thompson et al. 1937; Gardiner and Bell 1943; Armayor 1985; Garbrecht 1987; 1996.
7. Westermann 1917; Rostovtzeff 1922; Crawford 1971; Sharp 1999; Derda 2006.
8. Chronology is based on Shaw 2000: 479–83.
9. Tilley 1994, 18.
10. Zecchi 2001, 2010.
11. Tilley 1994, 18.
12. A useful presentation of the names of the Fayum can be found in Zecchi (2001: 233–240).
13. Helck 1956, 1586.
14. Faulkner 1962, 171.
15. Hannig 2003, 838; 2006, 1692.
16. Zecchi 2001, 238.
17. Wild 1971, 115.
18. Vandorpe 2004; Derda 2006.
19. Gardiner and Bell 1943; Rathbone 1996; Mueller 2002, 2003, 2004, 2005; Derda 2006; Kraemer 2010.
20. Reynolds and Wilson 1991, 1–34.

21. Reynolds and Wilson 1991, 18–39.
22. Reynolds and Wilson 1991, 49–90.
23. Ziolkowski 2007, 21.
24. Reynolds and Wilson 1991, 51–121; Ziolkowski 2007, 28.
25. Pfeiffer 1976, 2–14, 48–49; Reynolds and Wilson 1991, 123–58; Ziolkowski 2007, 28.
26. Pfeiffer 1976, 49; Reynolds and Wilson 1991, 123–158.
27. Pfeiffer 1976, 72–101; Reynolds and Wilson 1991, 164–206.
28. Thompson 2015, 58.
29. Thompson 2015, 64–73.
30. Ziolkowski 2007, 24.
31. Thompson 2015, 76.
32. Maspero 1899.
33. El Daly 2005, 6–8.
34. Uphill 2000; Vandorpe 2004.

Chapter 2

1. Bender 1995, 2.
2. Muir 1999, 3; Johnson 2007, 5, 9.
3. Johnson 2007, 24.
4. Muir 1999, 25–28; Johnson 2007, 40–49; Wylie 2007, 30–40.
5. Wylie 2007, 19–30, 54.
6. Hodder 2001.
7. Trigger 2006.
8. Shanks and Tilley 1987; Tilley 1994.
9. Bender 1995.
10. Cosgrove and Daniels 1988.
11. Wylie 2007, 13.
12. Lilley 2011.
13. Jeffreys 1998.
14. Richards 1999.
15. Bender 1995, 9.
16. Said 2003.
17. Thomas 1995, 29.
18. Tilley 1994, 35–67; Wylie 2007, 14.
19. Tilley 1994, 31–33.
20. Cosgrove and Daniels 1988; Bender 1995.

Chapter 3

1. Ball 1942, 1.
2. Hendrickx and Vermeersch 2000.
3. Shirai 2010, 33–43.
4. Beadnell 1905.

5. Caton Thompson and Gardner 1929; Caton Thompson and Gardner 1934; Caton Thompson et al. 1937.
6. Sandford and Arkell 1929.
7. Wendorf and Schild 1976.
8. Ginter and Kozlowski 1986.
9. Wenke 1983; 1984; Wenke and Brewer 1992a.
10. Shirai 2010; Holdaway et al. 2016; Holdaway and Wendrich 2017.
11. Holdaway and Wendrich 2017, 18–19.
12. Holdaway and Wendrich 2017, 219.
13. Wenke and Brewer 1992.
14. Holdaway and Wendrich 2017, 214.
15. Holdaway and Wendrich 2017.
16. Shirai 2010, 44–51.
17. Shirai 2010, 44–45.
18. Shirai 2010, 45–49.
19. Holdaway and Wendrich 2017, 25.
20. Midant-Reynes 2000; Shirai 2010, 49–50.
21. Shirai 2010, 50–51.
22. Personal Communication, Guilio Lucarini 2017.
23. Moeller 2016, 59–64.
24. Bard 2000.
25. Hassan and Tassie 2006.
26. Quirke 2005, 3–6.
27. Harrell and Brown 1995; Bloxam and Heldal 2007.
28. Harrell and Brown 1995.
29. Harrell and Brown 1995, 83.
30. Harrell and Brown 1995.
31. Borchardt 1900.
32. Leclant and Clerc 1988, 336; Muhlestein 2015, 252–53.
33. Cwiek 1997, 21.
34. Petrie 1913, 21–22.
35. Lepsius, 3–7.
36. Sethe 1933, 1–7.
37. Goedicke 1971, 149–50.
38. De Morgan 1903, 23.
39. "Giza Archives. Tomb G2150."
40. Der Manuelian 2006; see also "Giza Archives. Tomb G2150."
41. Kanawati and McFarlane 1993, 42–44.
42. Petrie 1898, fig. 21; Kanawati and McFarlane 1993, 52–53.
43. Fraser 1902, 67.
44. Fraser 1902, 76.
45. Sethe 1908, 217; 1910, 337; Faulkner 1969, 84, 236.
46. Seidlmayer 2000.

47. Griffith 1889, fig. 11, line 30.
48. El-Khadragy and Kahl 2004.
49. Malleson 2007.
50. Callender 2000.
51. Callender 2000, 164; Hewison 2008, 18.
52. Hassan and Tassie 2006, 40.
53. Romer 2017.
54. Hassan and Tassie 2006.
55. Zecchi 2010, 24.
56. Petrie 1889, 57.
57. Zecchi 2010, 26.
58. Vansleb 1678, 158–59.
59. Zecchi 2008, 373–375; Enmarch 2013, 21.
60. Zecchi 2010, 27–28.
61. Zecchi 2008, 382.
62. Enmarch 2013, 24.
63. Lacau and Chevrier 1969, plate 12.
64. Petrie 1890, 5.
65. Luft 1998, 1–2.
66. Quirke 1991, 142.
67. Luft 1998; Quirke 2005, 37.
68. Luft 1998.
69. Horváth 2009.
70. Quirke 1997; Luft 1998, 20–21.
71. Collier and Quirke 2002, 133.
72. Quirke 2005, 71, 88.
73. Petrie 1890, pl. 11.14.
74. Śliwa 1992.
75. Bresciani 1997, 9.
76. Bresciani 1997, 10.
77. Gallazzi 1994.
78. Gallazzi 1994.
79. See the current IFAO project webpage for an introduction to the site: "Tebtynis, IFAO Project."
80. Salmon 1901, 49–50.
81. Habachi 1940, 731.
82. Petrie 1889, 54.
83. Habachi 1937.
84. Zecchi 2010, 43.
85. Zecchi 2010, 43.
86. Petrie 1889, 57.
87. Zecchi 2010, 39.
88. Zecchi 2010, 40–41.

89. Zecchi 2010, 72.
90. Zecchi 2010, 79–81.
91. Zecchi 2010, 80.
92. Belzoni 1820, 383.
93. Lane 2000, 234.
94. Petrie et al. 1912, 28.
95. Petrie et al. 1912, 29.
96. Uphill 2000, 21.
97. Uytterhoeven 2009.
98. For inventories of statues fragments and inscriptions, see Uphill (2000) and Blom-Boer (2006).
99. Lepsius, 138, e.
100. Zecchi 2010, 157–170.
101. Lange and Schäfer 1908, 255–256.
102. Lange and Schäfer 1908, 196–198.
103. Lange and Schäfer 1902, 85.
104. Lange and Schäfer 1902, 91.
105. Wild 1971, 92.
106. Wild 1971, 99, 115.
107. Wild 1971, 107–109.
108. Zecchi 2006, 137–44; 2010, 94.
109. Zecchi 2006, 138.
110. Zecchi 2006, 141; 2010, 92–93.
111. Delange 1987, 133–135.
112. Delange 1987, 138–39.
113. Delange 1987, 70–71.
114. Wild 1971.
115. Wild 1971.
116. Delange 1987.
117. Delange 1987.
118. Delange 1987.
119. Caminos 1956.
120. Parkinson 2002, 226–34; Quirke 2004, 206.
121. Petrie 1909, 6–7.
122. Farag 1980.
123. Steven Snape suggests the mortuary temple of Amenemhat II at Dahshur as a potential original location (personal communication, 2017).
124. Quirke 2004, 206; Baines 2013, 197.
125. Baines 2013, 195.
126. Quirke 2004, 206.
127. Parkinson 2002, 231.
128. Quirke 2004, 206.

129. Quirke 2004, 208.
130. Quirke 2004, 212.
131. Quirke 2004, 213.
132. Quirke 2004, 215.
133. Quirke 2004, 212–17.
134. Quirke 2004, 215.
135. Quirke 2004, 212–13.
136. Quirke 2004, 213.
137. "Ramesseum Papyri."
138. Gardiner 1957, 45–48.
139. Gardiner 1957, 48–54.
140. Gardiner 1957, 46.
141. Gardiner 1957, 46–54.
142. Callender 2000, 172.
143. Bourriau 2000.
144. Thomas 1981, 1–2.
145. Thomas 1981, 2.
146. Thomas 1981, 3.
147. Shaw 2011.
148. Thanks are due to all my colleagues in the Liverpool and IFAO archaeological missions at Gurob, especially Dr. Ian Shaw, Dr. Marine Yoyotte, and Ms. Jan Picton, with whom I enjoyed many discussions about the site and its history during work at the site in 2005–17.
149. Kemp 1978; Lacovara 1997.
150. Kemp 1978; Lacovara 1997.
151. A list can be found in Kemp (1978).
152. Shaw 2011.
153. Hagen forthcoming. I am grateful to Dr. Fredrik Hagen for kindly sending me a pre-publication draft of his chapter.
154. Griffith 1898, 91–98.
155. Hagen and Soliman 2018.
156. Gardiner 1948a, vii–xiii.
157. Yoyotte 2012, 363.
158. Helck 1956, 1586–88; Charles 1960.
159. Dziobek and Raziq 1990.
160. Bryan 1991, 104–105, 245; 2006, 101.
161. Petrie and Brunton 1924, pl. 53.
162. Bryan 1991, 104, 266.
163. Bryan 1991, 103.
164. Bryan 1991, 105.
165. Charles 1960, 4; Parkinson 2002, 228.
166. Gardiner 1948b, 1.
167. Gardiner 1948b, 9; Katary 1989, xxi.

168. Gardiner 1948b, 1–2.
169. Gardiner 1948b, 1; Katary 1989, xxi. It is unknown what type of land *khato* refers to.
170. Gardiner 1948b, 11.
171. Numbers marked with § indicate the line number given in Gardiner 1948c, Volume III.
172. Gardiner 1948b, 47.
173. Gardiner 1947, 1–37.
174. Taylor 2000, 331–333.
175. Taylor 2000, 333–35.
176. Taylor 2000, 353.
177. Grimal 1981, xi.
178. Beinlich 2013, 27.
179. Beinlich 2013, 27–28.
180. Beinlich 2013, 28.
181. Jasnow 2013, 86.
182. Schulz 2013.
183. Beinlich 2013, 32–34.
184. Jasnow 2013, 79.
185. Jasnow 2013, 83.
186. Jasnow 2013, 86.
187. Tait 2003, 195.
188. Harrell and Brown 1992.
189. Beinlich 2013, 32.
190. Tait 2003.
191. Beinlich 1991, 54.
192. Beinlich 1991, 59–64.
193. Beinlich 2013.
194. Beinlich 1991, 229,§912.
195. Tait 2003, 188.

Chapter 4

1. Herodotus 1954, 161–62.
2. Jones 1932, 97–99.
3. Taylor 2000.
4. Lloyd 2000a; Taylor 2000; Manning 2010, 27, 51.
5. Lloyd 1982.
6. Lloyd 1975, 157; Harley and Woodward 1987; Romm 1998, 14–15.
7. Waters 1985, 16–17.
8. Waters 1985; Herodotus 2003, ix.
9. Herodotus 2003, xi–xiii; Baragwanath and de Bakker 2012, 2.
10. Easterling and Knox 1985, 427.
11. Earley 2016.

12. West 1980, 11.
13. Fergerson 1975, 16; Haller 2007.
14. Edwards 1993.
15. Waters 1985, 1–13.
16. Romm 1998, 12–31.
17. Lloyd 1975, 148.
18. Wilson 1970, 2; Waters 1985, 79; Romm 1998.
19. Spiegelberg 1927.
20. Eyre 1991.
21. Armayor 1978; 1985; Fehling 1989.
22. Lloyd 1975, 143–53.
23. Lloyd 1975, 142–49; Redfield 1985, 107; Romm 1998, 92.
24. Waters 1985; Eyre 1991.
25. Wilson 1970, 5.
26. Harrison 2007, 48–53.
27. Flory 1980; Redfield 1985, 102.
28. "Oxyrhynchus Online."
29. Earley 2016, 122–23.
30. Waters 1985, 52; Romm 1998, 41–42.
31. Lloyd 1975, 75.
32. Waters 1985, 52.
33. Lloyd 1975; Waters 1985, 52, 89.
34. Herodotus 1954, 106.
35. Herodotus 1954, 129.
36. Herodotus 1954, 139.
37. Herodotus 1954, 160–161.
38. Recent work suggests that the lake is in fact supplied by a deep spring (personal communication, Dr. Roger Flower, 2011).
39. Herodotus 1954, 161–162.
40. Herodotus 1954, 162.
41. Lloyd 1975; Eyre 1991.
42. Armayor 1985.
43. Armayor 1985, 2.
44. Armayor 1985, 4.
45. Armayor 1985, 2–8.
46. Waters 1985, 153.
47. Vansleb 1678.
48. Brown 1892, 1.
49. Brugsch 1892; 1893.
50. Brugsch 1872.
51. Brugsch 1892.
52. Caton Thompson and Gardner 1929, 20.
53. Caton Thompson and Gardner 1929; Caton Thompson et al. 1937.

54. Gardiner and Bell 1943.
55. Cruz-Uribe 1992.
56. Vandorpe 2004.
57. Beinlich 1991.
58. Faulkner 1962, 171.
59. Hannig 2003, 838; 2006, 1692.
60. Gardiner and Bell 1943, 42.
61. Vansleb 1678, 1.
62. Lane 2000, 234.
63. Uphill 2000, 1–2.
64. Uphill 2000.
65. "A Virtual Exploration of the Lost Labyrinth."
66. Beinlich 2013, 72.
67. Beinlich 1991.
68. Lloyd 2000a, 388–90.
69. Lloyd 2000b.
70. Derda 2006, 3.
71. Mueller 2002, 108.
72. Wilfong 2014, 1.
73. Mueller 2005; Monson 2013.
74. Davoli 2012, 163.
75. Davoli 2012, 154.
76. Monson 2013, 91.
77. Verhoogt 1998, Monson 2013.
78. Mueller 2002; Bagnall and Rathbone 2004, 128; Manning 2010, 47; Davoli 2012, 153–55.
79. Bagnall and Rathbone 2004, 152–153.
80. Vansleb 1678, 153.
81. Davoli and Ahmad 2006; Davoli 2012, 156.
82. Arnold 1999, 155.
83. Arnold 1999, 159, 253.
84. Davoli 2012, 156.
85. Davoli 2012.
86. Mueller 2002; 2003; 2004; 2005.
87. "Fayum Papyri."
88. Verhoogt 1998; Bagnall and Rathbone 2004, 147–152; Davoli 2012, 158.
89. Monson 2002, 53.
90. Davoli 1998, 117–20; Bitelli et al. 2003, 6–7.
91. Davoli 1998, 117–137; Bagnall and Rathbone 2004, 135; Pernigotti 2005, 30; Hewison 2008, 97.
92. Bitelli et al. 2003, 12–18.
93. Bitelli et al. 2003, 24.
94. Bagnall and Rathbone 2004, 135–136; Davoli 2012, 157–58.

95. My thanks to Dr. Gehad for sharing his findings with me.
96. Bagnall and Rathbone 2004, 135–136; Davoli 2012, 157–58.
97. Rostovtzeff 1922.
98. Bagnall and Rathbone 2004, 137.
99. Davoli 2005, 29; Carpasso and Davoli 2012, 11–18.
100. Carpasso and Davoli 2012, figs. 19, 24.
101. Davoli 2005.
102. Davoli 2007.
103. Jasnow 2013, 82.
104. Bagnall and Rathbone 2004, 138–140.
105. Cestari 2010, 33.
106. Schwartz and Wild 1950, 70.
107. Casanova 1975; Sharp 1999, 160–161; Bagnall and Rathbone 2004, 141; Davoli 2012, 157–58.
108. Sharp 1999, 160–161.
109. Bagnall and Rathbone 2004, 142–43; Davoli 2012, 161.
110. Bagnall and Rathbone 2004, 143–46; Bresciani et al. 2010.
111. Bagnall and Rathbone 2004, 152.
112. Westermann 1917.
113. Clarysse 2010.
114. Dielman 2011.
115. Uytterhoeven 2009.
116. Herklotz 2012, 11.
117. "Tebtunis Papyrus I.33."
118. Peacock 2000, 422.
119. Lewis 1983, 9–83.
120. Davoli 2012, 155.
121. Lewis 1983, 90.
122. Oldfather 1960, vii–ix; Sacks 1990, 6; Chamoux and Bertrac 1993, ix; Muntz 2017, 1–2.
123. Oldfather 1960, xiii.
124. Chamoux and Bertrac 1993, xv.
125. Sacks 1990, 3–4; Muntz 2017, 16–21.
126. Muntz 2017, 83–116.
127. Chamoux and Bertrac 1993, xiii–xv.
128. Vogel 1888.
129. Oldfather 1960, xvi.
130. Lewis 1983, 90.
131. Oldfather 1960, 181–183.
132. Oldfather 1960, 211.
133. Oldfather 1960, 227.
134. Oldfather 1960, 289.
135. Oldfather 1960, 303.

136. Oldfather 1960, 303–305.
137. Dueck 2000, 2–30; Dueck et al. 2005, 1.
138. Dueck 2000, 62.
139. Dover 1980, 148–50.
140. Dueck 2000, 31–84.
141. Dueck 2000; Dueck et al. 2005, 1–4.
142. Dueck 2000, 64; Roseman 2005.
143. Dueck et al. 2005, 1–4.
144. "Oxyrhynchus Online."
145. Jones 1917, xxxix–xli; Diller 1935.
146. Jones 1917, 185.
147. Jones 1932, 15.
148. Jones 1932, 97.
149. Jones 1932, 97–99.
150. Jones 1932, 103–105.
151. Jones 1932, 103–105.
152. Jones 1932, 107.
153. Jones 1932, 113.
154. Shotter 1968.
155. Hadas 2003, 75.
156. Shotter 1968, 207; Venning 2011, 380.
157. Herklotz 2012, 15.
158. Hadas 2003, 75.
159. Shotter 1968, 206.
160. Silberman 1988, vii–xxx; Romer 1998, 1–4, 22.
161. Gormley et al. 1984.
162. Gormley et al. 1984; Silberman 1988, xlii–li; Romer 1998, 27–30.
163. Romer 1998, 50.
164. Romer 1998, 12–13.
165. Bowder 1980, 169; Murphy 2004, 2–4.
166. Murphy 2004, 4–5, 53–54, 60–65.
167. Murphy 2004, 15–18, 53, 73.
168. Mayhoff 1906; Beaujeu 1950.
169. Rackham 1938, xii–xiii.
170. Rackham 1961, 255–57.
171. Rackham 1961, 267.
172. Toomer 1975, 186–202.
173. Berggren and Jones 2000, 23.
174. Berggren and Jones 2000, 42–44; Mittenhuber 2010, 96.
175. Toomer 1975, 202; Berggren and Jones 2000, 50–52.
176. Mittenhuber 2010, 95–103.
177. Stevenson 1932, 100–104.
178. Derda 2006, 6–42.

179. Derda 2006, 62–71.
180. Arnold 1999, 253, 270.
181. Davoli 2012, 163.
182. Dielman 2011.
183. Doxiadis 1995, 13.
184. Cheshire 2013, 117.
185. "UCLA Fayum Project."
186. Wilfong 2014.
187. I am grateful to Sebastián Encina, collections manager at the Kelsey Museum, for allowing me to spend some time examining this collection in July 2017.
188. Bagnall and Rathbone 2004, 131–134.
189. Pollard 1988.
190. Bagnall and Rathbone 2004, 138–140; Davoli 2012, 160.
191. Bresciani et al. 2010.
192. Jasnow 2013, 82.
193. Taplin 2000, 27–51.
194. Lewis 1983, 59–64.
195. Watterson 1988, 16–32.
196. Watterson 1988, 33–44.
197. For a history of the Fayum monasteries see Abbott 1937.
198. Watterson 1988, 48–53; Bagnall and Rathbone 2004, 19.

Chapter 5

1. Davies 1672, 177–78.
2. Bouriant 1895, 741–42.
3. Maspero 1899.
4. El Daly 2005, 6–8.
5. Dawood 1999, 3.
6. Duri 1983, 22–24.
7. Cahen 1990, 192; Kennedy 1998, 63.
8. El Daly 2005, 165.
9. Torrey 1932, 1.
10. Torrey 1932, 9–16.
11. Torrey 1932, 2; Rosenthal 1971.
12. Torrey 1901, 280; 1932, 6–7; El Daly 2005, 165.
13. El Daly 2005, 165.
14. Kennedy 1998, 63.
15. Torrey 1901, 283.
16. Torrey 1901, 284.
17. Ibn 'Abd al-Hakam 871[1922], 14–16.
18. Ibn 'Abd al-Hakam 871[1922], 15.
19. Kennedy 1991.

20. Bianquis 1998, 91; Kennedy 1998, 80–85.
21. Hopkins 1990, 301.
22. Hopkins 1990, 306; Rekaya 1991, 336–37. The Mu'tazila (theological) movement was founded in Basra in 748, and had considerable influence in the Abbasid period (Gimaret 1993). These scholars believed in seeking rational explanation of the laws of nature.
23. Tibbetts 1992, 95.
24. Vernet 1978, 1070; Sani 1982, 1–3; Aini 1985, 16; Hopkins 1990, 305.
25. Ahmad 1991, 577; Tibbetts 1992, 99.
26. Jafri 1985, 57.
27. Jafri 1985, 58; Tibbetts 1992, 97.
28. Tibbetts 1992, 105; Ahmad 1995, 22.
29. Aini 1985, 16.
30. Hopkins 1990, 307.
31. Hopkins 1990, 309, 308.
32. Kennedy 1991, 161.
33. Kennedy 1991, 161.
34. Gabrieli 1960, 176; Bonebakker 1990, 16.
35. de Meynard 1865, 10–13; Hadj-Sadok 1971, 839; Ahmad 1995, 58; El Daly 2005, 166.
36. Tibbetts 1992, 91; Ahmad 1995, 59.
37. Tibbetts 1992, 91; Ahmad 1995, 58.
38. Netton 2008, 257–58.
39. Tibbetts 1992, 91.
40. de Meynard 1865, 9.
41. de Meynard 1865, 9–15; Hadj-Sadok 1971, 839; Ahmad 1995, 59.
42. de Meynard 1865, 202–203.
43. Wiet 1937, vii; El Daly 2005, 166.
44. Zaman 2001, 257; Netton 2008, 687–688.
45. Netton 2008, 687–88.
46. Zaman 2001, 258.
47. Wiet 1937, xx.
48. Wiet 1937, xiii–xiv.
49. Wiet 1937, 2–3; Hopkins 1990, 309.
50. Wiet 1937, 185.
51. This is the standard accepted translation of the title, but there is dispute over this issue (Khalidi 1975: 2).
52. Pellat 1991, 784.
53. Ahmad 1995, 62.
54. Pellat 1991, 785.
55. Pellat 1991, 784; Ahmad 1995, 61; El Daly 2005, 170.
56. Pellat 1991.
57. Other copies of this edition were made in 1302, 1303, and 1313.

58. Pellat 1991, 784–89; Ahmad 1995, 61.
59. de Vaux 1896, ii; Pellat 1991.
60. Ahmad 1953, 63.
61. Ahmad 1954a; Khalidi 1975; Pellat 1991, 784–89.
62. de Vaux 1896, v; Ahmad 1953, 61–2; 1991, 579.
63. Khalidi 1975, 14.
64. Ahmad 1953; Khalidi 1975, 70.
65. Ahmad 1953, 71–77.
66. Ahmad 1954b.
67. Ahmad 1953, 63.
68. Khalidi 1975, 15.
69. Ahmad 1953; 1954a, 509; Pellat 1965, 4–5.
70. Bianquis 1998.
71. Pellat 1965, 293.
72. Pellat 1965, §773.
73. Pellat 1965, §774, §778.
74. Pellat 1965, §775.
75. Pellat 1965, §776, §781.
76. Pellat 1965, §782.
77. Pellat 1965, §783.
78. Pellat 1965, §784.
79. Pellat 1965, §787.
80. Khalidi 1975.
81. Pellat 1965, §788.
82. Pellat 1991, §797.
83. Pellat 1965, §798.
84. Wiet 1953, 4.
85. El Daly 2005, 170.
86. de Vaux 1984.
87. Wiet 1953, 5; de Vaux 1984, 29.
88. de Vaux 1984, 308.
89. de Vaux 1984, 323.
90. de Vaux 1984, 323–24.
91. de Vaux 1984, 324.
92. Halm 1991, 162; Kennedy 1991, 161.
93. Halm 1991, 162–64.
94. Dunlop 1960; Tibbetts 1992, 108–29.
95. Dunlop 1960; Ahmad 1995, 75–79.
96. Ahmad 1995, 76–78.
97. Kramers 1932; Tibbetts 1992, 110.
98. The twenty-first map covers the whole Islamic Empire.
99. Tibbetts 1992, 114.
100. Tibbetts 1992, 115.

101. Miquel 1978, 222.
102. Miquel 1978, 223; Tibbetts 1992, 109.
103. Mordtmann 1845, xiii.
104. Miquel 1978, 223.
105. Mordtmann 1845, v; Tibbetts 1992, 109–11, 131–32.
106. Tibbetts 1992, 112.
107. Ahmad 1995, 79.
108. Mordtmann 1845, 27–31.
109. Tibbetts 1992, 112.
110. Ahmad 1991, 581.
111. Tibbetts 1992, 115.
112. Tibbetts 1992, 115.
113. Kramers and Wiet 1925, xii; Miquel 1971, 787; Tibbetts 1992, 110–111.
114. Miquel 1971, 787; Tibbetts 1992, 110.
115. Miquel 1971, 787; Ahmad 1995, 85.
116. Miquel 1971, 787.
117. Tibbetts 1992, 112.
118. Kramers and Wiet 1925, xiv, 142; Ahmad 1991, 582.
119. Kramers and Wiet 1925, xvii.
120. Tibbetts 1992, 108, 132–34.
121. Tibbetts 1992, 135.
122. Tibbetts 1992, 113.
123. Tibbetts 1992, 134.
124. Kramers and Wiet 1925, 145.
125. Kramers and Wiet 1925, 157.
126. Kramers and Wiet 1925, 158.
127. Kramers and Wiet 1925.
128. Collins 1994, xiii.
129. Tibbetts 1992, 111, 134; Collins 1994, xiii, xxi.
130. Netton 2008, 449.
131. Collins 1994, 177.
132. Tibbetts 1992, 122–23.
133. Collins 1994, 1–5.
134. Tibbetts 1992, 110.
135. Collins 1994, 177–90.
136. Collins 1994, 185.
137. Collins 1994, 191.
138. Ahmad 1991, 584.
139. Boilot 1960, 1236; Ahmad 1991, 584; El Daly 2005, 171–72.
140. Halm 1991, 163.
141. Oman 1971, 1032; Ahmad 1992, 156.
142. Oman 1971, 1032; Netton 2008, 275.
143. Ahmad 1992, 157.

144. Aziz 1975, 78.
145. Ahmad 1992, 159.
146. Jaubert 1975, xxi.
147. Ahmad 1992, 159–60; 1995, 164–65.
148. Ahmad 1992, 156, 163.
149. Jaubert 1975, xix–xx.
150. Jaubert 1975, 129.
151. Jaubert 1975, 308–09.
152. Jaubert 1975, 309–11.
153. Bednarski 2005, 15.
154. Halm 1991, 163–64; Chamberlain 1998, 212–15.
155. Chamberlain 1998.
156. Ragib 1974, 205–206.
157. Wiet 1953, 1; Ragib 1974; Bosworth 1993.
158. Wiet 1953, 2–3.
159. Wiet 1953.
160. Wiet 1953, 4.
161. Davies 1672, 87–88.
162. Davies 1672, 177–78.
163. Davies 1672, 177–78.
164. Davies 1672, 178–79.
165. Davies 1672, 182.
166. Davies 1672, 182.
167. Davies 1672, 181–84.
168. Davies 1672, 185–86.
169. Davies 1672, 186–88.
170. Zeki-Bey 1899, 257; König 1996, 191.
171. Zeki-Bey 1899, 258; König 1996, 192.
172. Moritz 1899.
173. König 1996, 207.
174. König 1996, 205–10.
175. König 1996, 213.
176. König 1996, 213–17.
177. Salmon 1901, 37–72; Keenan 2005, 209.
178. Haarman 1991, 165–66; Northrup 1998, 248.
179. Rosenthal 1991, 193; El Daly 2005, 180.
180. El Daly 2005, 180.
181. Bouriant 1895, v.
182. Bouriant 1895, vi.
183. Bouriant 1895, 727–28.
184. Bouriant 1895, 728–29.
185. Bouriant 1895, 729–30.
186. Bouriant 1895, 730–33.

187. Bouriant 1895, 734.
188. Bouriant 1895, 735.
189. Bouriant 1895, 735.
190. Bouriant 1895, 740.
191. This may well be the work titled *Fada'il Misr*.
192. Bouriant 1895, 741–42.
193. Benjamin 1995, 254–55.
194. Holt 1965, 873.
195. Friedländer 1893, 180.
196. Benjamin 1995, 254–55.
197. Golb 1965, 270.

Chapter 6

1. St. John 1853, 261.
2. Lenoir 1873, 137.
3. Díaz-Andreu 2007, 32.
4. Wolff 2003, 1–13.
5. Pfeiffer 1976, 38, 48–49; Reynolds and Wilson, N. G. 1991, 122–49.
6. Ziolkowski 2007, 24.
7. Gonzales 1977, 188, 650.
8. Burri 1971, 31, 41.
9. Blount 1636, 55.
10. Yarrow 1967, 3.
11. Harrigan 2008, 24, 27, 30.
12. Yarrow 1967, 6–9; Díaz-Andreu 2007, 38.
13. Matar 2014, 17.
14. Irwin 2006, 87–103.
15. Dannenfelt 1959, 22.
16. Moser 2006, 11–13.
17. Winter 1992, 17.
18. Fedden 1958, 9.
19. Sandys 1673.
20. Ellison 2002, 250–57; 2008.
21. Pougeois 1869, 9; Carré 1956, 29.
22. Carré 1956, 29–37.
23. Irwin 2006, 111.
24. Carré 1956, 29.
25. Carré 1956, 30.
26. Vansleb 1678.
27. Vansleb 1678, 148–49.
28. Vansleb 1678, 153–56.
29. Vansleb 1678, 153–155.
30. Vansleb 1678, 155.

31. Vansleb 1678, 156–57.
32. Vansleb 1678, 158–59.
33. Vansleb 1678, 162.
34. Vansleb 1678, 161–63.
35. Vansleb 1678, 164–68.
36. Carré 1956, 44.
37. Duranton in Lucas 1998, 7–11.
38. Bierbrier 2012, 342.
39. Lucas 1998; 2002; 2004.
40. Carré 1956, 44; Duranton in Lucas 1998, 9.
41. Lucas 2002, 187.
42. Lucas 2002, 187.
43. Lucas 2002, 187–90.
44. Lucas 2002, 192–94.
45. Lucas 2002, 194–96.
46. Lucas 2002, 196.
47. Lucas 2002, 196–98.
48. Lucas 2002, 190.
49. Lucas 2004, 200–201.
50. Lucas 2004, 201–204.
51. Lucas 2004, 205–13.
52. Lucas 2004, 213–16.
53. Lucas 2002, 218.
54. Leask 2002, 2.
55. Díaz-Andreu 2007, 41.
56. Leask 2002, 2–22.
57. Moussa-Mahmoud 1988, 95–97.
58. Leask 2002, 30–31; Moser 2006, 1–35.
59. Milton 2008.
60. Rogers 2008.
61. Addison 1712a; Sambrook 1986, 130–32.
62. Addison 1712b.
63. Varney 1999, 171.
64. Watson 1970, 13–14.
65. Baigent 2008.
66. Bierbrier 2012, 438–39.
67. Pococke 1743, iii; Fedden 1958, 13; Leask 2002, 34.
68. Pococke 1743; Leask 2002, 34.
69. Pococke 1743, 57.
70. Pococke 1743, 57–59.
71. Pococke 1743, 60–63.
72. Pococke 1743, 64–65.
73. Pococke 1743, 66.

74. Pococke 1743, 66–67.
75. Oldfather 1960, 313.
76. Lloyd 1975; Leask 2002, 115.
77. Leask 2002, 116, 121.
78. Godlewska 1995.
79. Bednarski 2005, 95.
80. Godlewska 1995, 15.
81. Godlewska 1995, 12.
82. Jomard 1812.
83. Godlewska 1995.
84. Leask 2002, 103; Said 2003, 63.
85. Leask 2002, 106, 108; Reid 2002, 31.
86. Leask 2002, 129.
87. Leask 2002, 130; Reid 2002, 37–39.
88. Moser 2006, 33–64; Díaz-Andreu 2007, 42–49.
89. Díaz-Andreu 2007, 44–46.
90. Díaz-Andreu 2007, 50.
91. Díaz-Andreu 2007, 62.
92. Goldschmidt 2000, 98; Bierbrier 2012, 282.
93. Jomard 1812, 3–4.
94. Jomard 1812, 6–12.
95. Jomard 1812, 14–18.
96. Jomard 1812, 19–21.
97. Mayes 2003.
98. Bierbrier 2012, 52–53.
99. Mayes 2003.
100. Leask 2002, 136.
101. Belzoni 1820, 378–9.
102. Belzoni 1820, 379–82.
103. Belzoni 1820, 381–82.
104. Belzoni 1820, 382–86.
105. Belzoni 1820, 387–88.
106. Belzoni 1820, 389–90.
107. Belzoni 1820, 390–91.
108. Williams 1964, 49.
109. Leask 2002, 128–34.
110. Lockman 2004, 68; Irwin 2006, 146–49.
111. Lockman 2004, 75–76.
112. Mazuel 1937, 5–6; Bierbrier 2012, 334–35.
113. Linant de Bellefonds 1843.
114. Thompson 2010, 7–16.
115. Irwin 2006, 163.
116. Thompson 2010, 101.

117. Thompson 2010.
118. Lane 2000, xv–xvi.
119. Lane 2000, xviii–xx.
120. Lane 2000, ix–xxxi.
121. Thompson 2010, 22–25.
122. Lane 2000, ix–xi; Thompson 2010, 53–75.
123. Lane 2000, xiii–xiv.
124. Thompson 2010, 90–91.
125. Lane 2000, 230; Thompson 2010, 185.
126. Lane 2000, 230–31.
127. Lane 2000, 232–33.
128. Lane 2000, 234–37.
129. Lane 2000, 237–39.
130. Lane 2000, 240.
131. Lane 2000, 239–42.
132. Lane 2000, 242.
133. Lane 2000, 242–45; Thompson 2010, 203.
134. Leask 1992, 14.
135. Cranston 1994, 61–62.
136. Oerlemans 2004, 151.
137. Leask 1992, 23.
138. Buckingham also visited Egypt, and in his autobiography includes a short reference to his trip to the Fayum, which rivaled that of St. John in its poetic nature, including references to Virgil and a paradise-like landscape. As his discussion of the Fayum was exceptionally brief it is not included here (Buckingham 1855: 171–74).
139. All St. John poems referred to here are published in *Oriental Herald and Colonial Review* (1824) or *Oriental Herald and Journal of General Literature* (1825–27), some under a pseudonym 'Bion.'
140. Dr. Rachel Shulkins 2009 personal communication.
141. St. John 1834, xiv.
142. St. John 1834, 235.
143. St. John 1834, 211.
144. St. John 1834, 211.
145. St. John 1834, 218.
146. St. John 1834, 218.
147. St. John 1834, 223.
148. St. John 1853, 261.
149. St. John 1834, 229.
150. St. John 1834, 231–32.
151. St. John 1834, 238–39.
152. St. John 1834, 245.
153. St. John 1834, 245–48.

154. St. John 1834, 252.
155. St. John 1834, 251–55.
156. St. John 1834, 256–67.
157. St. John 1854, 3.
158. Thornton 1994, 99.
159. Lenoir 1873, 2.
160. Lenoir 1873, 85.
161. Lenoir 1873, 104–11.
162. Lenoir 1873, 112–14.
163. Lenoir 1873, 114.
164. Lenoir 1873, 114.
165. Lenoir 1873, 114–15.
166. Lenoir 1873, 114–15.
167. Lenoir 1873, 119.
168. Lenoir 1873, 115–24.
169. Lenoir 1873, 124–27.
170. Lenoir 1873, 134.
171. Lenoir 1873, 134.
172. Lenoir 1873, 137.
173. Behdad 1994, 35.
174. Wilkinson 1843.
175. Behdad 1994, 40–41.
176. Drower 1995, 3–26.
177. Drower 1995, 26–34.
178. Drower 1995, 34–40.
179. Drower 1995, 101–28.
180. Drower 1995, 60–62.
181. Petrie 1889, 1.
182. Petrie 1889, 1–2.
183. Petrie 1932, 87–88; Drower 1995, 132–33.
184. Petrie 1932, 88–90; Drower 1995, 133–35.
185. Drower 1995, 137.
186. Petrie 1890, 5.
187. Drower 1995, 149.
188. Drower 1995, 199–201.
189. Anon 1911.
190. Various 1884.
191. Cope Whitehouse 1881.
192. Cope Whitehouse 1881, 1–2.
193. Cope Whitehouse 1882a, 20–21.
194. Cope Whitehouse 1882a.
195. Cope Whitehouse 1882b.
196. Cope Whitehouse 1883.

197. Cope Whitehouse 1883.
198. Cope Whitehouse 1884a.
199. See the full bibliography for Cope Whitehouse.
200. Cope Whitehouse 1886b; 1887.
201. Cope Whitehouse 1886b, 15.
202. Cope Whitehouse 1885e; 1885f.
203. See list of anonymous articles in *Engineering* in Bibliography.
204. Cope Whitehouse 1893.

Further Reading

General Information

Cwiek, A. 1997. "Fayum in the Old Kingdom." *Göttinger Miszellen* 160:17–22.

Davoli, P. 1998. *L'Archaeologia Urbana nel Fayyum di età Ellenistica e Romana.* Bologna: Generoso Procaccini.

———. 2012. "The Archaeology of the Fayum." In *The Oxford Handbook of Roman Egypt*, edited by C. Riggs, 152–70. Oxford: Oxford University Press.

Derda, T. 2006. *Administration of the Fayum under Roman Rule: The Journal of Juristic Papyrology, Supplement VII.* Warsaw: University of Warsaw Press.

Hassan, F., and G. Tassie. 2006. "Modelling Environmental and Settlement Change in the Fayum." *Egyptian Archaeology* 29: 37–40.

Hewison, R.N. 2008. *The Fayum: History and Guide.* 4th ed. Cairo: American University in Cairo Press.

Holt, P.M. 1965. "al-Fayum." In *Encyclopaedia of Islam.* New ed., vol. 2. Leiden: Brill.

Shaw, I., ed. 2000. *The Oxford History of Ancient Egypt.* Oxford: Oxford University Press.

Shirai, N. 2010. *The Archaeology of the First Farmer-Herders in Egypt: New Insights into the Fayum Epipaleolithic and Neolithic.* Leiden: Leiden University Press.

Zecchi, M. 2001. *Geographia Religiosa del Fayyum: Dalle Origini al IV Secolo A.C.* Bologna: Editrice La Mandragora.

———. 2010. *Sobek of Shedet: The Crocodile God in the Fayyum in the Dynastic Period.* Todi: Tau Editrice.

Archaeological Sites

Madinat al-Fayum

Habachi, L. 1937. "Une 'Vaste Salle' d'Amenemhat III à Kiman-Fares (Fayoum)." *Annales du Service des Antiquités de l'Égypte* 37: 85–95.

Petrie, W.M.F. 1889. *Hawara, Biahmu and Arsinoe.* London: Field and Tuer, Leadenhall Press.

Kom W, Kom K

Caton-Thompson, G., and E. Gardner. 1934. *The Desert Fayum*. London: Royal Anthropological Institute of Great Britain and Northern Ireland.

Holdaway, S., R. Phillipps, J. Emmitt, and W. Wendrich. 2016. "The Fayum Revisited: Reconsidering the Role of the Neolithic Package, Fayum North Shore, Egypt." *Quaternary International* 410: 173–80.

Holdaway, S., and W. Wendrich. 2017. *The Desert Fayum Reinvestigated: The Early to Mid-Holocene Landscape Archaeology of the Fayum North Shore, Egypt*. Los Angeles: UCLA Cotsen Institute of Archaeology Press.

Widan al-Faras, Umm al-Sawan

Bloxham, E., and T. Heldal. 2007. "The Industrial Landscape of the Northern Faiyum Desert as a World Heritage Site: Modelling the 'Outstanding Universal Value' of Third Millennium BC Stone Quarrying in Egypt." *World Archaeology* 39, no. 3: 305–23.

Harrell, J.A., and T.M. Brown. 1995. "An Old Kingdom Basalt Quarry at Widan el-Faras and the Quarry Road to Lake Moeris." *Journal of the American Research Center in Egypt* 32: 71–91.

Qasr al-Sagha

Sliwa, J. 1992. "The Middle Kingdom Settlement at Qasr el-Sagha, 1979–1988." *Studies in Ancient Art and Civilization* 5: 19–38.

Seila

Borchardt, L. 1900. "Die Pyramide von Silah." *Annales du Service des Antiquités de l'Égypte* 1: 211–14.

Muhlstein, K. 2015. "Transitions in Pyramid Orientation: New Evidence from the Seila Pyramid." *Studien zur altägyptische Kultur* 44: 249–58.

Abgig/Bebig

Enmarch, R. 2013. "The Traces of the Main Inscription on the Abgig Monument of Senwosret I." In *Decorum and Experience: Essays in Ancient Culture for John Baines*, edited by E. Frood and A. McDonald. Oxford: Griffith Institute.

Zecchi, M. 2008. "The Monument of Abgig." *Studien zur altägyptische Kultur* 37: 373–85.

Lahun/Kahun

Petrie, W.M.F. 1890. *Kahun, Gurob and Hawara*. London: Kegan Paul, Trench, Trubner and Co.

Quirke, S. 2005. *Lahun: A Town in Egypt 1800 BC, and the History of Its Landscape*. London: Golden House Publications.

———. 1998. *Lahun Studies*. Reigate: SIA.

Biahmu/al-Sanam

Habachi, L. 1937. "The Monument of Biahmu." *Annales du Service des Antiquités de l'Égypte* 40: 721–32.

Petrie, W.M.F. 1889. *Hawara, Biahmu and Arsinoe*. London: Field and Tuer, Leadenhall Press.

Kom Khelwa

Bresciani, E. 1997–98. "Kuelua l'Indagine e le Scoperte." *Egitto e Vicino Oriente* 20–21: 7–49.

Hawara

Blom-Boer, I. 2006. *Die Tempelanlage Amenemhets III. in Hawara: Das Labyrinth—Bestandsaufname und Auswertung der Architektur- und Inventarfragmente*. Leiden: Nederlands Instituut voor het Nabije Oosten.

Doxiadis, E. 1995. *The Mysterious Fayum Portraits: Faces from Ancient Egypt*. London: Thames and Hudson.

Petrie, W.M.F. 1889. *Hawara, Biahmu and Arsinoe*. London: Field and Tuer, Leadenhall Press.

———. 1890. *Kahun, Gurob and Hawara*. London: Kegan Paul, Trench, Trubner and Co.

Petrie, W.M.F., G.A. Wainwright, and E. Mackay. 1912. *The Labyrinth, Gerzeh and Mazghuneh*. London: School of Archaeology in Egypt.

Uphill, E.P. 2000. *Pharaoh's Gateway to Eternity: The Hawara Labyrinth of King Amenemhat III*. London: Keegan Paul International.

Uytterhoeven, I. 2009. *Hawara in the Graeco-Roman Period: Life and Death in a Fayum Village*. Leuven: Peeters.

Madinat al-Gurob

Kemp, B.J. 1978. "The Harim-Palace at Madinat el-Ghurab." *Zeitschrift für* ägyptische *Sprache und Altertumskunde* 105, no. 1: 122–33.

Lacovara, P. 1997. "Gurob and the New Kingdom 'Harim' Palace." In *Ancient Egypt the Aegean and the Near East: Studies in Honor of Martha Rhoads Bell*, vol. 2, edited by J. Phillips, 297–305. San Antonio: Van Siclen.

Petrie, W.M.F. 1890. *Kahun, Gurob and Hawara*. London: Kegan Paul, Trench, Trubner and Co.

Shaw, I. 2011. "Seeking the Ramesside Royal Harem: New Fieldwork at Madinat el-Gurob." In *Ramesside Studies in Honour of K.A. Kitchen*, edited by M. Collier and S. Snape, 453–63. Chorley: Rutherford Press.

Thomas, A. 1981. *Gurob: A New Kingdom Town*. Warminster: Aris and Phillips.

Madinat Madi

Bresciani, E., and A. Giammarusti. 2012. *I Templi di Madinat Madi nel Fayum*. Pisa: Pisa University Press.

Bresciani, E., R. Ali, and A. Giammarusti. 2010. *Madinat Madi Archaeological Guide*. Verona: Geodia.

Umm al-Burigat (Tebtunis)

Gallazzi, C. 1994. "Tebtunis: Piecing Together 3,000 Years of History." *Egyptian Archaeology* 5: 27–29. http://www.ifao.egnet.net/archeologie/tebtynis/#en.

Kom Aushim (Karanis)

Wilfong, T.G. 2014. *Karanis Revealed: Discovering the Past and Present of a Michigan Excavation in Egypt*. Ann Arbor: Kelsey Museum.

Dimai (Soknopaios Nesos)

Carpasso, M., and P. Davoli. 2012. *Soknopaiou Nesos Project I (2003–2009)*. Pisa: Fabrizio Serra Editore.

Qasr Qarun (Dionysias)

Schwartz, J. 1949. "Fouilles à Kasr-Karoun (Fevrier-Mars 1948)." *Bulletin de l'Institut Français d'Archéologie Orientale* 48: 57–63.

Schwartz, J., and H. Wild. 1950. *Qasr-Qarun/Dionysias 1948*. Cairo: Institut Français d'Archéologie Orientale.

Kom Umm al-Atl (Bacchias)

Bitelli, G., M. Capasso, P. Davoli, S. Pernigotti, and L. Vituari. 2003. *The Bologna and Lecce Universities Joint Archaeological Mission in Egypt: Ten Years of Excavations at Bakchias (1993–2002)*. Naples: Graus Editore.

Pernigotti, S. 2005. *Villaggi dell'Egitto Antico I. Bakchias*. Bologna: Editrice La Mandragora.

Kom/Kharabet Ihrit (Theadelphia)

Sharp, M. 1999. "The Village of Theadelphia in the Fayum: Land and Population in the Second Century." *Proceedings of the British Academy* 96: 159–92.

Landscape of the Lake: Texts

Lahun Papyri

Collier, M., and S. Quirke. 2002. *The UCL Lahun Papyri: Letters—BAR International Series 1083*. Oxford: Archaeopress.

———. 2004. *The UCL Lahun Papyri: Religious, Literary, Legal, Mathematical and Medical—BAR International Series 1209*. Oxford: Archaeopress.

———. 2006. *The UCL Lahun Papyri: Accounts—BAR International Series 1471*. Oxford: Archaeopress.

Griffith, F.L. 1898. *Hieratic Papyri from Kahun and Gurob (Principally of the Middle Kingdom)*. London: Bernard Quaritch.

Middle Kingdom Statues

Delange, E. 1987. *Catalogue des Statues Égyptiennes du Moyen Empire 2060–1560 avant J.C.* Paris: Editions de la Réunion des Musées Nationaux Paris.

Wild, H. 1971. "Quatre Statuettes du Moyen Empire dans une Collection Privée de Suisse." *Bulletin de l'Institut Français d'Archéologie Orientale* 69: 89–130.

'Sporting King' and 'Fishing and Fowling'

Caminos, R.A. 1956. *Literary Fragments in the Hieratic Script*. Oxford: Griffith Institute.

Parkinson, R.B. 2002. *Poetry and Culture in Middle Kingdom Egypt: A Dark Side to Perfection*. London: Continuum.

Quirke, S. 2004. *Egyptian Literature 1800 BC: Questions and Readings*. London: Golden House Publications.

Wilbour Papyrus

Gardiner, A.H. 1948a. *Ramesside Administrative Documents*. Oxford: Oxford University Press.

———. 1948b. *The Wilbour Papyrus, Volume II, Commentary*. Oxford: Oxford University Press.

———. 1948c. *The Wilbour Papyrus, Volume III, Translation*. Oxford: Oxford University Press.

Katary, S. 1989. *Land Tenure in the Ramesside Period*. London: Kegan Paul International.

Onomastica

Gardiner, A.H. 1947. *Ancient Egyptian Onomastica, Text, Volume 1*. Oxford: Oxford University Press.

Hymn to Sobek

Gardiner, A.H. 1957. "Hymn to Sobk in a Ramesseum Papyrus." *Revue d'Egyptologie* 11: 43–56.

Tomb of Sobekhotep, TT63

Bryan, B. 2006. "Administration in the Reign of Tuthmose III." In *Tuthmose III: A New Biography*, edited by E. Cline and D. O'Connor, 69–122. Michigan: University of Michigan.

Dziobek, E., and M.A. Raziq. 1990. *Das Grab des Sobekhotep: Theben Nr. 63*. Mainz: Philip von Zabern.

Gurob Papyri

Gardiner, A.H. 1948. *Ramesside Administrative Documents*. Oxford: Oxford University Press.

Griffith, F.L. 1898. *Hieratic Papyri from Kahun and Gurob (Principally of the Middle Kingdom)*. London: Bernard Quaritch.

Hagen, F., and D. Soliman. 2018. "Archives in Ancient Egypt, 250–1000 BCE." In *Manuscripts and Archives. Comparative Views on Record Keeping* edited by A. Bausi, C. Brockmann, M. Friedrich, and S. Kienitz, 71-170. Berlin: De Gruyter.

The Book of Fayum

Beinlich, H. 1991. *Das Buch vom Fayum, Textband*, Ägyptologische *Abhandlung 51*. Wiesbaden: Otto Harrassowitz.

Beinlich, H., R. Schulz, and A. Wieszorek, eds. 2013. *Egypt's Mysterious Book of the Faiyum*. Dettlebach: J.H. Röll.

Tait, J. 2003. "The 'Book of Fayum': Mystery in a Known Landscape." In *Mysterious Lands*, edited by D. O'Connor and S. Quirke, 183–202. London: UCL Press.

Changing Landscape: Accounts

Herodotus, *Histories*

Armayor, O.K. 1985. *Herodotus' Autopsy of the Fayum, Lake Moeris and the Labyrinth of Egypt*. Amsterdam: J.C. Geiben.

Herodotus. 1954. *The Histories*. Translated by A. de Sélincourt. London: Penguin Books.

Priestley, J., and V. Zali, eds. 2016. *Brill Companion to the Reception of Herodotus in Antiquity and Beyond*. Leiden: Brill.

Lloyd, A.B. 1975. *Herodotus Book II*. Leiden: Brill.

Romm, J. 1998. *Herodotus*. Yale: Yale University Press.

Waters, K.H. 1985. *Herodotos the Historian: His Problems, Methodology and Originality*. London: Croom Helm.

Papyrus

Tebtunis I.33, Letter from Hermias to Horos: http://papyri.info/ddbdp/p.tebt;1;33.

Diodorus Siculus

Chamoux, F., and P. Bertrac. 1993. *Diodore de Sicile: Bibliothèque Historique*. Paris: Les Belles Lettres.

Muntz, C. 2017. *Diodorus Siculus and the World of the Late Roman Republic*. New York: Oxford University Press.

Oldfather, C.H. 1960. *Diodorus of Sicily*. London: William Heineman.

Sacks, K.A. 1990. *Diodorus Siculus and the First Century*. Princeton: Princeton University Press.

Strabo

Dueck, D. 2000. *Strabo of Amasia: A Greek Man of Letters in Augustan Rome*. London: Routledge.
Dueck, D., H. Lindsay, and S. Pothecary. 2005. *Strabo's Cultural Geography: The Making of a Kolossourgia*. Cambridge: Cambridge University Press.
Jones, H. 1917. *The Geography of Strabo*. Vol. 1. London: William Heineman.
———. 1932. *The Geography of Strabo*. Vol. 8. London: William Heineman.

Pomponius Mela

Romer, F.C. 1998. *Pomponius Mela's Description of the World*. Michigan: University of Michigan.
Silberman, A. 1988. *Pomponius Mela Chorographie*. Paris: Les Belles Lettres.

Pliny

Murphy, T. 2004. *Pliny the Elder's Natural History: The Empire in the Encyclopedia*. Oxford: Oxford University Press.
Rackham, H. 1938. *Pliny: Natural History*. Vol. 1. London: William Heineman.
———. 1961. *Pliny: Natural History*. Vol. 2. London: William Heineman.

Claudius Ptolemy

Berggren, J.L., and A. Jones. 2000. *Ptolemy's Geography: An Annotated Translation of the Theoretical Chapters*. Princeton: Princeton University Press.
Jones, A., ed. 2010. *Ptolemy in Perspective: Use and Criticism of His Work from Antiquity to the Nineteenth Century*. New York: Springer.
Stevenson, E.L. [1991]1932. *Claudius Ptolemy: The Geography*. New York: Dover.

Legendary Landscape: Accounts

Ibn 'Abd al-Hakam

Torrey, C.C. 1901. "The Mohammedan Conquest of Egypt and North Africa in the Years 643–705 A.D. Translated from the Original Arabic of Ibn Abd El-Hakem." In *Biblical and Semitic Studies: Critical and Historical Essays by the Members of the Semitic and Biblical Faculty of Yale University*. New Haven: Yale University Press.
———. 1932. *The History and Conquest of Egypt, North Africa and Spain Known as the Futūh Misr of Ibn 'Abd Al-Hakam*. New Haven: Yale University Press.

al-Khwarizmi

Aini, K.S. 1985. *Al-Khwarizmi's Map of the World Based on "Kitab Surat Al-Ard."* Srinagar: Donish Publishers.

Ibn Khurradadhbih

De Meynard, C.B. 1865. *Le Livre des Routes et des Provinces, par Ibn-Khordadebeh*. Paris: Imprimerie Impériale.

al-Ya'qubi

Wiet, G. 1937. *Ya'kūbī: Les Pays*. Paris: Imprimerie Nationale.

al-Mas'udi

Ahmad, S.M. 1953. "Al-Mas'udi's Contributions to Medieval Arab Geography." *Islamic Culture* 37, no. 2: 61–77.

———. 1954a. "Travels of Abu'l Hasan 'Ali b. Al-Husayn Al-Mas'udi." *Islamic Culture* 38, no. 4: 509–24.

———. 1954b. "Al-Mas'udi's Contributions to Medieval Arab Geography: Some Sources of His Knowledge." *Islamic Culture* 38, no. 1: 265–86.

De Vaux, C. 1896. *Maçoudi: Le Livre de l'Avertissement et de la Revision*. Paris: l'Imprimerie Nationale.

Pellat, C. 1962–65. *Mas*'ūdī*: Les Prairies d'Or.* Vols. 1–2. Trans. B. de Meynard and P. de Courteille. Paris: Société Asiatique.

Akhbar al-zaman

De Vaux, C. 1984. *L'Abrégé des Merveilles*. Paris: Sindbad.

al-Istakhri

Mordtmann, A.D. 1845. *Das Buch der Länder von Schech Ebu Ishak El Farisi El Isztachri*. Hamburg: Raues Haus.

Ibn Hawkal

Kramers, J.H., and G. Wiet. 1925. *Configuration de la Terre (Kitab Surat al-Ard)*. Paris: G.P. Maisonneuve et Larose.

al-Muqaddasi

Collins, B.A. 1994. *Al-Muqaddisi: The Best Divisions for Knowledge of the Regions.* Reading: Garnet Publishing.

al-Idrisi

Ahmad, S.M. 1992. "Cartography of Al-Sharīf Al-Idrisi." In *The History of Cartography, vol. 2, Cartography in the Traditional Islamic and South Asian Societies*, edited by J.B. Harley and D. Woodward, 156–74. Chicago: University of Chicago Press.

Jaubert, P.A. 1975. *La Géographie d'Édrisi.* Amsterdam: Philo Press.

al-Murtada

Davies, J. 1672. *The Egyptian History, Treating of the Pyramids, the Inundation of the Nile, and Other Prodigies of Egypt, according to the Opinions and Traditions of the Arabians Written Originally in the Arabian Tongue by Murtadi, the Son of Gaphiphus, Rendered into French by Monsieur Vattier . . . and Thence Faithfully Done into English by J. Davies*. London: Printed for R.B. by Thomas Basset.

Ragib, Y. 1974. "L'Auteur de L'Égypte de Murtadi Fils Du Gaphiphe." *Arabica* 21, no. 2: 203–209.

al-Nabulsi

Keenan, J.G. 2005. "Landscape and Memory: Al-Nabulsi's Tarikh Al-Fayyum." *Bulletin of the American Society of Papyrologists* 42: 203–12.

König, I. 1996. "Die Oase al-Fayyum nach 'Uthman Ibrahim an Nabulusi: Ein Beitrag zur Wirtschaftsgeschichte Ägyptens um die Mitte des 13. Jahrhunderts n. Chr." *Zeitschrift für Geschichte der Arabisch-Islamischen Wissenschaften*: 190–253.

Moritz, B. 1988. *Description du Fayoum au VIIme Siècle de l'Hêgire par 'Osmân il Naboulsi il Safadi*. Cairo: Imprimerie Nationale.

Salmon, G. 1901. "Répertoire Géographique de la Province du Fayyoûm d'après le Kitâab Târikh al Fayyoûm d'an-Naboulsi." *Bulletin de l'Institut Français d'Archaéologie Orientale* 1: 37–72.

Zeki-Bey, A. 1899. "Une Description Arabe du Fayoum au VIIe Siècle de l'Hégire." *Bulletin de la Société Khédiviale de Géographie* 5, no. 5: 235–95.

al-Maqrizi

Bouriant, U. 1895. *Description Topographique et Historique de l'Égypte*. Parts 1 and 2. Leiden: Brill.

Explored Landscape: Accounts

J.M. Vansleb

Vansleb, J.M. 1677. *Nouvelle Relation en Forme de Journal d'un Voyage Fait en* Égypte *en 1672 et 1673*.

———. 1678. *The Present State of Egypt: Or a New Relation of a Late Voyage into that Kingdom*.

Paul Lucas

Lucas, P. 1719. *Voyage dans la Turquie, l'Asie, Sourie, Haute el Basse* Égypte. Amsterdam: Steenhower and Uytwerp.

———. 1998. *Voyage du Sieur Paul Lucas dans le Levant*. Saint-Étienne: Université de Saint-Étienne.

———. 2002. *Deuxième Voyage du Sieur Paul Lucas dans le Levant*. Saint-Étienne: Université de Saint-Étienne.

———. 2004. *Troisième Voyage du Sieur Paul Lucas dans le Levant*. Saint-Étienne: Université de Saint-Étienne.

Richard Pococke

Pococke, R. 1743–45. *A Description of the East, and Some Other Countries*. London: printed for the author by W. Bowyer.

Edme François Jomard

Jomard, E.F. 1812. *Mémoire sur le Lac de Moeris Comparé au Lac du Fayoum.*

Giovanni Battista Belzoni

Belzoni, G.B. 1820. *Narrative of the Operations and Recent Discoveries within the Pyramids Temples, Tombs and Excavations in Egypt and Nubia.* London: J. Murray.

Linant de Bellefonds

De Bellefonds, L. 1843. *Mémoires sur le Lac Moeris présenté et lu à la Société égyptienne le 5 juillet 1842.* Alexandrie: A.E. Oxanne, published in translation by D. Borrer (1845) in *A Journey from Naples to Jerusalem by way of Athens, Egypt and the Peninsula of Sinai*, 545–79. London: J. Madden and Co.

———. 1872–73. *Mémoires sur les Principaux Travaux d'Utilité Publique Executés en* Égypte *depuis la Plus Haute Antiquité jusqu'à nos Jours.* Paris: Libraire Scientifique et Maritime.

Edward William Lane

Lane, E.W. 2000. *Description of Egypt*. Cairo: American University in Cairo Press.

Thompson, J. 2010. *Edward William Lane, 1801–1876: The Life of the Pioneering Egyptologist and Orientalist.* Cairo: American University in Cairo Press.

James Augustus St. John

St. John, J.A. 1834. *Egypt and Mohammed Ali or Travels in the Valley of the Nile.* London: Longman Rees.

———. 1853. *Isis: An Egyptian Pilgrimage*. London: Longman, Brown, Green and Longmans.

Paul Marie Lenoir

Lenoir, P.M. 1872. *Le Fayoum, le Sinaï et Pétra: Expédition dans la Moyenne Égypte et l'Arabie Pétrée*. Paris: Henri Plon.

———. 1873. *The Fayoum: or, Artists in Egypt.* London: Henry S. King & Co.

Flinders Petrie

Drower, M.S. 1995. *Flinders Petrie: A Life in Archaeology.* Madison: University of Wisconsin.

Petrie, W.M.F. 1889. *Hawara, Biahmu and Arsinoe.* London: Field and Tuer, Leadenhall Press.

———. 1890. *Kahun, Gurob and Hawara.* London: Kegan Paul, Trench, Trubner and Co.

———. 1932. *Seventy Years in Archaeology.* New York: Henry Holt and Co.

Petrie, W.M.F., G.A. Wainwright, and E. Mackay. 1912. *The Labyrinth, Gerzeh and Mazghuneh.* London: School of Archaeology in Egypt.

Frederick Cope Whitehouse

Cope Whitehouse, F. 1882. "Lake Moeris: From Recent Explorations in the Moeris Basin and the Wadi Fadhi." *Bulletin of the American Geographical Society* 14: 85–108.

———. 1883. "Communication on Lake Moeris (Part One)." *Proceedings of the Society for Biblical Archaeology*, May 5, 169–76.

———. 1884b. "Latest Researches in the Moeris Basin." *Proceedings of the Royal Geographical Society and Monthly Record of Geography*, October.

———. 1884c. "The Fayoum and the Land of Goshen." *The Churchman*, November 29, 2–3.

———. 1885c. "The Bahr Jusuf and the Prophecy of Joseph." *Proceedings of the Society for Biblical Archaeology*, November 3, 6–25.

———. 1885e. "Moeris: The Great Reservoir of Middle Egypt." *Proceedings of the U.S. Naval Institute* 33: 325–29.

———. 1885f. *Moeris: Wonder of the World.* New York: John Wiley & Sons.

———. 1886a. "Researches in the Moeris Basin." *Proceedings of the Society for Biblical Archaeology*, June 1, 201–10.

———. 1888. "The Raiyan Reservoir: A Project for the Storage of Part of the Nile Flood." *Engineering* 46: 267.

———. 1890. "The Raiyan Escape and Impounding Reservoir, Middle Egypt." *Engineering* 50: 334–35.

———. 1893. "The Moeris Papyri." *Proceedings of the Society for Biblical Archaeology*, November 7, 20–24.

Complete Bibliography

Anon. 1885. "Lake Moeris: Justification of Herodotus by the Recent Researches of Mr. Cope Whitehouse." *Bulletin of the Khedival Geographical Society 1883*, 1–8.

Anon. 1911. "F. Cope Whitehouse, Egyptologist, Dead." *New York Times*, 17 November.

Anon. 1885. "Impounding the Nile Floods." *Engineering* 40, 11 September, 241–44.

Anon. 1887. "Irrigation in Lower Egypt (Part One)." *Engineering* 44, 2 September, 259–61.

Anon. 1887. "Irrigation in Lower Egypt (Part Two)." *Engineering* 44, 9 September, 283–86.

Anon. 1891. "Storage Reservoirs in Egypt." *Engineering* 52, 16 October, 450–51.

Anon. 1893. "Irrigation in Egypt." *Engineering* 55, 6 January, 18–20.

Abbott, N. 1937. *The Monasteries of the Fayyūm*. Chicago: University of Chicago Press.

Addison, J. 1712a. *The Spectator* 387.

———. 1712b. *The Spectator* 411.

Ahmad, S.M. 1953. "Al-Mas'udi's Contributions to Medieval Arab Geography." *Islamic Culture* 37, no. 2: 61–77.

———. 1954a. "Travels of Abu'l Hasan 'Ali b. Al-Husayn Al-Mas'udi." *Islamic Culture* 38, no. 4: 509–24.

———. 1954b. "Al-Mas'udi's Contributions to Medieval Arab Geography: Some Sources of His Knowledge." *Islamic Culture* 38, no. 1: 265–86.

———. 1991. "Djugrafiya." In *Encyclopaedia of Islam, New Edition Volume 3*, 575–87. Leiden: Brill.

———. 1992. "Cartography of Al-Sharīf Al-Idrisi." In *The History of Cartography, vol. 2: Cartography in the Traditional Islamic and South Asian Societies*, edited by J.B. Harley and D. Woodward, 156–74. Chicago: University of Chicago Press.

———. 1995. *A History of Arab-Islamic Geography (9th–16th Century A.D.)*. Amman: al-Bayt University.

Aini, K.S. 1985. *Al-Khwarizmi's Map of the World Based on "Kitab Surat Al-Ard."* Srinagar: Donish Publishers.

Armayor, O.K. 1978. "Did Herodotus Ever Go to Egypt?" *Journal of the American Research Center in Egypt* 15: 59–73.

———. 1985. *Herodotus' Autopsy of the Fayum, Lake Moeris and the Labyrinth of Egypt*. Amsterdam: J.C. Geiben.

Arnold, D. 1999. *Temples of the Last Pharaohs*. Oxford: Oxford University Press.

Aziz, A. 1975. *A History of Islamic Sicily*. Edinburgh: Edinburgh University Press.

Bagnall, R.S., and D.W. Rathbone. 2004. *Egypt from Alexander to the Copts*. London: British Museum Press.

Baigent, E. 2008. "Richard Pococke (1704–1765)." In *Oxford Dictionary of National Biography*. Oxford: Oxford University Press.

Baines, J. 2013. *High Culture and Experience in Ancient Egypt*. Bristol: Equinox.

Ball, J. 1942. *Egypt in the Classical Geographers*. Cairo: Government Press.

Baragwanath, E., and M. de Bakker. 2012. *Myth Truth and Narrative in Herodotus*. Oxford: Oxford University Press.

Bard, K. 2000. "The Emergence of the Egyptian State (c. 3200–2686 BC)." In *The Oxford History of Ancient Egypt*, edited by I. Shaw, 61–88. Oxford: Oxford University Press.

Beadnell, H.J.L. 1905. *The Topography and Geology of the Fayum Province of Egypt*. Cairo: Survey Department of Egypt.

Beaujeu, J. 1950. *Pline l'Ancien: Histoire Naturelle*. Book 1. Paris: Les Belles Lettres.

Bednarski, A. 2005. *Holding Egypt: Tracing the Reception of the Description de l'Égypte in Nineteenth-Century Great Britain*. London: Golden House Publications.

Behdad, A. 1994. *Belated Travellers: Orientalism in the Age of Colonial Dissolution*. Cork: Cork University Press.

Beinlich, H. 1991. *Das Buch vom Fayum, Textband*. Ägyptologische Abhandlung 51. Wiesbaden: Otto Harrassowitz.

———. 2013. "The Book of Faiyum." In *Egypt's Mysterious Book of the Faiyum*, edited by H. Beinlich, R. Schulz, and A. Wieczorek, 27–77. Dettlebach: J.H. Röll.

Belzoni, G.B. 1820. *Narrative of the Operations and Recent Discoveries within the Pyramids, Temples, Tombs and Excavations in Egypt and Nubia*. London.

Bender, B. 1995. *Landscape: Politics and Perspectives*. Oxford: Berg.

Benjamin, S. 1995. *The World of Benjamin of Tudela: A Medieval Mediterranean Travelogue*. Madison: Associated University Press.

Berggren, J.L., and A. Jones. 2000. *Ptolemy's Geography: An Annotated Translation of the Theoretical Chapters*. Princeton: Princeton University Press.

Bianquis, T. 1998. "Autonomous Egypt from Ibn Tūlūn to Kāfūr, 868–969." In *The Cambridge History of Egypt, Volume 1: Islamic Egypt, 640–1571*, edited by C. Petry, 86–119. Cambridge: Cambridge University Press.

Bierbrier, M.L. 2012. *Who Was Who in Egyptology*. 4th ed. London: Egypt Exploration Society.

Bitelli, G., M. Capasso, P. Davoli, S. Pernigotti, and L. Vittuari. 2003. *The Bologna and Lecce Universities Joint Archaeological Mission in Egypt: Ten Years of Excavations at Bakchias (1993–2002)*. Naples: Graus Editore.

Blount, H. 1636. *A Voyage into the Levant*. London: John Legate.

Bloxam, E., and T. Heldal. 2007. "The Industrial Landscape of the Northern Faiyum Desert as a World Heritage Site: Modelling the 'Outstanding Universal Value' of Third Millennium BC Stone Quarrying in Egypt." *World Archaeology* 39, no. 3: 305–23.

Boilot, D.J. 1960. "Al-Bīrunī." In *Encyclopaedia of Islam New Edition*, vol. 1, 1236–38. Leiden: Brill.

Bonebakker, S.A. 1990. "Adab and the Concept of Abbasid Belle-Lettres." In *Cambridge History of Arabic Literature: Abbasid Belle-Lettres*, edited by J. Ashtiany et al., 16–30. Cambridge: Cambridge University Press.

Borchardt, L. 1900. "Die Pyramide von Silah." *Annales du Service des Antiquités de l'Égypte* 1: 211–14.

Bosworth, C.E. 1993. "Al-Murtadā b. Al-'Afīf." In *Encyclopaedia of Islam, New Edition Volume 3*, 634–35. Leiden: Brill.

Bouriant, U. 1895. *Description Topographique at Historique de L'Égypte*. Parts 1 and 2. Leiden: Brill.

Bourriau, J. 2000. "The Second Intermediate Period." In *The Oxford History of Ancient Egypt*, edited by I. Shaw, 184–217. Oxford: Oxford University Press.

Bowder, D. 1980. *Who Was Who in the Roman World*. Oxford: Phaidon.

Bresciani, E. 1997–98. "Kuelua l'Indagine e le Scoperte." *Egitto e Vicino Oriente* 20–21: 7–49.

Bresciani, E., A. Radwan, A. Giammarusti, and H. el-Leithy. 2010. *Madinat Madi Archaeological Guide*. Verona: Geodia.

Brown, R.H. 1892. *The Fayûm and Lake Moeris*. London: Edward Stanford.

Brugsch, H. 1872. "Das altägyptische 'Seeland.'" *Zeitschrift für ägyptische Sprache und Altertumskunde* 10: 89–91.

———. 1892. "Der Moeris-See" (Part One). *Zeitschrift für ägyptische Sprache und Altertumskunde* 30: 65–78.

———. 1893. "Der Moeris-See" (Part Two). *Zeitschrift für ägyptische Sprache und Altertumskunde* 31: 17–31.

Bryan, B. 1991. *The Reign of Tuthmose IV*. Baltimore: Johns Hopkins Press.

———. 2006. "Administration in the Reign of Tuthmose III." In *Tuthmose III: A New Biography*, edited by E. Cline and D. O'Connor, 69–122. Michigan: University of Michigan.

Buckingham, J.S. 1855. *Autobiography of James Silk Buckingham; Including His Voyages, Travels, Adventures, Speculations, Successes and Failures, Faithfully and Frankly Narrated*. Vol. 1. London: Longman, Brown, Green and Longmans.

Burri, C. 1971. *Voyages en Égypte: Des Années 1589, 1590 et 1591. Le Venitien Anonyme. Le Seigneur de Villamont. Le Hollandais Jan Sommer.* Translated by Carla Burri, Nadine Sauneron, Paul Bleser; Introduction and Notes by Carla Burri and Serge Sauneron. Cairo: Institut Français d'Archéologie Orientale.

Cahen, C. 1990. "History and Historians." In *The Cambridge History of Arabic Literature. Religion, Learning and Science in the 'Abbasid Period*, edited by M.J.L. Young, J.D. Latham, and R.B. Serjeant, 188–232. Cambridge: Cambridge University Press.

Callender, G. 2000. "The Middle Kingdom Renaissance (c. 2055–1650 BC)." In *The Oxford History of Ancient Egypt*, edited by I. Shaw, 148–83. Oxford: Oxford University Press.

Caminos, R.A. 1956. *Literary Fragments in the Hieratic Script*. Oxford: Griffith Institute.

Carpasso, M., and P. Davoli. 2012. *Soknopaiou Nesos Project I (2003–2009)*. Pisa: Fabrizio Serra Editore.

Carré, J.-M. 1956. *Voyageurs et Écrivains Français en Égypte, Tome Premier: Du Début à la Fin de la Domination Turque (1517–1840)*. Cairo: Institut Français d'Archéologie Orientale.

Casanova, G. 1975. "Theadelphia e l'Archivio di Harthotes: Ricerche su un Villaggio Egiziano fra il IIIa e il Ip." *Aegyptus* 55, no. 1: 70–158.

Caton Thompson, G., and E. Gardner. 1929. "Recent Work on the Problem of Lake Moeris." *The Geographical Journal* 73, no. 1: 20–58.

———. 1934. *The Desert Fayum*. London: Royal Anthropological Institute of Great Britain and Northern Ireland.

Caton Thompson, G., E. Gardner, and S.A. Husayyin. 1937. "Lake Moeris: Re-investigations and Some Comments." *Bulletin de l'Institut de l'Égypte* 19: 243–303.

Cestari, I. 2010. *Villaggi dell'Egitto Antico III: Dionysias*. Imola: Editrice La Mandragora.

Chamberlain, M. 1998. "The Crusader Era and the Ayyūbid Dynasty." In *The Cambridge History of Egypt, Volume 1: Islamic Egypt, 640–1571*, edited by C. Petry, 211–41. Cambridge: Cambridge University Press.

Chamoux, F., and P. Bertrac. 1993. *Diodore de Sicile: Bibliothèque Historique*. Livre I. Paris: Les Belles Lettres.

Charles, C.-P. 1960. "La Statue-Cube de Sobek-Hotep Gouverneur du Fayoum." *Revue d'Égyptologie* 12: 1–26.

Cheshire, W. 2013. "Art and Artists in the Fayum in the Ptolemaic and Roman Periods." In *Egypt's Mysterious Book of Fayum*, edited by H. Beinlich, R. Schultz, and A. Wieczorek, 105–122. Dettlebach: J.H. Röll.

Clarysse, W. 2010. "Language Diversity in the Archive of the Engineers Kleon and Tehodoros." In *The Language of the Papyri*, edited by T.V. Evans and D.D. Obbink, 35–50. Oxford: Oxford University Press.

Colla, E. 2008. *Conflicted Antiquities: Egyptology, Egyptomania, Egyptian Modernity.* Durham: Duke University Press.

Collier, M., and S. Quirke. 2002. *The UCL Lahun Papyri: Letters.* BAR International Series 1083. Oxford: Archaeopress.

Collins, B.A. 1994. *Al-Muqaddisi: The Best Divisions for Knowledge of the Regions.* Reading: Garnet Publishing.

Cope Whitehouse, F. 1881. *"The Pyramids, Bahr Yusuf, Moeris, the Labyrinth and the Sphinx."* Printed privately.

———. 1882a. "Lake Moeris: From Recent Explorations in the Moeris Basin and the Wadi Fadhi." *Bulletin of the American Geographical Society* 14: 85–108. Reprinted privately as p1–27.

———. 1882b. "Communication on Lake Moeris (Part Two)." *Proceedings of the Society for Biblical Archaeology,* June 6: 124–32.

———. 1883. "Communication on Lake Moeris (Part One)." *Proceedings of the Society for Biblical Archaeology,* May 5: 169–76.

———. 1884a. "Pithom-Moeris." *The Churchman,* January 26. Reprinted privately.

———. 1884b. "Latest Researches in the Moeris Basin." *Proceedings of the Royal Geographical Society and Monthly Record of Geography,* October, 1–6. Reprinted privately.

———. 1884c. "The Fayoum and the Land of Goshen." *The Churchman,* November 29, 2–3.

———. 1885a. *"Where Is the Land of Goshen? Lecture Delivered before the American Institute of Christian Philosophy, January 8th 1885."* Printed privately.

———. 1885b. "Mar-Moeris, West of Oxyrhyncus-Behnesa." *Proceedings of the Society for Biblical Archaeology,* March 3, 112–21.

———. 1885c. "The Bahr Jusuf and the Prophecy of Joseph." *Proceedings of the Society for Biblical Archaeology,* November 3, 6–25.

———. 1885d. "Communication from Mr. Cope Whitehouse." *Proceedings of the Society for Biblical Archaeology,* December 1, 57–58.

———. 1885e. "Moeris: The Great Reservoir of Middle Egypt." *Proceedings of the U.S. Naval Institute* 33: 325–29.

———. 1885f. *Moeris: Wonder of the World.* New York: John Wiley & Sons.

———. 1886a. "Researches in the Moeris Basin." *Proceedings of the Society for Biblical Archaeology,* June 1, 201–10.

———. 1886b. "The Lake of Moeris and the Patriarch Joseph, Communicated by F. Cope Whitehouse Esq." *Cambridge Antiquarian Society's Communication* 6, no. 2.

———. 1887. "La Bahr Youssouf: d'Après les Traditions Musulmanes." *Bulletin de l'Institut Égyptien.* Reprinted privately.

———. 1888. "The Raiyan Reservoir: A Project for the Storage of Part of the Nile Flood." *Engineering* 46, 14 September, 267.

———. 1890. "The Raiyan Escape and Impounding Reservoir, Middle Egypt." *Engineering* 50, 19 September, 334–35.

———. 1893. "The Moeris Papyri." *Proceedings of the Society for Biblical Archaeology* 16, November 7, 20–24.

Cosgrove, D.E., and S. Daniels. 1988. *The Iconography of Landscape: Essays on the Symbolic Representation, Design and Use of Past Environments*. Cambridge: Cambridge University Press.

Cranston, M. 1994. *The Romantic Movement*. Oxford: Blackwell.

Crawford, D. 1971. *Kerkeosiris: An Egyptian Village in the Ptolemaic Period*. Cambridge: Cambridge University Press.

Cruz-Uribe, E.D. 1992. "The Lake of Moeris: A Reprise." *Life in a Multicultural Society: Egypt from Cambyses to Constantine and Beyond*, edited by J. Johnson, 63–66. Chicago: Oriental Institute of the University of Chicago Studies in Ancient Oriental Civilization.

Cwiek, A. 1997. "Fayum in the Old Kingdom." *Göttinger Miszellen* 160: 17–22.

Dannenfelt, K.H. 1959. "Egypt and Egyptian Antiquities in the Renaissance." *Studies in the Renaissance* 6: 7–27.

Davies, J. 1672. *The Egyptian History, Treating of the Pyramids, the Inundation of the Nile, and Other Prodigies of Egypt, According to the Opinions and Traditions of the Arabians Written Originally in the Arabian Tongue by Murtadi, the Son of Gaphiphus, Rendered into French by Monsieur Vattier . . . and Thence Faithfully Done into English by J. Davies*. London.

Davoli, P. 1998. *L'Archaeologia Urbana nel Fayyum di Età Ellenistica e Romana*. Bologna: Generoso Procaccini.

———. 2005. "New Excavations at Soknopaiou Nesos: The 2003 Season." In *Tebtynis and Soknopaiu Nesos: Leben im römerzeitlichen Faijum*, edited by S. Lippert and M. Schentuleit, 29–39. Wiesbaden: Harrassowitz.

———. 2007. "The Temple Area of Soknopaiou Nesos." In *New Archaeological and Papyrological Researches on the Fayum*, edited by M. Carpasso and P. Davoli, 95–124. Milan: Congedo Editore.

———. 2012. "The Archaeology of the Fayum." In *The Oxford Handbook of Roman Egypt*, edited by C. Riggs, 152–70. Oxford: Oxford University Press.

Davoli, P., and N.M. Ahmad. 2006. "On Some Monuments from Kiman Fares (Madinat El-Fayum)." *Studi di Egittologia e di Papiriologia* 3: 81–110.

Dawood, N.J. 1999. *The Koran, Translated with Notes*. 2nd, rev. ed. London: Penguin.

De Meynard, C.B. 1865. *Le Livre des Routes et des Provinces, par Ibn-Khordadebeh*. Paris: Imprimerie Impériale.

De Morgan, J. 1903. *Fouilles à Dahchour 1894–1895*. Vienna: Holshausen.

De Vaux, C. 1896. *Maçoudi: Le Livre de l'Avertissement et de la Revision*. Paris: l'Imprimerie Nationale.

———. 1984. *L'Abrégé des Merveilles*. Paris: Sindbad.

Delange, E. 1987. *Catalogue des Statues Égyptiennes du Moyen Empire 2060–1560 avant J.C.* Paris: Reunion des Musées Nationaux.

Der Manuelian, P. 2006. "A Re-Examination of Reisner's Nucleus Cemetery Concept at Giza: Preliminary Remarks on Cemetery G2100." In *The Old Kingdom: Art and Archaeology*. Prague: Academy of Sciences of the Czech Republic.

Derda, T. 2006. *Administration of the Fayum under Roman Rule: The Journal of Juristic Papyrology, Supplement VII.* Warsaw: University of Warsaw.

Díaz-Andreu, M. 2007. *A World History of Nineteenth-century Archaeology: Nationalism, Colonialism and the Past*. Oxford: Oxford University Press.

Dielman, J. 2011. "A Guide to Greco-Roman Hawara in the Fayum and Its Death Industry." *Journal of Roman Studies* 24: 810–15.

Diller, A. 1935. "Codex B of Strabo." *American Journal of Philology* 56, no. 2: 97–102.

Dover, K.J. 1980. *Ancient Greek Literature*. Oxford: Oxford University Press.

Doxiadis, E. 1995. *The Mysterious Fayum Portraits: Faces from Ancient Egypt*. London: Thames and Hudson.

Drower, M.S. 1995. *Flinders Petrie: A Life in Archaeology*. Madison: University of Wisconsin.

Dueck, D. 2000. *Strabo of Amasia: A Greek Man of Letters in Augustan Rome*. London: Routledge.

Dueck, D., H. Lindsay, and S. Pothecary. 2005. *Strabo's Cultural Geography: The Making of a Kolossourgia*. Cambridge: Cambridge University Press.

Dumont, H.J., and G.M. El-Shabrawy. 2009. "The Fayum Depression and Its Lakes." In *The Nile: Origin, Environment, Limnology and Human Use*, edited by H.J. Dumont, 95–124. New York: Springer.

Dunlop, D.M. 1960. "Al-Balkhi." In *Encyclopaedia of Islam New Edition, Volume 1*. Leiden: Brill.

Duri, A.A. 1983. *The Rise of Historical Writing among the Arabs*, edited and translated by L.I. Conrad. Princeton: Princeton University Press.

Dziobek, E., and M.A. Raziq. 1990. *Das Grab des Sobekhotep: Theben Nr. 63*. Mainz: Philip von Zabern.

Earley, B. 2016. "Herodotus in Renaissance France." In *Brill Companion to the Reception of Herodotus in Antiquity and Beyond*, edited by J. Priestley and V. Zali, 120–42. Leiden: Brill.

Easterling, P.E., and B.M.W. Knox. 1985. *The Cambridge History of Classical Literature I: Greek Literature*. Cambridge: Cambridge University Press.

Edwards, A.T. 1993. "Homer's Ethical Geography: Country and City in the Odyssey." *Transactions of the American Philological Association* 123: 27–78.

El Daly, O. 2005. *Egyptology: The Missing Millennium, Ancient Egypt in Medieval Arabic Writings*. London: UCL Press.

Ellison, J. 2002. *George Sandys: Travel, Colonialism and Tolerance in the Seventeenth Century*. Cambridge: D.S. Brewer.

———. 2008. "Sandys, George (1578–1644)." In *Oxford Dictionary of National Biography*. Oxford: Oxford University Press.

Enmarch, R. 2013. "The Traces of the Inscription on the Abgig Monument of Senwosret I." In *Decorum and Experience: Essays in Ancient Culture for John Baines*, edited by E. Frood and A. McDonald, 21–25. Oxford: Griffith Institute.

Eyre, C. 1991. "Review of Herodotus Book II Commentary 99–182 by Alan B. Lloyd." *Journal of Egyptian Archaeology* 77: 223–25.

Farag, S. 1980. "Une Inscription Memphite de la XIIe Dynastie." *Revue d'Egyptologie* 32: 75–83.

Faulkner, R.O. 1962. *A Concise Dictionary of Middle Egyptian*. Oxford: Griffith Institute.

———. 1969. *The Ancient Egyptian Pyramid Texts*. Oxford: Oxford University Press.

"Fayum Papyri." Trismegistos Project. http://www.trismegistos.org/fayum.

"Fayum Project." http://www.archbase.com/fayum/project.html.

Fedden, R. 1958. *English Travellers in the Near East: Writers and Their Work No. 97*. London: Longmans, Green & Co.

Fehling, D. 1989. *Herodotus and His "Sources": Citation, Invention and Narrative Art*. Leeds: Francis Cairns.

Fergerson, J.B. 1975. *Utopias of the Classical World*. London: Thames and Hudson.

Flory, S. 1980. "Who Read Herodotus' Histories?" *The American Journal of Philology* 1001, no. 1: 12–28.

Fraser, G. 1902. "The Early Tombs at Tehneh." *Annales du Service des Antiquités de l'Égypte* 3: 67–76.

Friedländer, M. 1893. "Life and Works of Saadia." *Jewish Quarterly Review* 5, no. 2: 177–99.

Gabrieli, F. 1960. "Adab." In *Encyclopaedia of Islam, New Edition, Volume 1*, 175–76. Leiden: Brill.

Gallazzi, C. 1994. "Tebtunis: Piecing Together 3,000 Years of History." *Egyptian Archaeology* 5: 27–29.

Garbrecht, G. 1996. "Historical Water Storage for Irrigation in the Fayum Depression (Egypt)." *Irrigation and Drainage Systems* 10: 47–76.

———. 1987. "Water Storage (Lake Moeris) in the Fayum Depression, Legend or Reality?" *Irrigation and Drainage Systems* 1: 143–57.

Gardiner, A.H. 1947. *Ancient Egyptian Onomastica, Text*. Vol. 1. Oxford: Oxford University Press.

———. 1948a. *Ramesside Administrative Documents*. Oxford: Oxford University Press.

———. 1948b. *The Wilbour Papyrus, Volume II, Commentary*. Oxford: Oxford University Press

———. 1948c. *The Wilbour Papyrus, Volume III, Translation*. Oxford: Oxford University Press.

———. 1957. "Hymn to Sobk in a Ramesseum Papyrus." *Revue d'Égyptologie* 11: 43–56.
Gardiner, A.H., and H.I. Bell. 1943. "The Name of Lake Moeris." *Journal of Egyptian Archaeology* 29: 37–50.
Gimaret, D. 1993. "Mu'tazila." *Encyclopaedia of Islam, New Edition, vol. 8*, 783–93. Leiden: Brill.
Ginter, B., and J.K. Kozlowski. 1986. "Kulturelle und paläoklimatische Sequenz in der Fayum-Depression: Eine zusammenfassende Darstellung der Forschungsarbeiten in den Jahren 1979–1981." *Mitteilungen des deutschen archäologischen Instituts, Abteilung Kairo* 42: 9–23.
"Giza Archives. Tomb G2150." http://www.giza-pyramids.org/view/sites/asitem/search@/2/siteNumber-asc?t:state:flow=6c39c582-f66a-4b77-99fd-6ac259a36a87.
Godlewska, A. 1995. "Map, Text and Image: The Mentality of Enlightened Conquerors: A New Look at the *Description de l'Égypte*." *Transactions of the Institute of British Geographers, New Series* 20, no. 1: 5–28.
Goedicke, H. 1971. *Re-used Blocks from the Pyramids of Amenemhat I at Lisht*. New York: Metropolitan Museum of Art.
Golb, N. 1965. "The Topography of the Jews of Medieval Egypt." *Journal of Near Eastern Studies* 24, no. 1: 251–70.
Goldschmidt, A. 2000. *Biographical Dictionary of Modern Egypt*. Boulder: Lynne Rienner Publishers.
Gonzales, A. 1977. *Le Voyage en Égype du Père Antonius Gonzales, 1665–1666*. Translated by Charles Libois. Cairo: Institut Français d'Archéologie Orientale.
Gormley, C.M., M.A. Rouse, and R.H. Rouse. 1984. "The Medieval Circulation of *De Chorographia* of Pomponius Mela." *Medieval Studies* 46: 266–320.
Grajetzki, W. 2004. *Harageh, an Egyptian Burial Ground for the Rich, around 1800 BC*. London: Golden House Publications.
Griffith, F.L. 1889. *The Inscriptions of Siût and Dêr Rîfeh*. London: Trubner.
———. 1898. *Hieratic Papyri from Kahun and Gurob (Principally of the Middle Kingdom)*. London: Bernard Quaritch.
Grimal, N. 1981. *La Stèle Triomphale de Pi('ankh)y. JE 48862 & 47086 & 47089 au Musée du Caire*. Cairo: Institut Français d'Archéologie Orientale.
Haarman, U. 1991. "Misr: The Mamlūk Period 1250–1517." In *Encyclopaedia of Islam, New Edition, Volume 8*, 165–77. Leiden: Brill.
Habachi, L. 1937. "Une 'Vaste Salle' d'Amenemhat III a Kiman-Fares (Fayoum)." *Annales du Service des Antiquités de l'Égypte* 37: 85–95.
———. 1940. "The Monument of Biahmu." *Annales du Service des Antiquités de l'Égypte* 40: 721–32.
Hadas, M. 2003. *Tacitus: The Annals and the Histories*. New York: Modern Library.

Hadj-Sadok, M. 1971. "Ibn Khurradādhbih." In *Encyclopaedia of Islam, New Edition, vol. 3*, 839–40. Leiden: Brill.

Hagen, F., and D. Soliman 2018. "Archives in Ancient Egypt, 250–1000 bce." In *Manuscripts and Archives. Comparative Views on Record Keeping* edited by A. Bausi, C. Brockmann, M. Friedrich and S. Kienitz, 71-170. Berlin: De Gruyter. al-Hakem, Ibn 'Abd. 1922. *Futuh Misr*. ed. Torrey, C. New Haven: Yale Oriental Research Series III.

Haller, B.S. 2007. "Landscape Description in Homer's Odyssey." PhD diss., University of Pittsburgh.

Halm, H. 1991. "Misr; the Fatimid Period; and the Ayyubid Period." In *Encyclopaedia of Islam, New Edition, Volume* 7, 162–65. Leiden: Brill.

Hannig, R. 2003. Ägyptisches Wörterbuch I: *Altes Reich und erste Zwischenzeit*. Vol. 98. Kulturgeschichte der antiken Welt. Philip von Zabern.

———. 2006. Ägyptisches Wörterbuch II: *Mittleres Reich und zweite Zwischenzeit*. Vol. 112. Kulturgeschichte der antiken Welt. Philip von Zabern.

Harley, J.B., and D. Woodward. 1987. "The Foundations of Theoretical Cartography in Archaic and Classical Greece." In *The History of Cartography, Volume 1: Cartography in Prehistoric, Ancient and Medieval Europe and the Mediterranean*, edited by J.B. Harley and D. Woodward, 130–47. Chicago: University of Chicago Press.

Harrell, J.A., and T.M. Brown. 1995. "An Old Kingdom Basalt Quarry at Widan El-Faras and the Quarry Road to Lake Moeris." *Journal of the American Research Center in Egypt* 32: 71–91.

Harrell, J.A., and V. Brown. 1992. "The World's Oldest Surviving Geological Map: The 1150 BC Turin Papyrus from Egypt." *Journal of Geology* 100, no. 1: 3–18.

Harrigan, M. 2008. *Veiled Encounters: Representing the Orient in 17th-century French Travel Literature*. New York: Rodopi.

Harrison, T. 2007. "The Place of Geography in Herodotus' Histories." In *Travel, Geography and Culture in Ancient Greece Egypt and the Near East*, edited by C. Adams and J. Roy, 44–65. Oxford: Oxbow.

Hassan, F., and G. Tassie. 2006. "Modelling Environmental and Settlement Change in the Fayum." *Egyptian Archaeology* 29: 37–40.

Helck, W. 1956. *Urkunden der 18. Dynastie. Heft 18–19*. Leipzig: J.C. Hinrichs.

Hendrickx, S., and P. Vermeersch. 2000. "Prehistory: From the Palaeolithic to the Badarian Culture (c. 700,000–4000 BC)." In *The Oxford History of Ancient Egypt*, edited by I. Shaw. Oxford: Oxford University Press.

Herklotz, F. 2012. "Aegypto Capita: Augustus and the Annexation of Egypt." In *Oxford Handbook of Roman Egypt*, edited by C. Riggs, 11–21. Oxford: Oxford University Press.

Herodotus. 1954. *The Histories*. Translated by A. de Sélincourt. London: Penguin Books.

Hewison, R.N. 2008. *The Fayoum: History and Guide*. 4th ed. Cairo: American University in Cairo Press.

Hodder, I. 2001. *Archaeological Theory Today*. Cairo: Polity Press.

Holdaway, S., R. Phillipps, J. Emmitt, and W. Wendrich. 2016. "The Fayum Revisited: Reconsidering the Role of the Neolithic Package, Fayum North Shore, Egypt." *Quaternary International* 410: 173–80.

Holdaway, S., and W. Wendrich, eds. 2017. *The Desert Fayum Reinvestigated: The Early to Mid-Holocene Landscape Archaeology of the Fayum North Shore, Egypt*. Los Angeles: UCLA Cotsen Institute of Archaeology Press.

Holt, P.M. 1965. "Al-Fayum." In *Encyclopaedia of Islam, New Edition, Volume 2*, 872–73. Leiden: Brill.

Hopkins, J.F.P. 1990. "Geographical and Navigational Literature." In *The Cambridge History of Arabic Literature: Religion, Learning and Science in the 'Abbasid Period*, edited by M.J.L. Young, J.D. Latham, and R.B. Serjeant, 301–27. Cambridge: Cambridge University Press.

Horváth, Z. 2009. "Temple(s) and Town at El-Lahun: A Study of Ancient Toponyms in the El-Lahun Papyri." In *Archaism and Innovation: Studies in the Culture of Middle Kingdom Egypt*, edited by D.P. Silverman, W.K. Simpson, and J. Wegner, 171–203. New Haven and Philadelphia: Yale University and University of Pennsylvania.

Irwin, R. 2006. *For Lust of Knowing: The Orientalists and Their Enemies*. London: Allen Lane.

Jafri, S.R. 1985. "Introduction and Interpretation of the Map." In *Al-Khwarizmi's Map of the World Based on "Kitab Surat Al-Ard,"* edited by K.S. Aini, 57–68. Srinagar: Donish Publishers.

Jasnow, R. 2013. "Greco-Roman Period Demotic Texts from the Fayum and Their Relationship to the Book of Fayum." In *Egypt's Mysterious Book of Fayum*, edited by H. Beinlich, R. Schulz, and A. Wieczorek, 79–87. Dettlebach: J.H. Röll.

Jaubert, P.A. 1975. *La Géographie d'Édrisi*. Amsterdam: Philo Press.

Jeffreys, D. 1998. "The Topography of Heliopolis and Memphis: Some Cognitive Aspects." In *Stationen. Beiträge zur Kulturgeschichte Ägyptens. Rainer Stadelmann gewidmet*, edited by H. Guksch and D. Polz. Mainz: Philip von Zabern.

Johnson, M. 2007. *Ideas of Landscape*. Malden: Blackwell.

Jomard, E. 1812. *Mémoire sur le Lac de Moeris Comparé au Lac du Fayoum*.

Jones, H. 1917. *The Geography of Strabo*. Vol. 1. London: William Heinemann.

———. 1932. *The Geography of Strabo*. Vol. 8. London: William Heinemann.

Kanawati, N., and A. McFarlane. 1993. *Deshasha: The Tombs of Inti Shedu and Others*. Sydney: Australian Centre for Egyptology.

"Kanefer Stela." http://www.britishmuseum.org/research/collection_online/collection_object_details.aspx?objectId=111362&partId=1&searchText=1324&sortBy=fromDateDesc&page=1.

Katary, S. 1989. *Land Tenure in the Ramesside Period*. London: Kegan Paul International.

Keenan, J.G. 2005. "Landscape and Memory: Al-Nabulsi's Tarikh Al-Fayyum." *Bulletin of the American Society of Papyrologists* 42: 203–12.

Kemp, B.J. 1978. "The Harim-Palace at Madinat El-Ghurab." *Zeitschrift für ägyptische Sprache und Altertumskunde* 105, no. 1: 122–33.

Kennedy, H. 1991. "Misr; from the Abbasids to the Fatimids." In *Encyclopaedia of Islam, New Edition*, 160–62. Leiden: Brill.

———. 1998. "Egypt as a Province in the Islamic Caliphate, 641–86." In *The Cambridge History of Egypt, Volume 1: Islamic Egypt, 640–1571*, edited by C. Petry, 62–85. Cambridge: Cambridge University Press.

El-Khadragy, M., and J. Kahl. 2004. "The First Intermediate Period Tombs at Asyut Revisited." *Studien zur altägyptische Kultur* 32: 233–43.

Khalidi, T. 1975. *Islamic Historiography: The Histories of Mas*'ūdī. New York: State University of New York.

König, I. 1996. "Die Oase Al-Fayyum nach 'Uthman Ibrahim an Nabulusi: Ein Beitrag zur Wirtshcaftsgeschichte Ägyptens um die Mitte des 13. Jahrhunderts n. Chr." *Zeitschrift für Geschichte der Arabisch-Islamischen Wissenschaften* 10: 190–253.

Kraemer, B. 2010. "The Meandering Identity of the Fayum Canal: The Henet of Moeris / Dioryx Kleonos/Bahr Wardan/Abdul Wahbi." In *Proceedings of the Twenty-fifth International Congress of Papyrology, Ann Arbor, 2007*.

Kramers, J.H. 1932. "La Question Balhī–Istahrī–Ibn Hawkal et l'Atlas de l'Islam." *Acta Orientalia* 10: 9–30.

Kramers, J.H., and G. Wiet. 1925. *Configuration de la Terre (Kitab Surat al-Ard)*. Paris: G.P. Maisonneuve et Larose.

Lacau, P., and H. Chevrier. 1969. *Une Chapelle de Sésostris Ier à Karnak. Planches*. Cairo: Institut Français d'Archéologie Orientale.

Lacovara, P. 1997. "Gurob and the New Kingdom 'Harim' Palace." In *Ancient Egypt the Aegean and the Near East: Studies in Honor of Martha Rhoads Bell, Volume 2*, edited by J. Phillips, 297–305. San Antonio: Van Siclen.

Lane, E.W. 2000. *Description of Egypt*, edited by J. Thompson. Cairo: American University in Cairo Press.

Lange, H.O., and H. Schäfer. 1902. *Catalogue Général des Antiquités Égyptiennes du Musée du Caire. Nos 20001–20780: Grab- und Denksteine des mittleren Reichs, Theil I: Text zu no. 20001–20399*. Berlin: Reichsdruckerei.

———. 1908. *Catalogue Général des Antiquités Égyptiennes du Musée du Caire. Nos 20001–20780: Grab- Und Denksteine Des Mittleren Reichs, Theil II: Text Zu No. 20400–20780*. Berlin: Reichsdruckerei.

Leask, N. 1992. *British Romantic Writers and the East*. Cambridge: Cambridge University Press.

———. 2002. *Curiosity and the Aesthetics of Travel Writing 1770–1840*. Oxford: Oxford University Press.

Leclant, J., and G. Clerc. 1988. "Fouilles et Travaux en Égypte at au Soudan 1986–1987." *Orientalia* 57, no. 3: 307–404.

Lenoir, P. 1873. *The Fayoum or Artists in Egypt*. London: Henry S. King & Co.

Lepsius, K.R. *Denkmäler aus Aegypten und Aethiopian. Tafelwerke*. Vol. Abth. II. Band III. http://edoc3.bibliothek.uni-halle.de/lepsius/start.html.

———. *Denkmäler aus Aegypten und Aethiopian. Tafelwerke*. Vol. Abth II. Band IV. http://edoc3.bibliothek.uni-halle.de/lepsius/start.html.

Lewis, N. 1983. *Life in Egypt under Roman Rule*. Oxford: Clarendon Press.

Lilley, K. 2011. "Denis Cosgrove." In *Key Thinkers in Space and Place, 2nd ed.*, edited by P. Hubbard and R. Kitchin. Los Angeles: SAGE Publications.

Linant de Bellefonds, L.M.A. 1843. *Mémoires sur le Lac Moeris*. Alexandria: Imprimerie de A.E. Ozanne.

Lloyd, A.B. 1975. *Herodotus, Book II*. Leiden: Brill.

———. 1982. "The Inscription of Udjahorresnet, a Collaborator's Testament." *Journal of Egyptian Archaeology* 68: 166–80.

———. 2000a. "The Late Period." In *The Oxford History of Ancient Egypt*, edited by I. Shaw, 369–94. Oxford: Oxford University Press.

———. 2000b. "The Ptolemaic Period." In *The Oxford History of Ancient Egypt*, edited by I. Shaw, 395–421. Oxford: Oxford University Press.

Lockman, Z. 2004. *Contending Visions of the Middle East: The History and Politics of Orientalism*. Cambridge: Cambridge University Press.

Lucas, P. 1998. *Voyage du Sieur Paul Lucas dans le Levant*. Saint-Étienne: Université de Saint-Étienne.

———. 2002. *Deuxième Voyage du Sieur Paul Lucas dans le Levant*. Saint-Étienne: Université de Saint-Étienne.

———. 2004. *Troisième Voyage du Sieur Paul Lucas dans le Levant*. Saint-Étienne: Université de Saint-Étienne.

Luft, U. 1998. "The Ancient Town of El-Lahun." In *Lahun Studies*, edited by S. Quirke, 1–41. Reigate: SIA.

Malleson, C. 2007. "Investigating Ancient Egyptian Towns: A Case Study of Itj-tawy." In *Current Research in Egyptology 2005, Proceedings of the Sixth Annual Symposium. University of Cambridge 2005*, edited by R. Mairs and A. Stevenson, 90–104. Oxford: Oxbow Books.

Manning, J.G. 2010. *The Last Pharaohs: Egypt under the Ptolemies, 305–30 BC*. Princeton: Princeton University Press.

Maspero, G. 1899. "Review of Baron Carra de Vaux: l'Abrégé des Merveilles." *Journal des Savants*. February 1899: 69–86, 154–72, 277–78.

Matar, N. 2014. *Henry Stubbe and the Beginnings of Islam: The Originall and Progress of Mahometanism*. New York: Columbia University Press.

Mayes, S. 2003. *The Great Belzoni: The Circus Strongman Who Discovered Egypt's Ancient Treasures*. London: I.B. Tauris.

Mayhoff, C. 1906. *C. Plini Secundi Naturalis Historae*. Lipsae: Teubneri.

Mazuel, J. 1937. *L'Oeuvre Géographique de Linant de Bellefonds*. Cairo: Société Royale de Géographie d'Égypte.

Midant-Reynes, B. 2000. "The Naqada Period." In *The Oxford History of Ancient Egypt*, edited by I. Shaw, 44–60. Oxford: Oxford University Press.

Milton, J.R. 2008. "Locke, John (1632–1704)." In *Dictionary of National Biography*. Oxford: Oxford University Press.

Miquel, A. 1971. "Ibn Hawkal." In *Encyclopaedia of Islam, New Edition, vol. 3*, 786–88. Leiden: Brill.

———. 1978. "Al-Istakhri." In *Encyclopaedia of Islam, New Edition, vol. 4*, 222–23. Leiden: Brill.

Mittenhuber, F. 2010. "The Tradition of Texts and Maps in Ptolemy's Geography." In *Ptolemy in Perspective: Use and Criticism of His Work from Antiquity to the Nineteenth Century*, edited by A. Jones, 95–120. New York: Springer.

Moeller, N. 2016. *The Archaeology of Urbanism in Ancient Egypt: From the Predynastic to the End of the Middle Kingdom*. Cambridge: Cambridge University Press.

Monson, A. 2002. *From the Ptolemies to the Romans: Political and Economic Change in Egypt*. Cambridge: Cambridge University Press.

———. 2013. "Greeks in an Egyptian Landscape: The Faiyum under Ptolemaic and Roman Rule." In *Egypt's Mysterious Book of the Faiyum*, edited by H. Beinlich, R. Schulz, and A. Wieczorek, 89–104. Hildesheim: Roemer- und Pelizaeus-Museum.

Mordtmann, A.D. 1845. *Das Buch der Länder von Schech Ebu Ishak El Farisi El Isztachri*. Hamburg: Raues Haus.

Moritz, B. 1899. *Description du Fayoum au VIIme siècle de l'Hêgire par 'Osmân il Naboulsi il Safadi*. Cairo: Imprimerie Nationale.

Moser, S. 2006. *Wonderous Curiosities: Ancient Egypt at the British Museum*. Chicago: University of Chicago Press.

Moussa-Mahmoud, F. 1988. "English Travellers and the Arabian Nights." In *The Arabian Nights in English Literature: Studies in the Reception of the Thousand and One Nights into British Culture*, edited by P.L. Caracciolo, 95–110. Basingstoke: Macmillan.

Mueller, K. 2002. "Ptolemaic Settlements in Space: Settlement Size and Hierarchy in the Fayum." *Archiv für Papyrusforschung* 41, no. 8: 107–25.

———. 2003. "Mastering Matrices and Clusters: Locating Graeco-Roman Settlements in the Meris of Herakleides (Fayum/Egypt) by Monte-Carlo-Simulation." *Archiv für Papyrusforschung* 49, no. 2: 219–54.

———. 2004. "What's Your Position? Using Multi-Dimensional Scaling (MDS) and Geographical Information Systems (GIS) for Locating Ancient Settlements in the Meris of Polemon/Graeco-Roman Fayum." *Archiv für Papyrusforschung* 50, no. 2: 199–214.

———. 2005. "Redistricting the Ptolemaic Fayum, Egypt: From Nomarchies and Toparchies to Weighted Voronoi Tesselation." *Archiv für Papyrusforschung* 51, no. 1: 112–26.

Muhlestein, K. 2015. "Transitions in Pyramid Orientation: New Evidence from the Seila Pyramid." *Studien zur altägyptische Kultur* 44: 249–58.
Muir, R. 1999. *Approaches to Landscape*. Basingstoke: Macmillan.
Muntz, C. 2017. *Diodorus Siculus and the World of the Late Roman Republic*. New York: Oxford University Press.
Murphy, T. 2004. *Pliny the Elder's Natural History: The Empire in the Encyclopedia*. Oxford: Oxford University Press.
Netton, I.R. 2008. *Encyclopedia of Islamic Civilization and Religion*. London: Routledge.
Northrup, L.S. 1998. "The Bahrī Mamlūk Sultanate, 1250–1390." In *The Cambridge History of Egypt, Volume 1: Islamic Egypt 640–1517*, edited by C. Petry, 242–89. Cambridge: Cambridge University Press.
Oerlemans, O. 2004. *Romanticism and the Materiality of Nature*. Toronto: University of Toronto Press.
Oldfather, C.H. 1960. *Diodorus of Sicily*. London: William Heinemann.
Oman, G. 1971. "Al-Idrīsī." In *Encyclopaedia of Islam, New Edition, vol. 3*, 1032–53. Leiden: Brill.
"Oxyrhynchus Online." http://www.papyrology.ox.ac.uk/POxy.
Parkinson, R.B. 2002. *Poetry and Culture in Middle Kingdom Egypt: A Dark Side to Perfection*. London: Continuum.
Peacock, D. 2000. "The Roman Period." In *The Oxford History of Ancient Egypt*, edited by I. Shaw, 422–45. Oxford: Oxford University Press.
Pellat, C. 1965. *Mas'ūdī: Les Prairies d'Or Volume 2*. Translated by B. de Meynard and P. de Courteille. Paris: Société Asiatique.
———. 1991. "Al-Mas'udi." In *Encyclopaedia of Islam, New Edition, Volume 6*, 784–89. Leiden: Brill.
Pernigotti, S. 2005. *Villaggi dell'Egitto Antico I. Bakchias*. Bologna: La Mandragora.
Petrie, W.M.F. 1889. *Hawara, Biahmu and Arsinoe*. London: Field and Tuer, Leadenhall Press.
———. 1890. *Kahun, Gurob and Hawara*. London: Kegan Paul, Trench, Trubner and Co.
———. 1898. *Deshasheh 1897*. Egypt Exploration Fund Memoirs 15. London: Egypt Exploration Fund.
———. 1909. *Memphis I*. London: Bernard Quaritch.
———. 1913. *Tarkhan I and Memphis V*. London: British School of Archaeology in Egypt.
———. 1932. *Seventy Years in Archaeology*. New York: Henry Holt and Co.
Petrie, W.M.F., and G. Brunton. 1924. *Sedment I*. London: British School of Archaeology in Egypt.
Petrie, W.M.F., G.A. Wainwright, and E. Mackay. 1912. *The Labyrinth, Gerzeh and Mazghuneh*. British School of Archaeology in Egypt and Egyptian Research Account 18. London: School of Archaeology in Egypt.

Pfeiffer, R. 1976. *History of Classical Scholarship: From 1300 to 1850*. Oxford: Clarendon Press.

Pococke, R. 1743. *A Description of the East, and Some Other Countries*. London.

Pollard, N. 1988. "The Chronology and Economic Condition of Late Roman Karanis: An Archaeological Reassessment." *Journal of the American Research Center in Egypt* 35: 147–62.

Pougeois, A. 1869. *Vie et Voyages de Vansleb*. Paris: Librairie Académic.

Quirke, S. 1991. "'Townsmen' in the Middle Kingdom." *Zeitschrift für ägyptische Sprache und Altertumskunde* 118: 141–49.

———. 1997. "Gods in the Temple of the King: Anubis at Lahun." In *The Temple in Ancient Egypt*, edited by S. Quirke, 24–48. London: British Museum Press.

———. 2004. *Egyptian Literature 1800 BC: Questions and Readings*. London: Golden House Publications.

———. 2005. *Lahun: A Town in Egypt 1800 BC, and the History of Its Landscape*. London: Golden House Publications.

Rackham, H. 1938. *Pliny: Natural History*. Vol. 1. London: William Heinemann.

———. 1961. *Pliny: Natural History*. Vol. 2. London: William Heinemann.

Ragib, Y. 1974. "L'Auteur de l'Égypte de Murtadi Fils du Gaphiphe." *Arabica* 21, no. 2: 203–209.

Rathbone, D.W. 1996. "Towards a Historical Topography of the Fayum." In *Archaeological Research in Roman Egypt: The Proceedings of the Seventeenth Classical Colloquium of the Department of Greek and Roman Antiquities, British Museum, Held on 1-4th December 1993*, 50–56. JRA Supplementary Series 19. Michigan: Ann Arbor.

"Ramesseum Papyri." R.B. Parkinson. http://www.britishmuseum.org/research/publications/online_research_catalogues/rp/the_ramesseum_papyri.aspx.

Redfield, J. 1985. "Herodotus the Tourist." *Classical Philology* 80, no. 2: 97–118.

Reid, D.M. 2002. *Whose Pharaohs? Archaeology, Museums and Egyptian National Identity from Napoleon to World War I*. Berkeley: University of California Press.

Rekaya, M. 1991. "Al-Ma'mun." In *Encyclopaedia of Islam, New Edition, Volume 6*, 331–39. Leiden: Brill.

Reynolds, L.D., and N.G. Wilson. 1991. *Scribes and Scholars: A Guide to the Transmission of Greek and Latin Literature*. 3rd ed. Oxford: Clarendon Press.

Richards, J. 1999. "Conceptual Landscapes in the Egyptian Nile Valley." In *Archaeologies of Landscape: Contemporary Perspectives*, edited by W. Ashmore and A.B. Knapp, 83–100. Oxford: Blackwell.

Roeder, G. 1913. *Ägyptische Inschriften aus den königlichen Museen zu Berlin*. Vol. 1. Leipzig: J.C. Hinrichs.

Rogers, P. 2008. "Addison, Joseph (1672–1719)." In *Oxford Dictionary of National Biography*.

Romer, C. 2017. "The Nile in the Fayum: Strategies of Dominating and Using the Water Resources of the River in the Oasis of the Middle Kingdom and Graeco-Roman Period." In *The Nile: Natural and Cultural Landscape in Egypt*, edited by H. Willems and J.-M. Dahms, 171–91. Bielfeld: Transcript.

Romer, F.C. 1998. *Pomponius Mela's Description of the World*. Michigan: University of Michigan.

Romm, J. 1998. *Herodotus*. New Haven: Yale University Press.

Roseman, C.H. 2005. "Reflections of Philosophy: Strabo and Geographical Sources." In *Strabo's Cultural Geography: The Making of a Kolossougia*, edited by D. Dueck, H. Lindsay, and S. Pothecary, 27–41. Cambridge: Cambridge University Press.

Rosenthal, F. 1971. "Ibn 'Abd al-Hakam." In *Encyclopaedia of Islam, New Edition, Volume 3*, 674–75. Leiden: Brill.

———. 1991. "Al-Makrīzī." In *Encyclopaedia of Islam, New Edition, vol. 6*, 193–94. Leiden: Brill.

Rostovtzeff, M. 1922. *A Large Estate in Egypt in the Third Century B.C.: A Study in Economic History*. Madison: Madison. https://archive.org/details/cu31924013858661.

Sacks, K.A. 1990. *Diodorus Siculus and the First Century*. Princeton: Princeton University Press.

Said, E. 2003. *Orientalism*. London: Penguin Books.

Salmon, G. 1901. "Répertoire Géographique de la Province du Fayyoûm d'après le Kitâb Târikh Al Fayyoûm d'an-Naboulsi." *Bulletin de l'Institut Française d'Archaéologie Orientale* 1: 29–77.

Sambrook, J. 1986. *The Eighteenth Century: The Intellectual and Cultural Context of English Literature, 1700–1789*. London: Longmans.

Sandford, K.S., and W.J. Arkell. 1929. *Paleolithic Man and the Nile–Faiyum Divide*. Chicago: University of Chicago Press.

Sandys, G. 1673. *Sandys Travels*. London: John Williams Junior.

Sani, M. 1982. "The Life and Work of Al-Khwarizmi." *Menemui Matematik* 4, no. 1: 1–9.

Schulz, R. 2013. "The Creation of the World: On the Variety of Ancient Egyptian Creation Myths." In *Egypt's Mysterious Book of the Fayum*, edited by H. Beinlich, R. Schulz, and A. Wieczorek, 11–26. Dettlebach: J.H. Röll.

Schwartz, J., and H. Wild. 1950. *Qasr-Qarun/Dionysias 1948*. Fouilles Franco-Suisse 1. Cairo: Institut Français d'Archéologie Orientale.

Seidlmayer, S. 2000. "The First Intermediate Period." In *The Oxford History of Ancient Egypt*, edited by I. Shaw, 118–47. Oxford: Oxford University Press.

Sethe, K. 1908. *Die altaegyptischen Pyramidentexte nach dem Papierdrucken und Photographien des berliner Museums.* Vol. 1. Leipzig: J.C. Hinrichs

———. 1910. *Die altaegyptischen Pyramidentexte nach dem Papierdrucken und Photographien des berliner Museums.* Vol. 2. Leipzig: J.C. Hinrichs.

———. 1933. *Urkunden des alten Reichs.* Vol. 1. Leipzig: J.C. Hinrichs.

Shanks, M., and C. Tilley. 1987. *Social Theory and Archaeology.* Cambridge: Polity Press.

Sharp, M. 1999. "The Village of Theadelphia in the Fayum: Land and Population in the Second Century." *Proceedings of the British Academy* 96: 159–92.

Shaw, I. 2011. "Seeking the Ramesside Royal Harem: New Fieldwork at Madinat El-Gurob." In *Ramesside Studies in Honour of K.A. Kitchen*, edited by M. Collier and S. Snape, 453–63. Chorley: Rutherford Press.

Shiode, N., and W. Grajetzki. "A Virtual Exploration of the Lost Labyrinth." http://www.casa.ucl.ac.uk/digital_egypt/hawara/enco2000/enco2000_web.html.

Shirai, N. 2010. *The Archaeology of the First Farmer-Herders in Egypt: New Insights into the Fayum Epipaleolithic and Neolithic.* Leiden: Leiden University Press.

Shotter, D.C. 1968. "Tacitus, Tiberius and Germanicus." *Historia: Zeitschrift für alte Geschichte* 17, no. 2: 194–214.

Silberman, A. 1988. *Pomponius Mela: Chorographie.* Paris: Les Belles Lettres.

Śliwa, J. 1992. "The Middle Kingdom Settlement at Qasr El-Sagha, 1979–1988." *Studies in Ancient Art and Civilization* 5: 19–38.

Spiegelberg, W. 1927. *The Credibility of Herodotus' Account of Egypt in the Light of Egyptian Monuments.* Translated by A.M. Blackman. Oxford: Blackwell.

St. John, J.A. 1834. *Egypt, and Mohammed Ali; or, Travels in the Valley of the Nile.* Vol. 2. London: Longman Rees.

———. 1853. *Isis: An Egyptian Pilgrimage.* London: Longmans.

———. 1854. *The Philosophical Works of John Locke.* London: Bell.

Stevenson, E.L. 1932. *Claudius Ptolemy: The Geography.* New York: Dover.

Tait, J. 2003. "The 'Book of Fayum': Mystery in a Known Landscape." In *Mysterious Lands*, edited by D. O'Connor and S. Quirke, 183–202. London: UCL Press.

Taplin, O. 2000. *Literature in the Roman World.* Oxford: Oxford University Press.

Taylor, J. 2000. "The Third Intermediate Period." In *The Oxford History of Ancient Egypt*, edited by I. Shaw, 330–68. Oxford: Oxford University Press.

"Tebtynis, IFAO Project." http://www.ifao.egnet.net/archeologie/tebtynis/#en.

"Tebtunis Papyrus I.33." http://papyri.info/ddbdp/p.tebt;1;33.

Thomas, A. 1981. *Gurob: A New Kingdom Town.* Warminster: Aris and Phillips.

Thomas, J. 1995. "The Politics of Vision and the Archaeologies of Landscape." In *Landscape: Politics and Perspectives*, edited by B. Bender, 19–48. Oxford: Berg.

Thompson, J. 2010. *Edward William Lane 1801–1876: The Life of the Pioneering Egyptologist and Orientalist*. Cairo: American University in Cairo Press.

———. 2015. *Wonderful Things: A History of Egyptology*. Vol. 1. Cairo: American University in Cairo Press.

Thornton, L. 1994. *The Orientalists: Painter Travellers 1828–1908*. Paris: ACR.

Tibbetts, G.R. 1992. "'The Beginnings of a Cartographic Tradition' & 'The Balkhī School of Geographers.'" In *The History of Cartography, Volume 2: Cartography in the Traditional Islamic and South Asian Societies*, edited by J.B. Harley and D. Woodward, 90–136. Chicago: University of Chicago Press.

Tilley, C. 1994. *A Phenomenology of Landscape: Places, Paths and Monuments*. Oxford: Berg.

Toomer, G.J. 1975. "Ptolemais, Claudius." In *Dictionary of Scientific Biography, vol. 11*, edited by C.C. Gillispie, 186–206. New York: Charles Scribner's Sons.

Torrey, C.C. 1901. "The Mohammedan Conquest of Egypt and North Africa in the Years 643–705 A. D. Translated from the Original Arabic of Ibn Abd El-Hakem." In *Biblical and Semitic Studies: Critical and Historical Essays by the Members of the Semitic and Biblical Faculty of Yale University*, 279–330. New Haven: Yale University Press.

———. 1932. *The History and Conquest of Egypt, North Africa and Spain Known as the Futūh Misr of Ibn 'Abd Al-Hakam*. New Haven: Yale University Press.

Trigger, B.G. 2006. *A History of Archaeological Thought*. 2nd ed. Cambridge: Cambridge University Press.

Uphill, E.P. 2000. *Pharaoh's Gateway to Eternity: The Hawara Labyrinth of King Amenemhat III*. London: Kegan Paul International.

Uytterhoeven, I. 2009. *Hawara in the Graeco-Roman Period: Life and Death in a Fayum Village*. Orientalia Lovaniensia Analecta 174. Leuven: Peeters.

Vandorpe, K. 2004. "The Henet of Moeris and the Ancient Administrative Division of the Fayum in Two Parts." *Archiv für Papyrusforschung und verwandte Gebiete* 50, no. 1: 61–78.

Vansleb, J.M. 1678. *The Present State of Egypt: Or A New Relation of a Late Voyage into That Kingdom Performed in the Years 1672 and 1673*. London.

Various. 1884. "The Meeting of the Society of Civil Engineers at Buffalo. Collection of Newspaper Reports." Printed privately.

Varney, A. 1999. *Eighteenth-century Writers in Their World*. Basingstoke: Macmillan.

Venning, T. 2001. *Chronology of the Roman Empire*. London: Continuum.

Verhoogt, A.M.F.W. 1998. *Menches, Komogrammateus of Kerkeosiris: The Doings and Dealings of a Village Scribe in the Late Ptolemaic Period (120–110 B.C.)*. Leiden: Brill.

Vernet, J. 1978. "Al-Khwārazmī." In *Encyclopaedia of Islam, New Edition, Volume 4*, 1070–71. Leiden: Brill.

"Virtual Hawara." http://www.casa.ucl.ac.uk/digital_egypt/hawara/gallery.html.
Vogel, F. 1888. *Diodori Bibliotheca Historica*. Leipzig: Teubner.
Waters, K.H. 1985. *Herodotus the Historian: His Problems, Methodology and Originality*. London: Croom Helm.
Watson, J.R. 1970. *Picturesque Landscape and English Romantic Poetry*. London: Hutchinson Educational.
Watterson, B. 1988. *Coptic Egypt*. Edinburgh: Schottish Academic Press.
———Wendorf, F., and R. Schild. 1976. *Prehistory of the Nile Valley*. New York: Academic Press.
Wenke, R.J. 1983. "The Fayyum Archaeological Project: Preliminary Report of the 1981 Season." *Newsletter of the American Research Center in Egypt* 122: 25–40.
———. 1984. "Early Agriculture in the Southern Fayum Depression: Some Test Survey Results and Research Implications." In *Origin and Early Development of Food-producing Cultures in North-eastern Africa*, edited by L. Kryzaniak and M. Kobusiewicz, 193–98. Poznan: Poznan Archaeological Museum.
Wenke, R.J., and D.J. Brewer. 1992. "The Neolithic–Predynastic Transition in the Fayum Depression." In *Followers of Horus*, edited by R. Friedman and D. Adams, 175–84. Oxford: Oxbow Books.
West, M.L. 1980. "Homeric and Hesiodic Poetry." In *Ancient Greek Literature*, edited by K.J. Dover, 10–28. Oxford: Oxford University Press.
Westermann, W.L. 1917. "Land Reclamation in the Fayum under Ptolemies Philadelphus and Euergetes I." *Classical Philology* 12, no. 4: 426–30.
Wiet, G. 1953[1937]. *L'Égypte de Murtadi Fils du Gaphiphe*. Paris: l'Imprimerie Nationale.
———. 1937. *Ya'kūbī: Les Pays*. Cairo: Institut Français d'Archéologie Orientale.
Wild, H. 1971. "Quatre Statuettes du Moyen Empire dans une Collection Privée de Suisse." *Bulletin de l'Institut Français d'Archéologie Orientale* 69: 89–130.
Wilfong, T.G. 2014. *Karanis Revealed: Discovering the Past and Present of a Michigan Excavation in Egypt*. Ann Arbor: Kelsey Museum.
Wilkinson, J.G. 1843. *Modern Egypt and Thebes: Being a Description of Egypt*. London: John Murray.
Williams, R.D. 1964. "The Sixth Book of the Aeneid." *Greece and Rome* 11, no. 1: 48–63.
Wilson, J.A. 1970. *Herodotus in Egypt*. Leiden: Nederlands Instituut voor het Nabije Oosten.
Winter, M. 1992. *Egyptian Society under Ottoman Rule 1517–1798*. London: Routledge.
Wolff, A. 2003. *How Many Miles to Babylon? Travels and Adventures to Egypt and Beyond from 1300 to 1640*. Liverpool: Liverpool University Press.

Wylie, J. 2007. *Landscape*. London: Routledge.

Yarrow, P.J. 1967. *A Literary History of France, vol. 2: The Seventeenth Century*. London: Ernest Benn.

Yoyotte, M. 2012. "Le Harem Royal dans l'Égypte Ancienne: Enquête Philologique, Archéologique et Prosopographique." PhD diss., La Sorbonne University.

Zaman, M.Q. 2001. "Al-Ya'kūbī." In *Encyclopaedia of Islam, New Edition, Volume 11*, 257–58. Leiden: Brill.

Zecchi, M. 2001. *Geographia Religiosa del Fayyum: Dalle origini al IV Secolo A.C.* Bologna: La Mandragora.

———. 2006. "Osiris in the Fayyum." In *Fayyum Studies* 2, 117–46.

———. 2008. "The Monument of Abgig." *Studien zur altägyptische Kultur* 37: 373–85.

———. 2010. *Sobek of Shedet: The Crocodile God in the Fayyum in the Dynastic Period.* Todi: Tau.

Zeki-Bey, A. 1899. "Une Description Arabe du Fayoum au VIIe Siècle de l'Hégire." *Bulletin de la Société Khédiviale de Géographie*, Ve Serie No. 5, 235–95.

Ziolkowski, J.M. 2007. "Middle Ages." In *A Companion to the Classical Tradition*, edited by C.W. Kallendorf, 17–43. Malden: Blackwell.

Index

Page numbers in bold refer to images. A number preceded by pl *refers to a numbered plate.*